TODD AND CRAIG'S

THE Perhapanauts™

GNO

East Baton Rouge Parish Library
Baton Rouge, Louisiana
THE PERHAPANAUTS created by Todd Dezago and Craig Rousseau

TODD AND CRAIG'S THE PERHAPANAUTS™

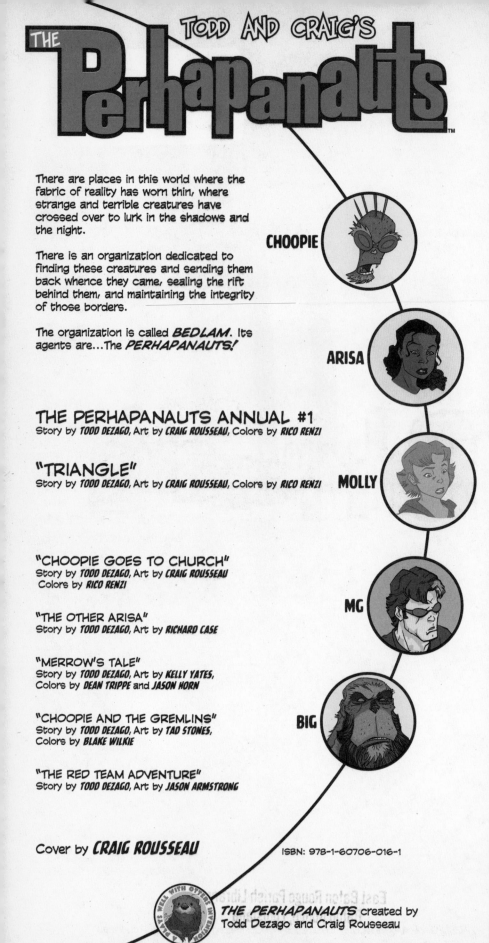

There are places in this world where the fabric of reality has worn thin, where strange and terrible creatures have crossed over to lurk in the shadows and the night.

There is an organization dedicated to finding these creatures and sending them back whence they came, sealing the rift behind them, and maintaining the integrity of those borders.

The organization is called *BEDLAM*. Its agents are...The *PERHAPANAUTS!*

CHOOPIE

ARISA

THE PERHAPANAUTS ANNUAL #1
Story by *TODD DEZAGO*, Art by *CRAIG ROUSSEAU*, Colors by *RICO RENZI*

"TRIANGLE"
Story by *TODD DEZAGO*, Art by *CRAIG ROUSSEAU*, Colors by *RICO RENZI*

MOLLY

"CHOOPIE GOES TO CHURCH"
Story by *TODD DEZAGO*, Art by *CRAIG ROUSSEAU*
Colors by *RICO RENZI*

"THE OTHER ARISA"
Story by *TODD DEZAGO*, Art by *RICHARD CASE*

MG

"MERROW'S TALE"
Story by *TODD DEZAGO*, Art by *KELLY YATES*,
Colors by *DEAN TRIPPE* and *JASON HORN*

"CHOOPIE AND THE GREMLINS"
Story by *TODD DEZAGO*, Art by *TAD STONES*,
Colors by *BLAKE WILKIE*

BIG

"THE RED TEAM ADVENTURE"
Story by *TODD DEZAGO*, Art by *JASON ARMSTRONG*

Cover by *CRAIG ROUSSEAU*

ISBN: 978-1-60706-016-1

THE PERHAPANAUTS created by
Todd Dezago and Craig Rousseau

IMAGE COMICS, INC. ★ ROBERT KIRKMAN – CHIEF OPERATING OFFICER ★ ERIK LARSEN – CHIEF FINANCIAL OFFICER ★ TODD McFARLANE – PRESIDENT ★ MARC SILVESTRI – CHIEF EXECUTIVE OFFICER ★ JIM VALENTINO – VICE-PRESIDENT ★ ERICSTEPHENSON – PUBLISHER ★ JOE KEATINGE – PR & MARKETING COORDINATOR ★ BRANWYN BIGGLESTONE – ACCOUNTS MANAGER ★ TYLER SHAINLINE – ADMIN. ASSISTANT ★ TRACI HUI – TRAFFIC MANAGER ★ ALLEN HUI – PRODUCTION MANAGER ★ DREW GILL – PRODUCTION ARTIST ★ JONATHAN CHAN – PRODUCTION ARTIST ★ MONICA HOWARD – PRODUCTION ARTIST ★ WWW.IMAGECOMICS.COM

THE PERHAPANAUTS, VOL. 1: TRIANGLE. First Printing. Published by Image Comics, Inc. Office of publication: 2134 Allston Way, 2nd Floor. Berkeley, CA 94704. Copyright © 2009 Todd Dezago and Craig Rousseau. All rights reserved. Originally published in single magazine form as THE PERHAPANAUTS ANNUAL #1 and THE PERHAPANAUTS #1–5. THE PERHAPANAUTS™ (including all prominent characters featured herein), its logo and all character likenesses are trademarks of Todd Dezago and Craig Rousseau, unless otherwise noted. Image Comics® and its logos are registered trademarks of Image Comics, Inc. All rights reserved. No part of this publication may be reproduced or transmitted, in any form or by any means (except for short excerpts for review purposes) without the express written permission of Image Comics, Inc. All names, characters, events and locales in this publication are entirely fictional. Any resemblance to actual persons (living or dead), events or places, without satiric intent, is coincidental. PRINTED IN CANADA. International RightsRepresentative:Christine Jensen(christine@gfloystudio.com)

foreword

Not so much a Foreword as a Thank You. I'll try to keep it short; I know you have this boss book you want to get into.

When Craig and I first launched *The Perhapanauts* out of Dark Horse those five long years ago, we were met with an apathy from their promotions department that upped the "Huh?" Factor for us. Their support for us while under their roof was close to non-existent. A few in-house ads appeared during our first run and none at all to announce our second. When we realized that they didn't even have copies of the Perhapanauts at their booth at conventions, we knew that we were destined for nothingness. We just didn't get it. Wouldn't it be in their best interest to promote our book? Ya think?

And so, after two narrowly-received, yet highly-acclaimed miniseries (Yes, Lads, they'll all be collected sometime next year...), we packed it in and took our gang of crazy cryptids on the road. At the time, Mike and I were finishing up liner notes and such on the *Tellos Colossal* when Image's PR and Marketing genius, Joe Keatinge, asked what was going on with the 'Haps. I told him and he said, Hey, ya want us to show you how to market a book? Erik Larsen later told me that he'd always wanted *The Perhapanauts* at Image, but didn't want to look like he was poaching from another company. But he mighta been punkin' me.

And so, through the efforts of these two guys—nd the unending patience of Eric Stephenson—The Perhapanauts made it to Image. They did, indeed, show us what really promoting a book is all about (You are a miracle-worker, Joe) and they, and everyone else at Image have made the transition, and the production of each issue, incredibly easy.

So this is a Thank You to them. To you guys for taking a chance on us. And to everyone on the production staff, ESPECIALLY Allen Hui, Production Manager (and our very favorite book designer!), Drew Gill, who apparently doesn't sleep, to Traci Hui, who makes sure that everything gets where it's going and, hopefully, on time, and to everyone else there at Image. Thank you for making us feel welcome and look good!

I'd say that's all, go ahead and read your stupid book, but Craig and I would also like to thank *you*, Dear Reader, for buying our book, for telling your friends, for being part of our family, and for following the adventures of these creepy and unlikely heroes in the first place!

Thank YOU!
todd dezago
elizaville ny
feb 19 2K9

Not short enough, huh? Sorry. We'd also like to thank everyone who pitched in on stories and art in this run; Dave Tata, Bob Almond, Blake Wilkie, Rich Case, Tad Stones, Kelly Yates, Dean Trippe, Jason Horn, Jason Armstrong, Jason Copland, Chris Summers, and of course, for his extraordinary work above and beyond the call of duty, Rico Renzi!

annual 2008

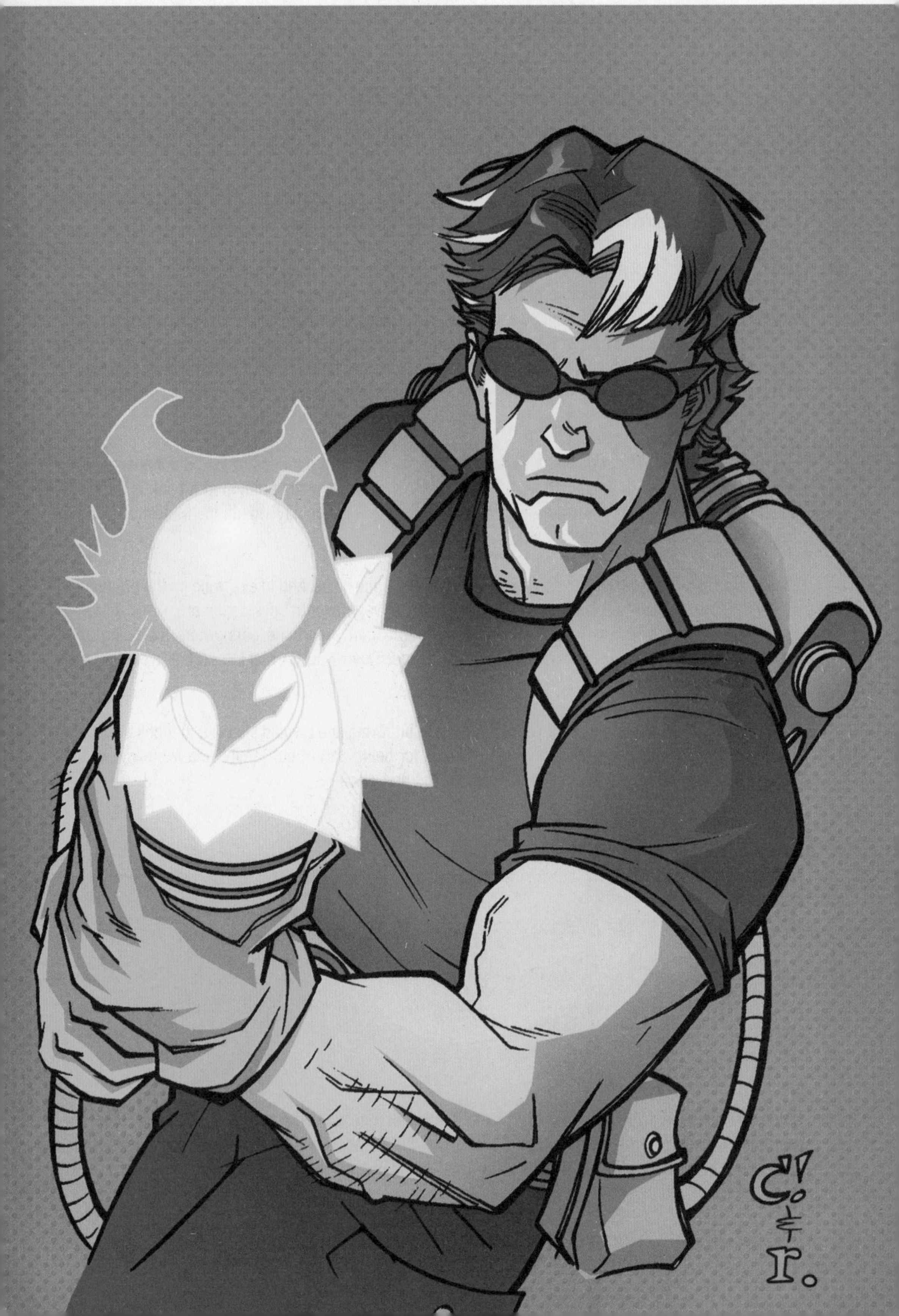

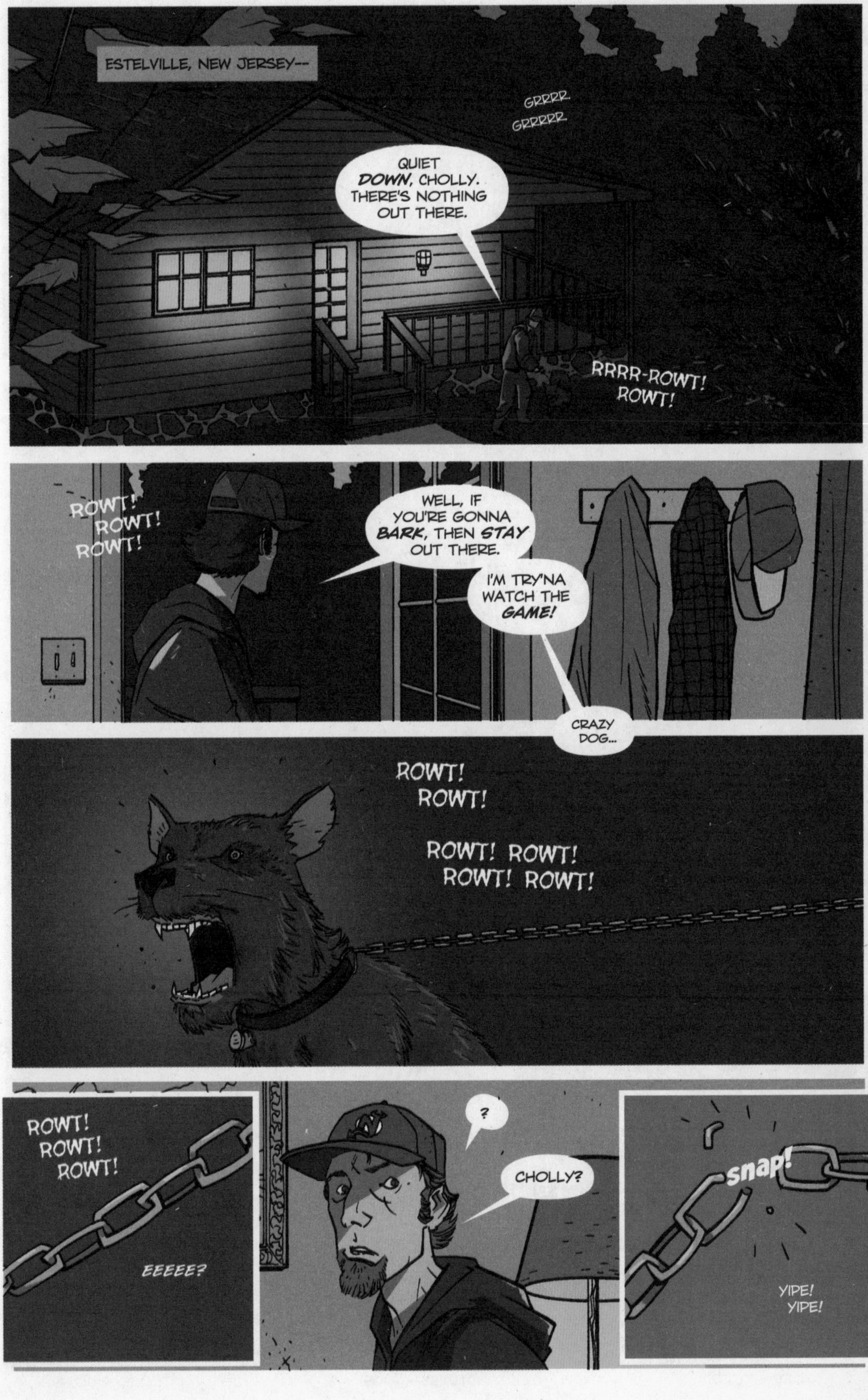
ESTELVILLE, NEW JERSEY--
GRRRR
GRRRRR
QUIET DOWN, CHOLLY. THERE'S NOTHING OUT THERE.
RRRR-ROWT! ROWT!
ROWT! ROWT! ROWT!
WELL, IF YOU'RE GONNA BARK, THEN STAY OUT THERE.
I'M TRY'NA WATCH THE GAME!
CRAZY DOG...
ROWT! ROWT!
ROWT! ROWT! ROWT! ROWT!
ROWT! ROWT! ROWT!
EEEEE?
?
CHOLLY?
SNAP!
YIPE! YIPE!

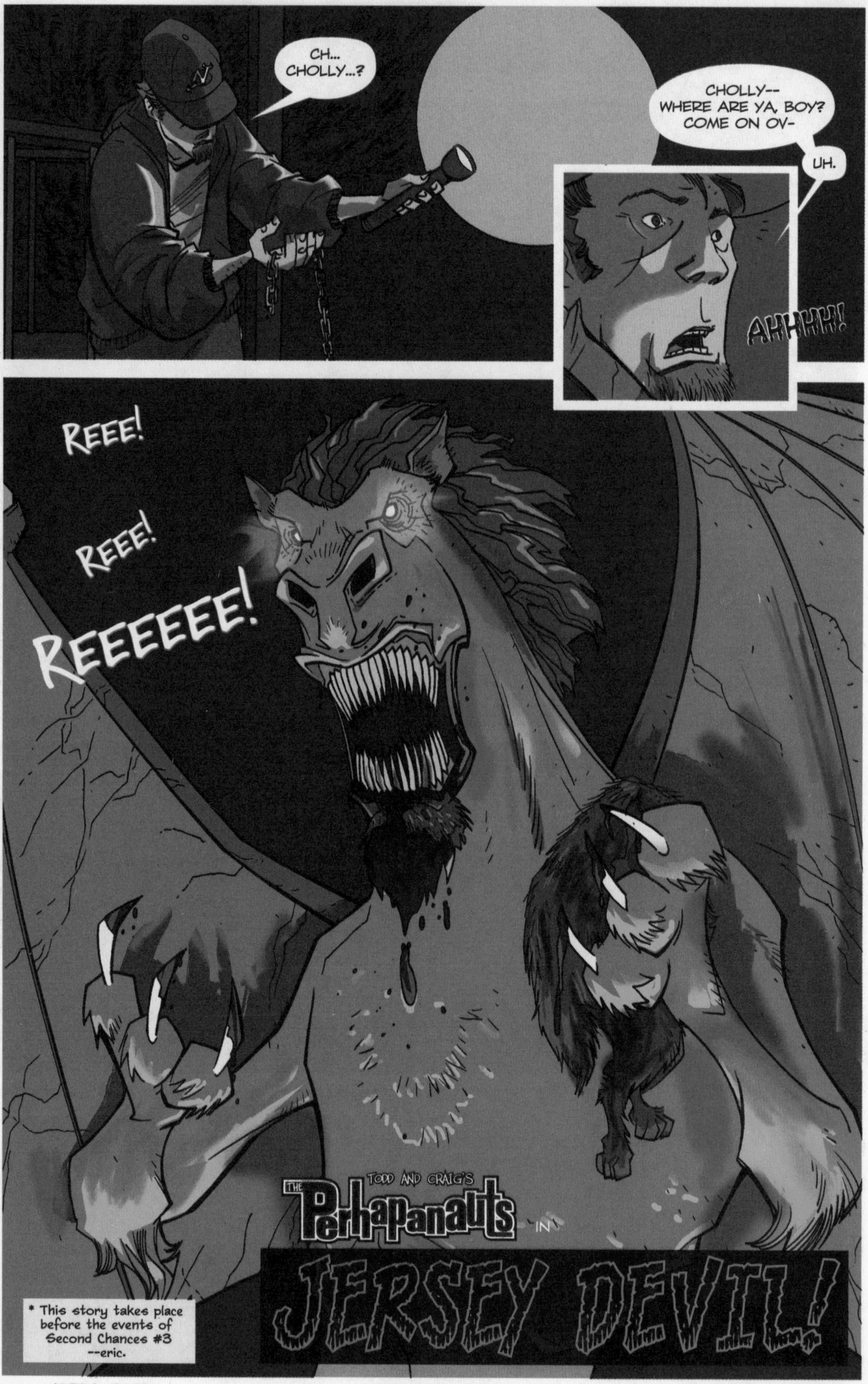
CH... CHOLLY...?
CHOLLY-- WHERE ARE YA, BOY? COME ON OV-
UH.
AHHHH!
REEE!
REEE!
REEEEEEE!
TODD AND CRAIG'S
THE Perhapanauts IN
JERSEY DEVIL!
* This story takes place before the events of Second Chances #3 --eric.

WORDS--TODD PICTURES--CRAIG COLORS--RICO 2K8

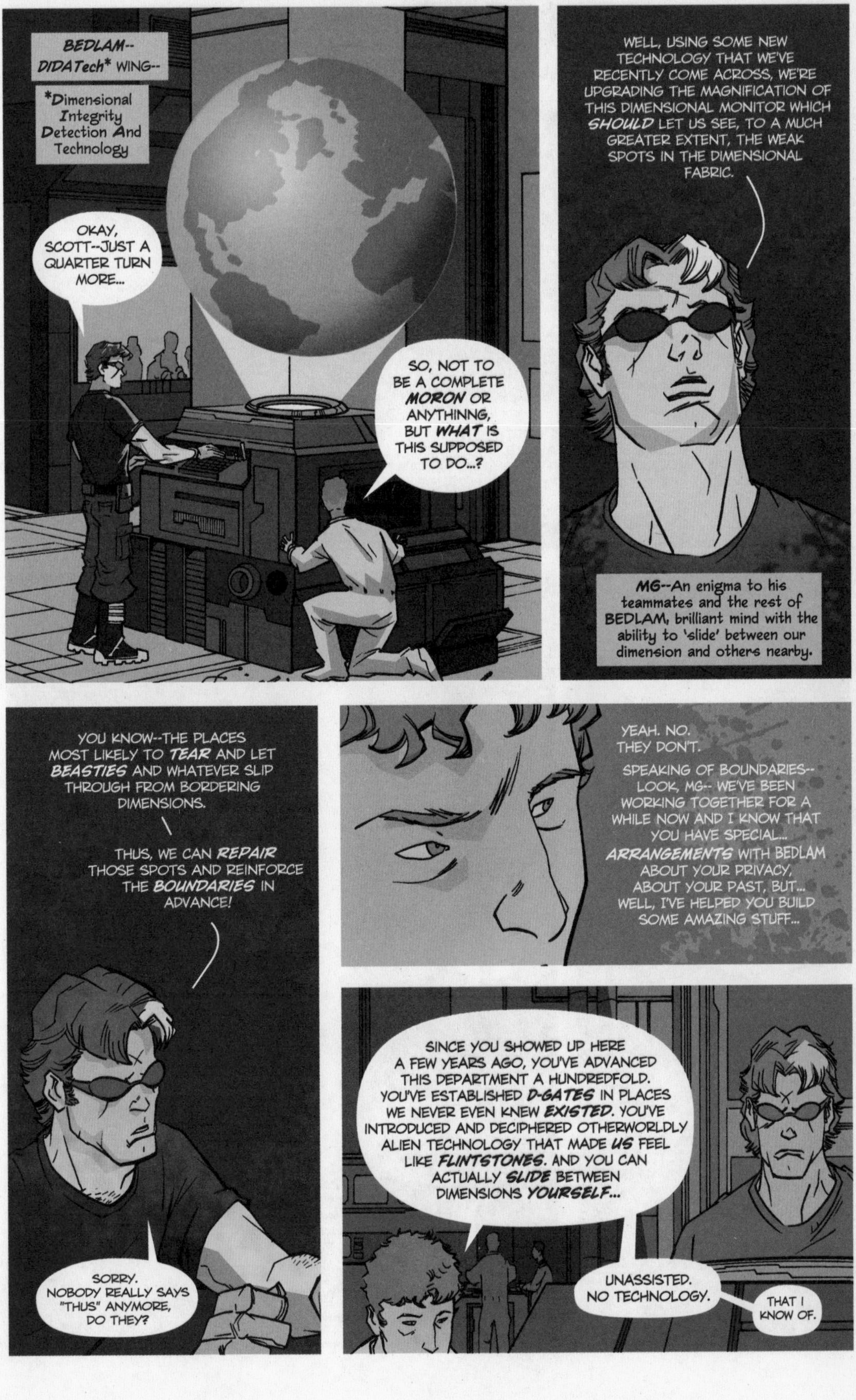
BEDLAM--
DIDATech* WING--
*Dimensional Integrity Detection And Technology
OKAY, SCOTT--JUST A QUARTER TURN MORE...
SO, NOT TO BE A COMPLETE MORON OR ANYTHINNG, BUT WHAT IS THIS SUPPOSED TO DO...?
WELL, USING SOME NEW TECHNOLOGY THAT WE'VE RECENTLY COME ACROSS, WE'RE UPGRADING THE MAGNIFICATION OF THIS DIMENSIONAL MONITOR WHICH SHOULD LET US SEE, TO A MUCH GREATER EXTENT, THE WEAK SPOTS IN THE DIMENSIONAL FABRIC.
MG--An enigma to his teammates and the rest of BEDLAM, brilliant mind with the ability to 'slide' between our dimension and others nearby.
YOU KNOW--THE PLACES MOST LIKELY TO TEAR AND LET BEASTIES AND WHATEVER SLIP THROUGH FROM BORDERING DIMENSIONS.
THUS, WE CAN REPAIR THOSE SPOTS AND REINFORCE THE BOUNDARIES IN ADVANCE!
SORRY. NOBODY REALLY SAYS "THUS" ANYMORE, DO THEY?
YEAH. NO. THEY DON'T.
SPEAKING OF BOUNDARIES-- LOOK, MG-- WE'VE BEEN WORKING TOGETHER FOR A WHILE NOW AND I KNOW THAT YOU HAVE SPECIAL... ARRANGEMENTS WITH BEDLAM ABOUT YOUR PRIVACY, ABOUT YOUR PAST, BUT... WELL, I'VE HELPED YOU BUILD SOME AMAZING STUFF...
SINCE YOU SHOWED UP HERE A FEW YEARS AGO, YOU'VE ADVANCED THIS DEPARTMENT A HUNDREDFOLD. YOU'VE ESTABLISHED D-GATES IN PLACES WE NEVER EVEN KNEW EXISTED. YOU'VE INTRODUCED AND DECIPHERED OTHERWORLDLY ALIEN TECHNOLOGY THAT MADE US FEEL LIKE FLINTSTONES. AND YOU CAN ACTUALLY SLIDE BETWEEN DIMENSIONS YOURSELF...
UNASSISTED. NO TECHNOLOGY.
THAT I KNOW OF.

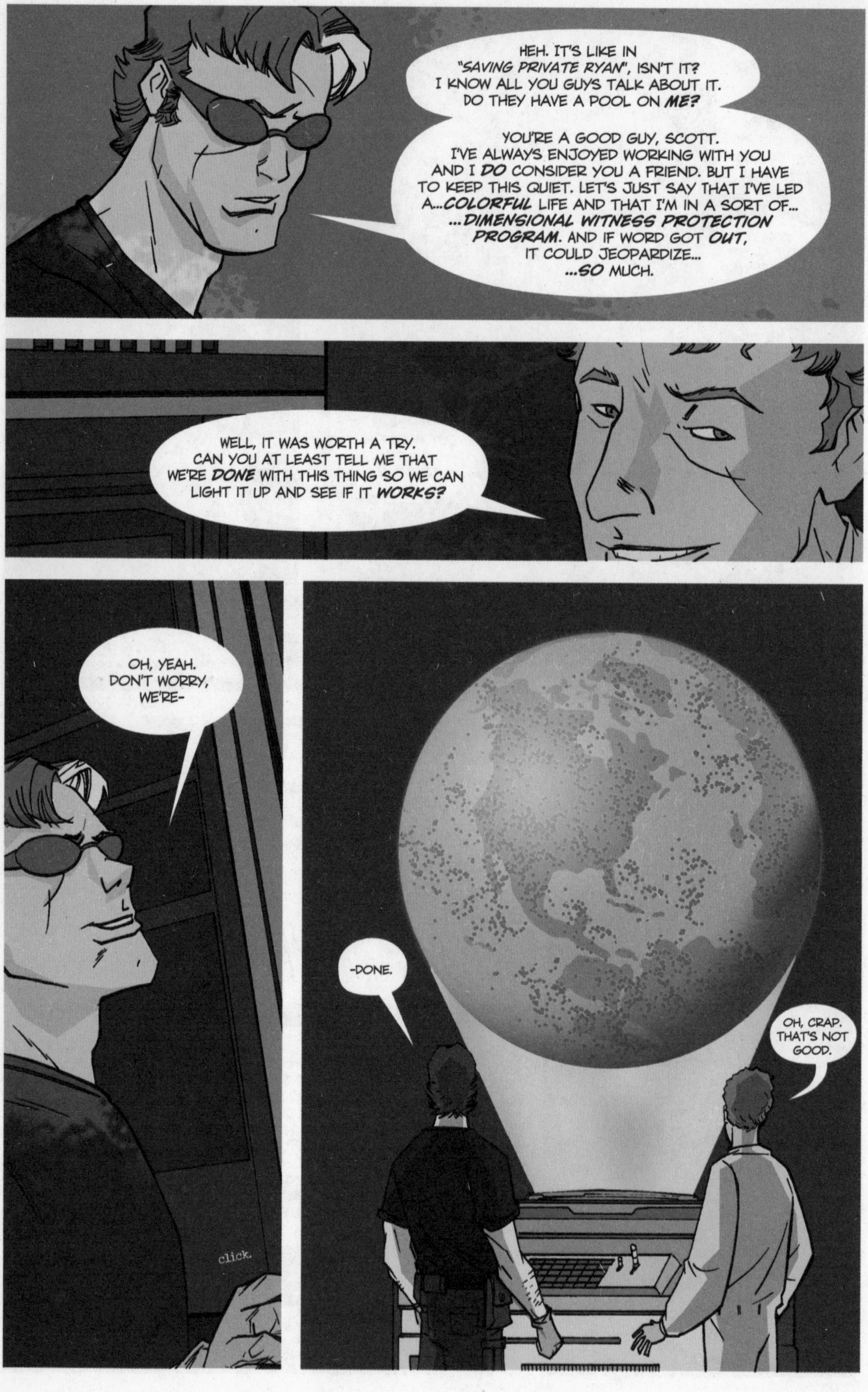
HEH. IT'S LIKE IN "SAVING PRIVATE RYAN", ISN'T IT? I KNOW ALL YOU GUYS TALK ABOUT IT. DO THEY HAVE A POOL ON ME?
YOU'RE A GOOD GUY, SCOTT. I'VE ALWAYS ENJOYED WORKING WITH YOU AND I DO CONSIDER YOU A FRIEND. BUT I HAVE TO KEEP THIS QUIET. LET'S JUST SAY THAT I'VE LED A...COLORFUL LIFE AND THAT I'M IN A SORT OF... ...DIMENSIONAL WITNESS PROTECTION PROGRAM. AND IF WORD GOT OUT, IT COULD JEOPARDIZE... ...SO MUCH.
WELL, IT WAS WORTH A TRY. CAN YOU AT LEAST TELL ME THAT WE'RE DONE WITH THIS THING SO WE CAN LIGHT IT UP AND SEE IF IT WORKS?
OH, YEAH. DON'T WORRY, WE'RE-
click.
-DONE.
OH, CRAP. THAT'S NOT GOOD.

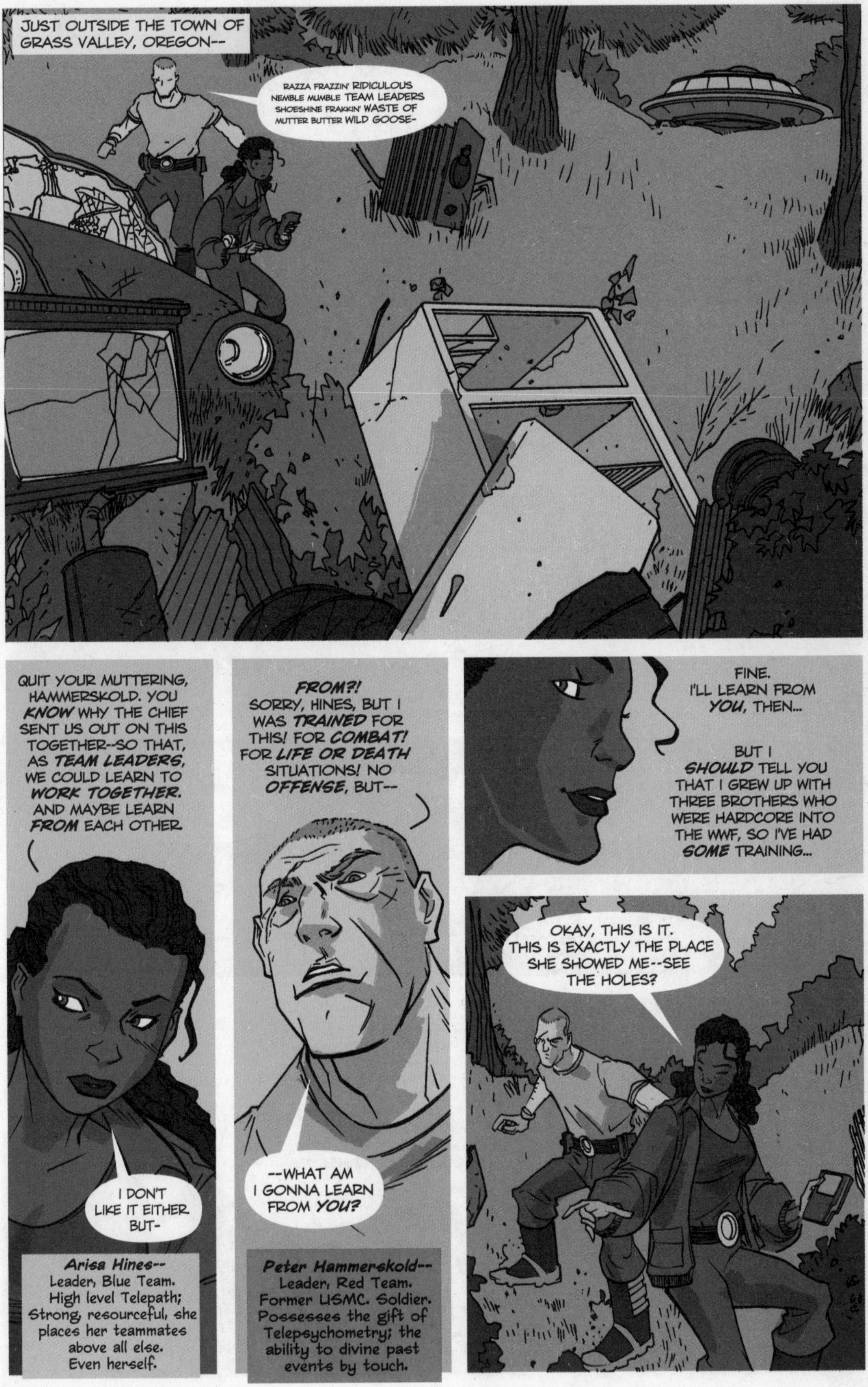

JUST OUTSIDE THE TOWN OF GRASS VALLEY, OREGON--
RAZZA FRAZZIN' RIDICULOUS NEMBLE MUMBLE TEAM LEADERS SHOESHINE FRAKKIN' WASTE OF MUTTER BUTTER WILD GOOSE-
QUIT YOUR MUTTERING, HAMMERSKOLD. YOU KNOW WHY THE CHIEF SENT US OUT ON THIS TOGETHER--SO THAT, AS TEAM LEADERS, WE COULD LEARN TO WORK TOGETHER. AND MAYBE LEARN FROM EACH OTHER.
I DON'T LIKE IT EITHER. BUT-
Arisa Hines-- Leader, Blue Team. High level Telepath; Strong, resourceful, she places her teammates above all else. Even herself.
FROM?! SORRY, HINES, BUT I WAS TRAINED FOR THIS! FOR COMBAT! FOR LIFE OR DEATH SITUATIONS! NO OFFENSE, BUT--
--WHAT AM I GONNA LEARN FROM YOU?
Peter Hammerskold-- Leader, Red Team. Former USMC. Soldier. Possesses the gift of Telepsychometry; the ability to divine past events by touch.
FINE. I'LL LEARN FROM YOU, THEN...
BUT I SHOULD TELL YOU THAT I GREW UP WITH THREE BROTHERS WHO WERE HARDCORE INTO THE WWF, SO I'VE HAD SOME TRAINING...
OKAY, THIS IS IT. THIS IS EXACTLY THE PLACE SHE SHOWED ME--SEE THE HOLES?

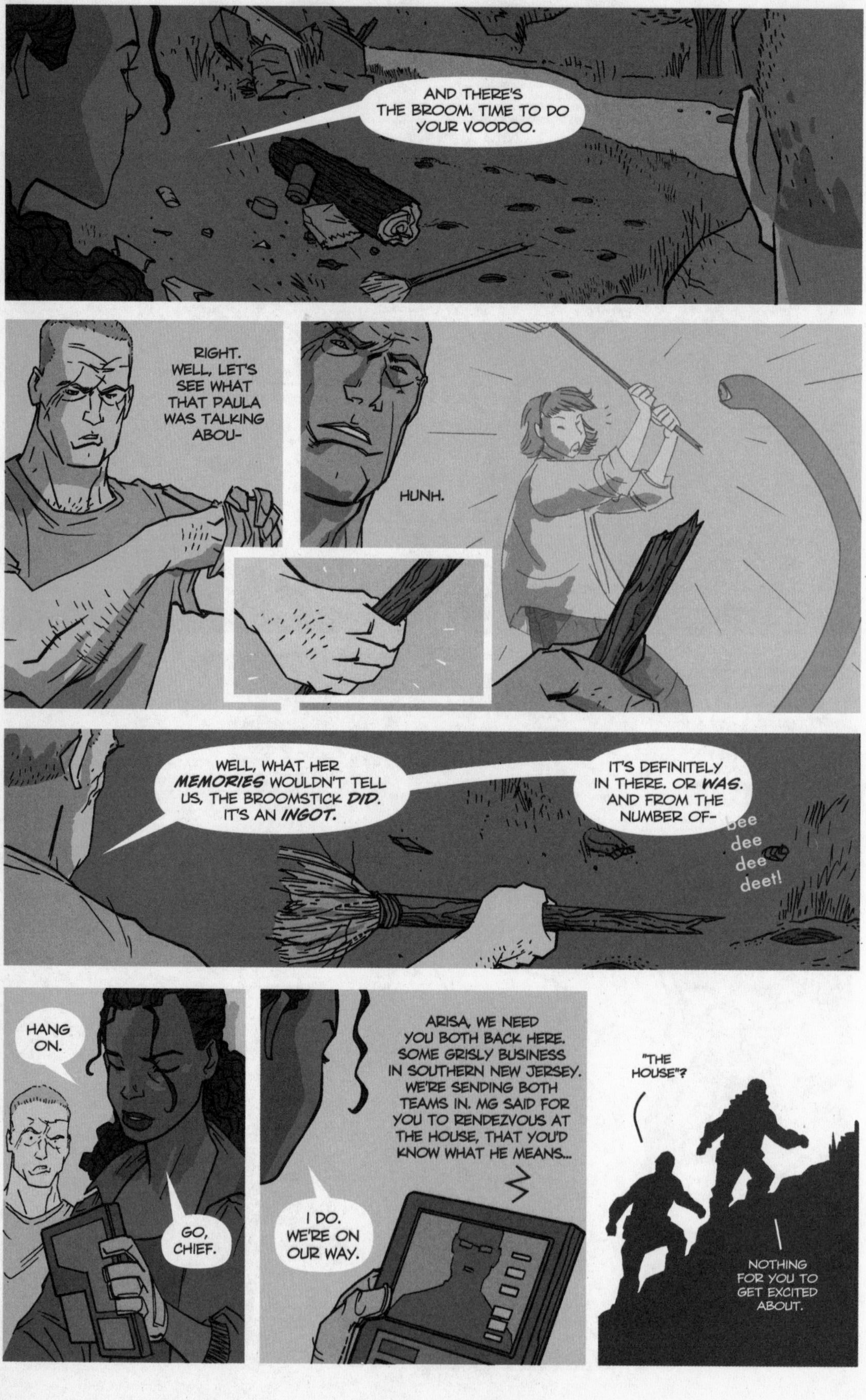
AND THERE'S THE BROOM. TIME TO DO YOUR VOODOO.
RIGHT. WELL, LET'S SEE WHAT THAT PAULA WAS TALKING ABOU-
HUNH.
WELL, WHAT HER MEMORIES WOULDN'T TELL US, THE BROOMSTICK DID. IT'S AN INGOT.
IT'S DEFINITELY IN THERE. OR WAS. AND FROM THE NUMBER OF-
bee dee dee deet!
HANG ON.
GO, CHIEF.
ARISA, WE NEED YOU BOTH BACK HERE. SOME GRISLY BUSINESS IN SOUTHERN NEW JERSEY. WE'RE SENDING BOTH TEAMS IN. MG SAID FOR YOU TO RENDEZVOUS AT THE HOUSE, THAT YOU'D KNOW WHAT HE MEANS...
I DO. WE'RE ON OUR WAY.
"THE HOUSE"?
NOTHING FOR YOU TO GET EXCITED ABOUT.

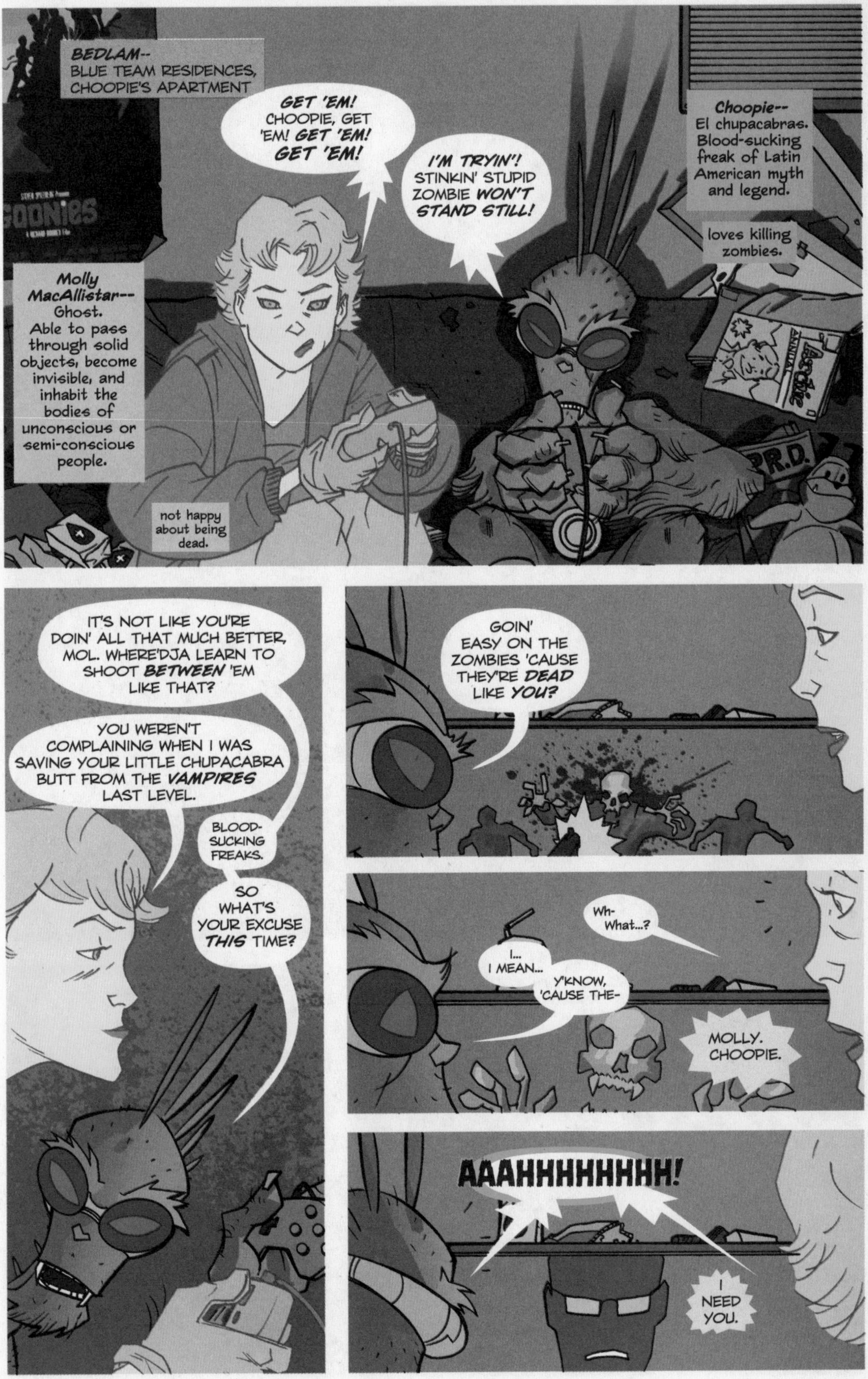

BEDLAM--
BLUE TEAM RESIDENCES, CHOOPIE'S APARTMENT
GET 'EM! CHOOPIE, GET 'EM! GET 'EM! GET 'EM!
I'M TRYIN'! STINKIN' STUPID ZOMBIE WON'T STAND STILL!
Choopie-- El chupacabras. Blood-sucking freak of Latin American myth and legend.
loves killing zombies.
Molly MacAllistar-- Ghost. Able to pass through solid objects, become invisible, and inhabit the bodies of unconscious or semi-conscious people.
not happy about being dead.
IT'S NOT LIKE YOU'RE DOIN' ALL THAT MUCH BETTER, MOL. WHERE'DJA LEARN TO SHOOT BETWEEN 'EM LIKE THAT?
YOU WEREN'T COMPLAINING WHEN I WAS SAVING YOUR LITTLE CHUPACABRA BUTT FROM THE VAMPIRES LAST LEVEL.
BLOOD-SUCKING FREAKS.
SO WHAT'S YOUR EXCUSE THIS TIME?
GOIN' EASY ON THE ZOMBIES 'CAUSE THEY'RE DEAD LIKE YOU?
Wh- What...?
I... I MEAN... Y'KNOW, 'CAUSE THE-
MOLLY. CHOOPIE.
AAAHHHHHHHH!
I NEED YOU.

YOU'RE TO RENDEZVOUS WITH MG IN THE DOCKING BAYS.

AND MOLLY, PLEASE STOP AND PICK-UP BIG ON YOUR WAY.

WHAT DO WE GOTTA GET BIG FOR?

WELL, WHEN *ARISA'S* AROUND, SHE ALERTS ALL OF US *TELEPATHICALLY* WHEN WE HAVE A MISSION, RIGHT?

SO, LIKE, WHEN SHE'S NOT AROUND, THE CHIEF HAS TO LET US KNOW SOME *OTHER* WAY...

AND SINCE BIG DOESN'T HAVE A *TV* OR ANY *ELECTRONICS* IN HIS APARTMENT...

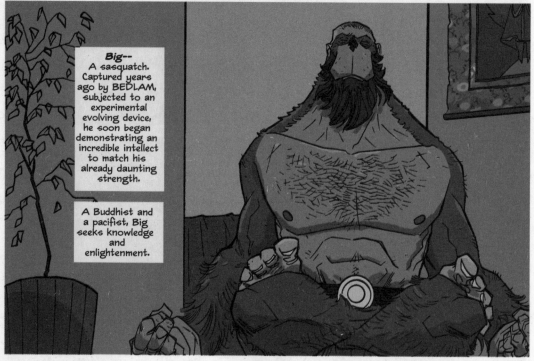

Big-- A sasquatch. Captured years ago by BEDLAM, subjected to an experimental evolving device, he soon began demonstrating an incredible intellect to match his already daunting strength.

A Buddhist and a pacifist, Big seeks knowledge and enlightenment.

BIG? IT'S MOLLY.

AND CHOOPIE!

Ah.

COME RIGHT IN. YOU BOTH KNOW THAT YOU'RE ALWAYS WELCOME.

I DO.

THE CHIEF WANTS US TO MEET MG IN THE BAYS.

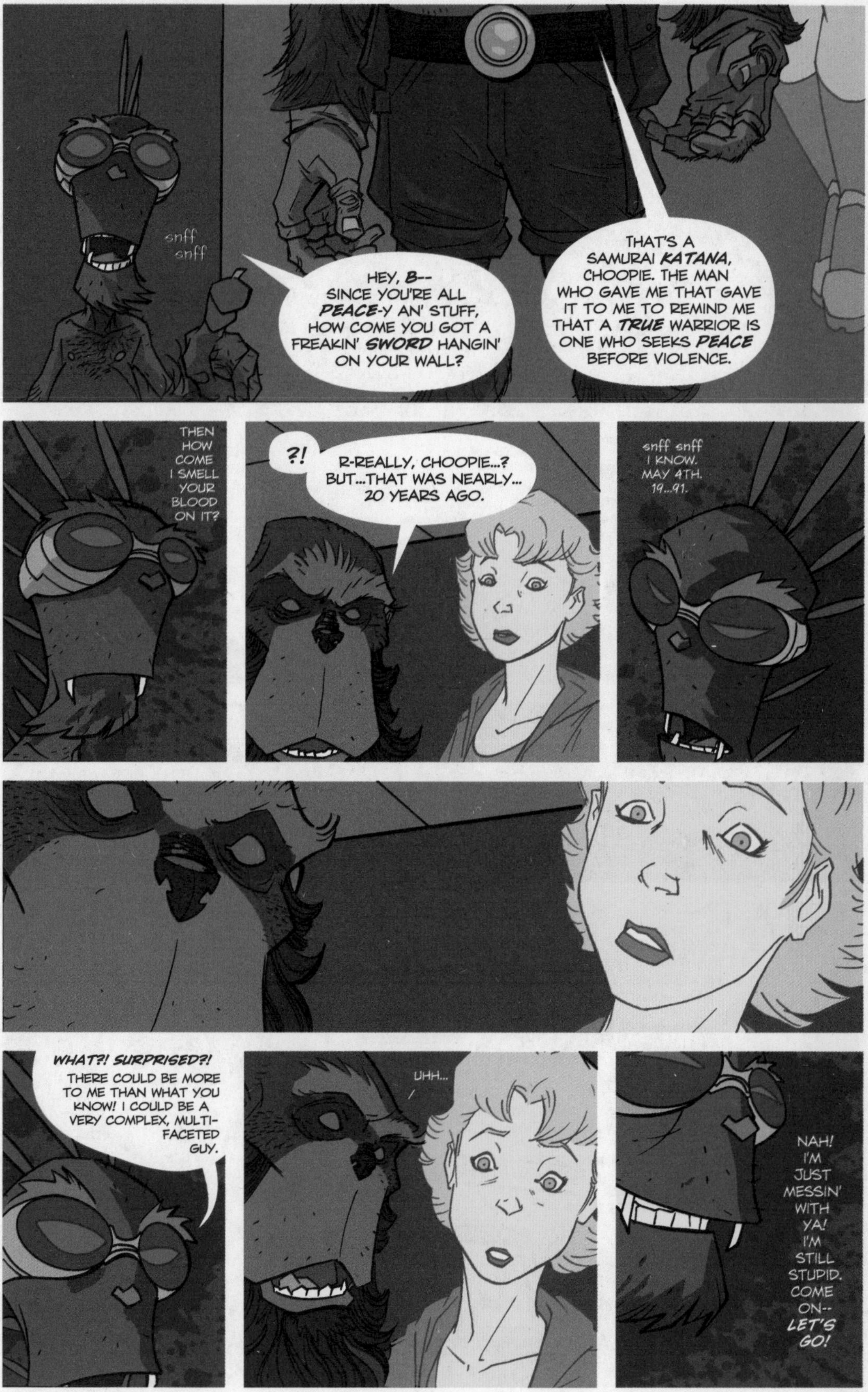
snff snff
HEY, B-- SINCE YOU'RE ALL PEACE-Y AN' STUFF, HOW COME YOU GOT A FREAKIN' SWORD HANGIN' ON YOUR WALL?
THAT'S A SAMURAI KATANA, CHOOPIE. THE MAN WHO GAVE ME THAT GAVE IT TO ME TO REMIND ME THAT A TRUE WARRIOR IS ONE WHO SEEKS PEACE BEFORE VIOLENCE.
THEN HOW COME I SMELL YOUR BLOOD ON IT?
?!
R-REALLY, CHOOPIE...? BUT...THAT WAS NEARLY... 20 YEARS AGO.
snff snff I KNOW. MAY 4TH. 19...91.
WHAT?! SURPRISED?! THERE COULD BE MORE TO ME THAN WHAT YOU KNOW! I COULD BE A VERY COMPLEX, MULTI-FACETED GUY.
UHH...
NAH! I'M JUST MESSIN' WITH YA! I'M STILL STUPID. COME ON-- LET'S GO!

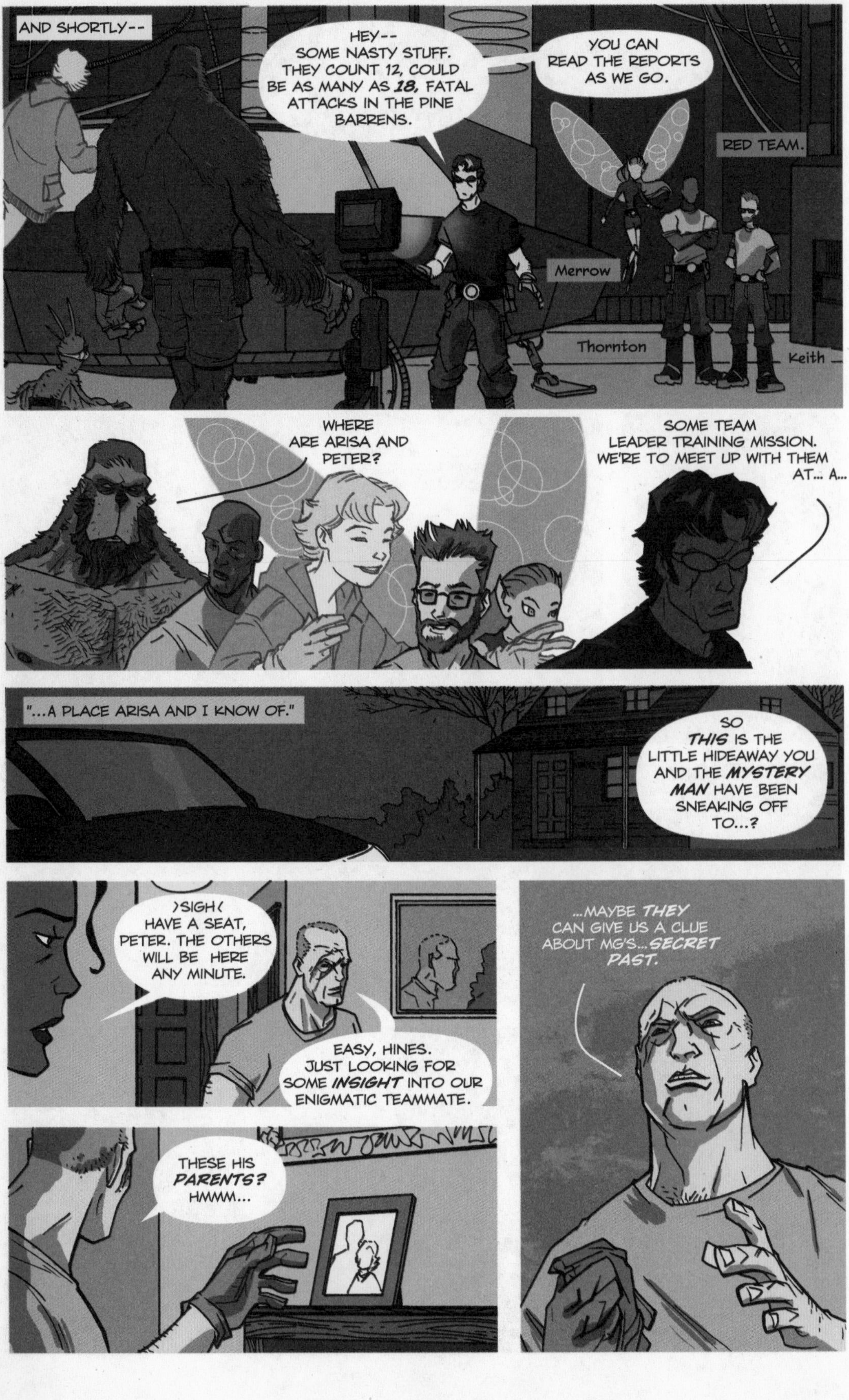
AND SHORTLY--
HEY-- SOME NASTY STUFF. THEY COUNT 12, COULD BE AS MANY AS 18, FATAL ATTACKS IN THE PINE BARRENS.
YOU CAN READ THE REPORTS AS WE GO.
RED TEAM.
Merrow
Thornton
Keith
WHERE ARE ARISA AND PETER?
SOME TEAM LEADER TRAINING MISSION. WE'RE TO MEET UP WITH THEM AT... A...
"...A PLACE ARISA AND I KNOW OF."
SO THIS IS THE LITTLE HIDEAWAY YOU AND THE MYSTERY MAN HAVE BEEN SNEAKING OFF TO...?
>SIGH< HAVE A SEAT, PETER. THE OTHERS WILL BE HERE ANY MINUTE.
EASY, HINES. JUST LOOKING FOR SOME INSIGHT INTO OUR ENIGMATIC TEAMMATE.
THESE HIS PARENTS? HMMM...
...MAYBE THEY CAN GIVE US A CLUE ABOUT MG'S...SECRET PAST.

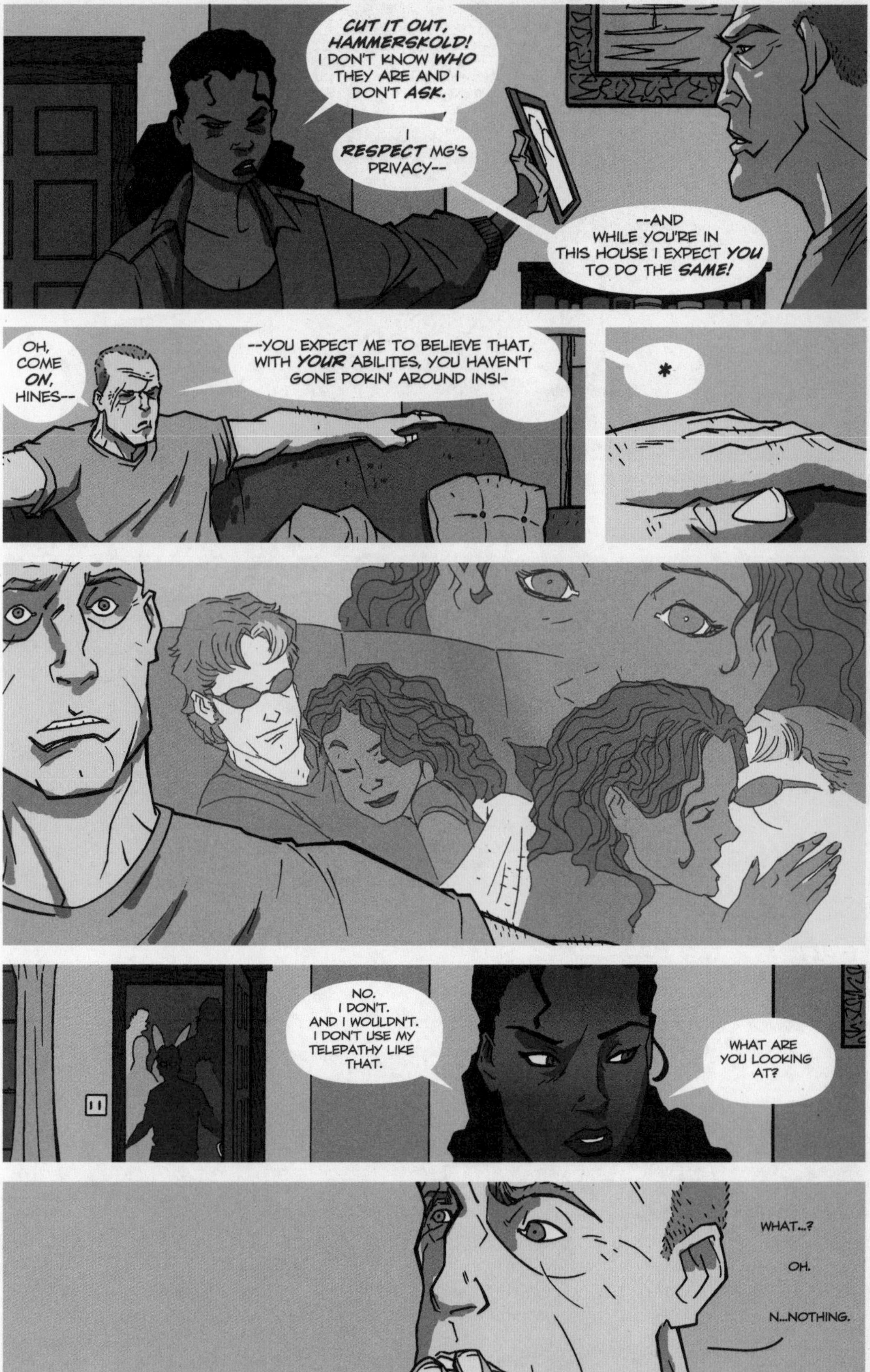

CUT IT OUT, HAMMERSKOLD! I DON'T KNOW WHO THEY ARE AND I DON'T ASK.
I RESPECT MG'S PRIVACY--
--AND WHILE YOU'RE IN THIS HOUSE I EXPECT YOU TO DO THE SAME!
OH, COME ON, HINES--
--YOU EXPECT ME TO BELIEVE THAT, WITH YOUR ABILITES, YOU HAVEN'T GONE POKIN' AROUND INSI-
*
NO. I DON'T. AND I WOULDN'T. I DON'T USE MY TELEPATHY LIKE THAT.
WHAT ARE YOU LOOKING AT?
WHAT...?
OH.
N...NOTHING.

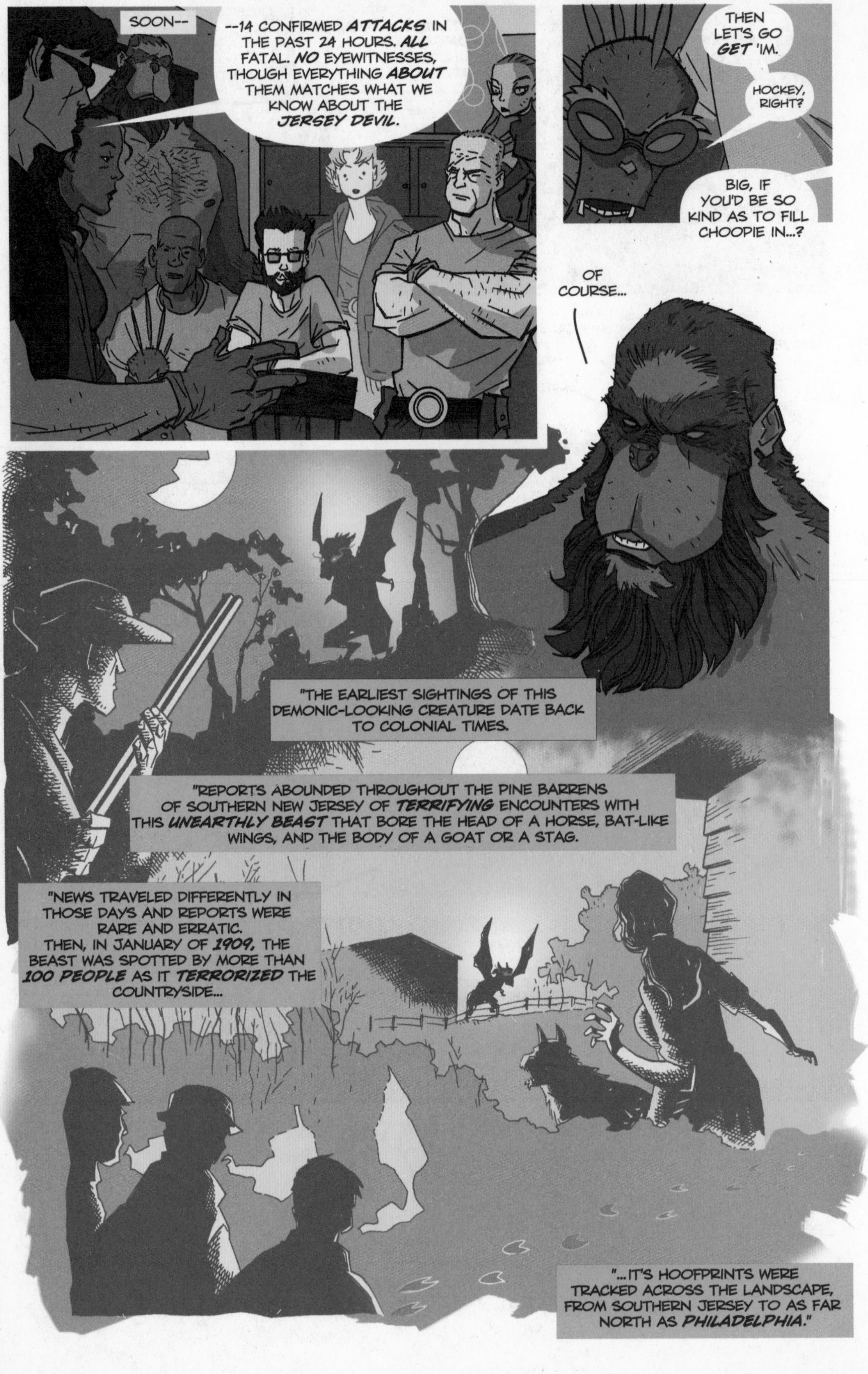
SOON--
--14 CONFIRMED ATTACKS IN THE PAST 24 HOURS. ALL FATAL. NO EYEWITNESSES, THOUGH EVERYTHING ABOUT THEM MATCHES WHAT WE KNOW ABOUT THE JERSEY DEVIL.
THEN LET'S GO GET 'IM.
HOCKEY, RIGHT?
BIG, IF YOU'D BE SO KIND AS TO FILL CHOOPIE IN...?
OF COURSE...
"THE EARLIEST SIGHTINGS OF THIS DEMONIC-LOOKING CREATURE DATE BACK TO COLONIAL TIMES.
"REPORTS ABOUNDED THROUGHOUT THE PINE BARRENS OF SOUTHERN NEW JERSEY OF TERRIFYING ENCOUNTERS WITH THIS UNEARTHLY BEAST THAT BORE THE HEAD OF A HORSE, BAT-LIKE WINGS, AND THE BODY OF A GOAT OR A STAG.
"NEWS TRAVELED DIFFERENTLY IN THOSE DAYS AND REPORTS WERE RARE AND ERRATIC. THEN, IN JANUARY OF 1909, THE BEAST WAS SPOTTED BY MORE THAN 100 PEOPLE AS IT TERRORIZED THE COUNTRYSIDE...
"...IT'S HOOFPRINTS WERE TRACKED ACROSS THE LANDSCAPE, FROM SOUTHERN JERSEY TO AS FAR NORTH AS PHILADELPHIA."

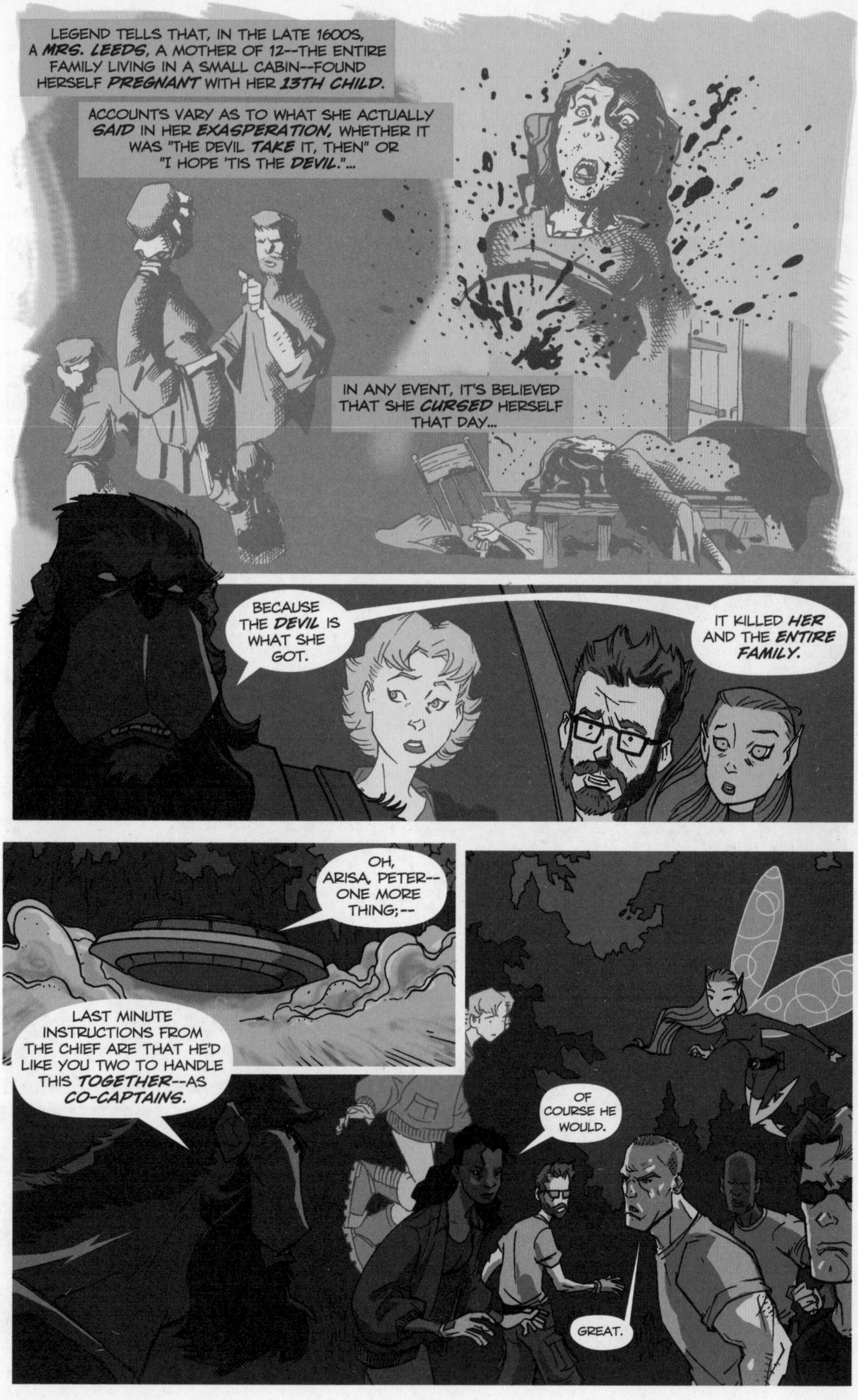
LEGEND TELLS THAT, IN THE LATE 1600S, A MRS. LEEDS, A MOTHER OF 12--THE ENTIRE FAMILY LIVING IN A SMALL CABIN--FOUND HERSELF PREGNANT WITH HER 13TH CHILD.
ACCOUNTS VARY AS TO WHAT SHE ACTUALLY SAID IN HER EXASPERATION, WHETHER IT WAS "THE DEVIL TAKE IT, THEN" OR "I HOPE 'TIS THE DEVIL."...
IN ANY EVENT, IT'S BELIEVED THAT SHE CURSED HERSELF THAT DAY...
BECAUSE THE DEVIL IS WHAT SHE GOT.
IT KILLED HER AND THE ENTIRE FAMILY.
OH, ARISA, PETER--ONE MORE THING;--
LAST MINUTE INSTRUCTIONS FROM THE CHIEF ARE THAT HE'D LIKE YOU TWO TO HANDLE THIS TOGETHER--AS CO-CAPTAINS.
OF COURSE HE WOULD.
GREAT.

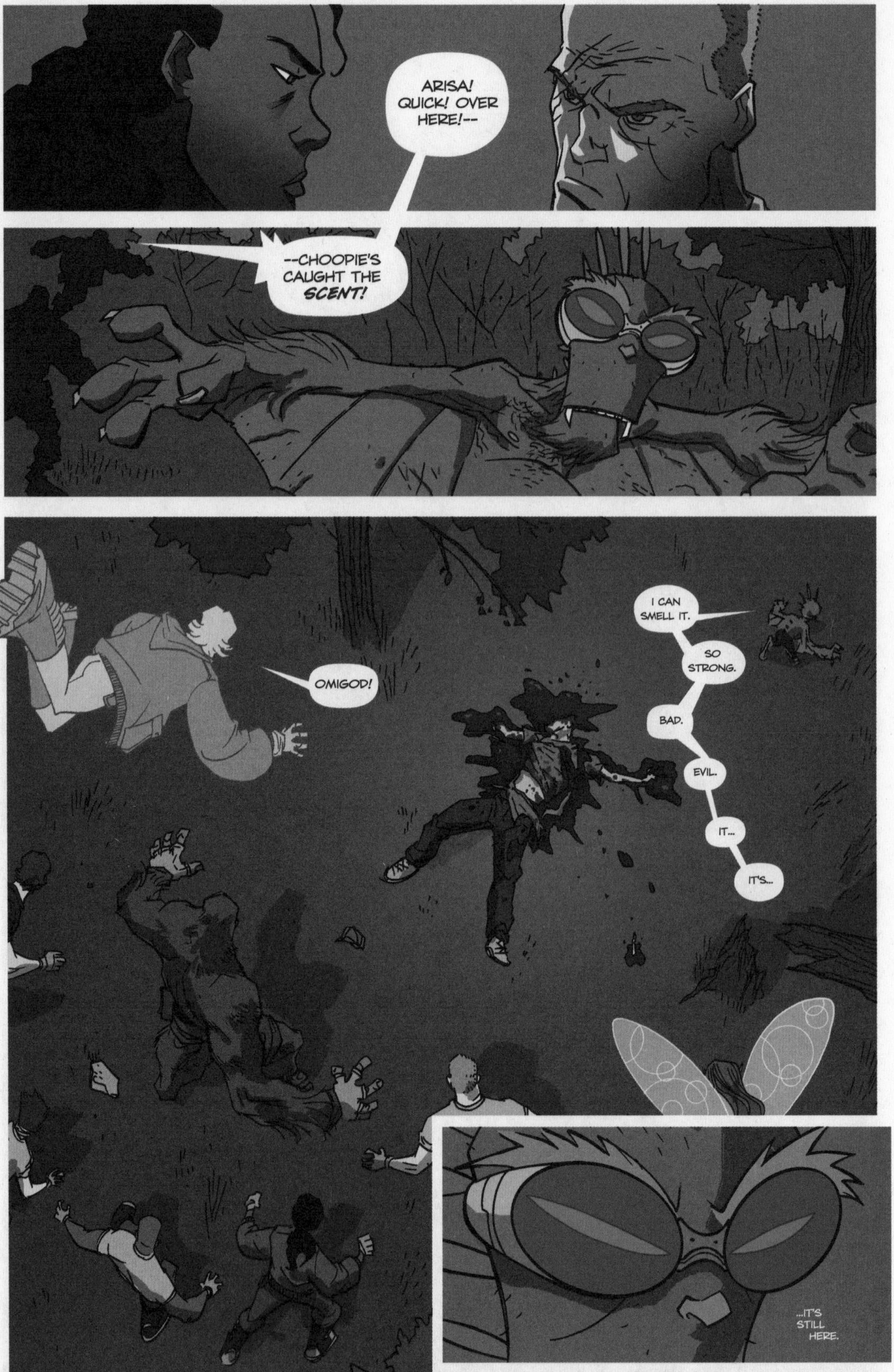
ARISA! QUICK! OVER HERE!--
--CHOOPIE'S CAUGHT THE SCENT!
OMIGOD!
I CAN SMELL IT.
SO STRONG.
BAD.
EVIL.
IT...
IT'S...
...IT'S STILL HERE.

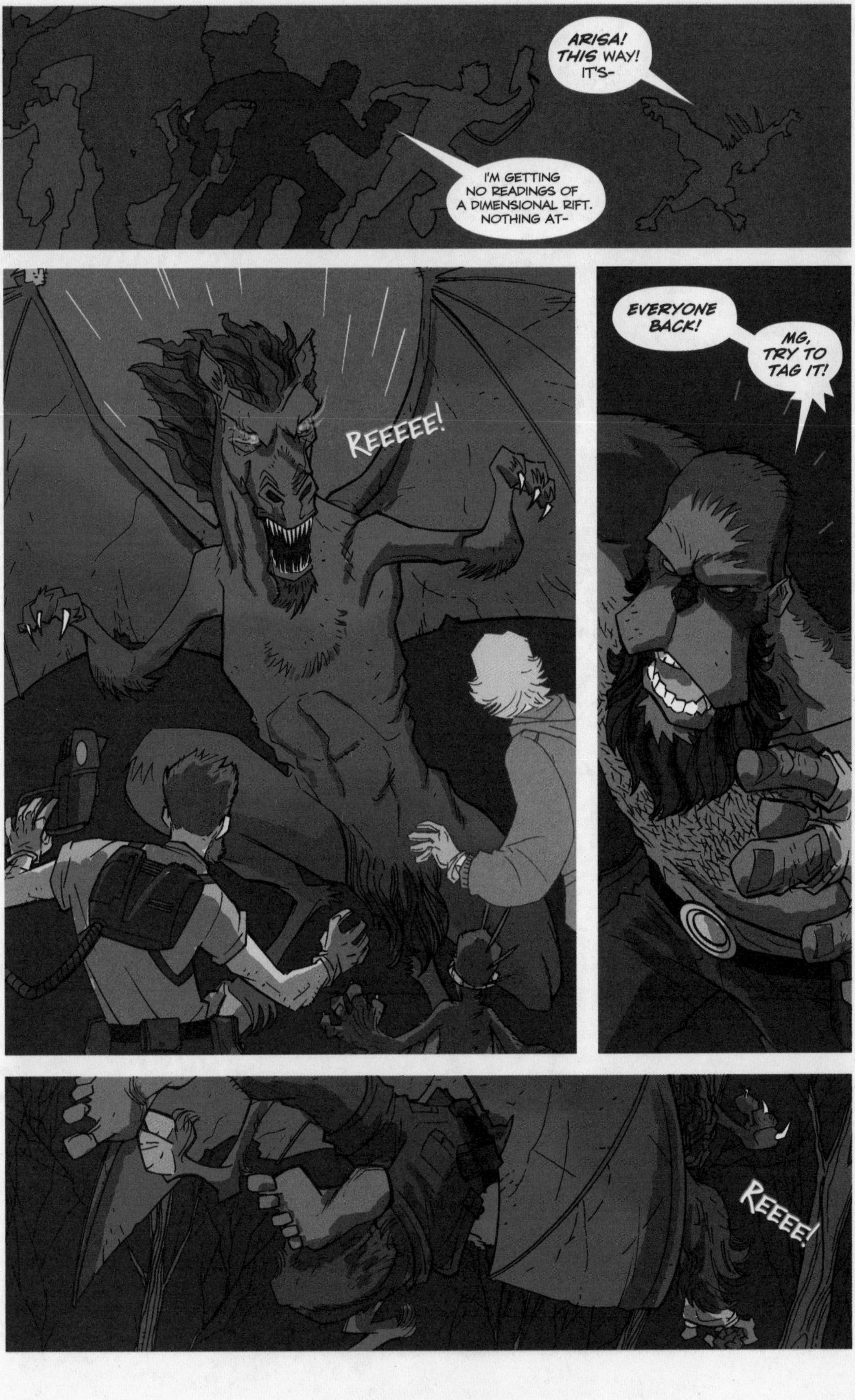
ARISA! THIS WAY! IT'S-
I'M GETTING NO READINGS OF A DIMENSIONAL RIFT. NOTHING AT-
REEEEE!
EVERYONE BACK!
MG, TRY TO TAG IT!
REEEE!

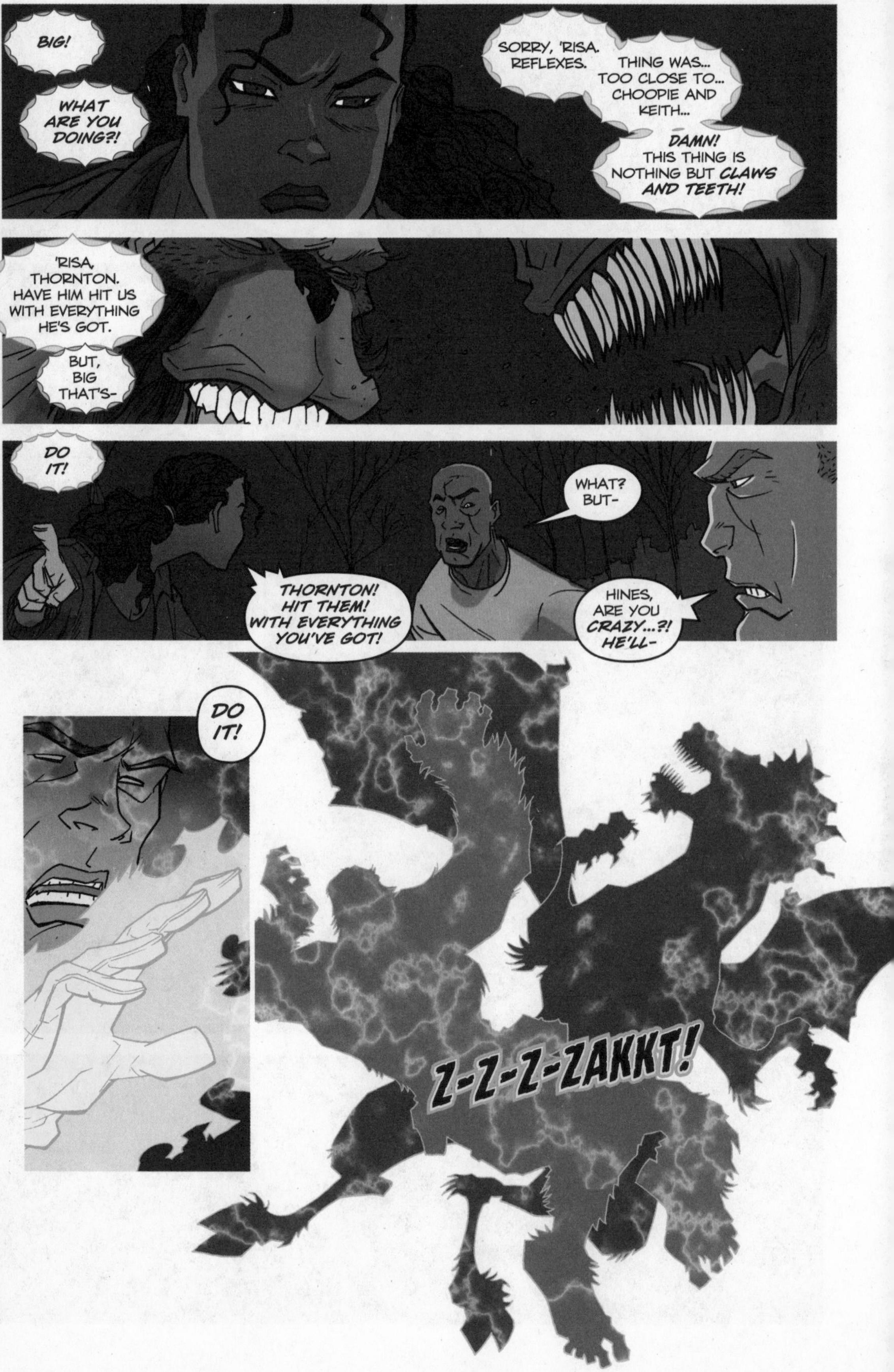
BIG!
WHAT ARE YOU DOING?!
SORRY, 'RISA. REFLEXES.
THING WAS... TOO CLOSE TO... CHOOPIE AND KEITH...
DAMN! THIS THING IS NOTHING BUT CLAWS AND TEETH!
'RISA, THORNTON. HAVE HIM HIT US WITH EVERYTHING HE'S GOT.
BUT, BIG THAT'S-
DO IT!
WHAT? BUT-
THORNTON! HIT THEM! WITH EVERYTHING YOU'VE GOT!
HINES, ARE YOU CRAZY...?! HE'LL-
DO IT!
Z-Z-Z-ZAKKT!

MG! KEITH! PLASMA-NET THAT *THING!*

BIG! ARE YOU—

CRISPY. I'M FRIED, BOTH PHYSICALLY AND MENTALLY. BUT I'LL LIVE.

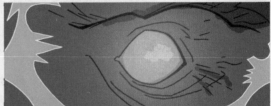

BUT *I* KNEW IT WAS COMING. LET'S HOPE THAT *THAT JOLT* WAS ENOUGH TO KEEP THAT THING *DOWN* FOR A—

MERDE!

WHERE'D IT GO?! WHERE—

krak!

AHHHH!

UHH!

thud!

whump!

GEH!

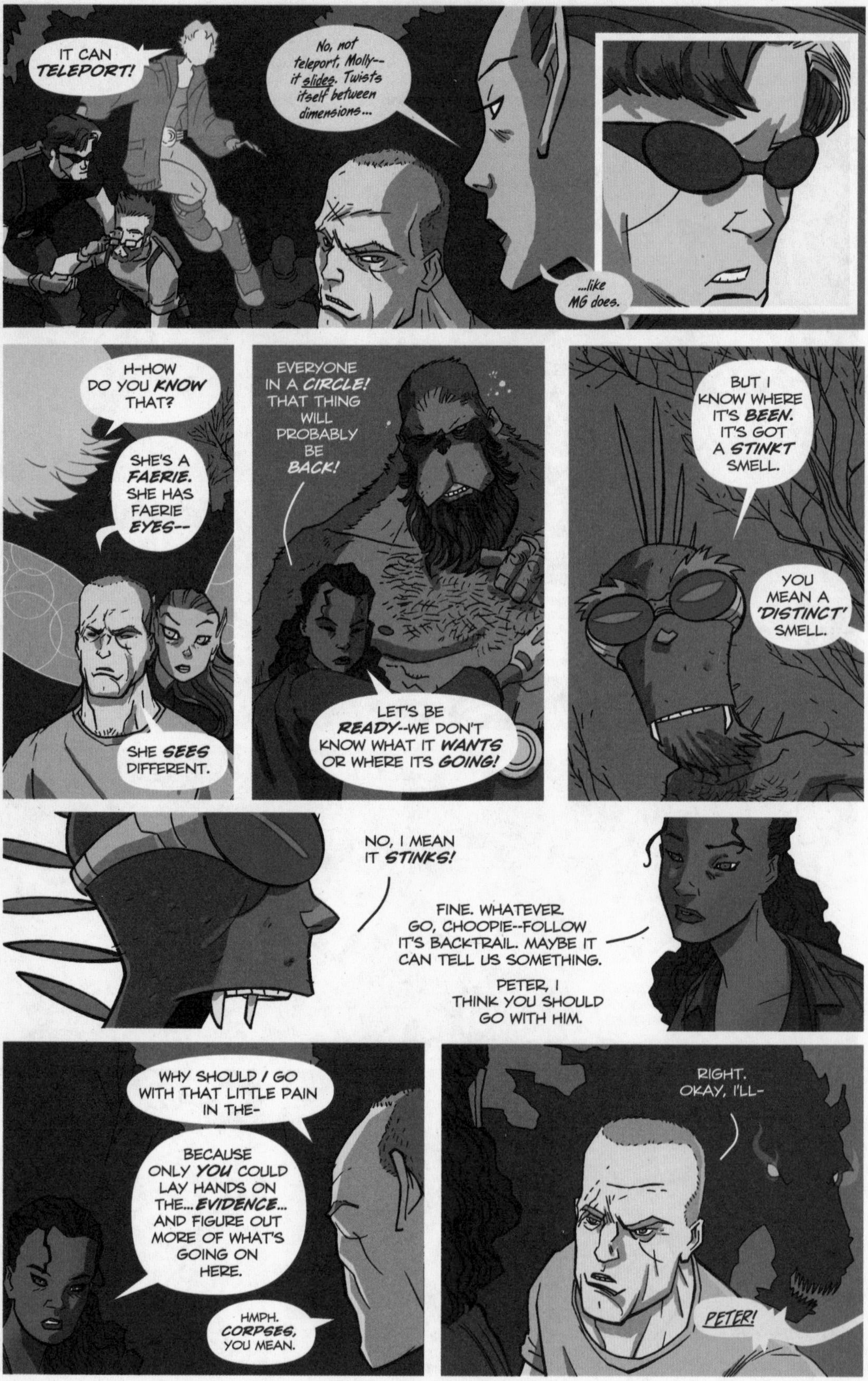

IT CAN TELEPORT!
No, not teleport, Molly--it slides. Twists itself between dimensions...
...like MG does.
H-HOW DO YOU KNOW THAT?
SHE'S A FAERIE. SHE HAS FAERIE EYES--
SHE SEES DIFFERENT.
EVERYONE IN A CIRCLE! THAT THING WILL PROBABLY BE BACK!
LET'S BE READY--WE DON'T KNOW WHAT IT WANTS OR WHERE ITS GOING!
BUT I KNOW WHERE IT'S BEEN. IT'S GOT A STINKT SMELL.
YOU MEAN A 'DISTINCT' SMELL.
NO, I MEAN IT STINKS!
FINE. WHATEVER. GO, CHOOPIE--FOLLOW IT'S BACKTRAIL. MAYBE IT CAN TELL US SOMETHING.
PETER, I THINK YOU SHOULD GO WITH HIM.
WHY SHOULD I GO WITH THAT LITTLE PAIN IN THE-
BECAUSE ONLY YOU COULD LAY HANDS ON THE...EVIDENCE... AND FIGURE OUT MORE OF WHAT'S GOING ON HERE.
HMPH. CORPSES, YOU MEAN.
RIGHT. OKAY, I'LL-
PETER!

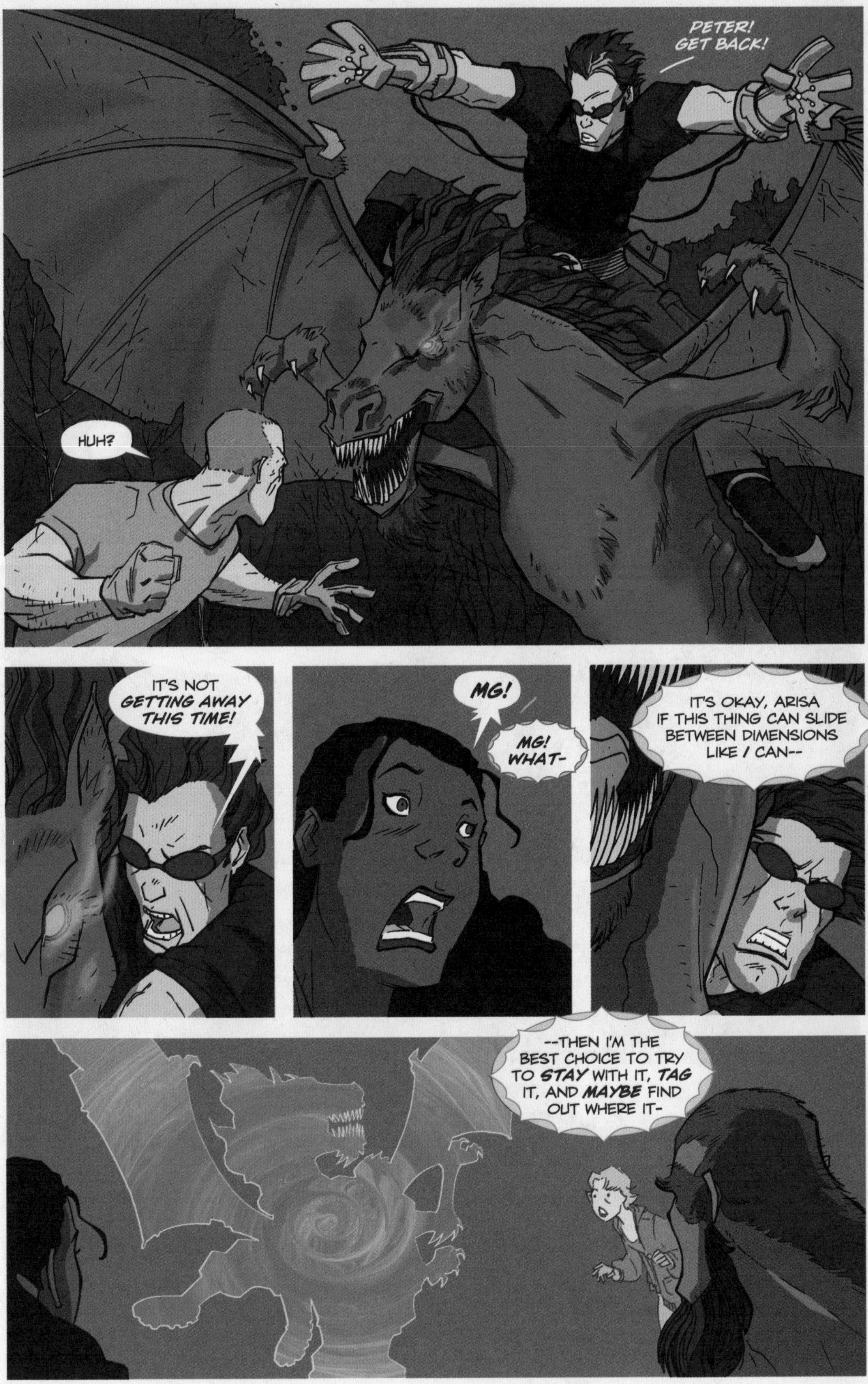
PETER! GET BACK!
HUH?
IT'S NOT GETTING AWAY THIS TIME!
MG!
MG! WHAT-
IT'S OKAY, ARISA IF THIS THING CAN SLIDE BETWEEN DIMENSIONS LIKE I CAN--
--THEN I'M THE BEST CHOICE TO TRY TO STAY WITH IT, TAG IT, AND MAYBE FIND OUT WHERE IT-

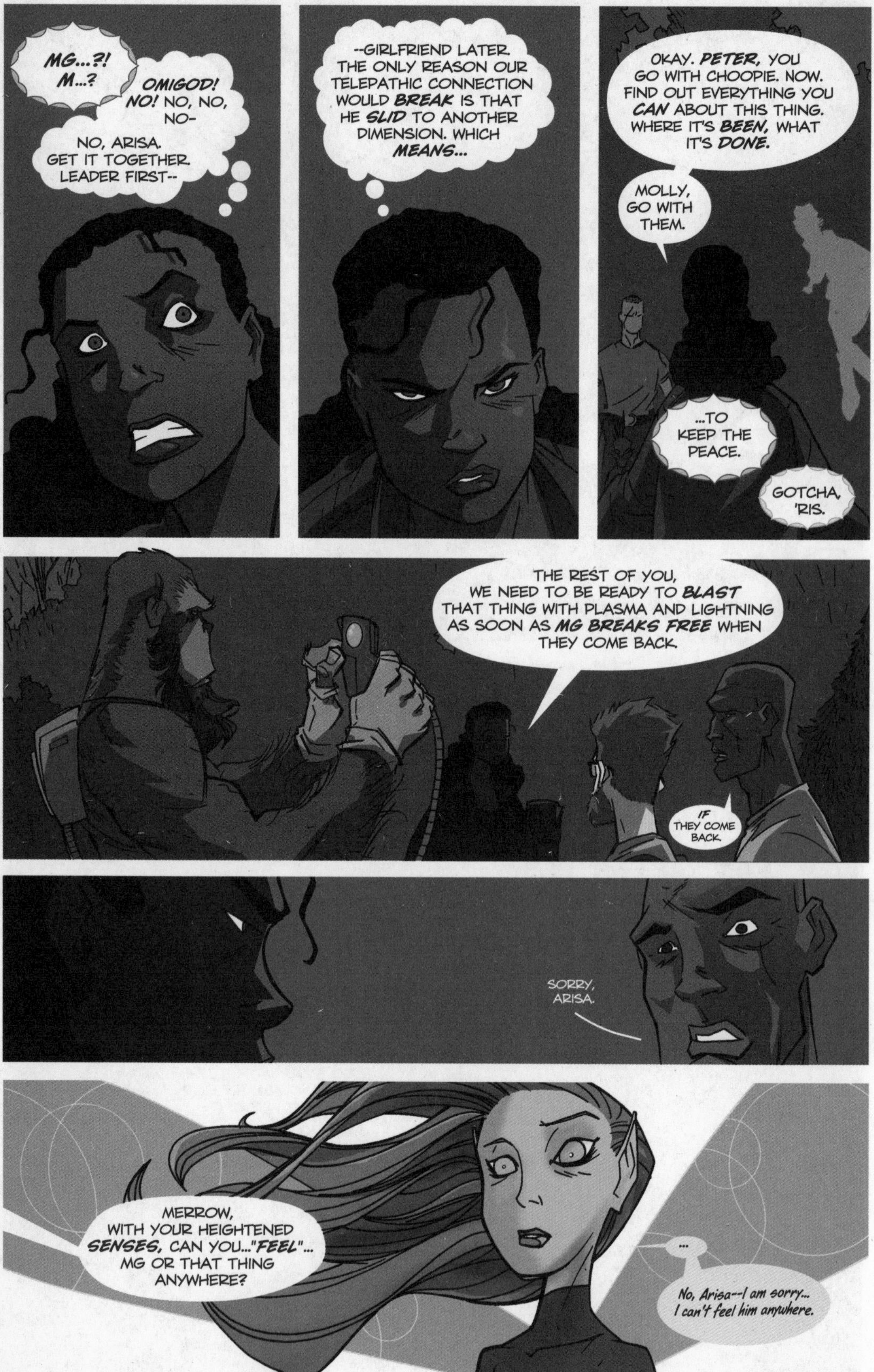
MG...?! M...?
OMIGOD! NO! NO, NO, NO-
NO, ARISA. GET IT TOGETHER. LEADER FIRST--
--GIRLFRIEND LATER. THE ONLY REASON OUR TELEPATHIC CONNECTION WOULD BREAK IS THAT HE SLID TO ANOTHER DIMENSION. WHICH MEANS...
OKAY. PETER, YOU GO WITH CHOOPIE. NOW. FIND OUT EVERYTHING YOU CAN ABOUT THIS THING. WHERE IT'S BEEN, WHAT IT'S DONE.
MOLLY, GO WITH THEM.
...TO KEEP THE PEACE.
GOTCHA, 'RIS.
THE REST OF YOU, WE NEED TO BE READY TO BLAST THAT THING WITH PLASMA AND LIGHTNING AS SOON AS MG BREAKS FREE WHEN THEY COME BACK.
IF THEY COME BACK.
SORRY, ARISA.
MERROW, WITH YOUR HEIGHTENED SENSES, CAN YOU..."FEEL"... MG OR THAT THING ANYWHERE?
...
No, Arisa--I am sorry... I can't feel him anywhere.

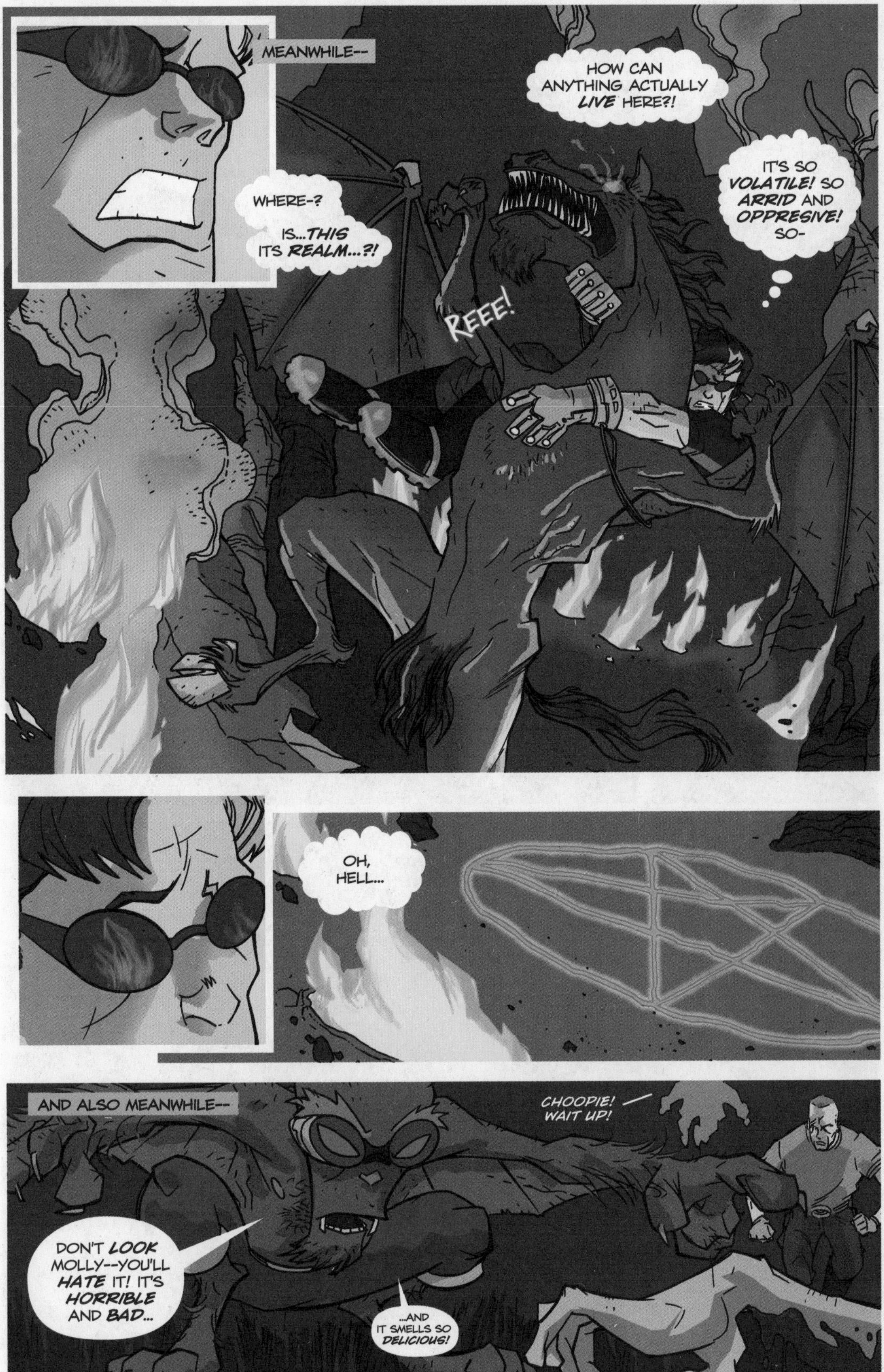
MEANWHILE--
HOW CAN ANYTHING ACTUALLY LIVE HERE?!
WHERE-? IS...THIS ITS REALM...?!
IT'S SO VOLATILE! SO ARRID AND OPPRESIVE! SO-
REEE!
OH, HELL...
AND ALSO MEANWHILE--
CHOOPIE! WAIT UP!
DON'T LOOK MOLLY--YOU'LL HATE IT! IT'S HORRIBLE AND BAD...
...AND IT SMELLS SO DELICIOUS!

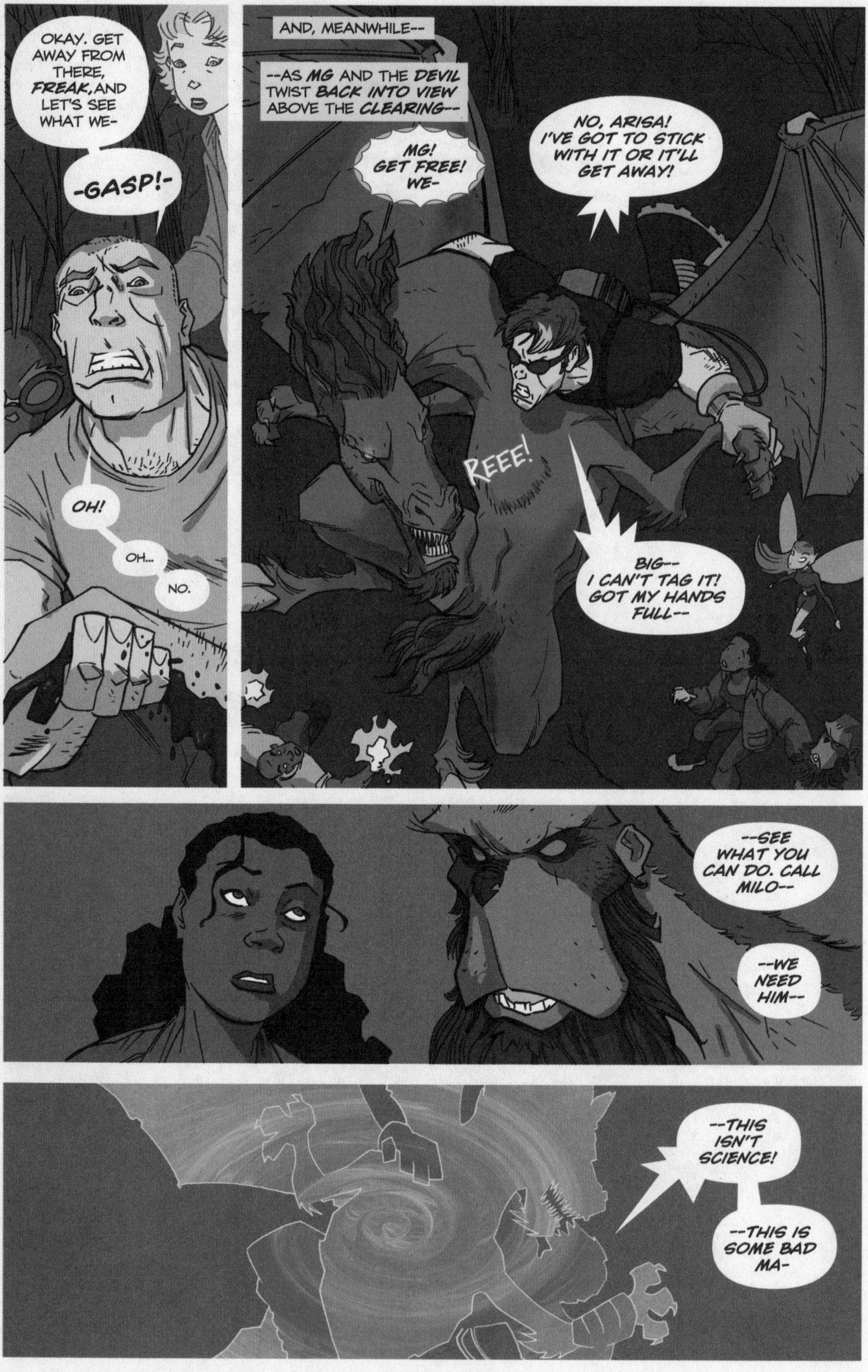
OKAY. GET AWAY FROM THERE, FREAK, AND LET'S SEE WHAT WE-
-GASP!-
OH!
OH...
NO.
AND, MEANWHILE--
--AS MG AND THE DEVIL TWIST BACK INTO VIEW ABOVE THE CLEARING--
MG! GET FREE! WE-
NO, ARISA! I'VE GOT TO STICK WITH IT OR IT'LL GET AWAY!
REEE!
BIG-- I CAN'T TAG IT! GOT MY HANDS FULL--
--SEE WHAT YOU CAN DO. CALL MILO--
--WE NEED HIM--
--THIS ISN'T SCIENCE!
--THIS IS SOME BAD MA-

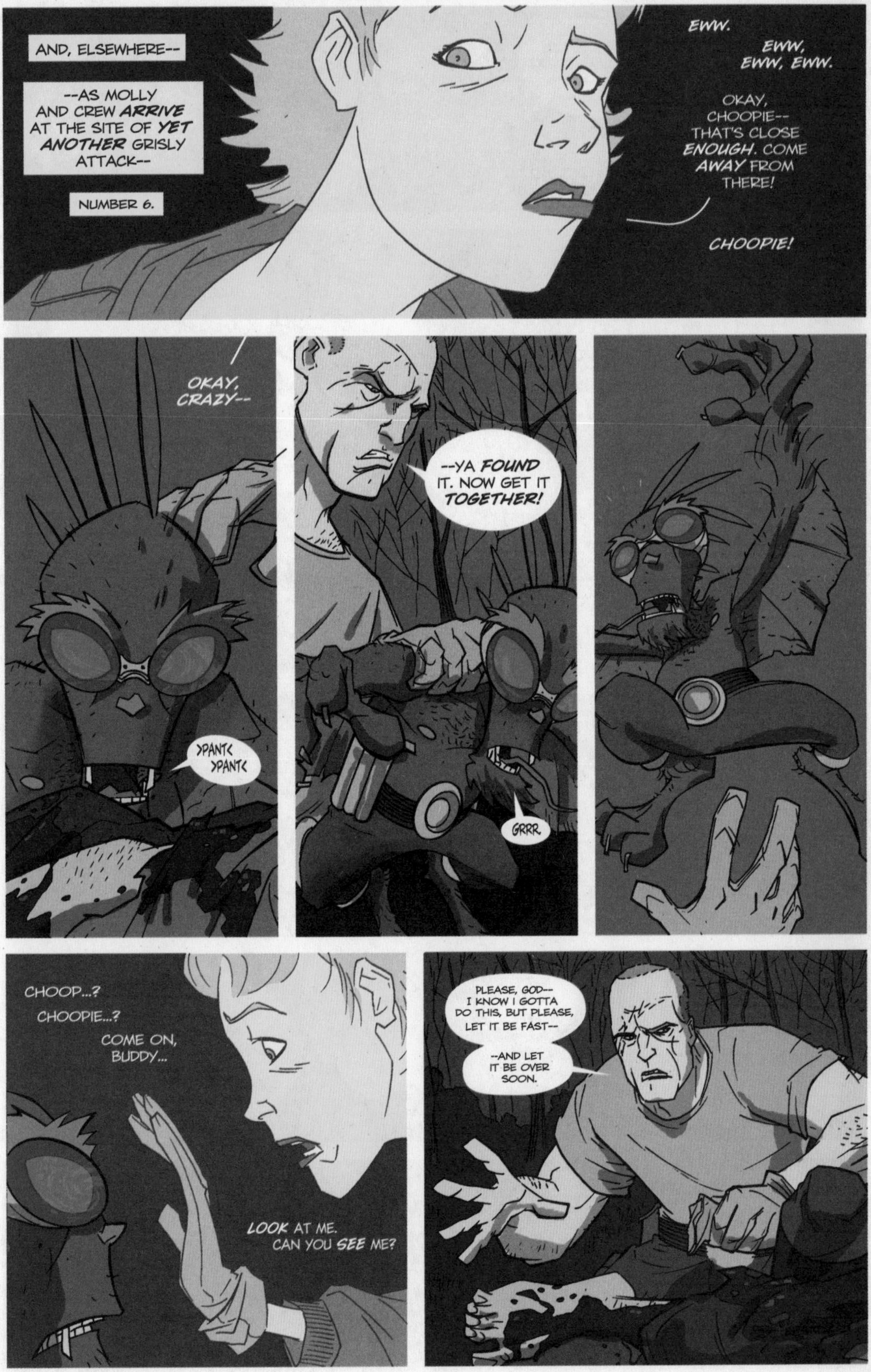
AND, ELSEWHERE--
--AS MOLLY AND CREW ARRIVE AT THE SITE OF YET ANOTHER GRISLY ATTACK--
NUMBER 6.
EWW.
EWW, EWW, EWW.
OKAY, CHOOPIE-- THAT'S CLOSE ENOUGH. COME AWAY FROM THERE!
CHOOPIE!
OKAY, CRAZY--
--YA FOUND IT. NOW GET IT TOGETHER!
>PANT< >PANT<
GRRR.
CHOOP...?
CHOOPIE...?
COME ON, BUDDY...
LOOK AT ME. CAN YOU SEE ME?
PLEASE, GOD-- I KNOW I GOTTA DO THIS, BUT PLEASE, LET IT BE FAST--
--AND LET IT BE OVER SOON.

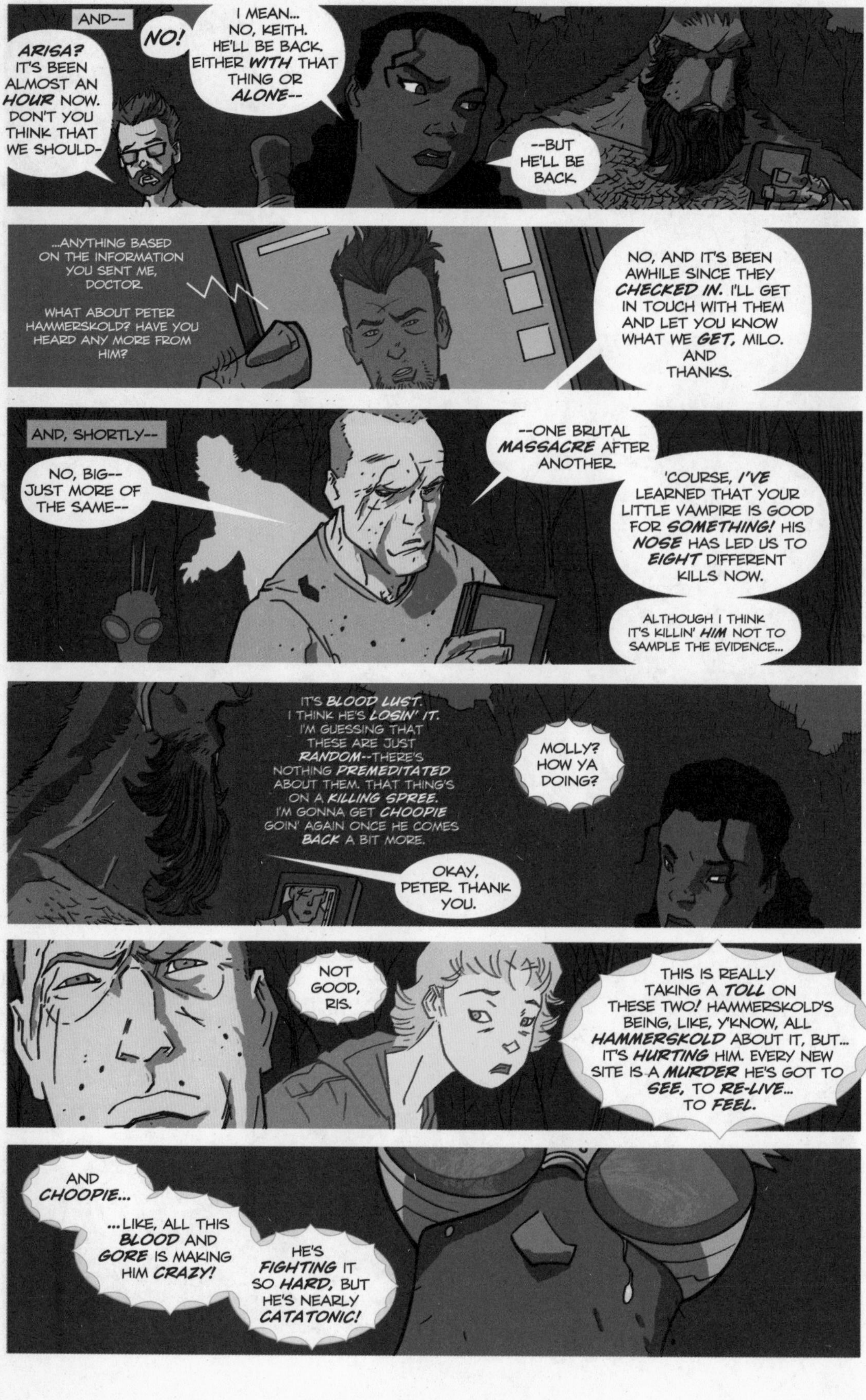
AND--
ARISA? IT'S BEEN ALMOST AN HOUR NOW. DON'T YOU THINK THAT WE SHOULD-
NO!
I MEAN... NO, KEITH. HE'LL BE BACK. EITHER WITH THAT THING OR ALONE--
--BUT HE'LL BE BACK.
...ANYTHING BASED ON THE INFORMATION YOU SENT ME, DOCTOR.
WHAT ABOUT PETER HAMMERSKOLD? HAVE YOU HEARD ANY MORE FROM HIM?
NO, AND IT'S BEEN AWHILE SINCE THEY CHECKED IN. I'LL GET IN TOUCH WITH THEM AND LET YOU KNOW WHAT WE GET, MILO. AND THANKS.
AND, SHORTLY--
NO, BIG-- JUST MORE OF THE SAME--
--ONE BRUTAL MASSACRE AFTER ANOTHER.
'COURSE, I'VE LEARNED THAT YOUR LITTLE VAMPIRE IS GOOD FOR SOMETHING! HIS NOSE HAS LED US TO EIGHT DIFFERENT KILLS NOW.
ALTHOUGH I THINK IT'S KILLIN' HIM NOT TO SAMPLE THE EVIDENCE...
IT'S BLOOD LUST. I THINK HE'S LOSIN' IT. I'M GUESSING THAT THESE ARE JUST RANDOM--THERE'S NOTHING PREMEDITATED ABOUT THEM. THAT THING'S ON A KILLING SPREE. I'M GONNA GET CHOOPIE GOIN' AGAIN ONCE HE COMES BACK A BIT MORE.
MOLLY? HOW YA DOING?
OKAY, PETER. THANK YOU.
NOT GOOD, RIS.
THIS IS REALLY TAKING A TOLL ON THESE TWO! HAMMERSKOLD'S BEING, LIKE, Y'KNOW, ALL HAMMERSKOLD ABOUT IT, BUT... IT'S HURTING HIM. EVERY NEW SITE IS A MURDER HE'S GOT TO SEE, TO RE-LIVE... TO FEEL.
AND CHOOPIE...
...LIKE, ALL THIS BLOOD AND GORE IS MAKING HIM CRAZY!
HE'S FIGHTING IT SO HARD, BUT HE'S NEARLY CATATONIC!

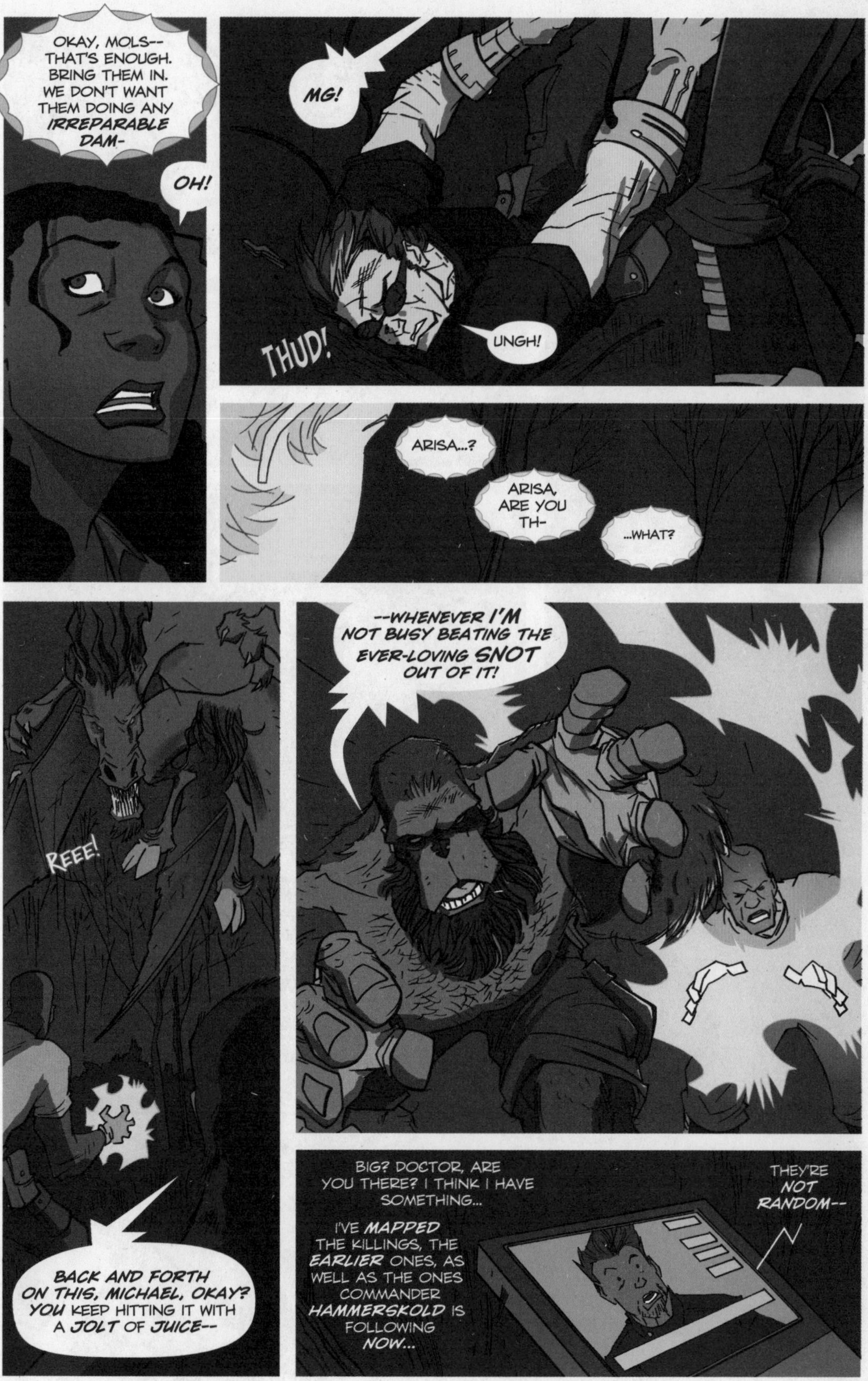
OKAY, MOLS-- THAT'S ENOUGH. BRING THEM IN. WE DON'T WANT THEM DOING ANY IRREPARABLE DAM-
OH!
MG!
THUD!
UNGH!
ARISA...?
ARISA, ARE YOU TH-
...WHAT?
REEE!
BACK AND FORTH ON THIS, MICHAEL, OKAY? YOU KEEP HITTING IT WITH A JOLT OF JUICE--
--WHENEVER I'M NOT BUSY BEATING THE EVER-LOVING SNOT OUT OF IT!
BIG? DOCTOR, ARE YOU THERE? I THINK I HAVE SOMETHING...
I'VE MAPPED THE KILLINGS, THE EARLIER ONES, AS WELL AS THE ONES COMMANDER HAMMERSKOLD IS FOLLOWING NOW...
THEY'RE NOT RANDOM--

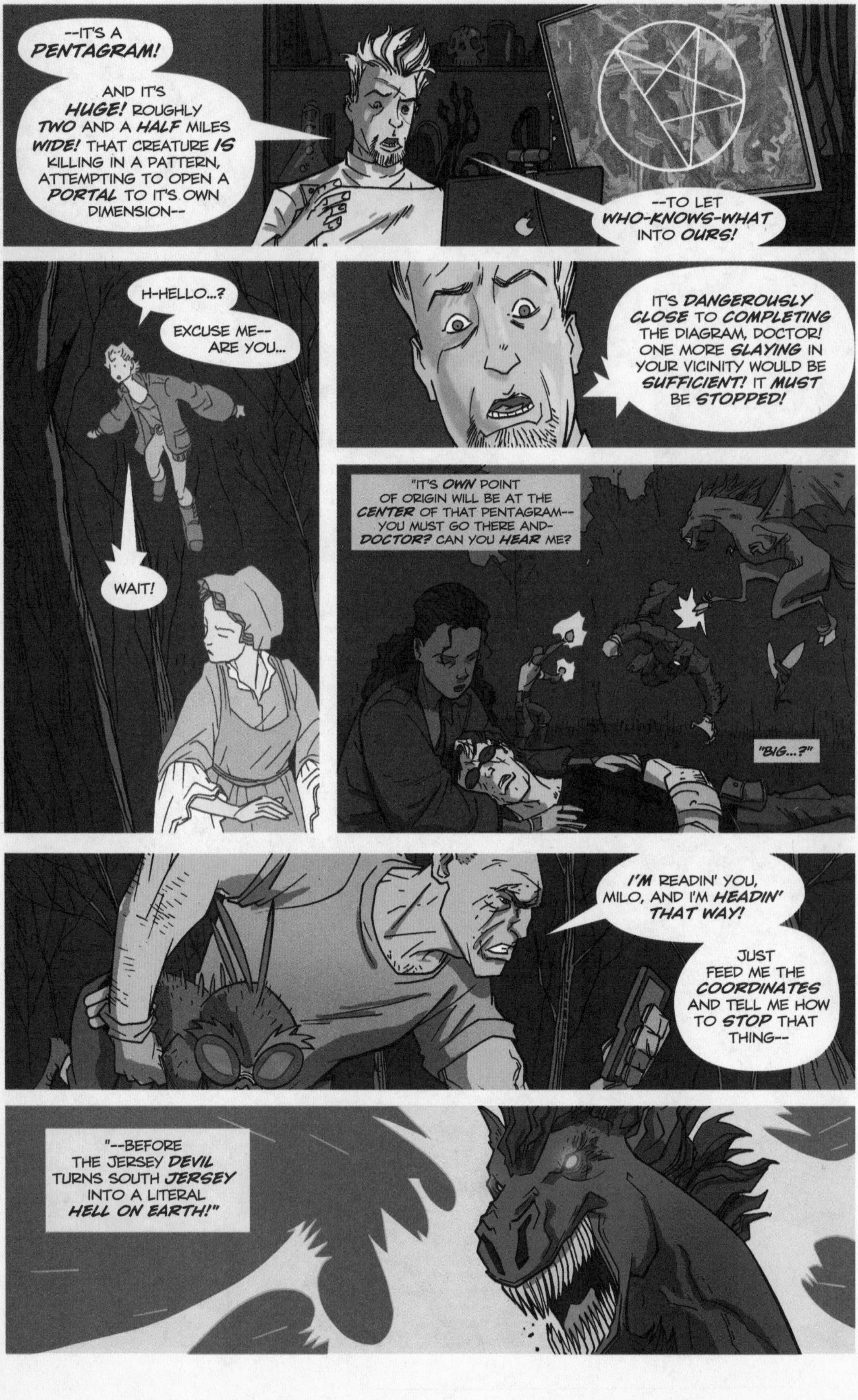
--IT'S A PENTAGRAM!
AND IT'S HUGE! ROUGHLY TWO AND A HALF MILES WIDE! THAT CREATURE IS KILLING IN A PATTERN, ATTEMPTING TO OPEN A PORTAL TO IT'S OWN DIMENSION--
--TO LET WHO-KNOWS-WHAT INTO OURS!
H-HELLO...?
EXCUSE ME-- ARE YOU...
WAIT!
IT'S DANGEROUSLY CLOSE TO COMPLETING THE DIAGRAM, DOCTOR! ONE MORE SLAYING IN YOUR VICINITY WOULD BE SUFFICIENT! IT MUST BE STOPPED!
"IT'S OWN POINT OF ORIGIN WILL BE AT THE CENTER OF THAT PENTAGRAM-- YOU MUST GO THERE AND- DOCTOR? CAN YOU HEAR ME?
"BIG...?"
I'M READIN' YOU, MILO, AND I'M HEADIN' THAT WAY!
JUST FEED ME THE COORDINATES AND TELL ME HOW TO STOP THAT THING--
"--BEFORE THE JERSEY DEVIL TURNS SOUTH JERSEY INTO A LITERAL HELL ON EARTH!"

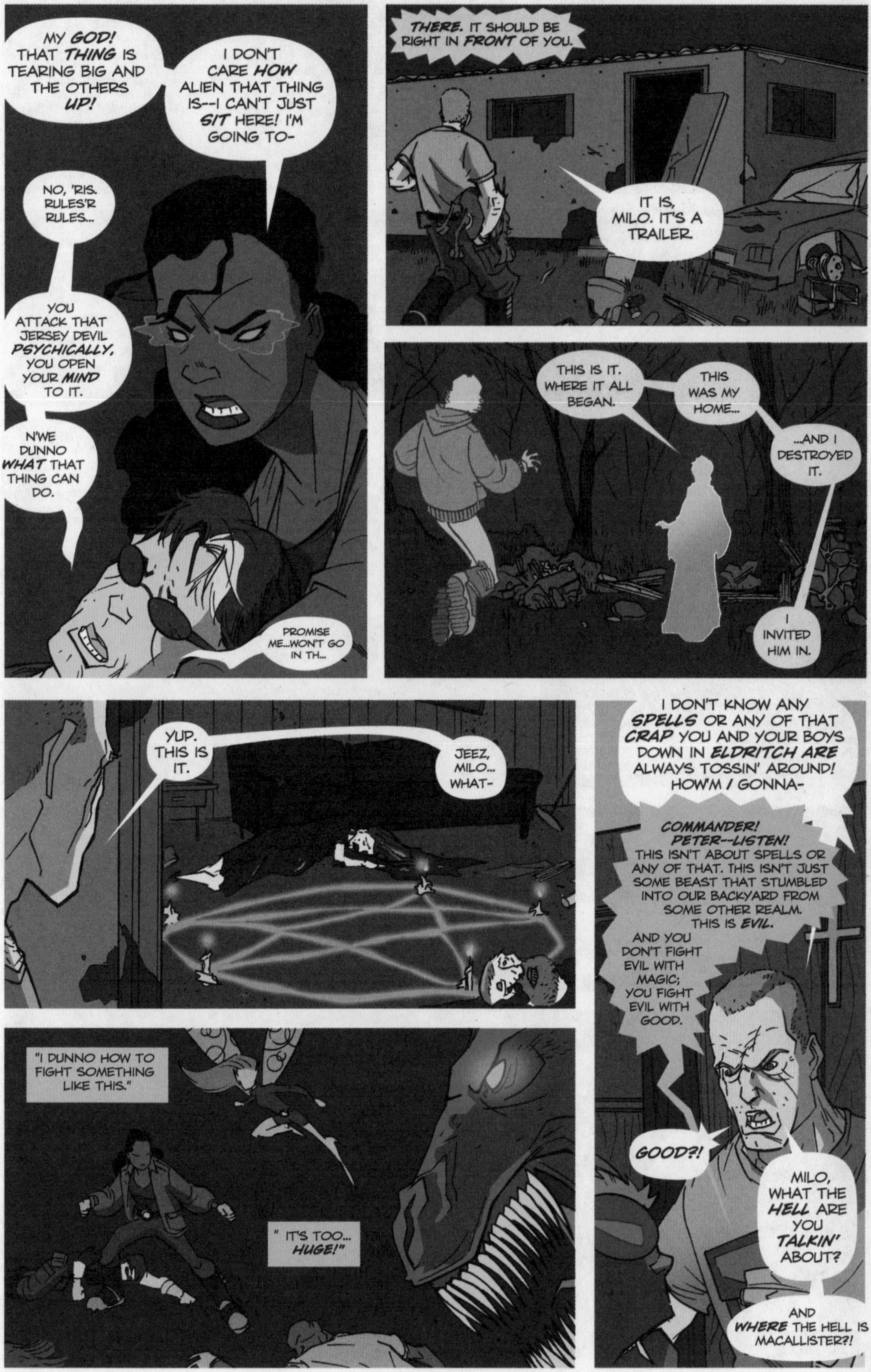
MY GOD! THAT THING IS TEARING BIG AND THE OTHERS UP!
I DON'T CARE HOW ALIEN THAT THING IS--I CAN'T JUST SIT HERE! I'M GOING TO-
NO, 'RIS. RULES'R RULES...
YOU ATTACK THAT JERSEY DEVIL PSYCHICALLY, YOU OPEN YOUR MIND TO IT.
N'WE DUNNO WHAT THAT THING CAN DO.
PROMISE ME...WON'T GO IN TH...
THERE. IT SHOULD BE RIGHT IN FRONT OF YOU.
IT IS, MILO. IT'S A TRAILER.
THIS IS IT. WHERE IT ALL BEGAN.
THIS WAS MY HOME...
...AND I DESTROYED IT.
I INVITED HIM IN.
YUP. THIS IS IT.
JEEZ, MILO... WHAT-
"I DUNNO HOW TO FIGHT SOMETHING LIKE THIS."
" IT'S TOO... HUGE!"
I DON'T KNOW ANY SPELLS OR ANY OF THAT CRAP YOU AND YOUR BOYS DOWN IN ELDRITCH ARE ALWAYS TOSSIN' AROUND! HOW'M I GONNA-
COMMANDER! PETER--LISTEN! THIS ISN'T ABOUT SPELLS OR ANY OF THAT. THIS ISN'T JUST SOME BEAST THAT STUMBLED INTO OUR BACKYARD FROM SOME OTHER REALM. THIS IS EVIL.
AND YOU DON'T FIGHT EVIL WITH MAGIC; YOU FIGHT EVIL WITH GOOD.
GOOD?!
MILO, WHAT THE HELL ARE YOU TALKIN' ABOUT?
AND WHERE THE HELL IS MACALLISTER?!

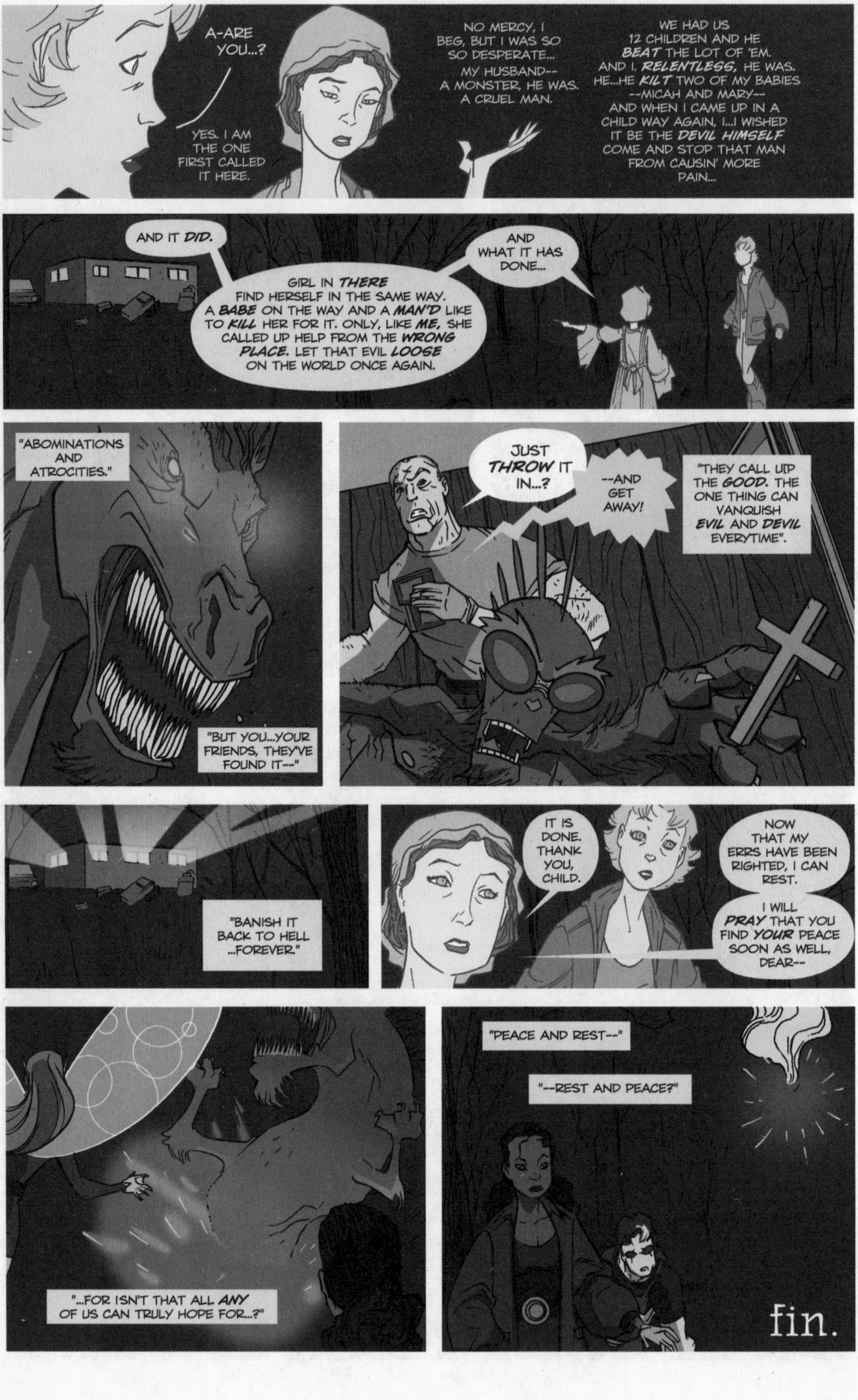
A-ARE YOU...?
YES. I AM THE ONE FIRST CALLED IT HERE.
NO MERCY, I BEG, BUT I WAS SO SO DESPERATE... MY HUSBAND-- A MONSTER, HE WAS. A CRUEL MAN.
WE HAD US 12 CHILDREN AND HE BEAT THE LOT OF 'EM. AND I. RELENTLESS, HE WAS. HE...HE KILT TWO OF MY BABIES --MICAH AND MARY-- AND WHEN I CAME UP IN A CHILD WAY AGAIN, I...I WISHED IT BE THE DEVIL HIMSELF COME AND STOP THAT MAN FROM CAUSIN' MORE PAIN...
AND IT DID.
GIRL IN THERE FIND HERSELF IN THE SAME WAY. A BABE ON THE WAY AND A MAN'D LIKE TO KILL HER FOR IT. ONLY, LIKE ME, SHE CALLED UP HELP FROM THE WRONG PLACE. LET THAT EVIL LOOSE ON THE WORLD ONCE AGAIN.
AND WHAT IT HAS DONE...
"ABOMINATIONS AND ATROCITIES."
"BUT YOU...YOUR FRIENDS, THEY'VE FOUND IT--"
JUST THROW IT IN...?
--AND GET AWAY!
"THEY CALL UP THE GOOD. THE ONE THING CAN VANQUISH EVIL AND DEVIL EVERYTIME".
"BANISH IT BACK TO HELL ...FOREVER."
IT IS DONE. THANK YOU, CHILD.
NOW THAT MY ERRS HAVE BEEN RIGHTED, I CAN REST.
I WILL PRAY THAT YOU FIND YOUR PEACE SOON AS WELL, DEAR--
"...FOR ISN'T THAT ALL ANY OF US CAN TRULY HOPE FOR...?"
"PEACE AND REST--"
"--REST AND PEACE?"
fin.

perhapanauts 1

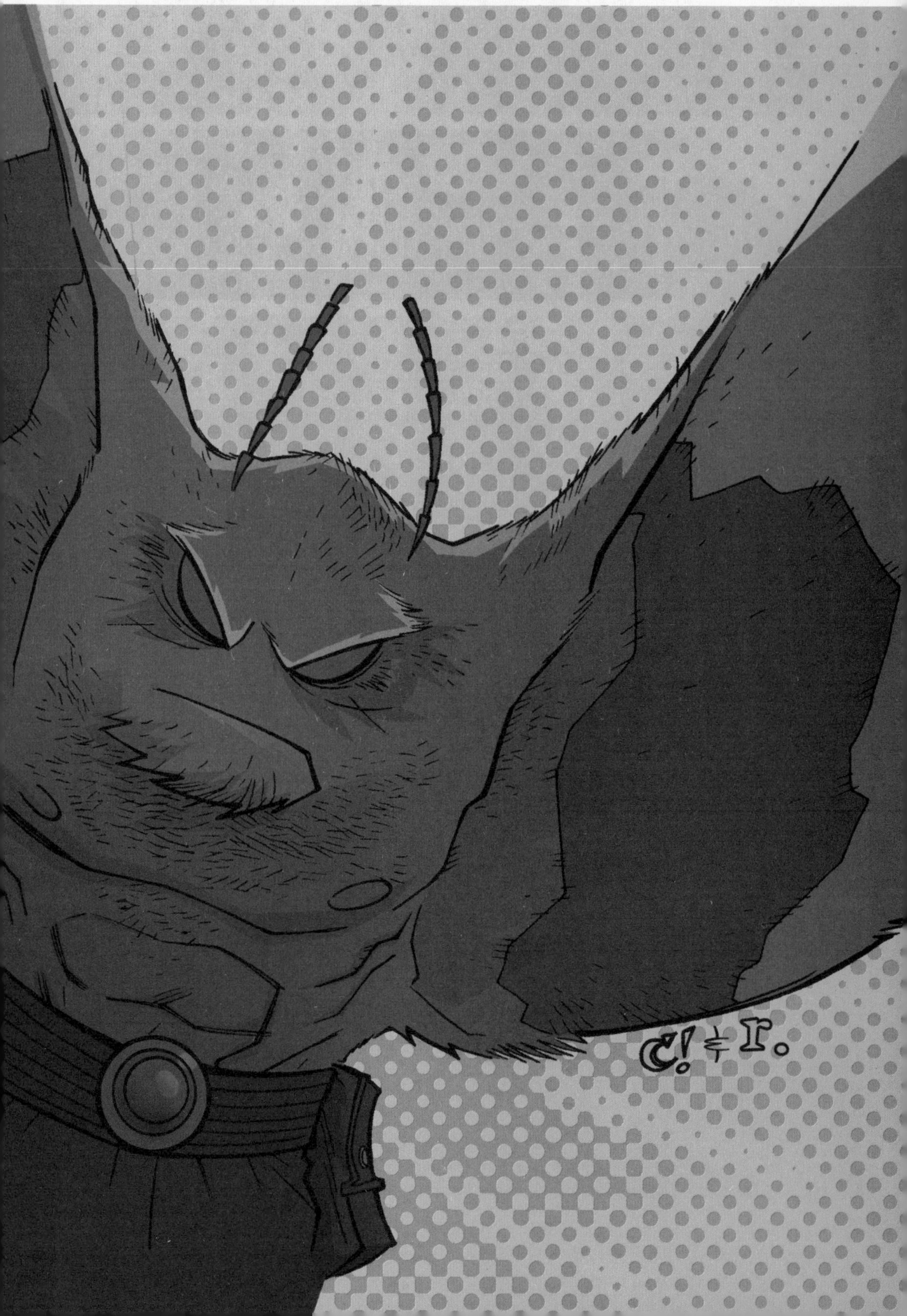
c! & r.

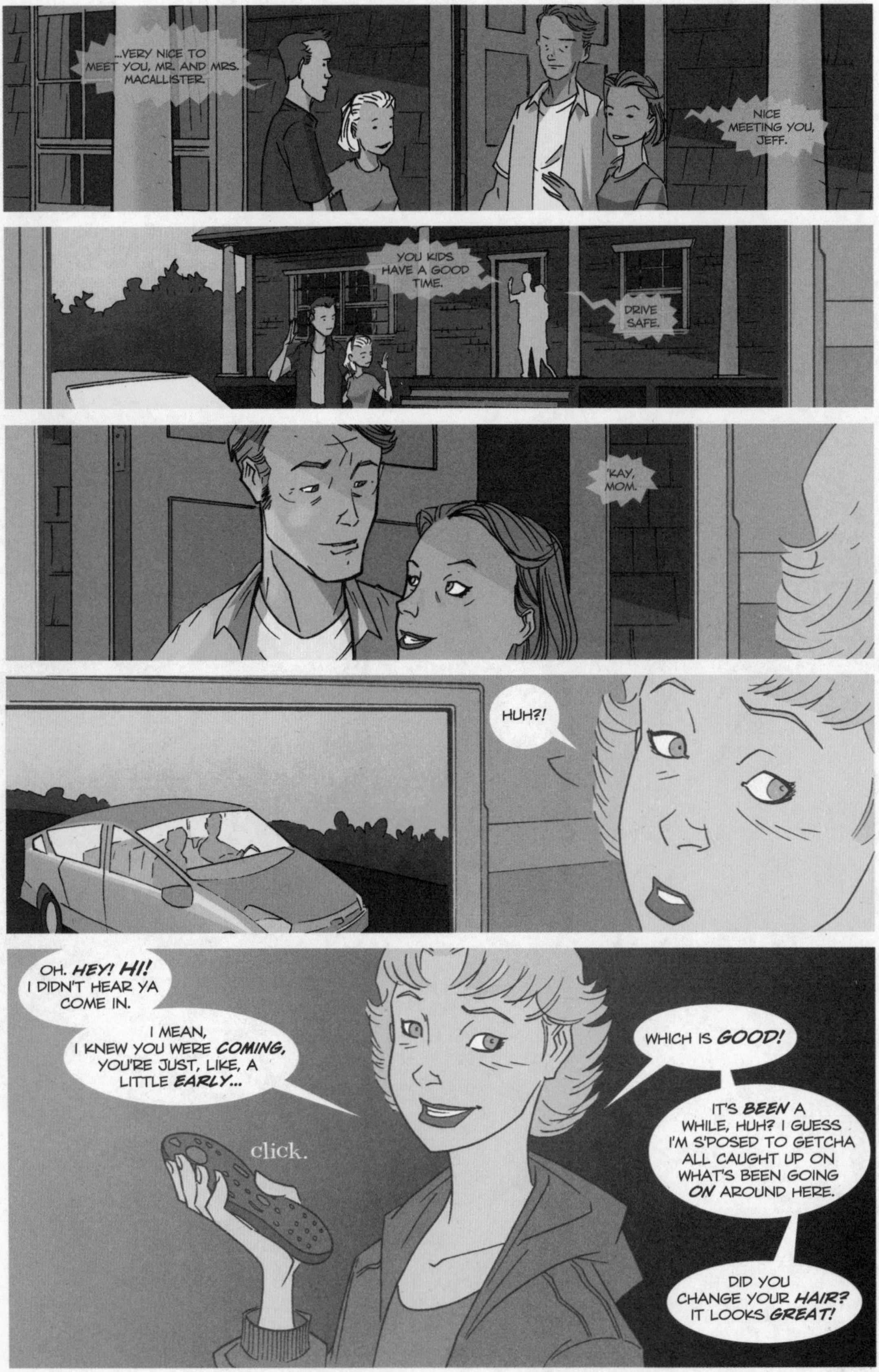
...VERY NICE TO MEET YOU, MR. AND MRS. MACALLISTER.
NICE MEETING YOU, JEFF.
YOU KIDS HAVE A GOOD TIME.
DRIVE SAFE.
'KAY, MOM.
HUH?!
OH. HEY! HI! I DIDN'T HEAR YA COME IN.
I MEAN, I KNEW YOU WERE COMING, YOU'RE JUST, LIKE, A LITTLE EARLY...
click.
WHICH IS GOOD!
IT'S BEEN A WHILE, HUH? I GUESS I'M S'POSED TO GETCHA ALL CAUGHT UP ON WHAT'S BEEN GOING ON AROUND HERE.
DID YOU CHANGE YOUR HAIR? IT LOOKS GREAT!

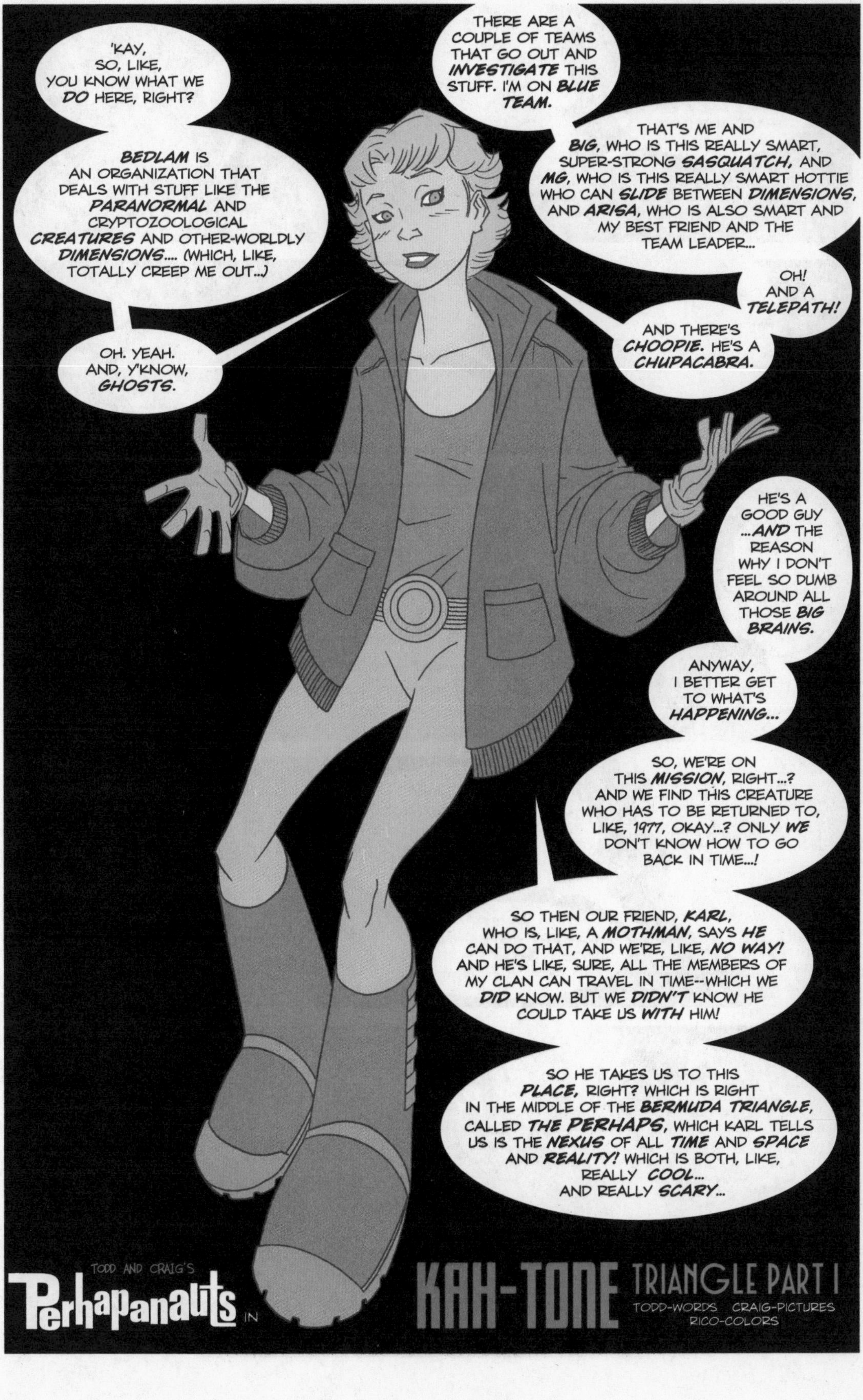
'KAY, SO, LIKE, YOU KNOW WHAT WE DO HERE, RIGHT?
BEDLAM IS AN ORGANIZATION THAT DEALS WITH STUFF LIKE THE PARANORMAL AND CRYPTOZOOLOGICAL CREATURES AND OTHER-WORLDLY DIMENSIONS.... (WHICH, LIKE, TOTALLY CREEP ME OUT...)
OH. YEAH. AND, Y'KNOW, GHOSTS.
THERE ARE A COUPLE OF TEAMS THAT GO OUT AND INVESTIGATE THIS STUFF. I'M ON BLUE TEAM.
THAT'S ME AND BIG, WHO IS THIS REALLY SMART, SUPER-STRONG SASQUATCH, AND MG, WHO IS THIS REALLY SMART HOTTIE WHO CAN SLIDE BETWEEN DIMENSIONS, AND ARISA, WHO IS ALSO SMART AND MY BEST FRIEND AND THE TEAM LEADER...
OH! AND A TELEPATH!
AND THERE'S CHOOPIE. HE'S A CHUPACABRA.
HE'S A GOOD GUY ...AND THE REASON WHY I DON'T FEEL SO DUMB AROUND ALL THOSE BIG BRAINS.
ANYWAY, I BETTER GET TO WHAT'S HAPPENING...
SO, WE'RE ON THIS MISSION, RIGHT...? AND WE FIND THIS CREATURE WHO HAS TO BE RETURNED TO, LIKE, 1977, OKAY...? ONLY WE DON'T KNOW HOW TO GO BACK IN TIME...!
SO THEN OUR FRIEND, KARL, WHO IS, LIKE, A MOTHMAN, SAYS HE CAN DO THAT, AND WE'RE, LIKE, NO WAY! AND HE'S LIKE, SURE, ALL THE MEMBERS OF MY CLAN CAN TRAVEL IN TIME--WHICH WE DID KNOW. BUT WE DIDN'T KNOW HE COULD TAKE US WITH HIM!
SO HE TAKES US TO THIS PLACE, RIGHT? WHICH IS RIGHT IN THE MIDDLE OF THE BERMUDA TRIANGLE, CALLED THE PERHAPS, WHICH KARL TELLS US IS THE NEXUS OF ALL TIME AND SPACE AND REALITY! WHICH IS BOTH, LIKE, REALLY COOL... AND REALLY SCARY...
TODD AND CRAIG'S
Perhapanauts IN
KAH-TONE TRIANGLE PART I
TODD-WORDS CRAIG-PICTURES
RICO-COLORS

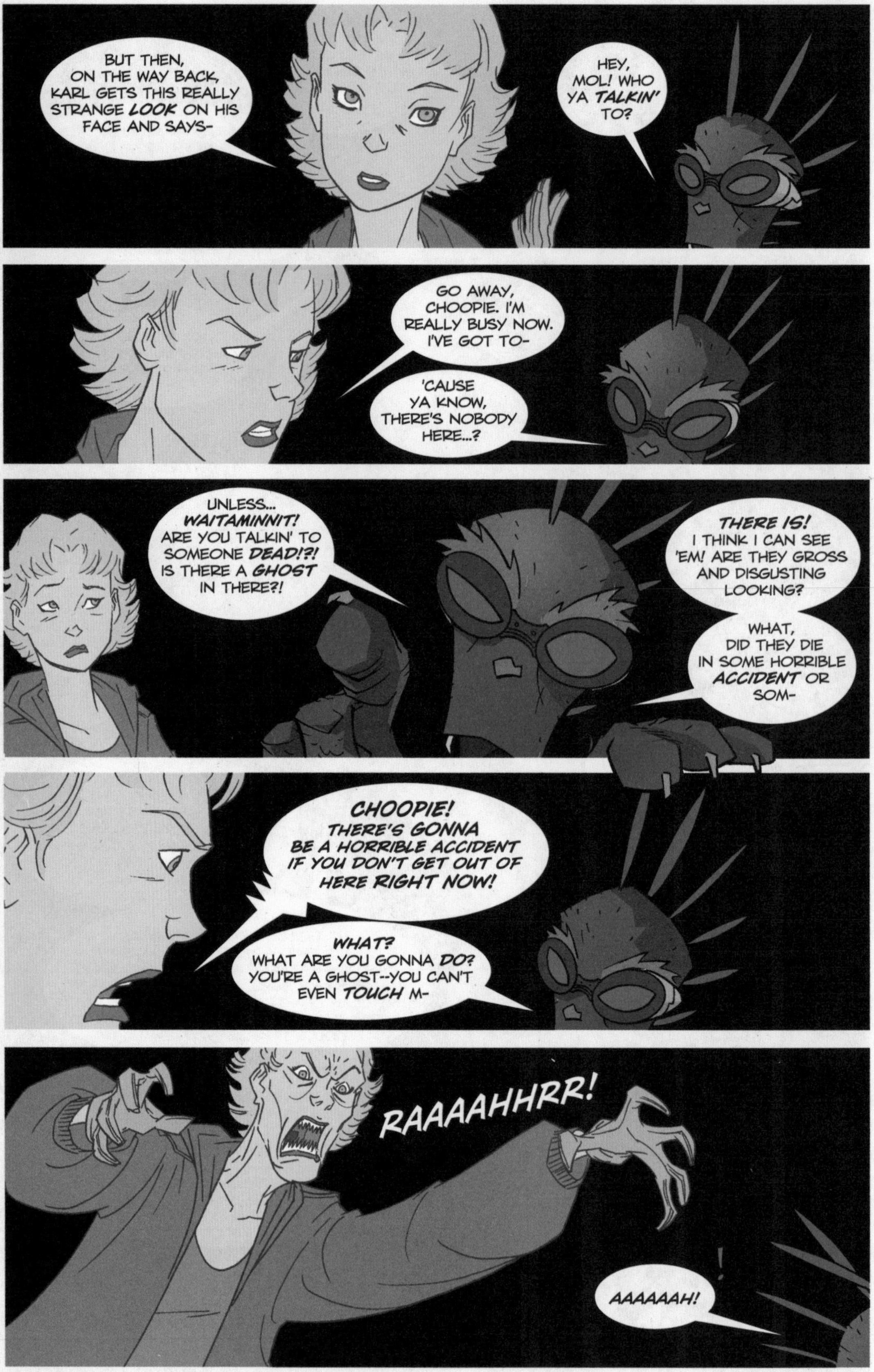
BUT THEN, ON THE WAY BACK, KARL GETS THIS REALLY STRANGE *LOOK* ON HIS FACE AND SAYS-
HEY, MOL! WHO YA *TALKIN'* TO?
GO AWAY, CHOOPIE. I'M REALLY BUSY NOW. I'VE GOT TO-
'CAUSE YA KNOW, THERE'S NOBODY HERE...?
UNLESS... *WAITAMINNIT!* ARE YOU TALKIN' TO SOMEONE *DEAD!?!* IS THERE A *GHOST* IN THERE?!
THERE IS! I THINK I CAN SEE 'EM! ARE THEY GROSS AND DISGUSTING LOOKING?
WHAT, DID THEY DIE IN SOME HORRIBLE *ACCIDENT* OR SOM-
CHOOPIE! THERE'S GONNA BE A HORRIBLE ACCIDENT IF YOU DON'T GET OUT OF HERE RIGHT NOW!
WHAT? WHAT ARE YOU GONNA *DO*? YOU'RE A GHOST--YOU CAN'T EVEN *TOUCH* M-
RAAAAHHRR!
!
AAAAAAH!

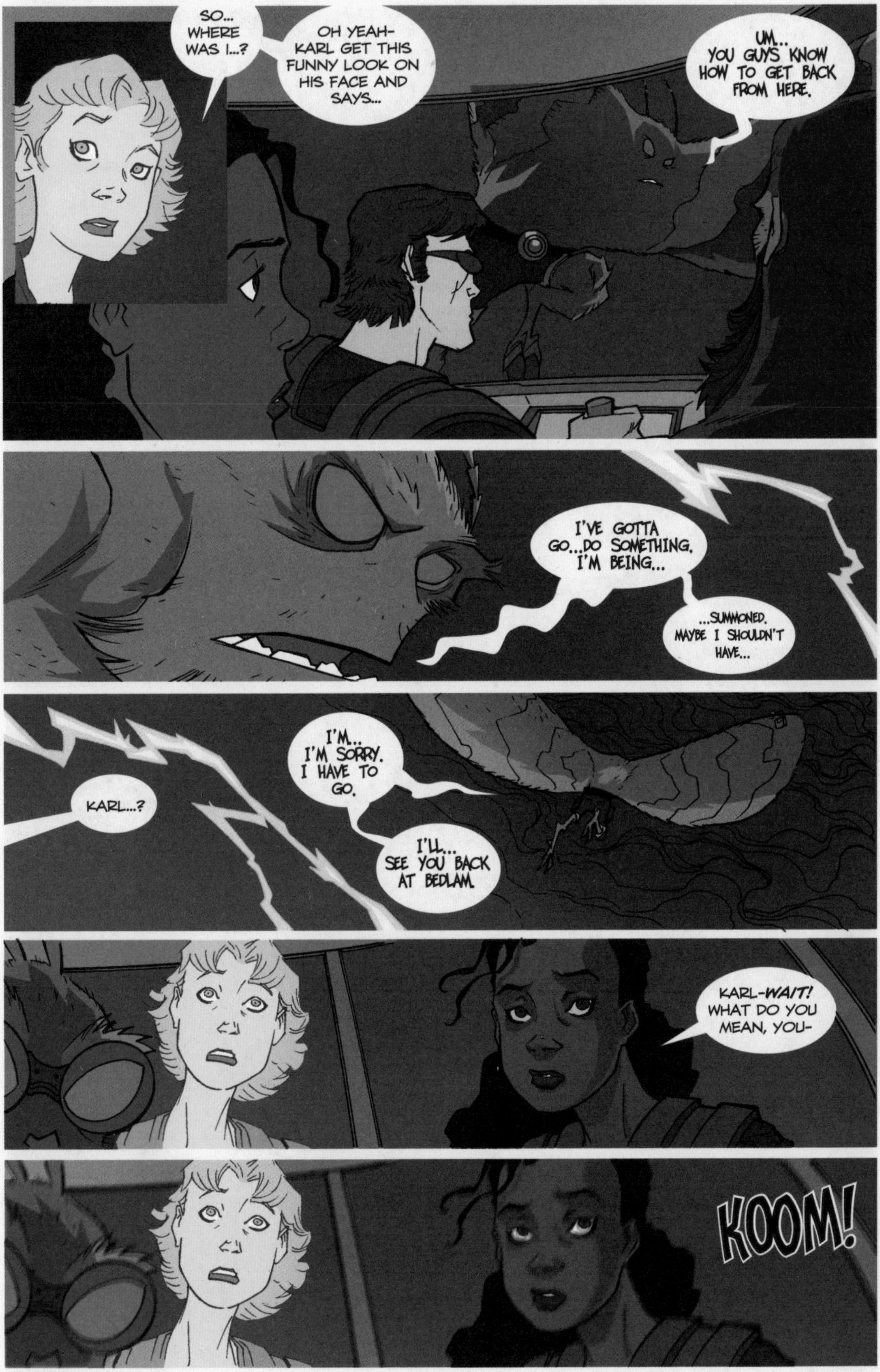
SO... WHERE WAS I...?
OH YEAH- KARL GET THIS FUNNY LOOK ON HIS FACE AND SAYS...
UM... YOU GUYS KNOW HOW TO GET BACK FROM HERE.
I'VE GOTTA GO...DO SOMETHING. I'M BEING...
...SUMMONED. MAYBE I SHOULDN'T HAVE...
KARL...?
I'M... I'M SORRY. I HAVE TO GO.
I'LL... SEE YOU BACK AT BEDLAM.
KARL-WAIT! WHAT DO YOU MEAN, YOU-
KOOM!

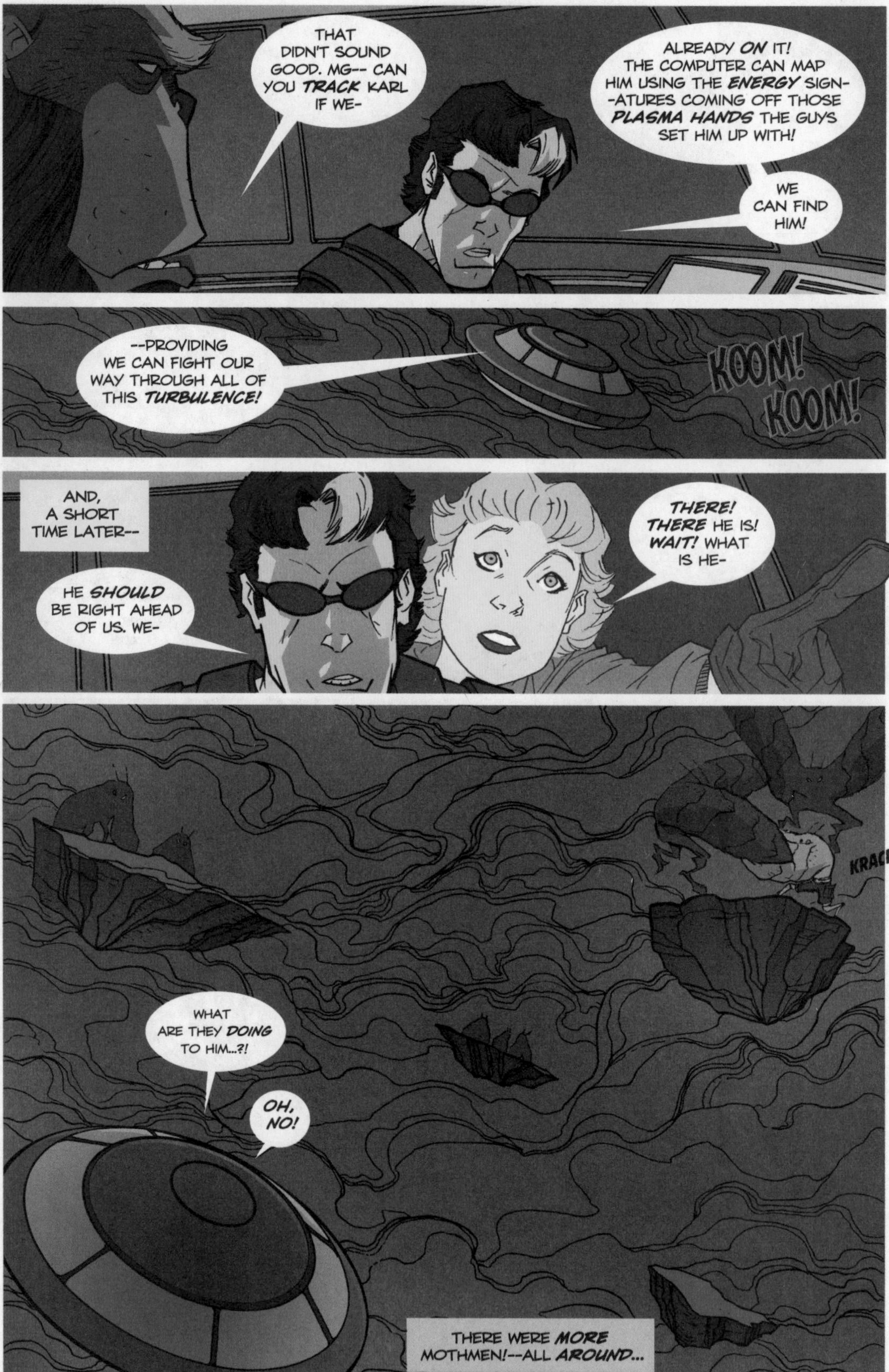
THAT DIDN'T SOUND GOOD. MG-- CAN YOU TRACK KARL IF WE-
ALREADY ON IT! THE COMPUTER CAN MAP HIM USING THE ENERGY SIGN--ATURES COMING OFF THOSE PLASMA HANDS THE GUYS SET HIM UP WITH!
WE CAN FIND HIM!
--PROVIDING WE CAN FIGHT OUR WAY THROUGH ALL OF THIS TURBULENCE!
KOOM! KOOM!
AND, A SHORT TIME LATER--
HE SHOULD BE RIGHT AHEAD OF US. WE-
THERE! THERE HE IS! WAIT! WHAT IS HE-
KRACK!
WHAT ARE THEY DOING TO HIM...?!
OH, NO!
THERE WERE MORE MOTHMEN!--ALL AROUND...

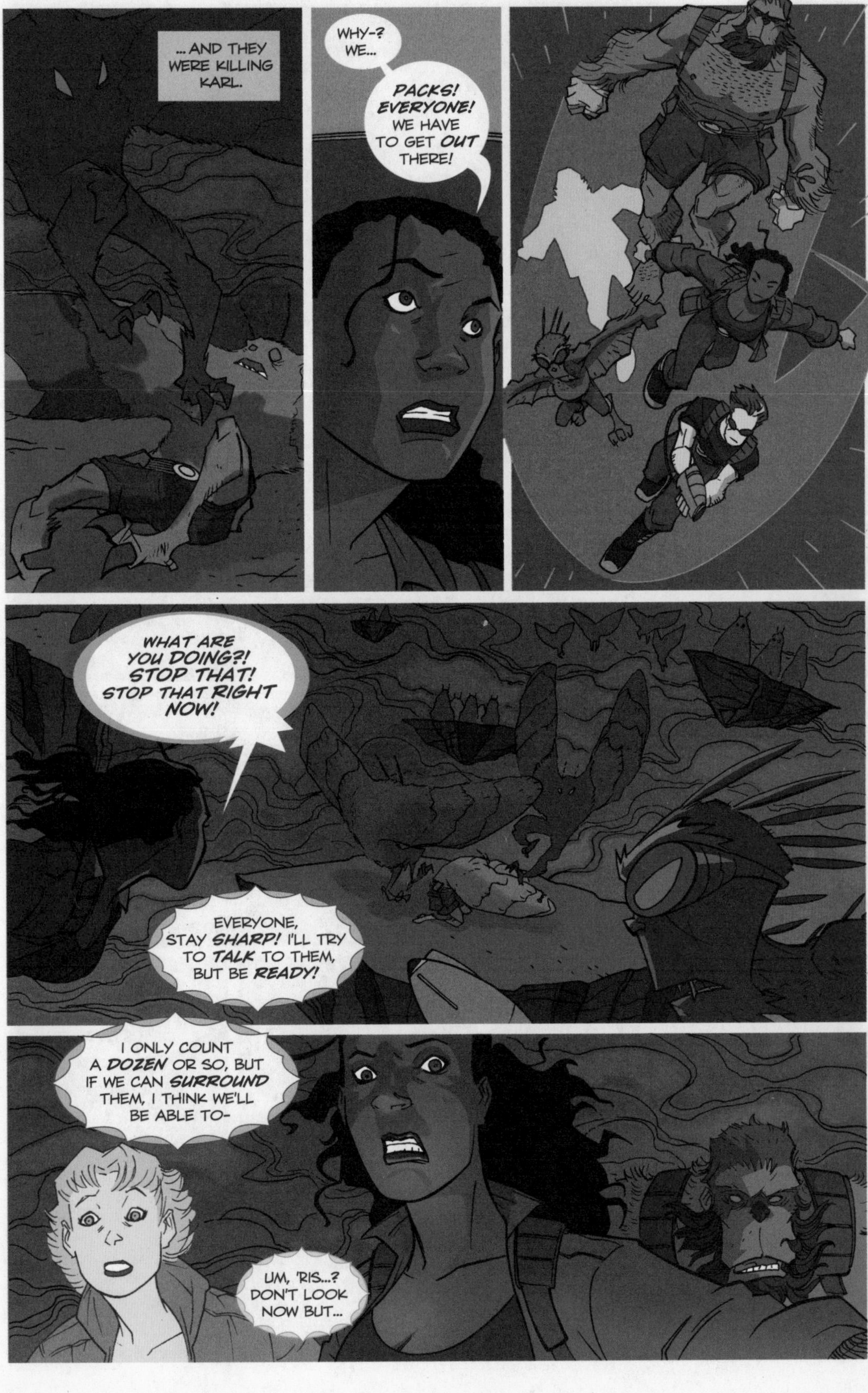
...AND THEY WERE KILLING KARL.
WHY-? WE...
PACKS! EVERYONE! WE HAVE TO GET OUT THERE!
WHAT ARE YOU DOING?! STOP THAT! STOP THAT RIGHT NOW!
EVERYONE, STAY SHARP! I'LL TRY TO TALK TO THEM, BUT BE READY!
I ONLY COUNT A DOZEN OR SO, BUT IF WE CAN SURROUND THEM, I THINK WE'LL BE ABLE TO-
UM, 'RIS...? DON'T LOOK NOW BUT...

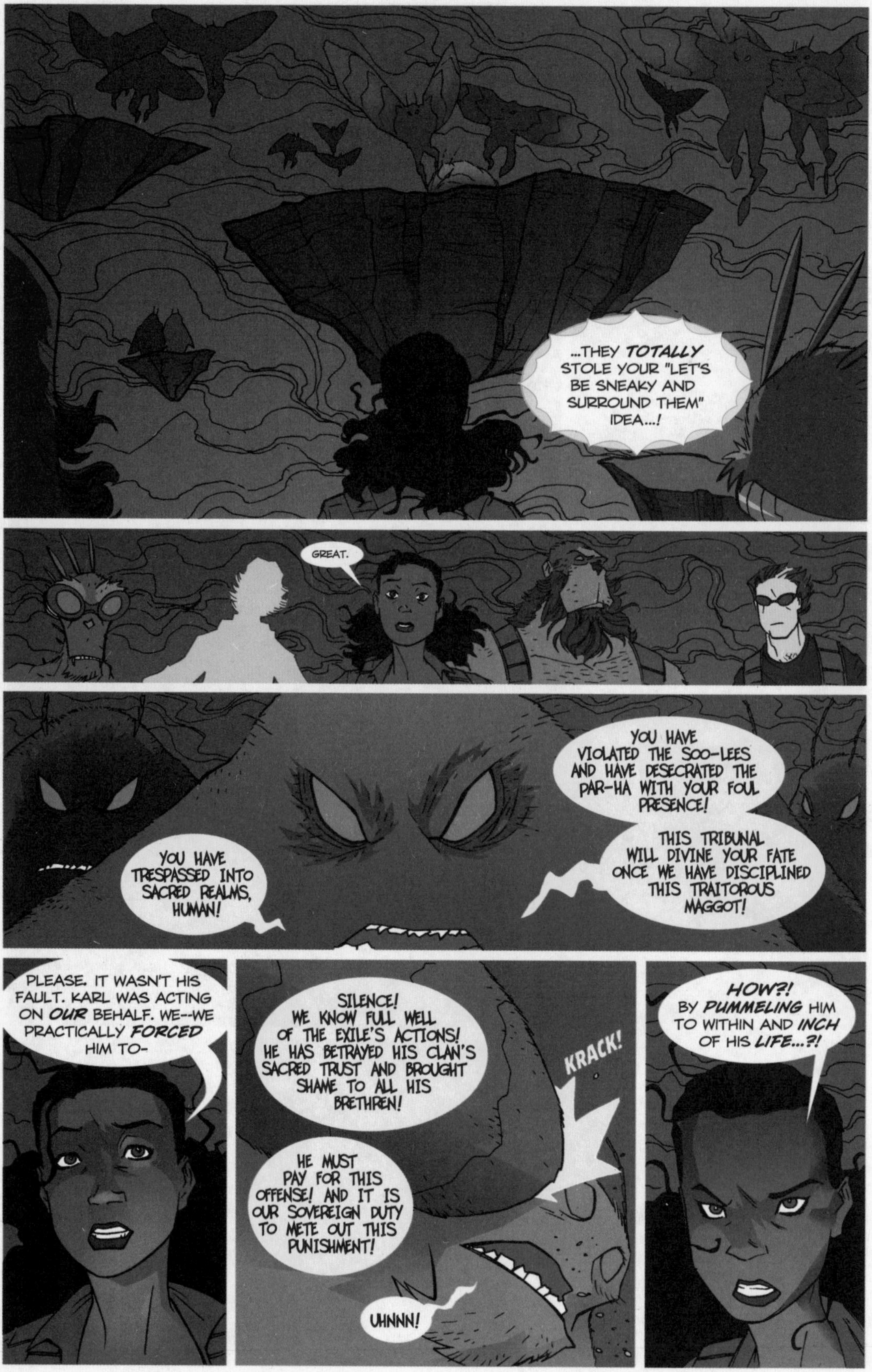
...THEY TOTALLY STOLE YOUR "LET'S BE SNEAKY AND SURROUND THEM" IDEA...!
GREAT.
YOU HAVE VIOLATED THE SOO-LEES AND HAVE DESECRATED THE PAR-HA WITH YOUR FOUL PRESENCE!
YOU HAVE TRESPASSED INTO SACRED REALMS, HUMAN!
THIS TRIBUNAL WILL DIVINE YOUR FATE ONCE WE HAVE DISCIPLINED THIS TRAITOROUS MAGGOT!
PLEASE. IT WASN'T HIS FAULT. KARL WAS ACTING ON OUR BEHALF. WE--WE PRACTICALLY FORCED HIM TO-
SILENCE! WE KNOW FULL WELL OF THE EXILE'S ACTIONS! HE HAS BETRAYED HIS CLAN'S SACRED TRUST AND BROUGHT SHAME TO ALL HIS BRETHREN!
KRACK!
HE MUST PAY FOR THIS OFFENSE! AND IT IS OUR SOVEREIGN DUTY TO METE OUT THIS PUNISHMENT!
UHNNN!
HOW?! BY PUMMELING HIM TO WITHIN AND INCH OF HIS LIFE...?!

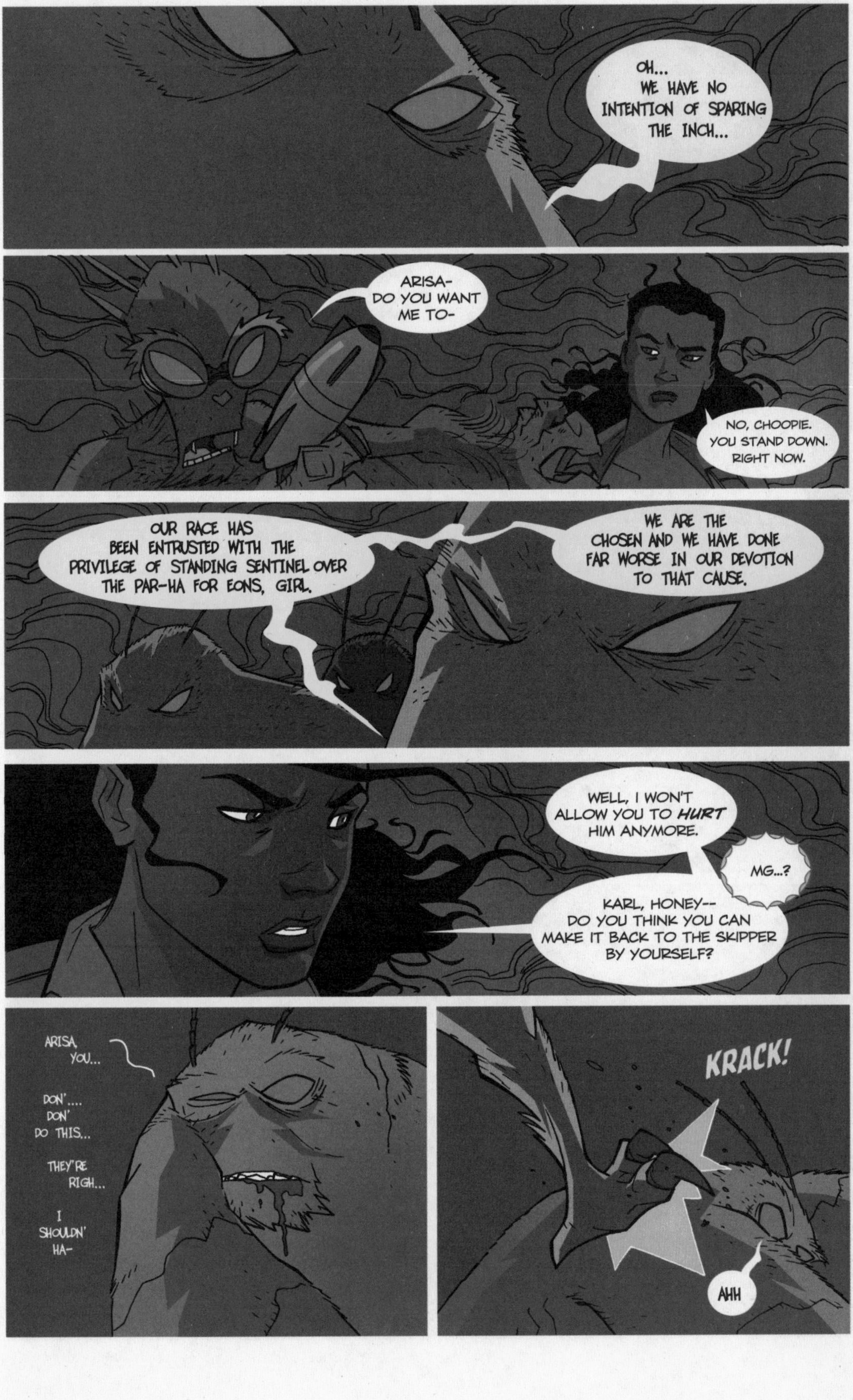
OH...
WE HAVE NO INTENTION OF SPARING THE INCH...
ARISA-
DO YOU WANT ME TO-
NO, CHOOPIE.
YOU STAND DOWN.
RIGHT NOW.
OUR RACE HAS BEEN ENTRUSTED WITH THE PRIVILEGE OF STANDING SENTINEL OVER THE PAR-HA FOR EONS, GIRL.
WE ARE THE CHOSEN AND WE HAVE DONE FAR WORSE IN OUR DEVOTION TO THAT CAUSE.
WELL, I WON'T ALLOW YOU TO *HURT* HIM ANYMORE.
MG...?
KARL, HONEY--
DO YOU THINK YOU CAN MAKE IT BACK TO THE SKIPPER BY YOURSELF?
ARISA, YOU...
DON'.... DON' DO THIS...
THEY'RE RIGH...
I SHOULDN' HA-
KRACK!
AHH

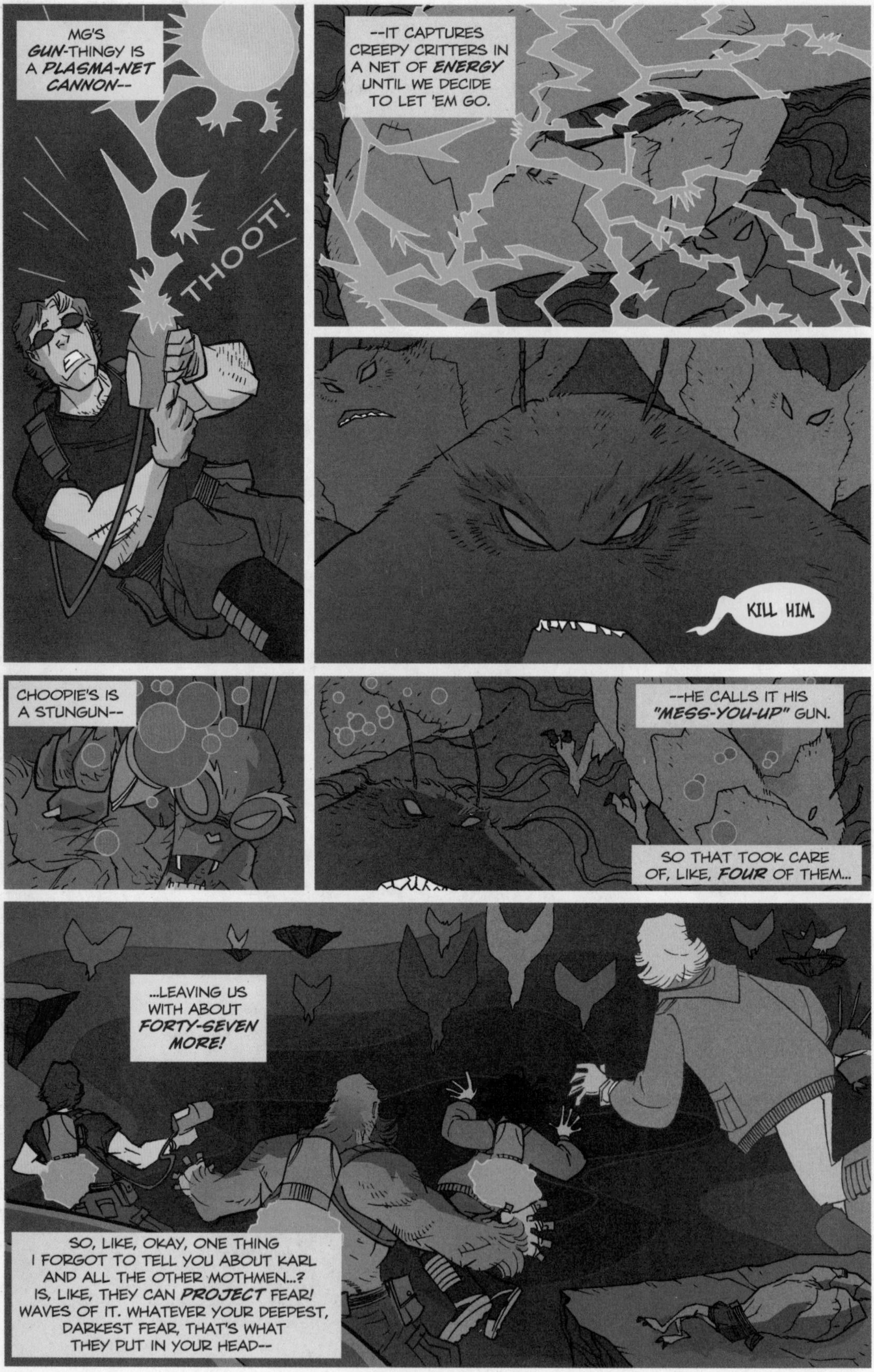
MG'S GUN-THINGY IS A PLASMA-NET CANNON--
THOOT!
--IT CAPTURES CREEPY CRITTERS IN A NET OF ENERGY UNTIL WE DECIDE TO LET 'EM GO.
KILL HIM.
CHOOPIE'S IS A STUNGUN--
--HE CALLS IT HIS "MESS-YOU-UP" GUN.
SO THAT TOOK CARE OF, LIKE, FOUR OF THEM...
...LEAVING US WITH ABOUT FORTY-SEVEN MORE!
SO, LIKE, OKAY, ONE THING I FORGOT TO TELL YOU ABOUT KARL AND ALL THE OTHER MOTHMEN...? IS, LIKE, THEY CAN PROJECT FEAR! WAVES OF IT. WHATEVER YOUR DEEPEST, DARKEST FEAR, THAT'S WHAT THEY PUT IN YOUR HEAD--

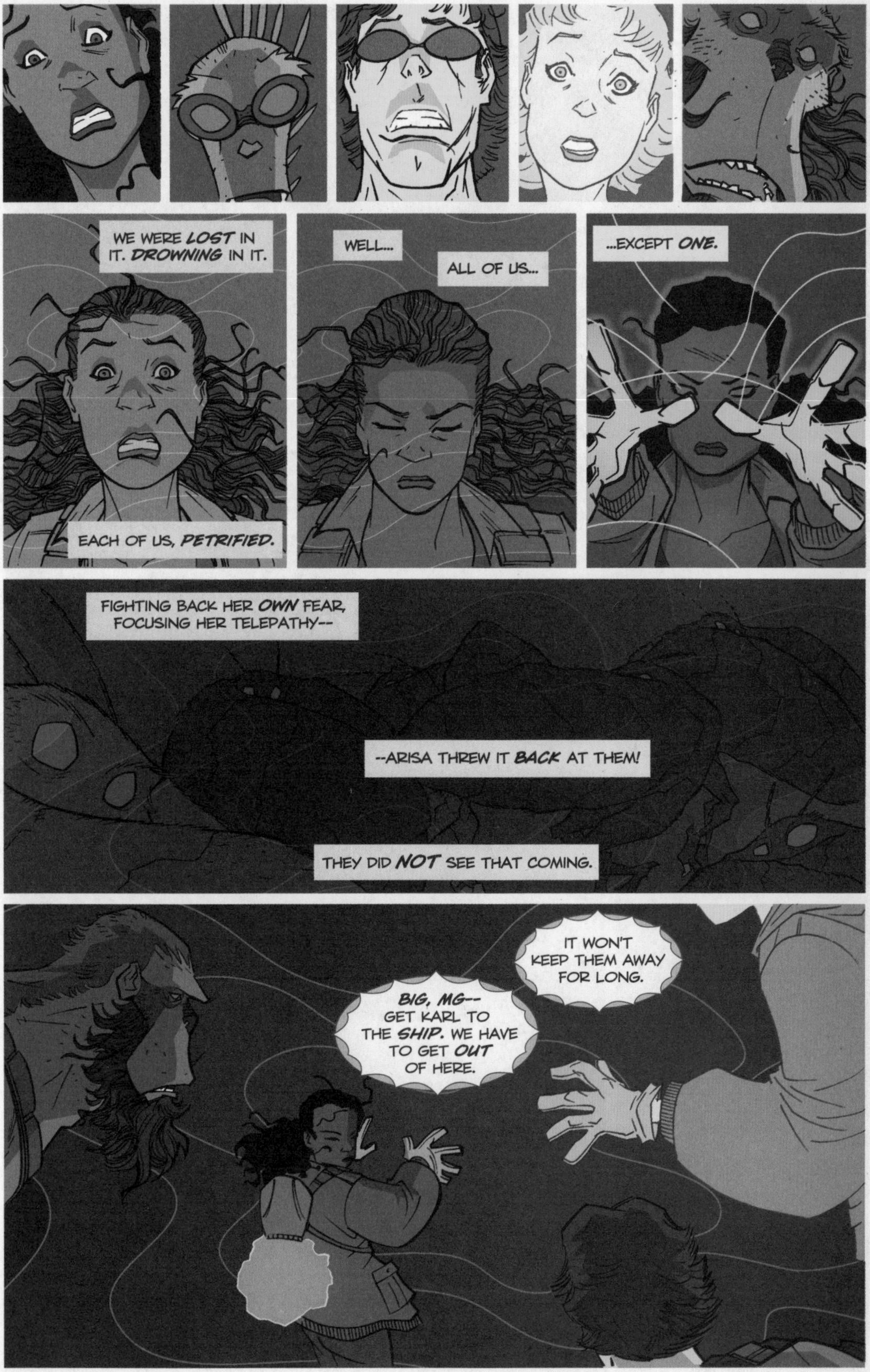
WE WERE LOST IN IT. DROWNING IN IT.
EACH OF US, PETRIFIED.
WELL...
ALL OF US...
...EXCEPT ONE.
FIGHTING BACK HER OWN FEAR, FOCUSING HER TELEPATHY--
--ARISA THREW IT BACK AT THEM!
THEY DID NOT SEE THAT COMING.
IT WON'T KEEP THEM AWAY FOR LONG.
BIG, MG-- GET KARL TO THE SHIP. WE HAVE TO GET OUT OF HERE.

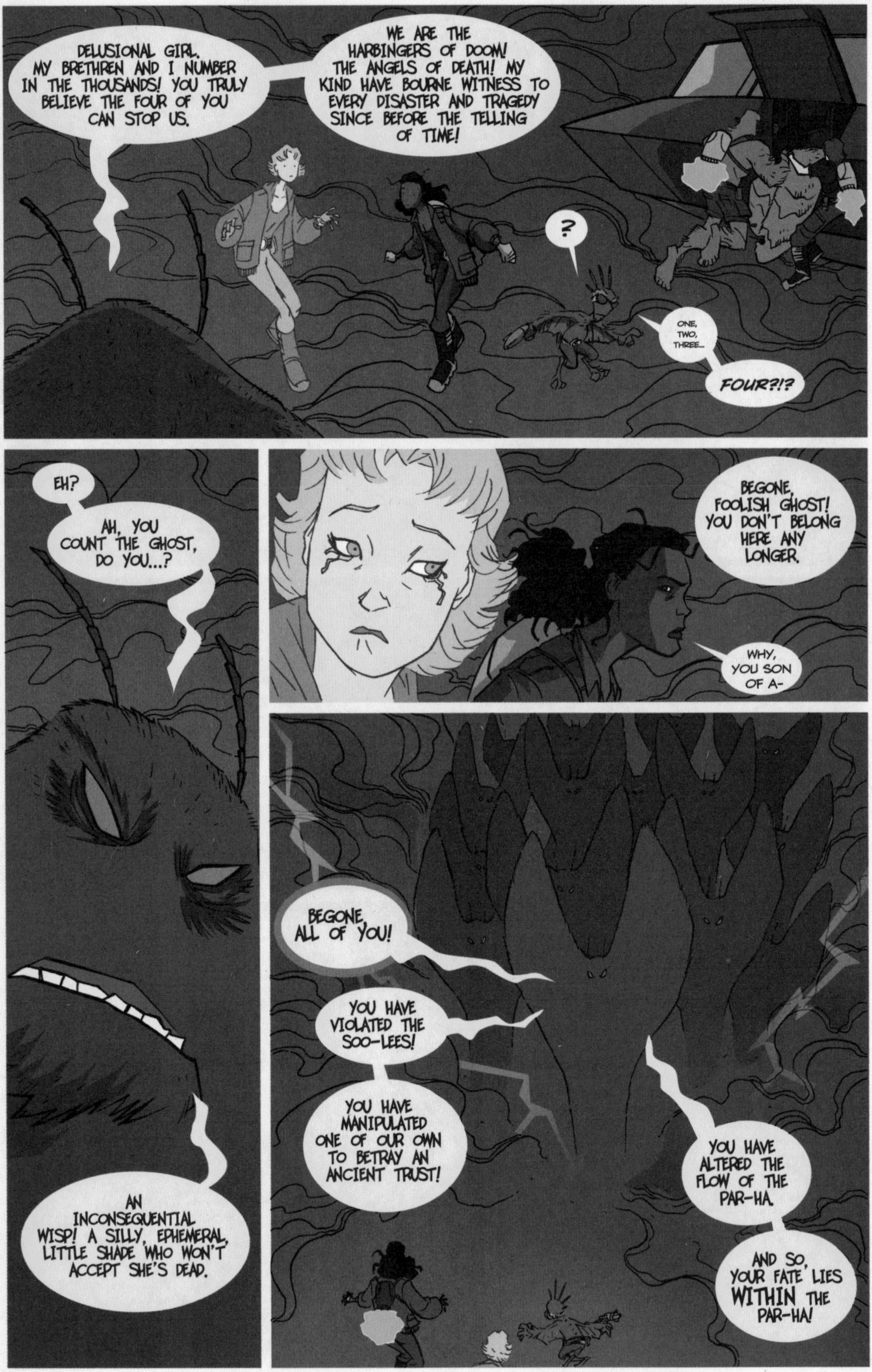
DELUSIONAL GIRL. MY BRETHREN AND I NUMBER IN THE THOUSANDS! YOU TRULY BELIEVE THE FOUR OF YOU CAN STOP US.
WE ARE THE HARBINGERS OF DOOM! THE ANGELS OF DEATH! MY KIND HAVE BOURNE WITNESS TO EVERY DISASTER AND TRAGEDY SINCE BEFORE THE TELLING OF TIME!
?
ONE, TWO, THREE...
FOUR?!?
EH?
AH, YOU COUNT THE GHOST, DO YOU...?
AN INCONSEQUENTIAL WISP! A SILLY, EPHEMERAL, LITTLE SHADE WHO WON'T ACCEPT SHE'S DEAD.
BEGONE, FOOLISH GHOST! YOU DON'T BELONG HERE ANY LONGER.
WHY, YOU SON OF A-
BEGONE, ALL OF YOU!
YOU HAVE VIOLATED THE SOO-LEES!
YOU HAVE MANIPULATED ONE OF OUR OWN TO BETRAY AN ANCIENT TRUST!
YOU HAVE ALTERED THE FLOW OF THE PAR-HA.
AND SO, YOUR FATE LIES WITHIN THE PAR-HA!

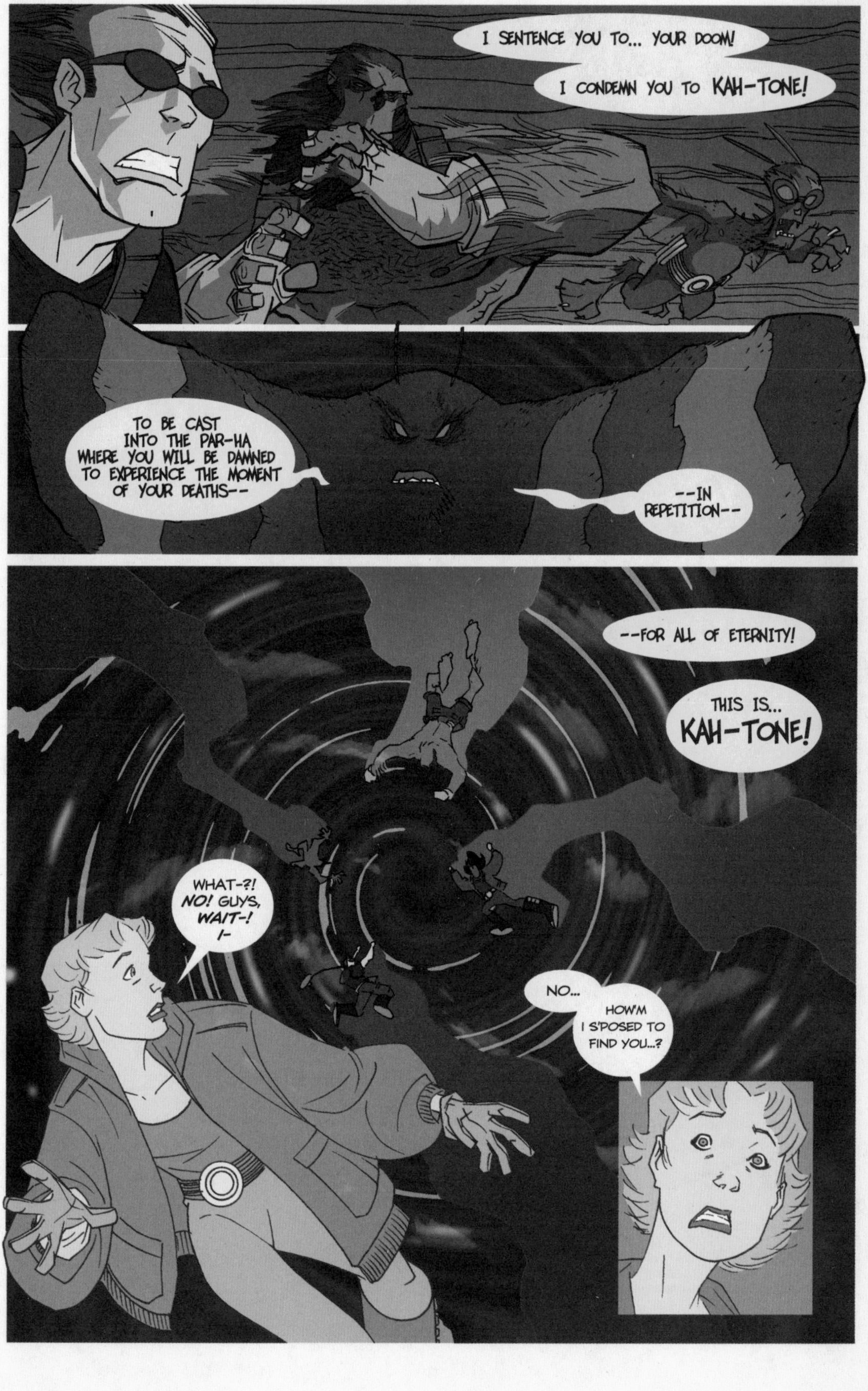
I SENTENCE YOU TO... YOUR DOOM!
I CONDEMN YOU TO KAH-TONE!
TO BE CAST INTO THE PAR-HA WHERE YOU WILL BE DAMNED TO EXPERIENCE THE MOMENT OF YOUR DEATHS--
--IN REPETITION--
--FOR ALL OF ETERNITY!
THIS IS... KAH-TONE!
WHAT-?! NO! GUYS, WAIT-! I-
NO...
HOW'M I S'POSED TO FIND YOU...?

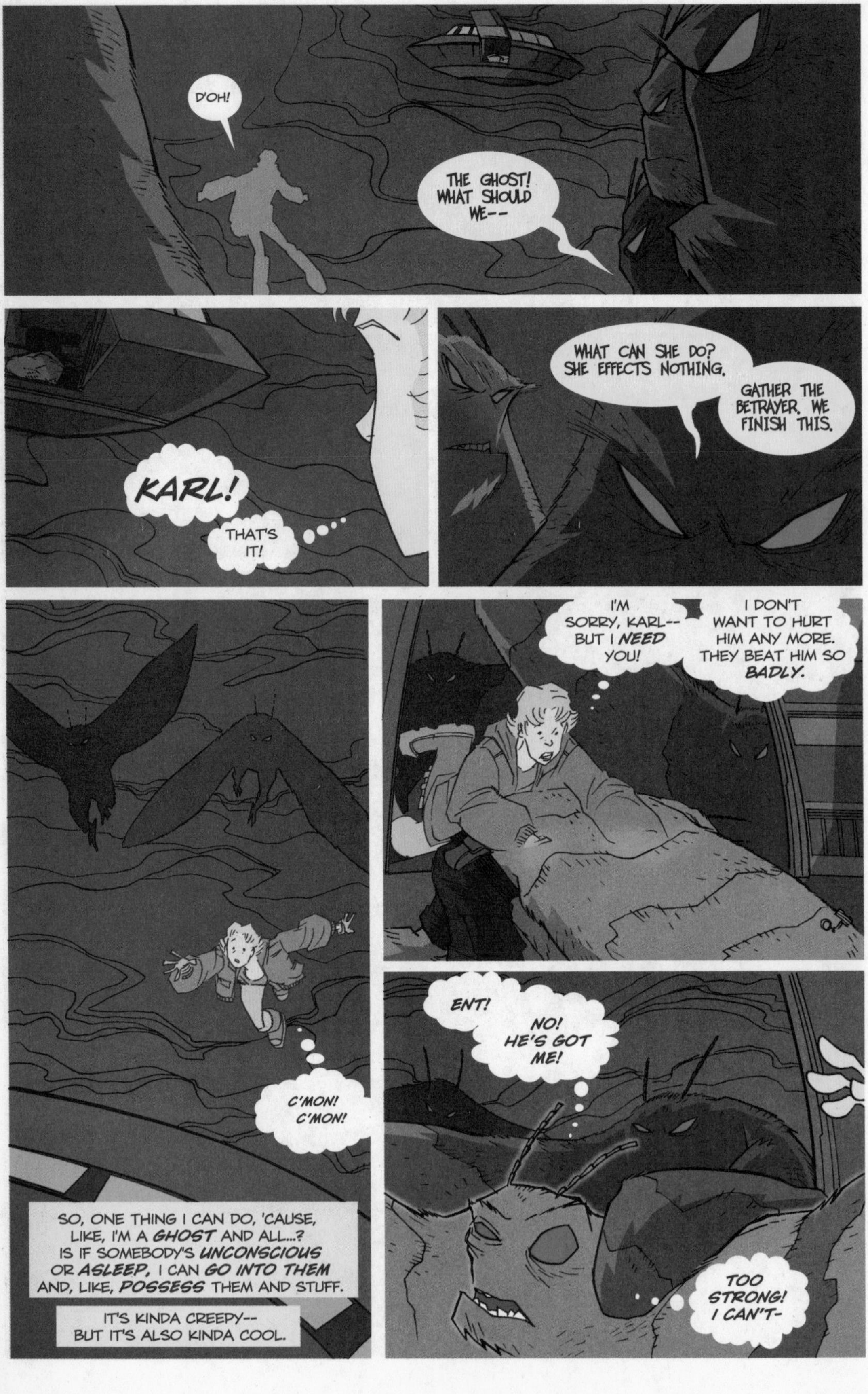
D'OH!
THE GHOST! WHAT SHOULD WE--
KARL!
THAT'S IT!
WHAT CAN SHE DO? SHE EFFECTS NOTHING.
GATHER THE BETRAYER. WE FINISH THIS.
SO, ONE THING I CAN DO, 'CAUSE, LIKE, I'M A GHOST AND ALL...? IS IF SOMEBODY'S UNCONSCIOUS OR ASLEEP, I CAN GO INTO THEM AND, LIKE, POSSESS THEM AND STUFF.
IT'S KINDA CREEPY-- BUT IT'S ALSO KINDA COOL.
C'MON! C'MON!
I'M SORRY, KARL-- BUT I NEED YOU!
I DON'T WANT TO HURT HIM ANY MORE. THEY BEAT HIM SO BADLY.
ENT!
NO! HE'S GOT ME!
TOO STRONG! I CAN'T-

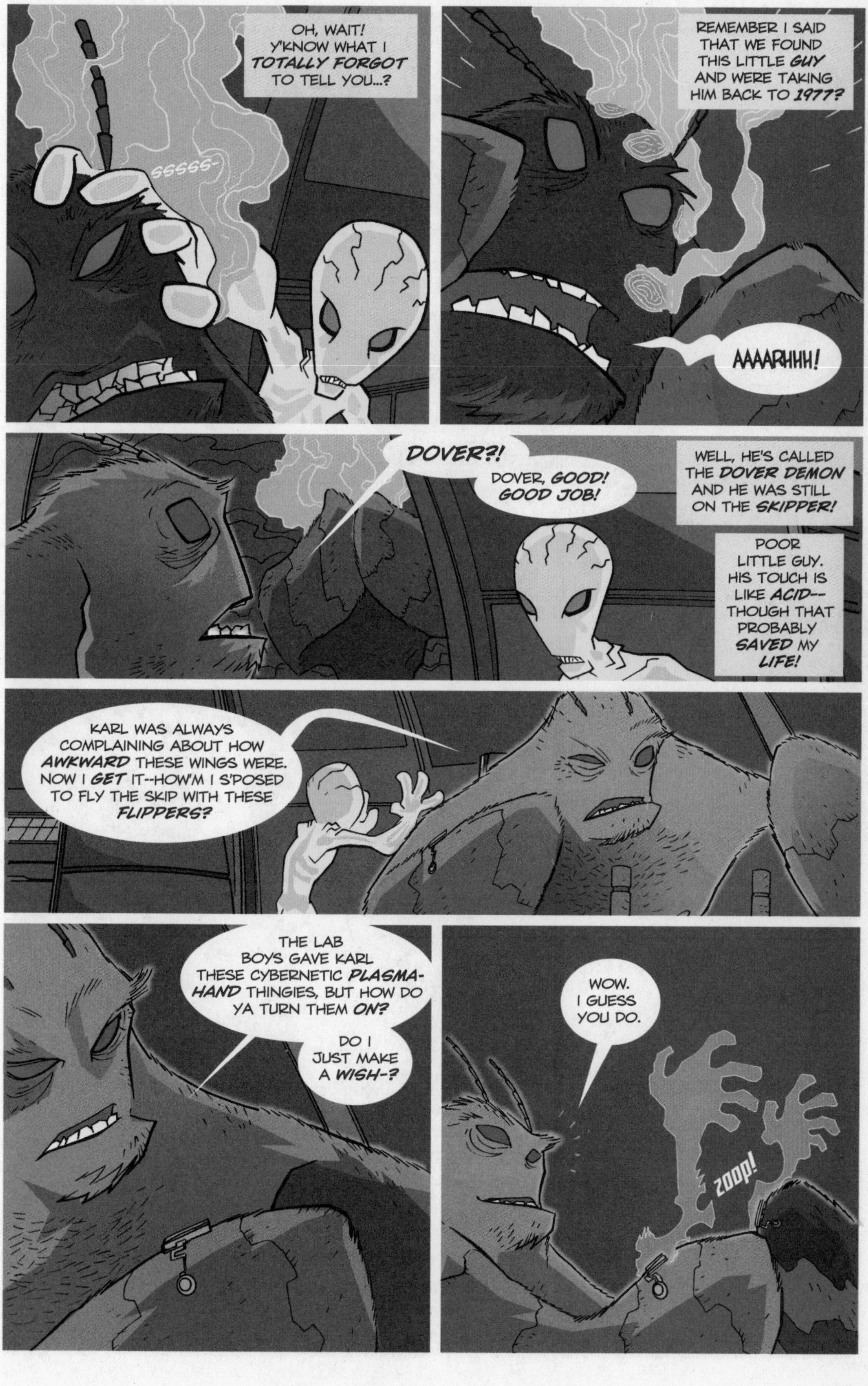
OH, WAIT! Y'KNOW WHAT I TOTALLY FORGOT TO TELL YOU...?
SSSSS-
REMEMBER I SAID THAT WE FOUND THIS LITTLE GUY AND WERE TAKING HIM BACK TO 1977?
AAAARHHH!
DOVER?!
DOVER, GOOD! GOOD JOB!
WELL, HE'S CALLED THE DOVER DEMON AND HE WAS STILL ON THE SKIPPER!
POOR LITTLE GUY. HIS TOUCH IS LIKE ACID-- THOUGH THAT PROBABLY SAVED MY LIFE!
KARL WAS ALWAYS COMPLAINING ABOUT HOW AWKWARD THESE WINGS WERE. NOW I GET IT--HOW'M I S'POSED TO FLY THE SKIP WITH THESE FLIPPERS?
THE LAB BOYS GAVE KARL THESE CYBERNETIC PLASMA-HAND THINGIES, BUT HOW DO YA TURN THEM ON?
DO I JUST MAKE A WISH-?
WOW. I GUESS YOU DO.
ZOOP!

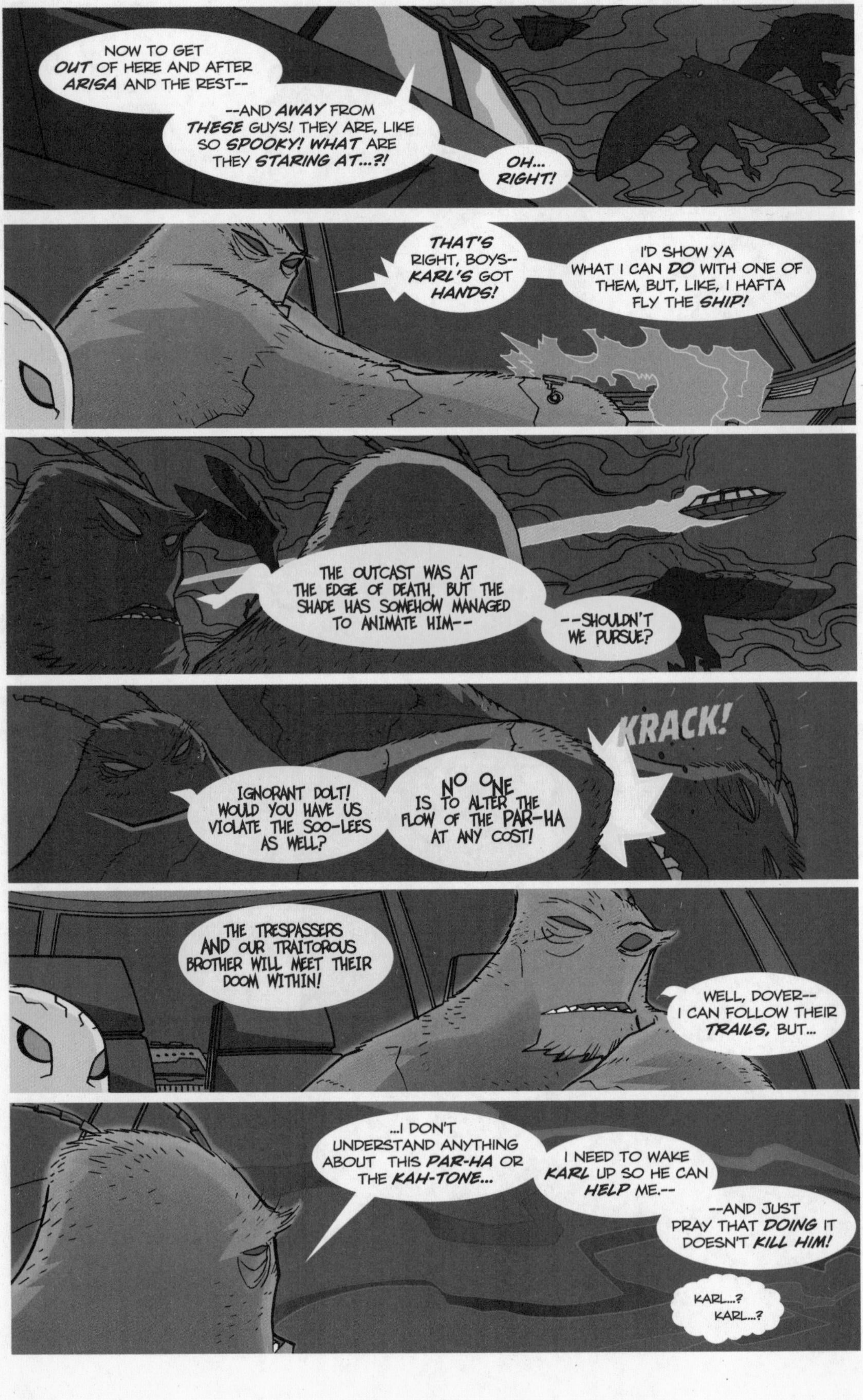

NOW TO GET OUT OF HERE AND AFTER ARISA AND THE REST--
--AND AWAY FROM THESE GUYS! THEY ARE, LIKE SO SPOOKY! WHAT ARE THEY STARING AT...?!
OH... RIGHT!
THAT'S RIGHT, BOYS-- KARL'S GOT HANDS!
I'D SHOW YA WHAT I CAN DO WITH ONE OF THEM, BUT, LIKE, I HAFTA FLY THE SHIP!
THE OUTCAST WAS AT THE EDGE OF DEATH, BUT THE SHADE HAS SOMEHOW MANAGED TO ANIMATE HIM--
--SHOULDN'T WE PURSUE?
KRACK!
IGNORANT DOLT! WOULD YOU HAVE US VIOLATE THE SOO-LEES AS WELL?
NO ONE IS TO ALTER THE FLOW OF THE PAR-HA AT ANY COST!
THE TRESPASSERS AND OUR TRAITOROUS BROTHER WILL MEET THEIR DOOM WITHIN!
WELL, DOVER-- I CAN FOLLOW THEIR TRAILS, BUT...
...I DON'T UNDERSTAND ANYTHING ABOUT THIS PAR-HA OR THE KAH-TONE...
I NEED TO WAKE KARL UP SO HE CAN HELP ME.--
--AND JUST PRAY THAT DOING IT DOESN'T KILL HIM!
KARL...? KARL...?

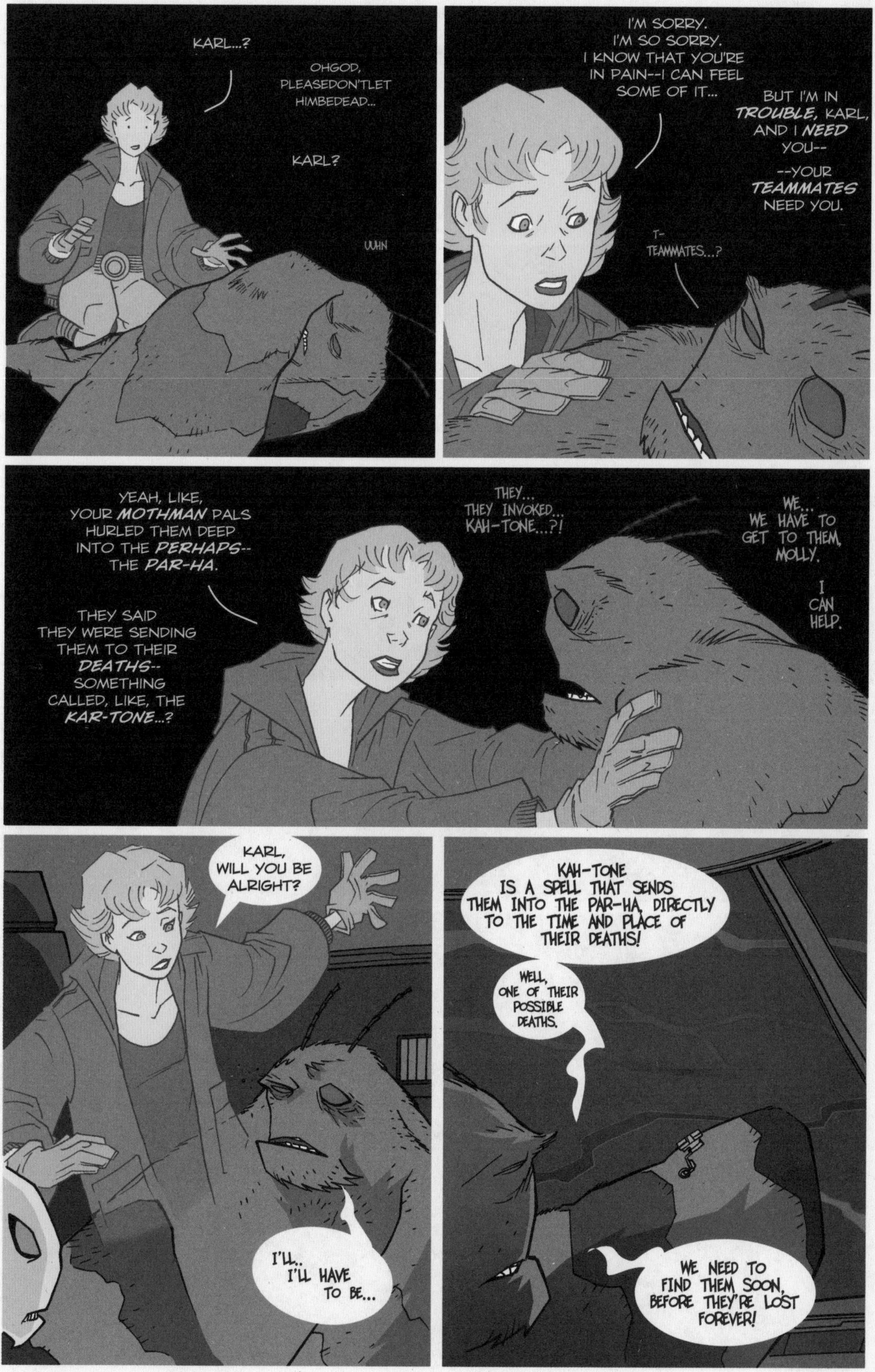
KARL...?
OHGOD, PLEASEDON'TLET HIMBEDEAD...
KARL?
UUHN
I'M SORRY. I'M SO SORRY. I KNOW THAT YOU'RE IN PAIN--I CAN FEEL SOME OF IT...
BUT I'M IN TROUBLE, KARL, AND I NEED YOU--
--YOUR TEAMMATES NEED YOU.
T- TEAMMATES...?
YEAH, LIKE, YOUR MOTHMAN PALS HURLED THEM DEEP INTO THE PERHAPS-- THE PAR-HA.
THEY SAID THEY WERE SENDING THEM TO THEIR DEATHS-- SOMETHING CALLED, LIKE, THE KAR-TONE...?
THEY... THEY INVOKED... KAH-TONE...?!
WE... WE HAVE TO GET TO THEM, MOLLY.
I CAN HELP.
KARL, WILL YOU BE ALRIGHT?
I'LL.. I'LL HAVE TO BE...
KAH-TONE IS A SPELL THAT SENDS THEM INTO THE PAR-HA, DIRECTLY TO THE TIME AND PLACE OF THEIR DEATHS!
WELL, ONE OF THEIR POSSIBLE DEATHS.
WE NEED TO FIND THEM SOON, BEFORE THEY'RE LOST FOREVER!

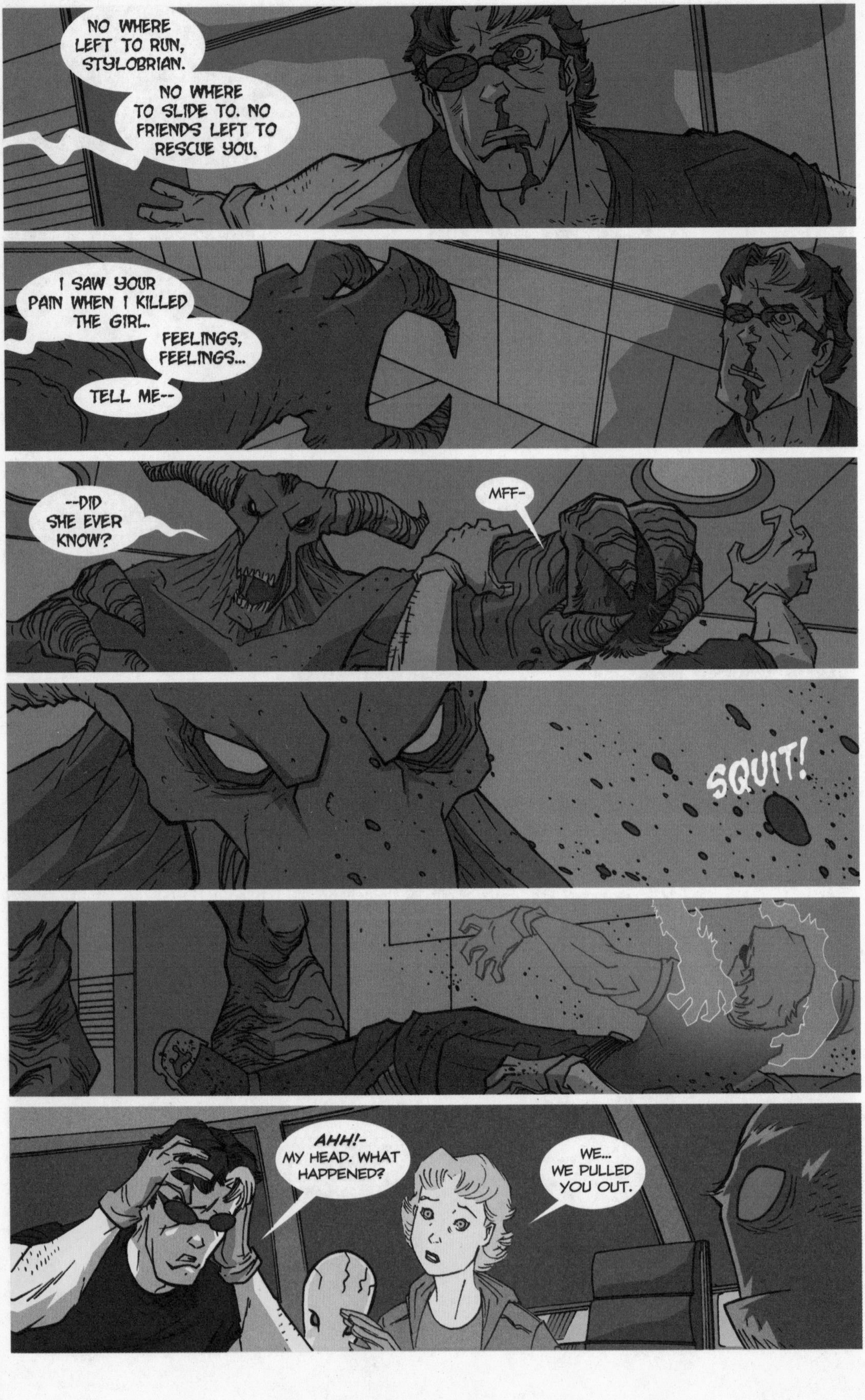
NO WHERE
LEFT TO RUN,
STYLOBRIAN.
NO WHERE
TO SLIDE TO. NO
FRIENDS LEFT TO
RESCUE YOU.
I SAW YOUR
PAIN WHEN I KILLED
THE GIRL.
FEELINGS,
FEELINGS...
TELL ME--
--DID
SHE EVER
KNOW?
MFF-
SQUIT!
AHH!-
MY HEAD. WHAT
HAPPENED?
WE...
WE PULLED
YOU OUT.

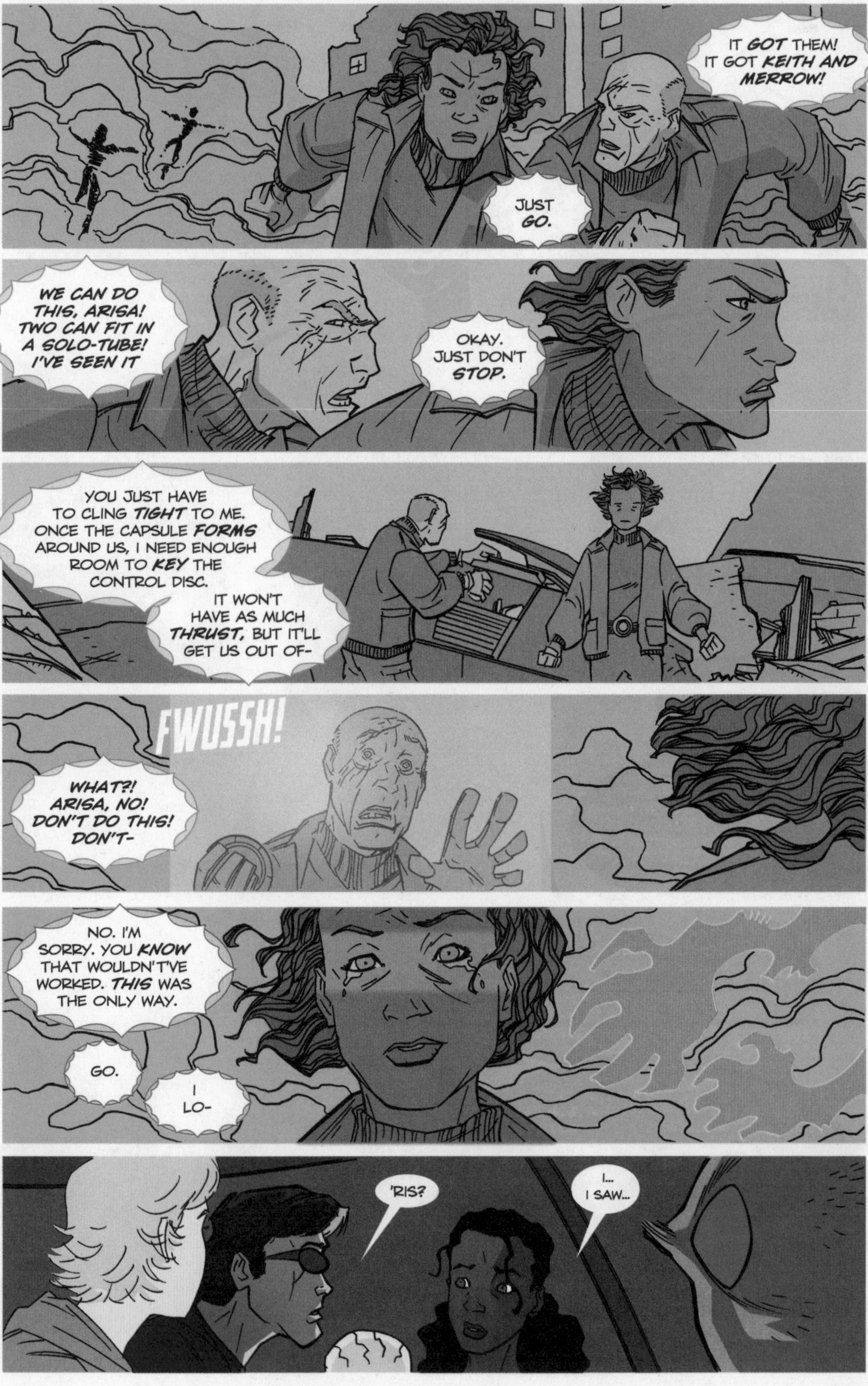

IT GOT THEM! IT GOT KEITH AND MERROW!
JUST GO.
WE CAN DO THIS, ARISA! TWO CAN FIT IN A SOLO-TUBE! I'VE SEEN IT
OKAY. JUST DON'T STOP.
YOU JUST HAVE TO CLING TIGHT TO ME. ONCE THE CAPSULE FORMS AROUND US, I NEED ENOUGH ROOM TO KEY THE CONTROL DISC.
IT WON'T HAVE AS MUCH THRUST, BUT IT'LL GET US OUT OF-
FWUSSH!
WHAT?! ARISA, NO! DON'T DO THIS! DON'T-
NO. I'M SORRY. YOU KNOW THAT WOULDN'T'VE WORKED. THIS WAS THE ONLY WAY.
GO.
I LO-
'RIS?
I... I SAW...

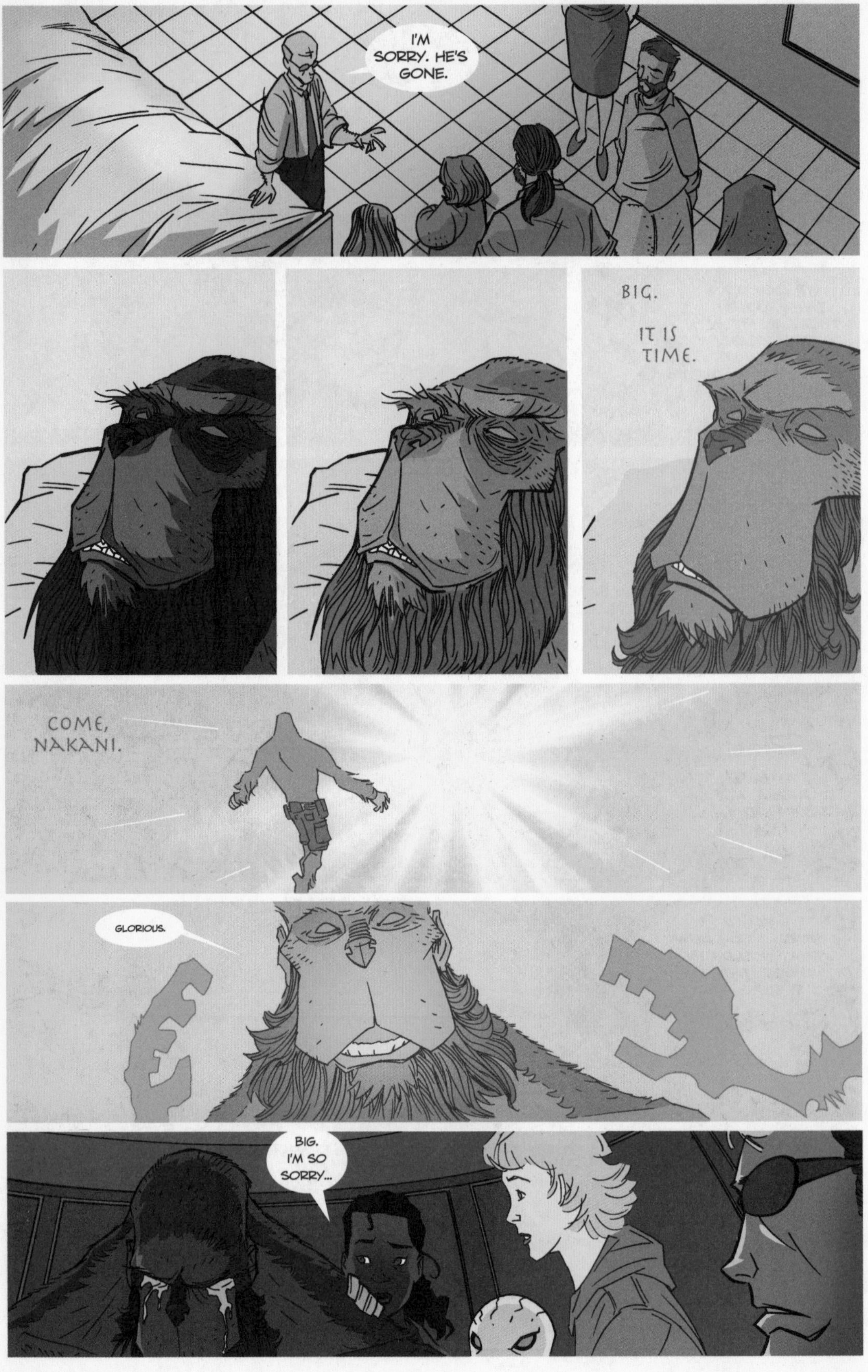
I'M SORRY. HE'S GONE.
BIG.
IT IS TIME.
COME, NAKANI.
GLORIOUS.
BIG. I'M SO SORRY...

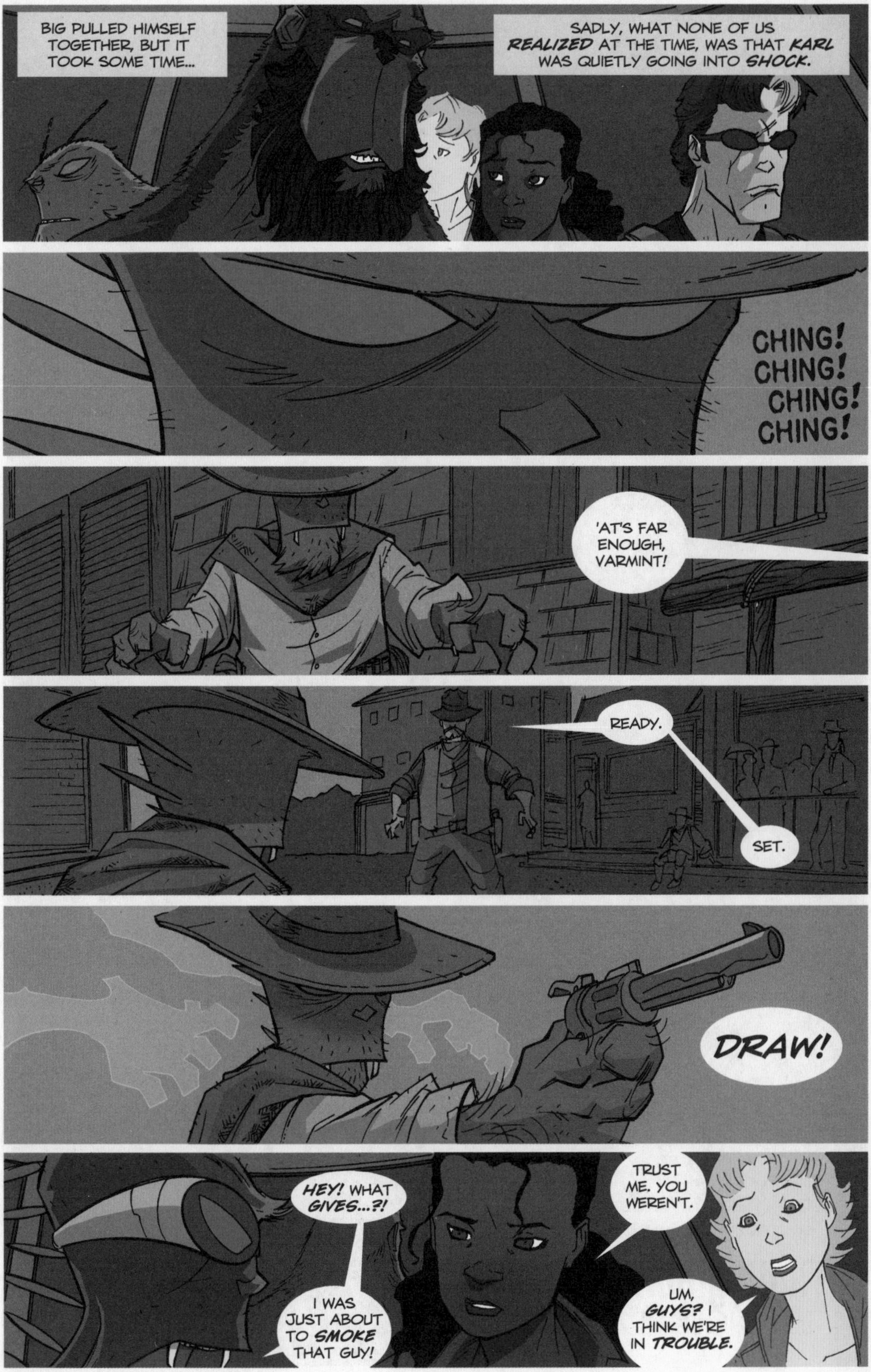
BIG PULLED HIMSELF TOGETHER, BUT IT TOOK SOME TIME...
SADLY, WHAT NONE OF US *REALIZED* AT THE TIME, WAS THAT *KARL* WAS QUIETLY GOING INTO *SHOCK*.
CHING! CHING! CHING! CHING!
'AT'S FAR ENOUGH, VARMINT!
READY.
SET.
DRAW!
HEY! WHAT *GIVES...?!*
I WAS JUST ABOUT TO *SMOKE* THAT GUY!
TRUST ME. YOU WEREN'T.
UM, *GUYS?* I THINK WE'RE IN *TROUBLE*.

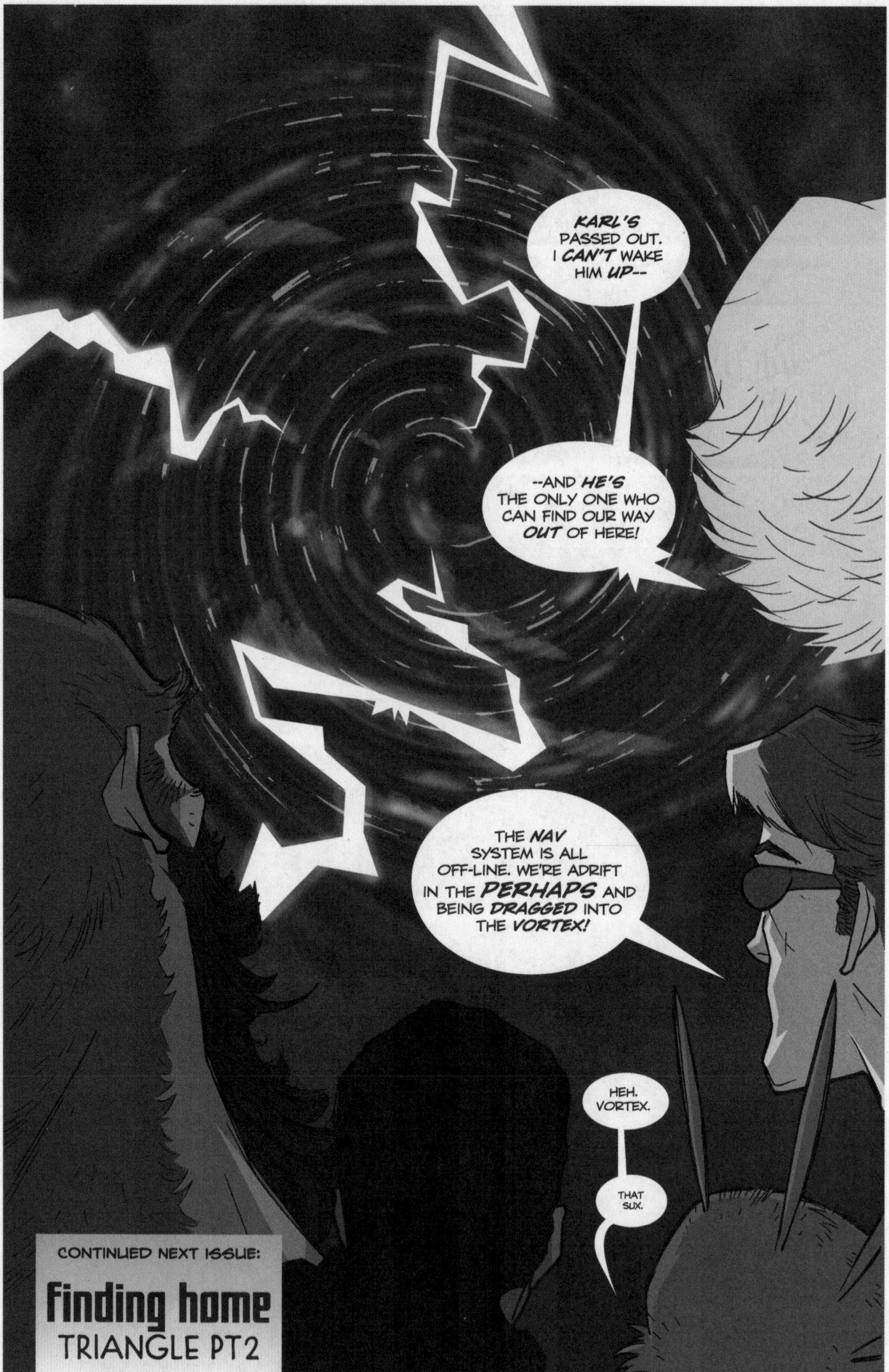
KARL'S PASSED OUT. I CAN'T WAKE HIM UP--
--AND HE'S THE ONLY ONE WHO CAN FIND OUR WAY OUT OF HERE!
THE NAV SYSTEM IS ALL OFF-LINE. WE'RE ADRIFT IN THE PERHAPS AND BEING DRAGGED INTO THE VORTEX!
HEH. VORTEX.
THAT SUX.
CONTINUED NEXT ISSUE:
finding home
TRIANGLE PT 2
SEE YA THEN!

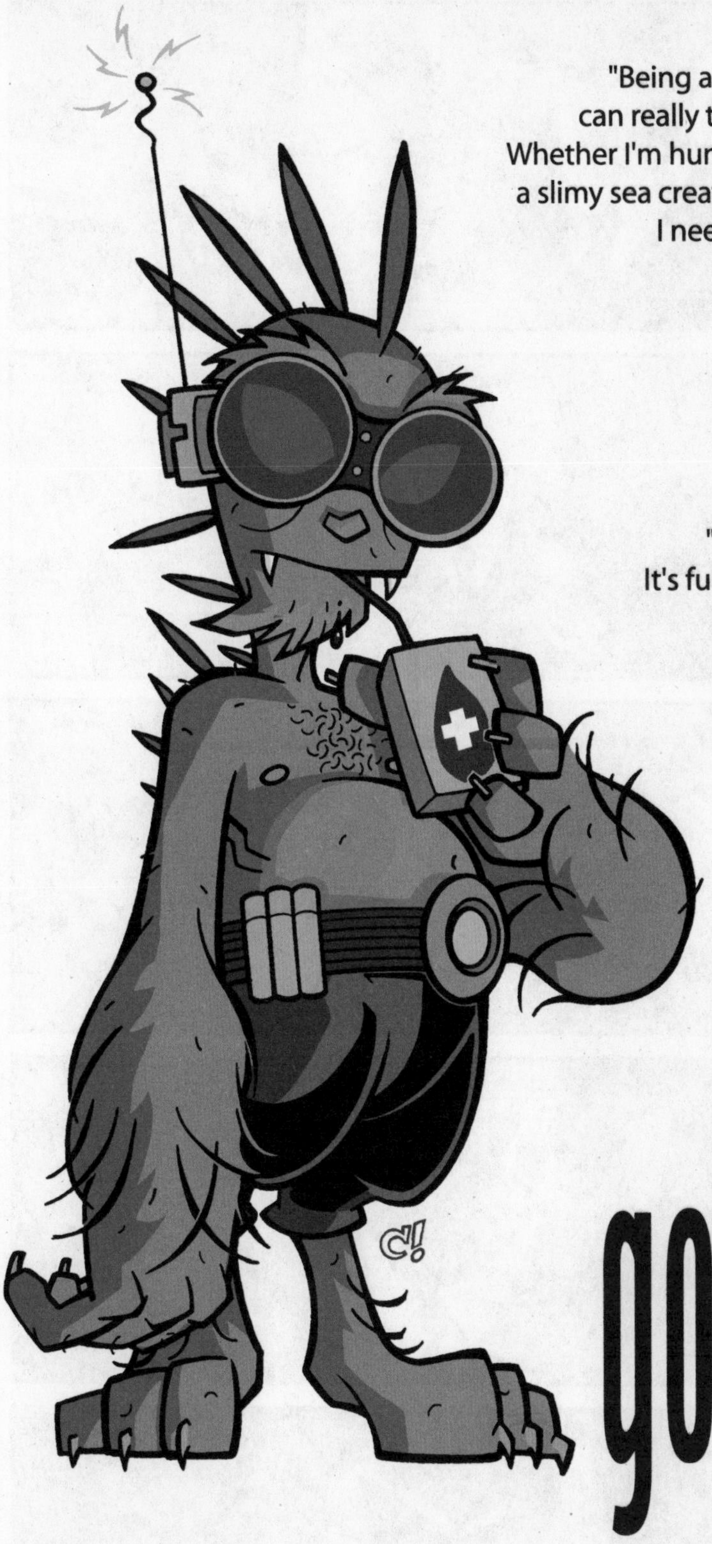

"Being a busy chupacabra
can really take it's toll on a guy.
Whether I'm hunting down a mothman or
a slimy sea creature or a stinkin' vampire,
I need my energy."

"That's why I drink blood.
It's fulla iron and minerals and, uh...
hemogoblins and stuff.
Plus, it tastes great!
It's the only way to start
my day."

got blood?

THE TODD AND CRAIG'S Perhapanauts

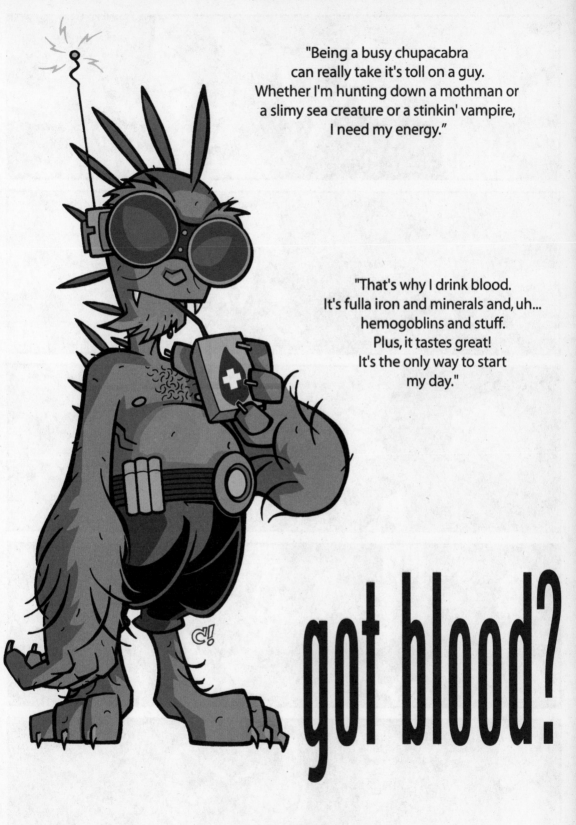

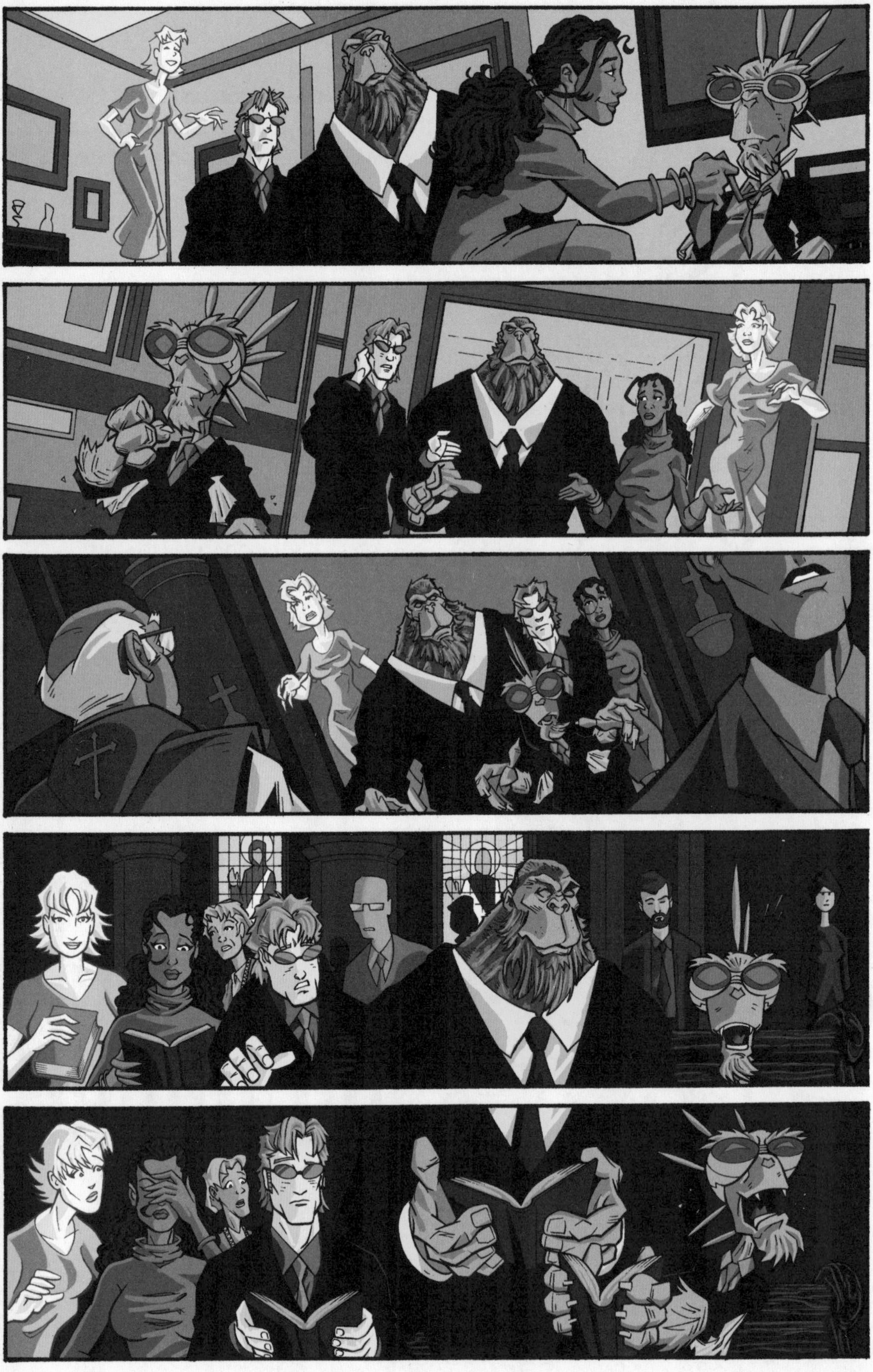

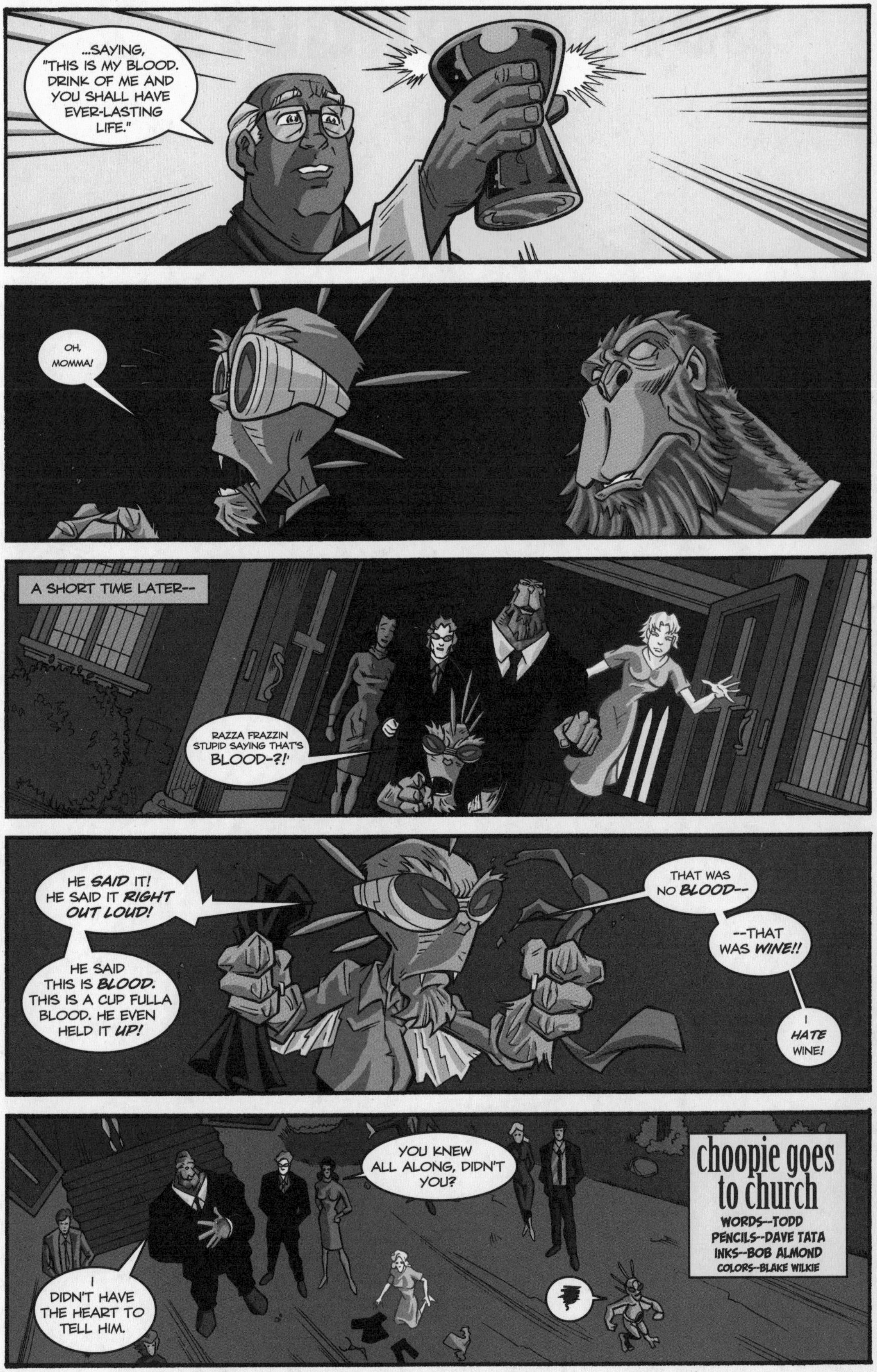
...SAYING, "THIS IS MY BLOOD. DRINK OF ME AND YOU SHALL HAVE EVER-LASTING LIFE."
OH, MOMMA!
A SHORT TIME LATER--
RAZZA FRAZZIN STUPID SAYING THAT'S BLOOD-?!'
HE SAID IT! HE SAID IT RIGHT OUT LOUD!
HE SAID THIS IS BLOOD. THIS IS A CUP FULLA BLOOD. HE EVEN HELD IT UP!
THAT WAS NO BLOOD--
--THAT WAS WINE!!
I HATE WINE!
YOU KNEW ALL ALONG, DIDN'T YOU?
I DIDN'T HAVE THE HEART TO TELL HIM.
choopie goes to church
WORDS--TODD
PENCILS--DAVE TATA
INKS--BOB ALMOND
COLORS--BLAKE WILKIE

perhapanauts 2

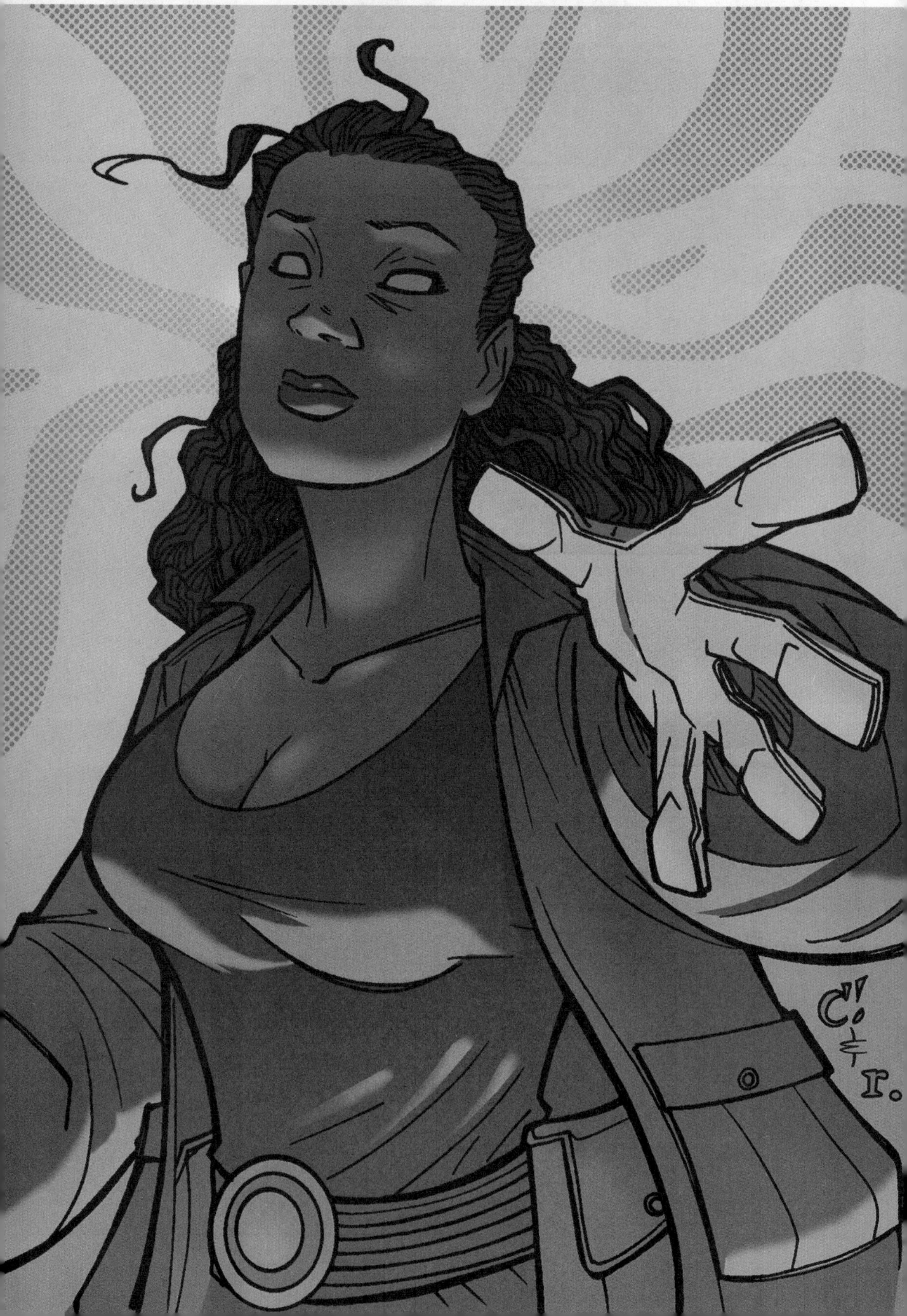

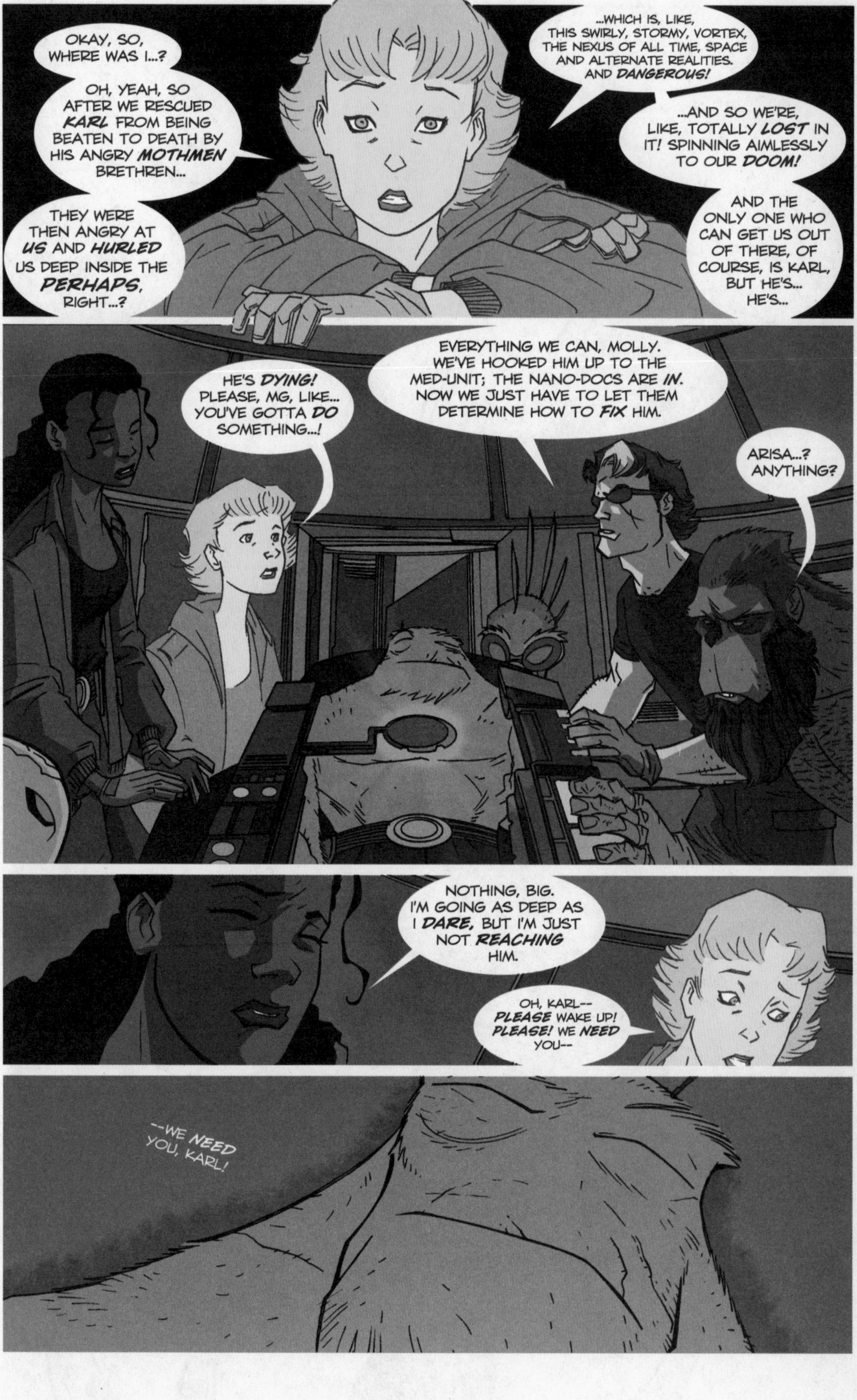
OKAY, SO, WHERE WAS I...?
OH, YEAH, SO AFTER WE RESCUED KARL FROM BEING BEATEN TO DEATH BY HIS ANGRY MOTHMEN BRETHREN...
THEY WERE THEN ANGRY AT US AND HURLED US DEEP INSIDE THE PERHAPS, RIGHT...?
...WHICH IS, LIKE, THIS SWIRLY, STORMY, VORTEX, THE NEXUS OF ALL TIME, SPACE AND ALTERNATE REALITIES. AND DANGEROUS!
...AND SO WE'RE, LIKE, TOTALLY LOST IN IT! SPINNING AIMLESSLY TO OUR DOOM!
AND THE ONLY ONE WHO CAN GET US OUT OF THERE, OF COURSE, IS KARL, BUT HE'S... HE'S...
HE'S DYING! PLEASE, MG, LIKE... YOU'VE GOTTA DO SOMETHING...!
EVERYTHING WE CAN, MOLLY. WE'VE HOOKED HIM UP TO THE MED-UNIT; THE NANO-DOCS ARE IN. NOW WE JUST HAVE TO LET THEM DETERMINE HOW TO FIX HIM.
ARISA...? ANYTHING?
NOTHING, BIG. I'M GOING AS DEEP AS I DARE, BUT I'M JUST NOT REACHING HIM.
OH, KARL-- PLEASE WAKE UP! PLEASE! WE NEED YOU--
--WE NEED YOU, KARL!

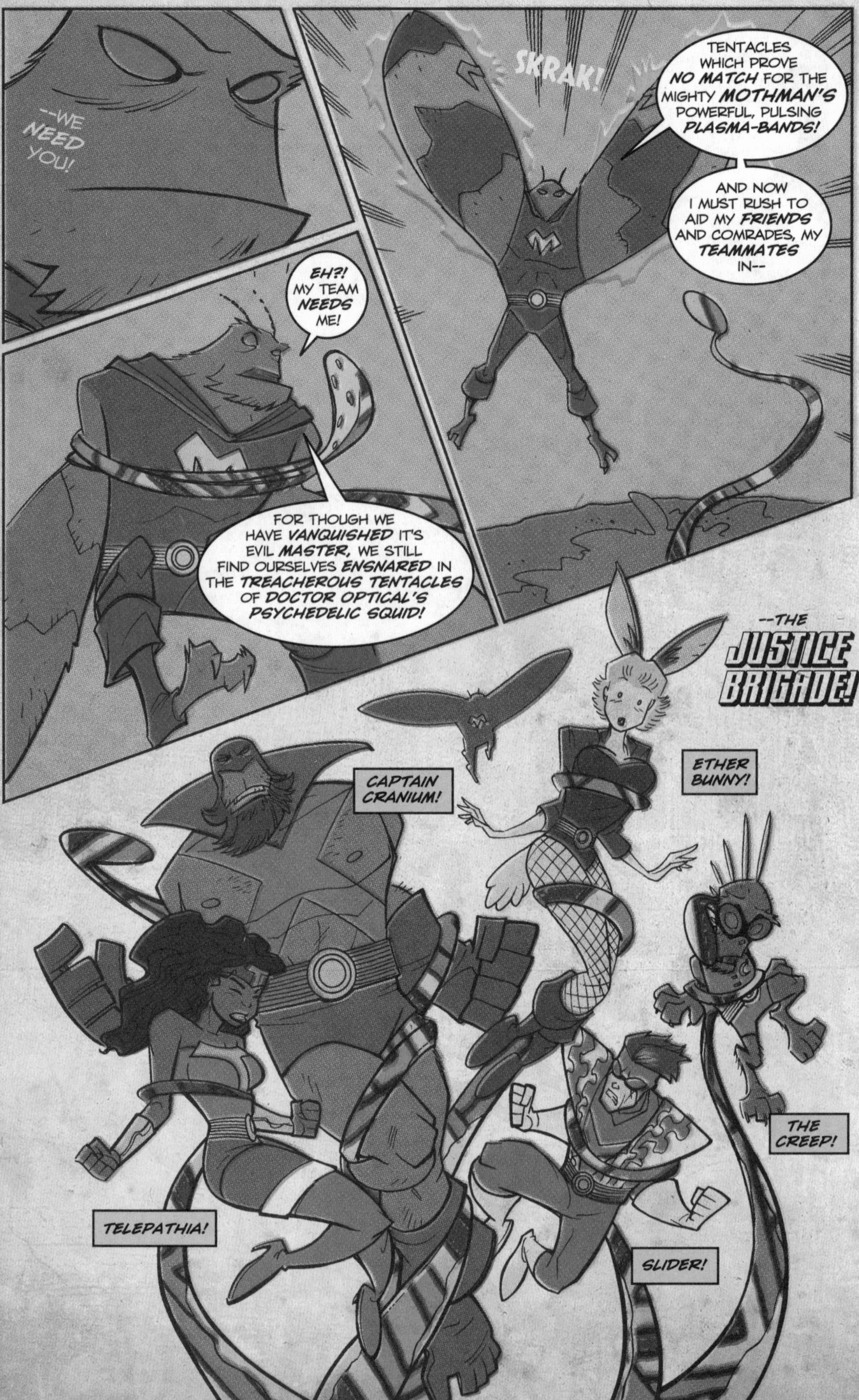
--WE NEED YOU!
SKRAK!
TENTACLES WHICH PROVE NO MATCH FOR THE MIGHTY MOTHMAN'S POWERFUL, PULSING PLASMA-BANDS!
AND NOW I MUST RUSH TO AID MY FRIENDS AND COMRADES, MY TEAMMATES IN--
EH?! MY TEAM NEEDS ME!
FOR THOUGH WE HAVE VANQUISHED IT'S EVIL MASTER, WE STILL FIND OURSELVES ENSNARED IN THE TREACHEROUS TENTACLES OF DOCTOR OPTICAL'S PSYCHEDELIC SQUID!
--THE JUSTICE BRIGADE!
CAPTAIN CRANIUM!
ETHER BUNNY!
THE CREEP!
TELEPATHIA!
SLIDER!

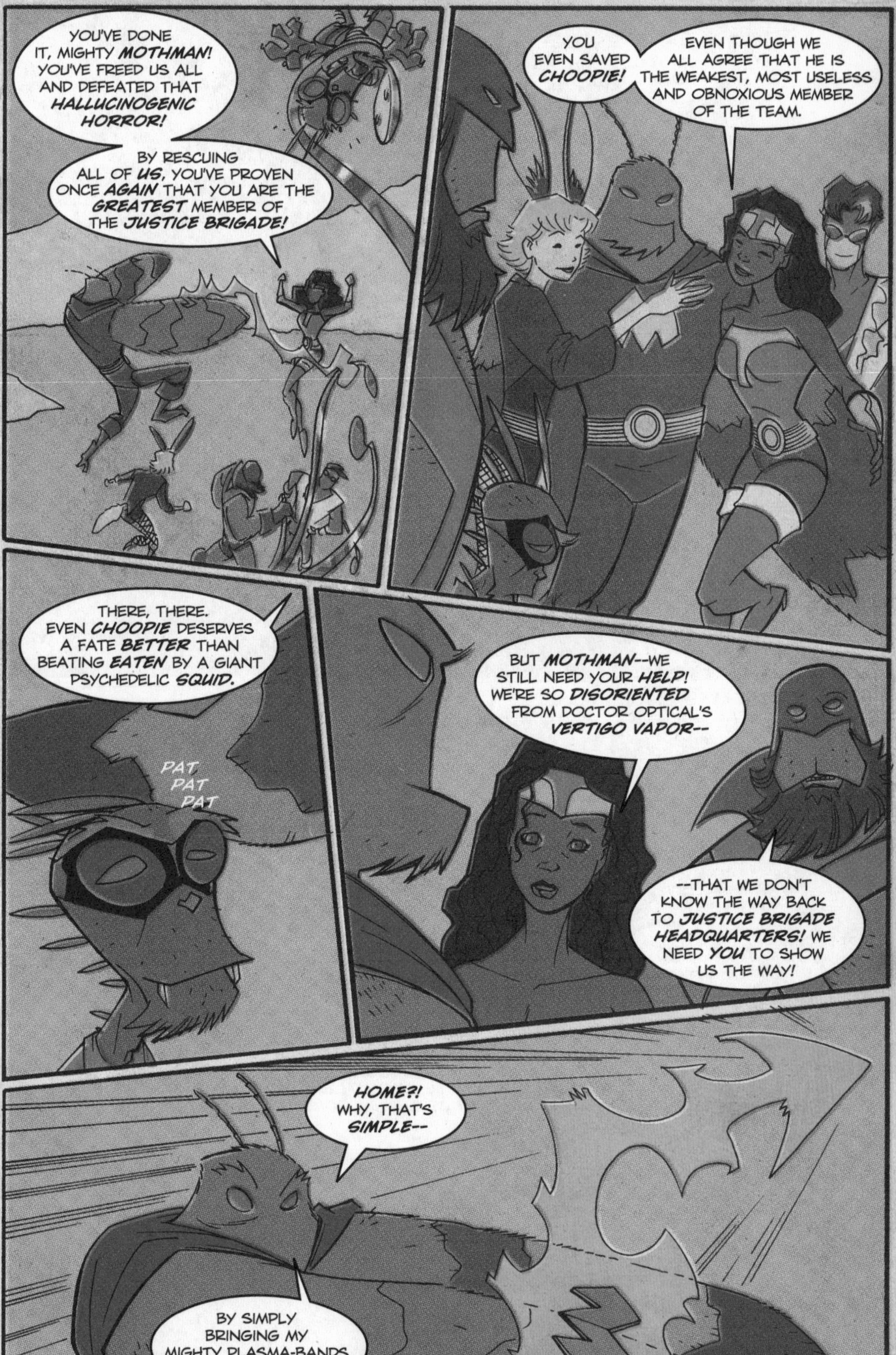
YOU'VE DONE IT, MIGHTY MOTHMAN! YOU'VE FREED US ALL AND DEFEATED THAT HALLUCINOGENIC HORROR!
BY RESCUING ALL OF US, YOU'VE PROVEN ONCE AGAIN THAT YOU ARE THE GREATEST MEMBER OF THE JUSTICE BRIGADE!
YOU EVEN SAVED CHOOPIE!
EVEN THOUGH WE ALL AGREE THAT HE IS THE WEAKEST, MOST USELESS AND OBNOXIOUS MEMBER OF THE TEAM.
THERE, THERE. EVEN CHOOPIE DESERVES A FATE BETTER THAN BEATING EATEN BY A GIANT PSYCHEDELIC SQUID.
PAT PAT PAT
BUT MOTHMAN--WE STILL NEED YOUR HELP! WE'RE SO DISORIENTED FROM DOCTOR OPTICAL'S VERTIGO VAPOR--
--THAT WE DON'T KNOW THE WAY BACK TO JUSTICE BRIGADE HEADQUARTERS! WE NEED YOU TO SHOW US THE WAY!
HOME?! WHY, THAT'S SIMPLE--
BY SIMPLY BRINGING MY MIGHTY PLASMA-BANDS TOGETHER...

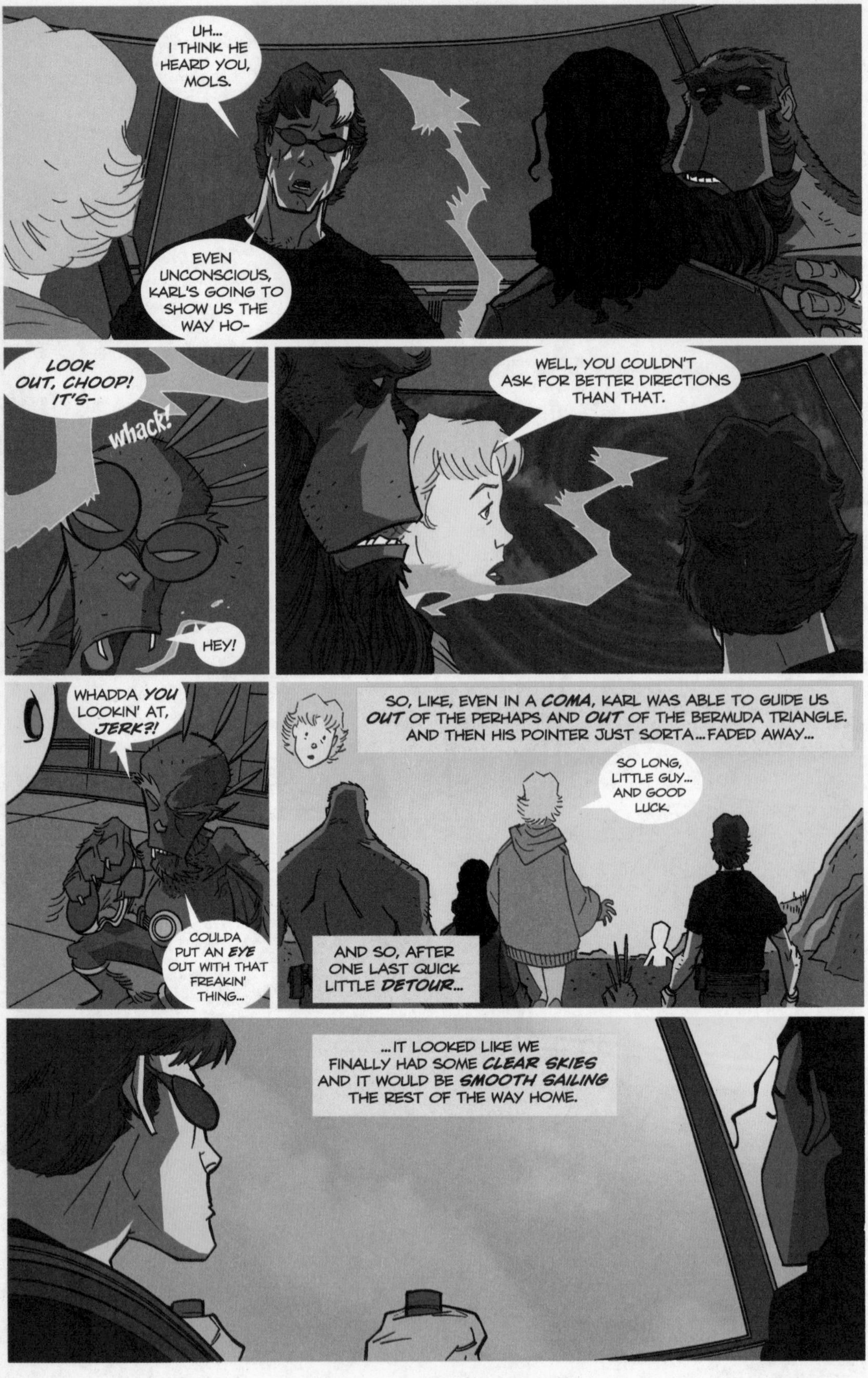
UH... I THINK HE HEARD YOU, MOLS.
EVEN UNCONSCIOUS, KARL'S GOING TO SHOW US THE WAY HO-
LOOK OUT, CHOOP! IT'S-
whack!
HEY!
WELL, YOU COULDN'T ASK FOR BETTER DIRECTIONS THAN THAT.
WHADDA YOU LOOKIN' AT, JERK?!
COULDA PUT AN EYE OUT WITH THAT FREAKIN' THING...
SO, LIKE, EVEN IN A COMA, KARL WAS ABLE TO GUIDE US OUT OF THE PERHAPS AND OUT OF THE BERMUDA TRIANGLE. AND THEN HIS POINTER JUST SORTA...FADED AWAY...
SO LONG, LITTLE GUY... AND GOOD LUCK.
AND SO, AFTER ONE LAST QUICK LITTLE DETOUR...
...IT LOOKED LIKE WE FINALLY HAD SOME CLEAR SKIES AND IT WOULD BE SMOOTH SAILING THE REST OF THE WAY HOME.

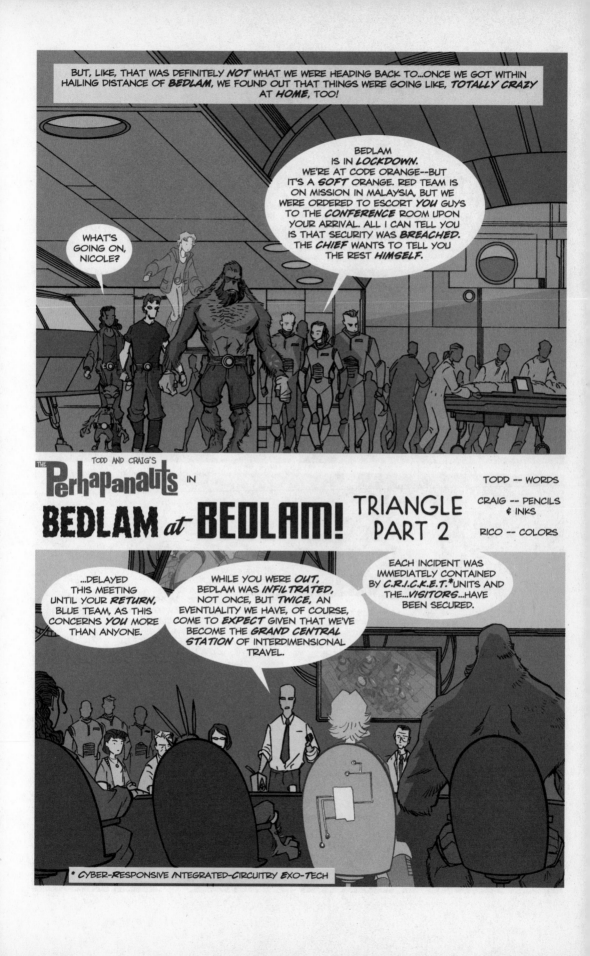

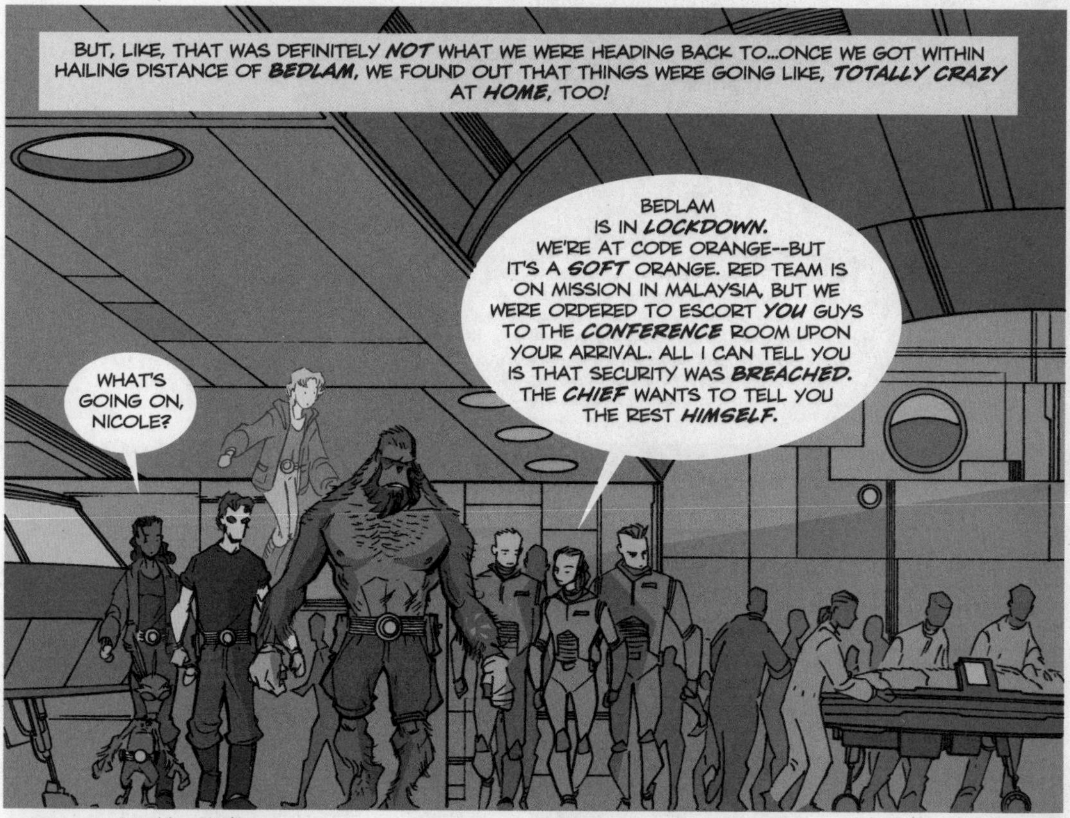
BUT, LIKE, THAT WAS DEFINITELY NOT WHAT WE WERE HEADING BACK TO...ONCE WE GOT WITHIN HAILING DISTANCE OF BEDLAM, WE FOUND OUT THAT THINGS WERE GOING LIKE, TOTALLY CRAZY AT HOME, TOO!
WHAT'S GOING ON, NICOLE?
BEDLAM IS IN LOCKDOWN. WE'RE AT CODE ORANGE--BUT IT'S A SOFT ORANGE. RED TEAM IS ON MISSION IN MALAYSIA, BUT WE WERE ORDERED TO ESCORT YOU GUYS TO THE CONFERENCE ROOM UPON YOUR ARRIVAL. ALL I CAN TELL YOU IS THAT SECURITY WAS BREACHED. THE CHIEF WANTS TO TELL YOU THE REST HIMSELF.

TODD AND CRAIG'S THE Perhapanauts IN

BEDLAM at BEDLAM! TRIANGLE PART 2

TODD -- WORDS

CRAIG -- PENCILS & INKS

RICO -- COLORS

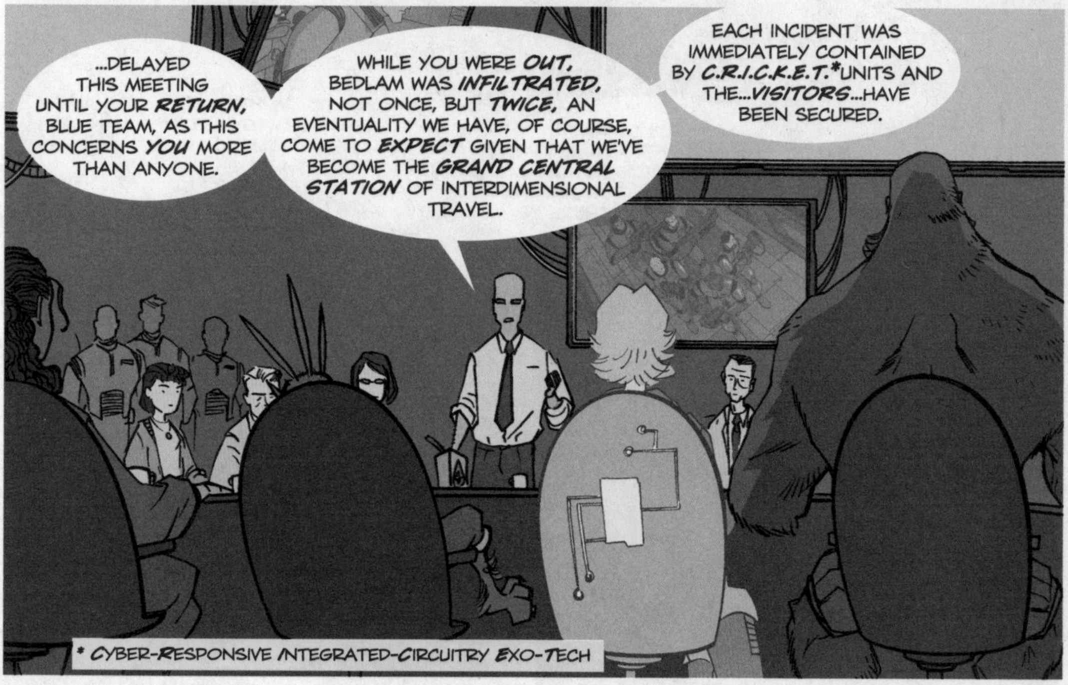
...DELAYED THIS MEETING UNTIL YOUR RETURN, BLUE TEAM, AS THIS CONCERNS YOU MORE THAN ANYONE.
WHILE YOU WERE OUT, BEDLAM WAS INFILTRATED, NOT ONCE, BUT TWICE, AN EVENTUALITY WE HAVE, OF COURSE, COME TO EXPECT GIVEN THAT WE'VE BECOME THE GRAND CENTRAL STATION OF INTERDIMENSIONAL TRAVEL.
EACH INCIDENT WAS IMMEDIATELY CONTAINED BY C.R.I.C.K.E.T.* UNITS AND THE...VISITORS...HAVE BEEN SECURED.
* CYBER-RESPONSIVE INTEGRATED-CIRCUITRY EXO-TECH

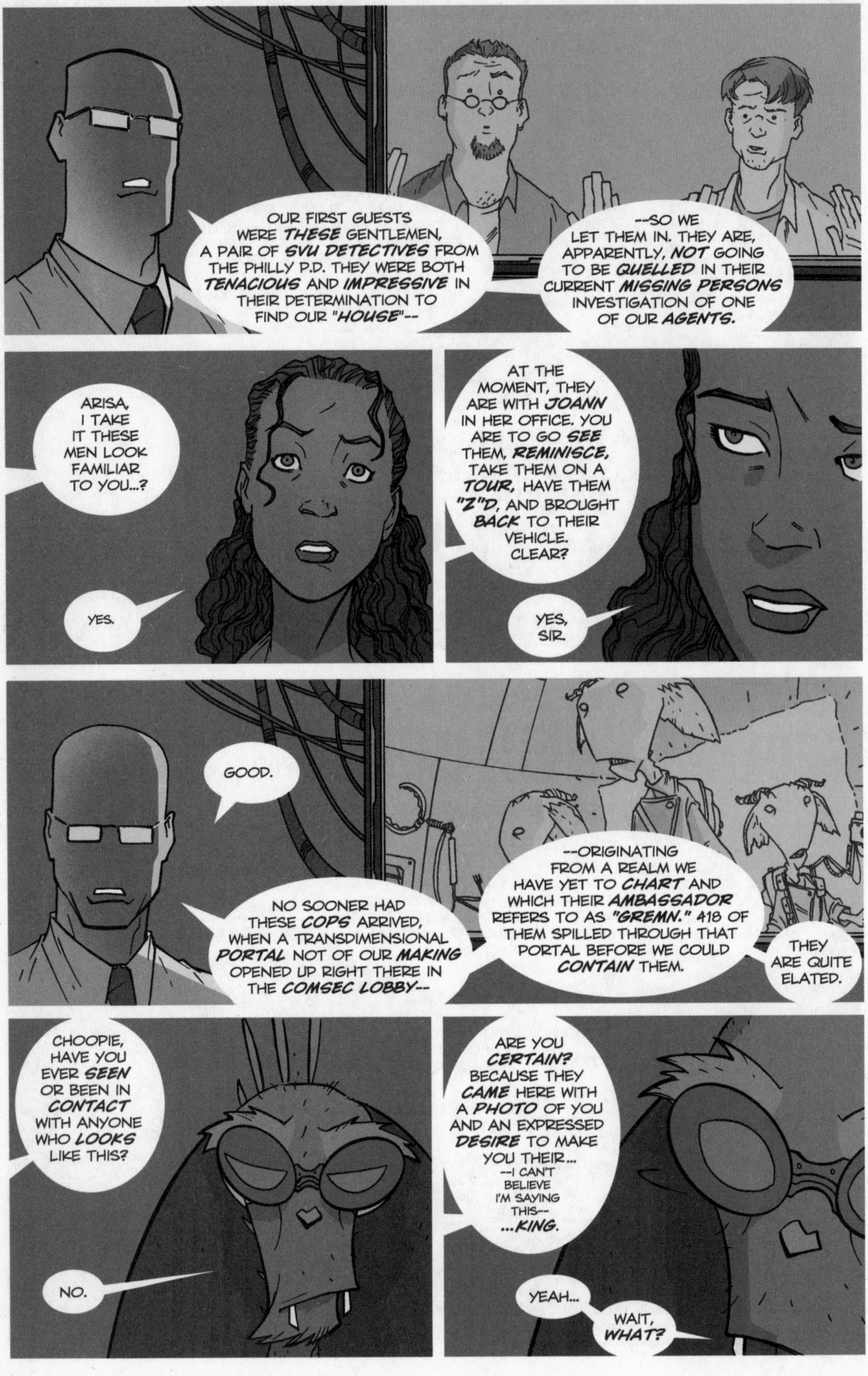
OUR FIRST GUESTS WERE THESE GENTLEMEN, A PAIR OF SVU DETECTIVES FROM THE PHILLY P.D. THEY WERE BOTH TENACIOUS AND IMPRESSIVE IN THEIR DETERMINATION TO FIND OUR "HOUSE"--
--SO WE LET THEM IN. THEY ARE, APPARENTLY, NOT GOING TO BE QUELLED IN THEIR CURRENT MISSING PERSONS INVESTIGATION OF ONE OF OUR AGENTS.
ARISA, I TAKE IT THESE MEN LOOK FAMILIAR TO YOU...?
YES.
AT THE MOMENT, THEY ARE WITH JOANN IN HER OFFICE. YOU ARE TO GO SEE THEM, REMINISCE, TAKE THEM ON A TOUR, HAVE THEM "Z"'D, AND BROUGHT BACK TO THEIR VEHICLE. CLEAR?
YES, SIR.
GOOD.
NO SOONER HAD THESE COPS ARRIVED, WHEN A TRANSDIMENSIONAL PORTAL NOT OF OUR MAKING OPENED UP RIGHT THERE IN THE COMSEC LOBBY--
--ORIGINATING FROM A REALM WE HAVE YET TO CHART AND WHICH THEIR AMBASSADOR REFERS TO AS "GREMN." 418 OF THEM SPILLED THROUGH THAT PORTAL BEFORE WE COULD CONTAIN THEM.
THEY ARE QUITE ELATED.
CHOOPIE, HAVE YOU EVER SEEN OR BEEN IN CONTACT WITH ANYONE WHO LOOKS LIKE THIS?
NO.
ARE YOU CERTAIN? BECAUSE THEY CAME HERE WITH A PHOTO OF YOU AND AN EXPRESSED DESIRE TO MAKE YOU THEIR... --I CAN'T BELIEVE I'M SAYING THIS-- ...KING.
YEAH...
WAIT, WHAT?

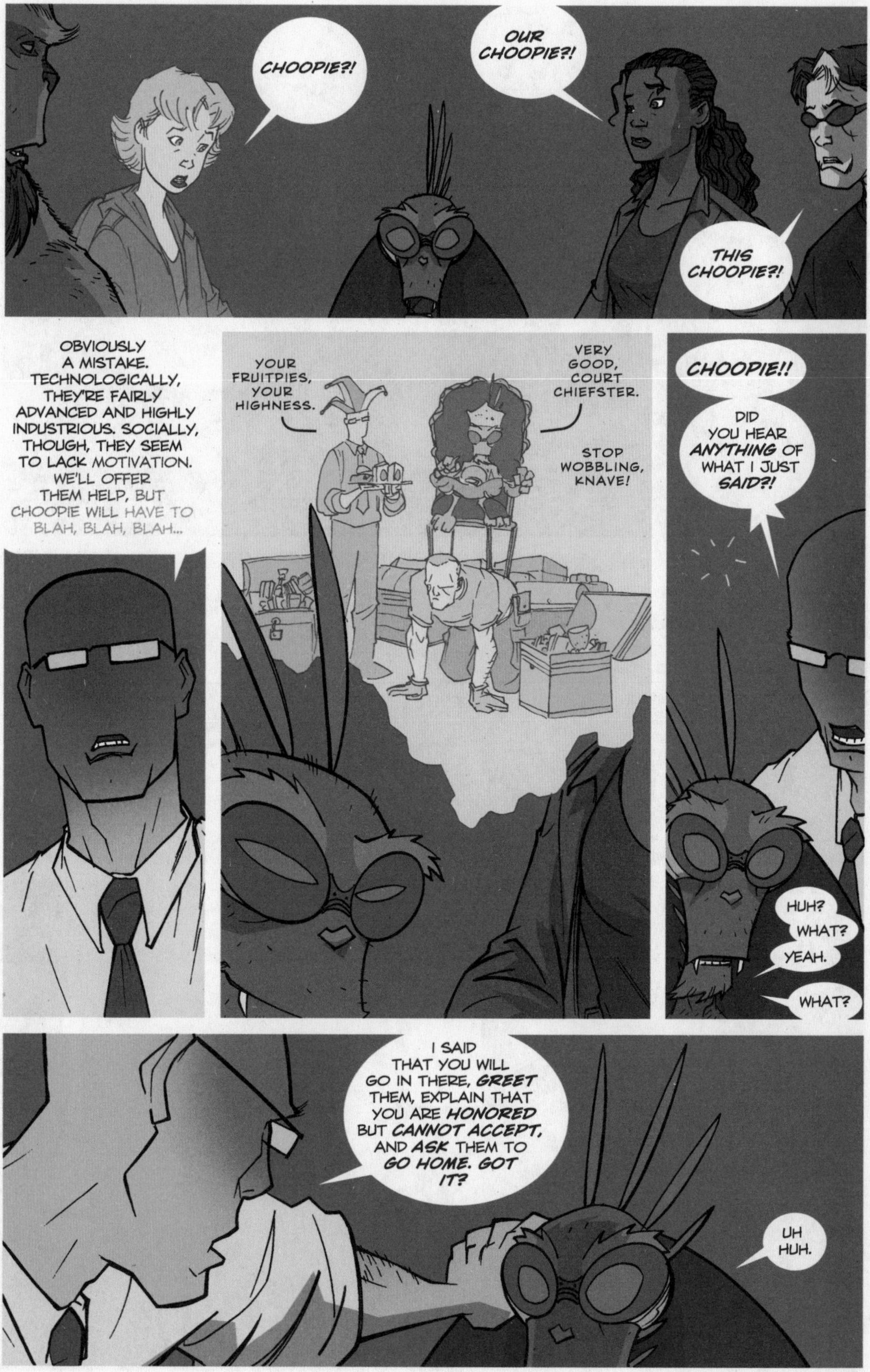
CHOOPIE?!
OUR CHOOPIE?!
THIS CHOOPIE?!
OBVIOUSLY A MISTAKE. TECHNOLOGICALLY, THEY'RE FAIRLY ADVANCED AND HIGHLY INDUSTRIOUS. SOCIALLY, THOUGH, THEY SEEM TO LACK MOTIVATION. WE'LL OFFER THEM HELP, BUT CHOOPIE WILL HAVE TO BLAH, BLAH, BLAH...
YOUR FRUITPIES, YOUR HIGHNESS.
VERY GOOD, COURT CHIEFSTER.
STOP WOBBLING, KNAVE!
CHOOPIE!!
DID YOU HEAR ANYTHING OF WHAT I JUST SAID?!
HUH?
WHAT?
YEAH.
WHAT?
I SAID THAT YOU WILL GO IN THERE, GREET THEM, EXPLAIN THAT YOU ARE HONORED BUT CANNOT ACCEPT, AND ASK THEM TO GO HOME. GOT IT?
UH HUH.

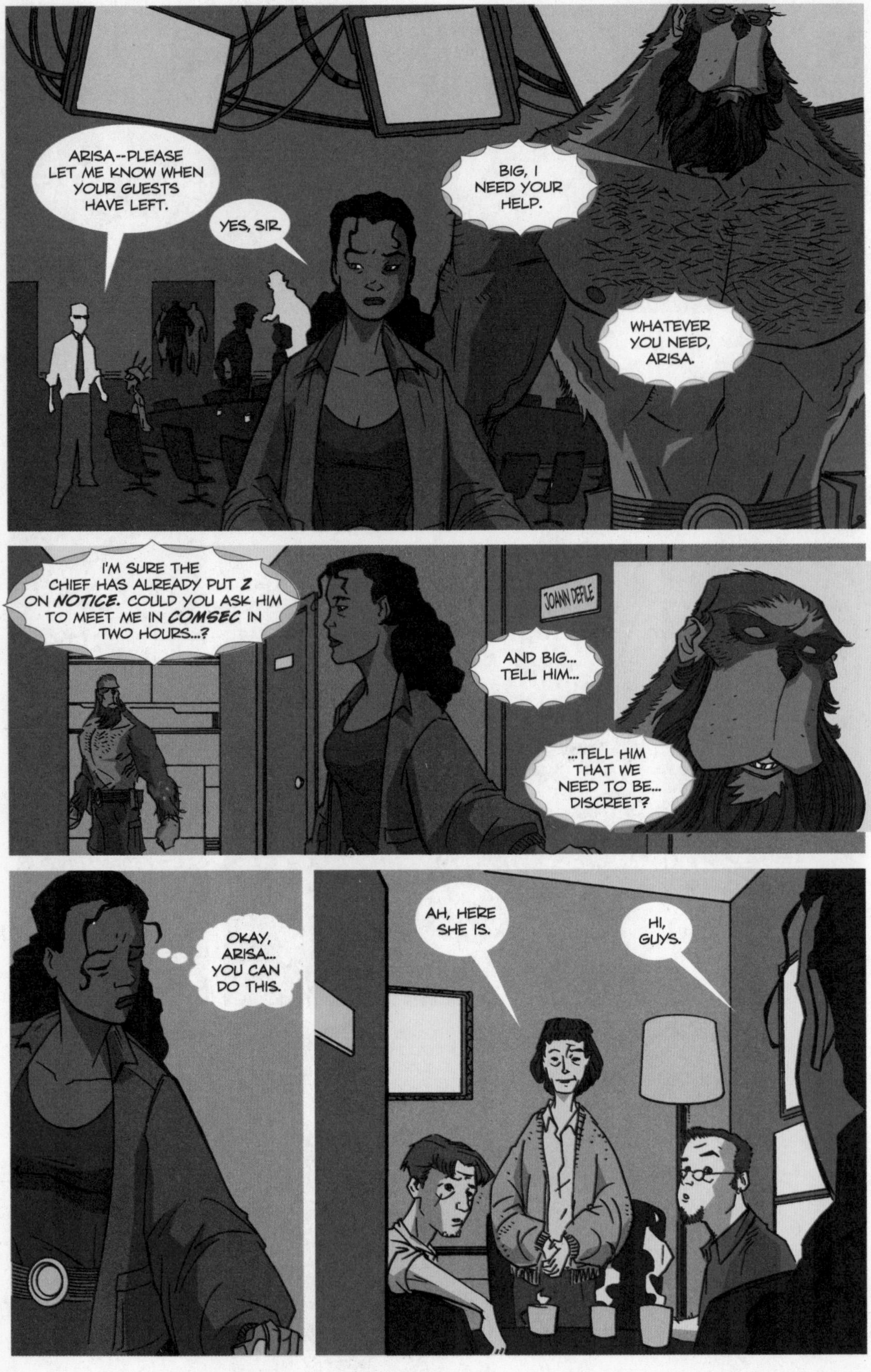
ARISA--PLEASE LET ME KNOW WHEN YOUR GUESTS HAVE LEFT.
YES, SIR.
BIG, I NEED YOUR HELP.
WHATEVER YOU NEED, ARISA.
I'M SURE THE CHIEF HAS ALREADY PUT Z ON NOTICE. COULD YOU ASK HIM TO MEET ME IN COMSEC IN TWO HOURS...?
JOANN DEFILE
AND BIG... TELL HIM...
...TELL HIM THAT WE NEED TO BE... DISCREET?
OKAY, ARISA... YOU CAN DO THIS.
AH, HERE SHE IS.
HI, GUYS.

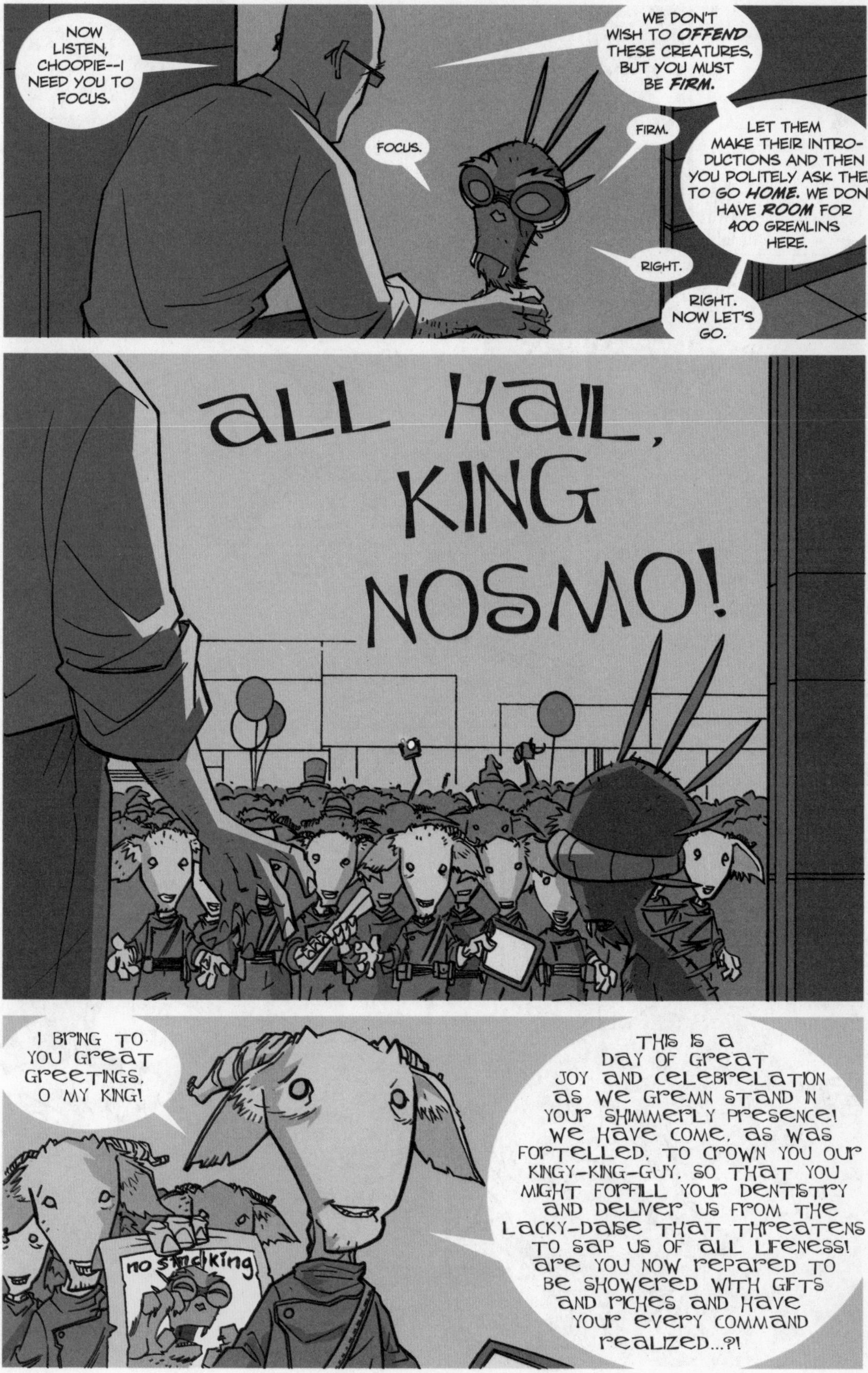

NOW LISTEN, CHOOPIE--I NEED YOU TO FOCUS.
WE DON'T WISH TO *OFFEND* THESE CREATURES, BUT YOU MUST BE *FIRM.*
FOCUS.
FIRM.
LET THEM MAKE THEIR INTRO-DUCTIONS AND THEN YOU POLITELY ASK THEM TO GO *HOME.* WE DON'T HAVE *ROOM* FOR 400 GREMLINS HERE.
RIGHT.
RIGHT. NOW LET'S GO.
ALL HAIL, KING NOSMO!
I BRING TO YOU GREAT GREETINGS, O MY KING!
THIS IS A DAY OF GREAT JOY AND CELEBRELATION AS WE GREMN STAND IN YOUR SHIMMERLY PRESENCE! WE HAVE COME, AS WAS FORTELLED, TO CROWN YOU OUR KINGY-KING-GUY, SO THAT YOU MIGHT FORFILL YOUR DENTISTRY AND DELIVER US FROM THE LACKY-DAISE THAT THREATENS TO SAP US OF ALL LIFENESS! ARE YOU NOW REPARED TO BE SHOWERED WITH GFTS AND RICHES AND HAVE YOUR EVERY COMMAND REALIZED...?!

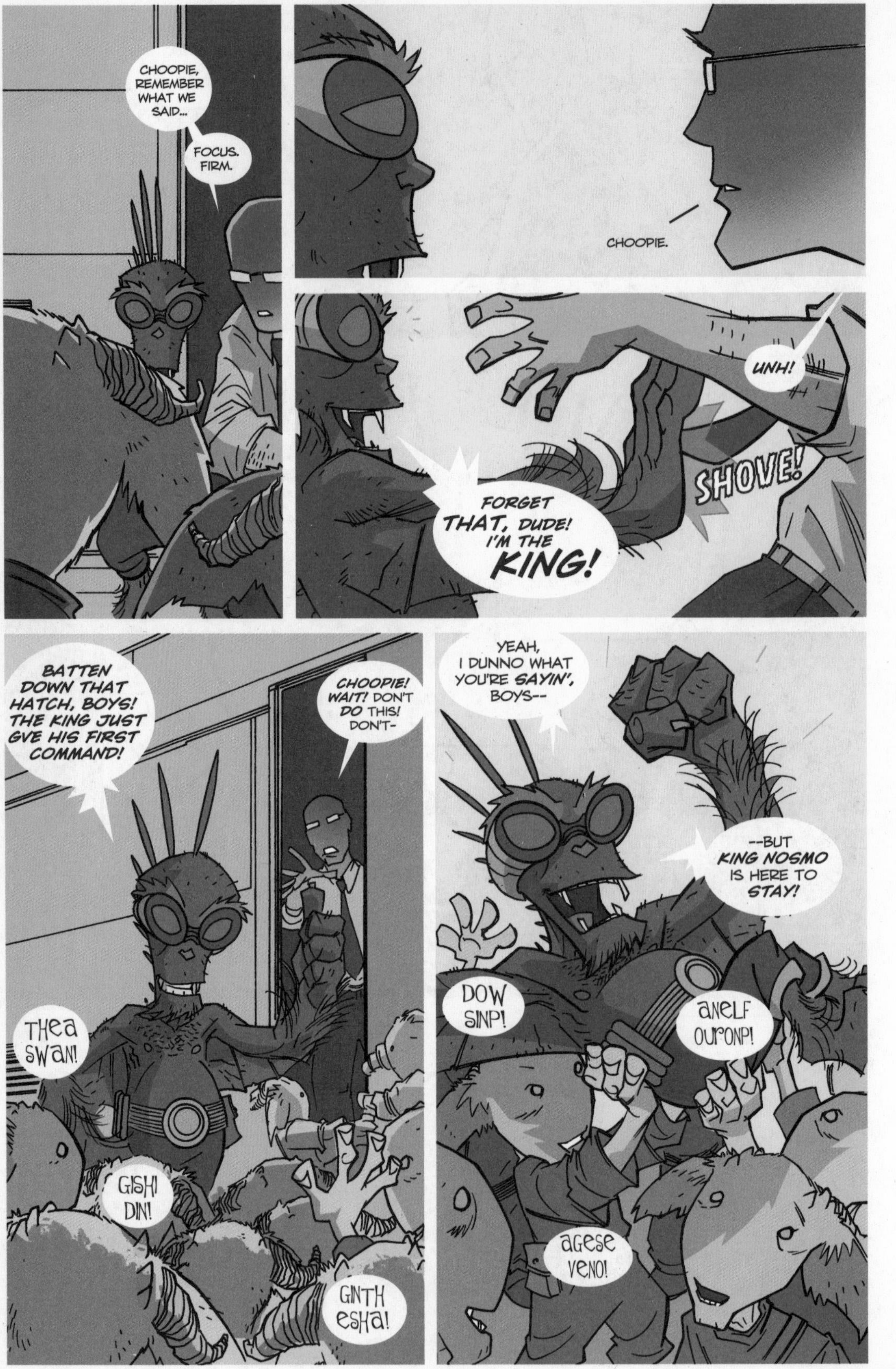
CHOOPIE, REMEMBER WHAT WE SAID...
FOCUS. FIRM.
CHOOPIE.
UNH!
SHOVE!
FORGET THAT, DUDE! I'M THE KING!
BATTEN DOWN THAT HATCH, BOYS! THE KING JUST GVE HIS FIRST COMMAND!
CHOOPIE! WAIT! DON'T DO THIS! DON'T-
THEA SWAN!
GISHI DIN!
GINTH ESHA!
YEAH, I DUNNO WHAT YOU'RE SAYIN', BOYS--
--BUT KING NOSMO IS HERE TO STAY!
DOW SINP!
ANELF OURONP!
AGESE VENO!

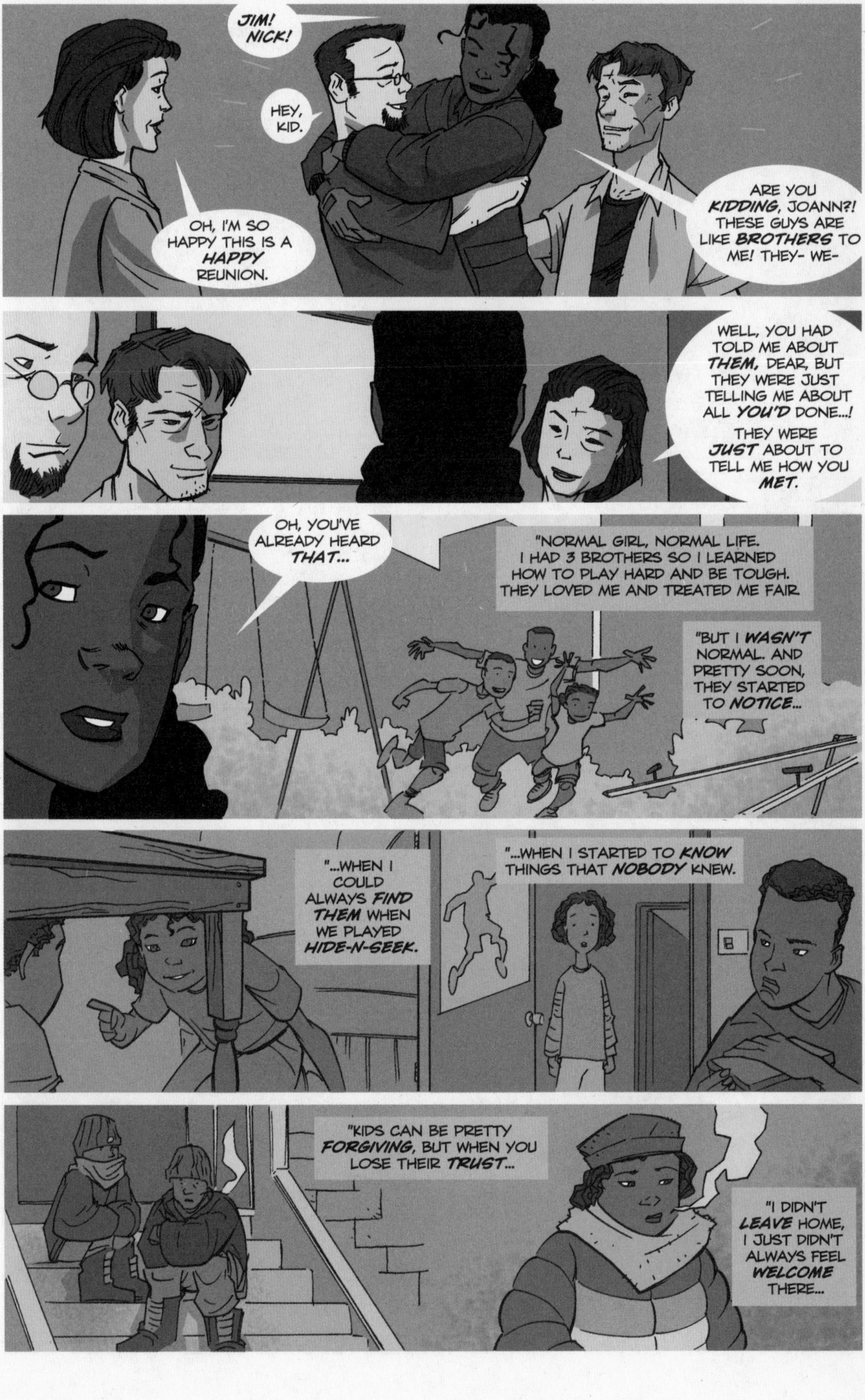
JIM! NICK!
HEY, KID.
OH, I'M SO HAPPY THIS IS A HAPPY REUNION.
ARE YOU KIDDING, JOANN?! THESE GUYS ARE LIKE BROTHERS TO ME! THEY- WE-
WELL, YOU HAD TOLD ME ABOUT THEM, DEAR, BUT THEY WERE JUST TELLING ME ABOUT ALL YOU'D DONE...!
THEY WERE JUST ABOUT TO TELL ME HOW YOU MET.
OH, YOU'VE ALREADY HEARD THAT...
"NORMAL GIRL, NORMAL LIFE. I HAD 3 BROTHERS SO I LEARNED HOW TO PLAY HARD AND BE TOUGH. THEY LOVED ME AND TREATED ME FAIR
"BUT I WASN'T NORMAL. AND PRETTY SOON, THEY STARTED TO NOTICE...
"...WHEN I COULD ALWAYS FIND THEM WHEN WE PLAYED HIDE-N-SEEK.
"...WHEN I STARTED TO KNOW THINGS THAT NOBODY KNEW.
"KIDS CAN BE PRETTY FORGIVING, BUT WHEN YOU LOSE THEIR TRUST...
"I DIDN'T LEAVE HOME, I JUST DIDN'T ALWAYS FEEL WELCOME THERE...

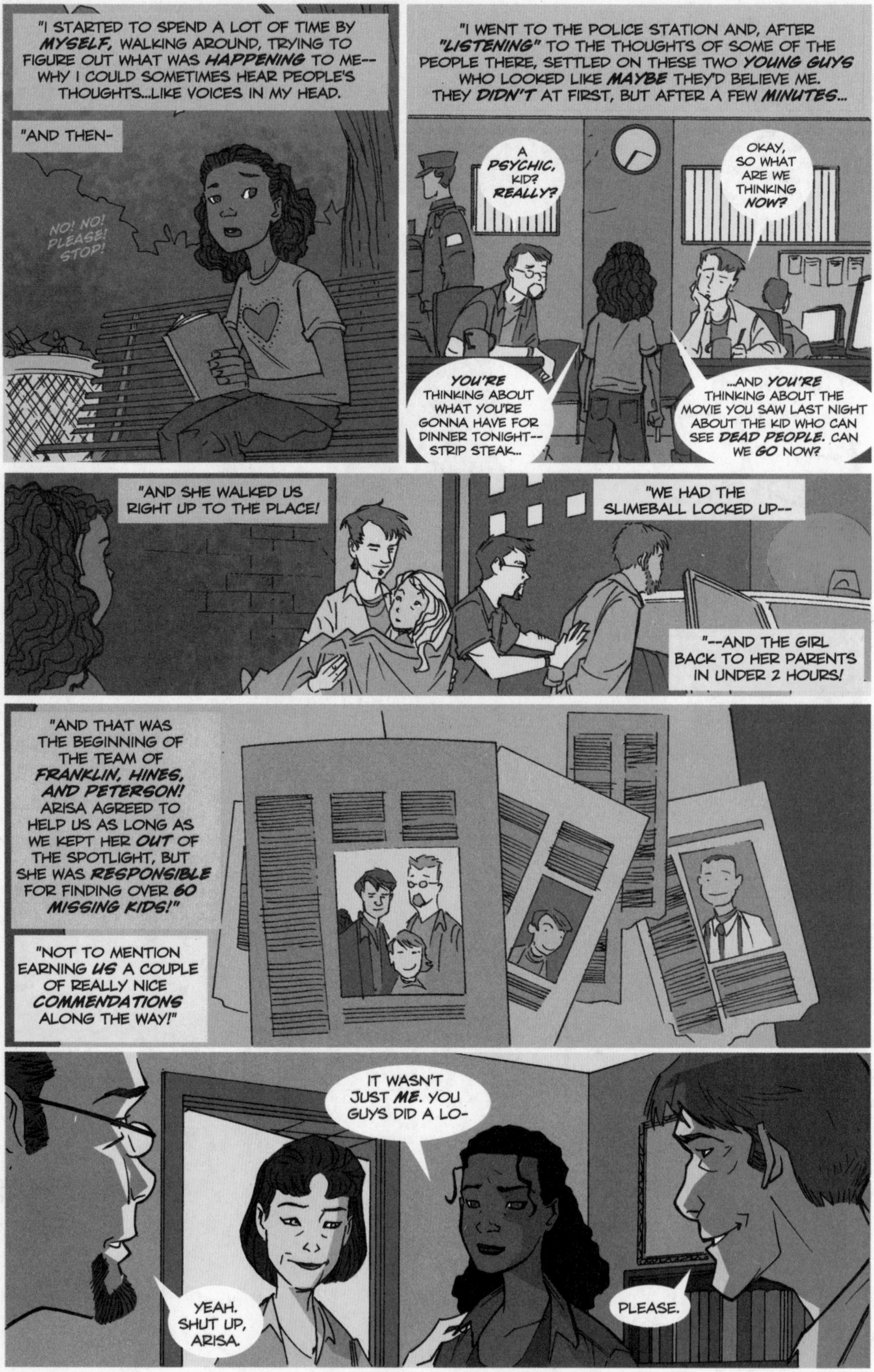
"I STARTED TO SPEND A LOT OF TIME BY MYSELF, WALKING AROUND, TRYING TO FIGURE OUT WHAT WAS HAPPENING TO ME--WHY I COULD SOMETIMES HEAR PEOPLE'S THOUGHTS...LIKE VOICES IN MY HEAD.
"AND THEN-
NO! NO! PLEASE! STOP!
"I WENT TO THE POLICE STATION AND, AFTER "LISTENING" TO THE THOUGHTS OF SOME OF THE PEOPLE THERE, SETTLED ON THESE TWO YOUNG GUYS WHO LOOKED LIKE MAYBE THEY'D BELIEVE ME. THEY DIDN'T AT FIRST, BUT AFTER A FEW MINUTES...
A PSYCHIC, KID? REALLY?
OKAY, SO WHAT ARE WE THINKING NOW?
YOU'RE THINKING ABOUT WHAT YOU'RE GONNA HAVE FOR DINNER TONIGHT--STRIP STEAK...
...AND YOU'RE THINKING ABOUT THE MOVIE YOU SAW LAST NIGHT ABOUT THE KID WHO CAN SEE DEAD PEOPLE. CAN WE GO NOW?
"AND SHE WALKED US RIGHT UP TO THE PLACE!
"WE HAD THE SLIMEBALL LOCKED UP--
"--AND THE GIRL BACK TO HER PARENTS IN UNDER 2 HOURS!
"AND THAT WAS THE BEGINNING OF THE TEAM OF FRANKLIN, HINES, AND PETERSON! ARISA AGREED TO HELP US AS LONG AS WE KEPT HER OUT OF THE SPOTLIGHT, BUT SHE WAS RESPONSIBLE FOR FINDING OVER 60 MISSING KIDS!"
"NOT TO MENTION EARNING US A COUPLE OF REALLY NICE COMMENDATIONS ALONG THE WAY!"
IT WASN'T JUST ME. YOU GUYS DID A LO-
YEAH. SHUT UP, ARISA.
PLEASE.

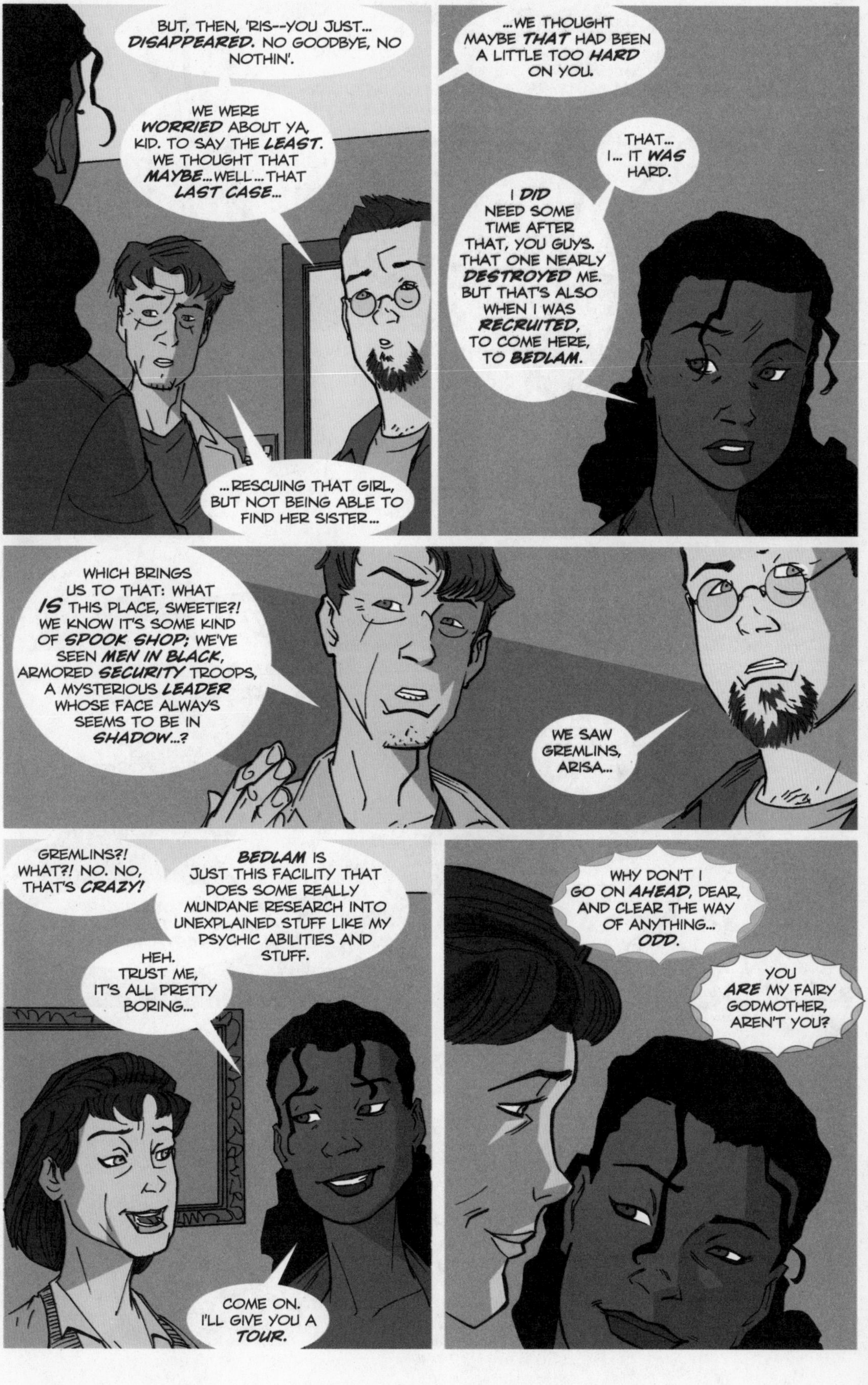
BUT, THEN, 'RIS--YOU JUST... DISAPPEARED. NO GOODBYE, NO NOTHIN'.
WE WERE WORRIED ABOUT YA, KID. TO SAY THE LEAST. WE THOUGHT THAT MAYBE...WELL...THAT LAST CASE...
...RESCUING THAT GIRL, BUT NOT BEING ABLE TO FIND HER SISTER...
...WE THOUGHT MAYBE THAT HAD BEEN A LITTLE TOO HARD ON YOU.
THAT... I... IT WAS HARD.
I DID NEED SOME TIME AFTER THAT, YOU GUYS. THAT ONE NEARLY DESTROYED ME. BUT THAT'S ALSO WHEN I WAS RECRUITED, TO COME HERE, TO BEDLAM.
WHICH BRINGS US TO THAT: WHAT IS THIS PLACE, SWEETIE?! WE KNOW IT'S SOME KIND OF SPOOK SHOP; WE'VE SEEN MEN IN BLACK, ARMORED SECURITY TROOPS, A MYSTERIOUS LEADER WHOSE FACE ALWAYS SEEMS TO BE IN SHADOW...?
WE SAW GREMLINS, ARISA...
GREMLINS?! WHAT?! NO. NO, THAT'S CRAZY!
BEDLAM IS JUST THIS FACILITY THAT DOES SOME REALLY MUNDANE RESEARCH INTO UNEXPLAINED STUFF LIKE MY PSYCHIC ABILITIES AND STUFF.
HEH. TRUST ME, IT'S ALL PRETTY BORING...
COME ON. I'LL GIVE YOU A TOUR.
WHY DON'T I GO ON AHEAD, DEAR, AND CLEAR THE WAY OF ANYTHING... ODD.
YOU ARE MY FAIRY GODMOTHER, AREN'T YOU?

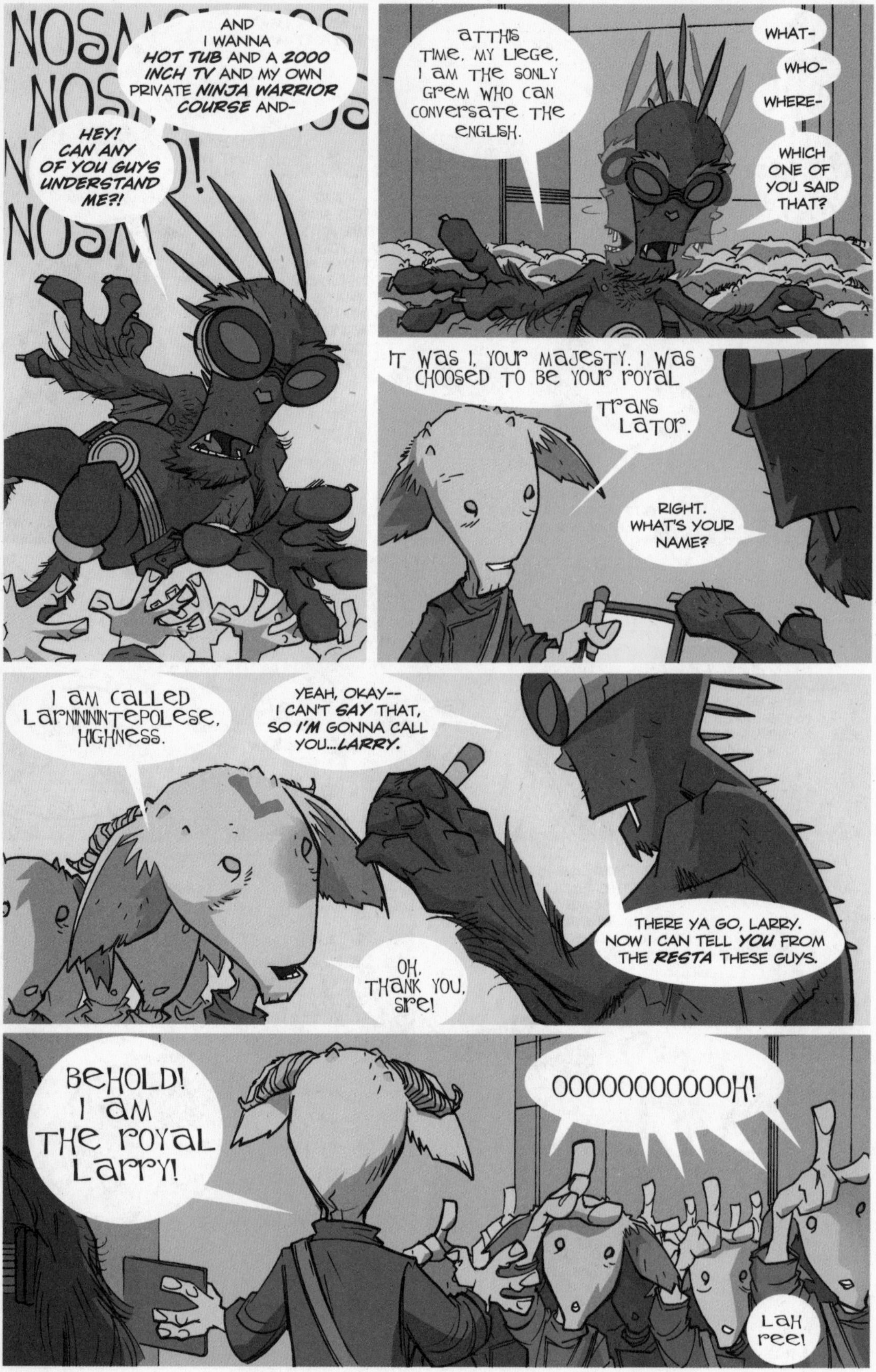
AND I WANNA HOT TUB AND A 2000 INCH TV AND MY OWN PRIVATE NINJA WARRIOR COURSE AND-
HEY! CAN ANY OF YOU GUYS UNDERSTAND ME?!
AT THIS TIME, MY LIEGE, I AM THE SONLY GREM WHO CAN CONVERSATE THE ENGLISH.
WHAT-
WHO-
WHERE-
WHICH ONE OF YOU SAID THAT?
IT WAS I, YOUR MAJESTY. I WAS CHOOSED TO BE YOUR ROYAL TRANS LATOR.
RIGHT. WHAT'S YOUR NAME?
I AM CALLED LARNINNINTEPOLESE, HIGHNESS.
YEAH, OKAY-- I CAN'T SAY THAT, SO I'M GONNA CALL YOU...LARRY.
THERE YA GO, LARRY. NOW I CAN TELL YOU FROM THE RESTA THESE GUYS.
OH, THANK YOU, SIRE!
BEHOLD! I AM THE ROYAL LARRY!
OOOOOOOOOOOH!
LAH REE!

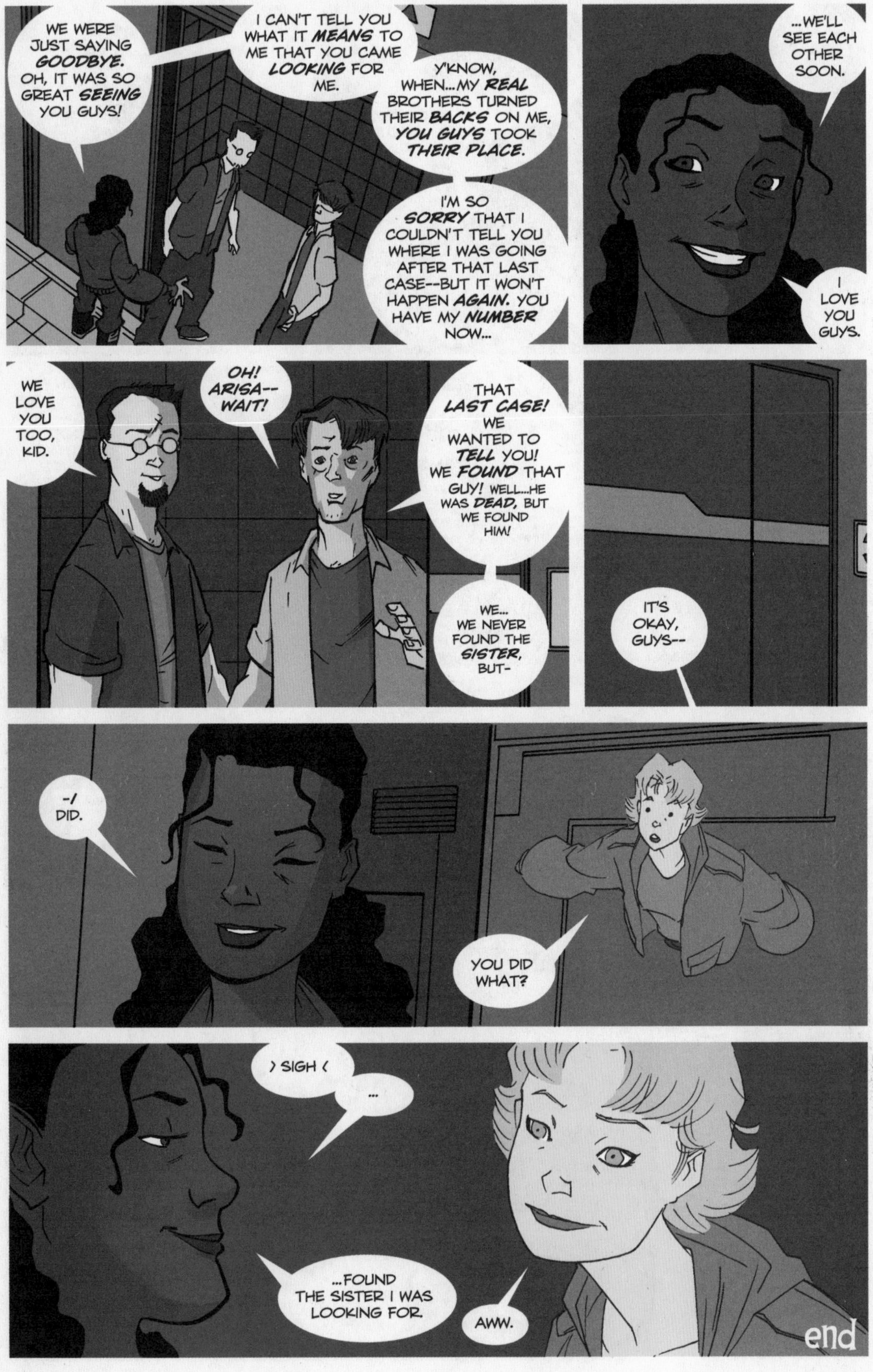
WE WERE JUST SAYING GOODBYE. OH, IT WAS SO GREAT SEEING YOU GUYS!
I CAN'T TELL YOU WHAT IT MEANS TO ME THAT YOU CAME LOOKING FOR ME.
Y'KNOW, WHEN...MY REAL BROTHERS TURNED THEIR BACKS ON ME, YOU GUYS TOOK THEIR PLACE.
I'M SO SORRY THAT I COULDN'T TELL YOU WHERE I WAS GOING AFTER THAT LAST CASE--BUT IT WON'T HAPPEN AGAIN. YOU HAVE MY NUMBER NOW...
...WE'LL SEE EACH OTHER SOON.
I LOVE YOU GUYS.
WE LOVE YOU TOO, KID.
OH! ARISA--WAIT!
THAT LAST CASE! WE WANTED TO TELL YOU! WE FOUND THAT GUY! WELL...HE WAS DEAD, BUT WE FOUND HIM!
WE... WE NEVER FOUND THE SISTER, BUT-
IT'S OKAY, GUYS--
-I DID.
YOU DID WHAT?
› SIGH ‹
...
...FOUND THE SISTER I WAS LOOKING FOR.
AWW.
end

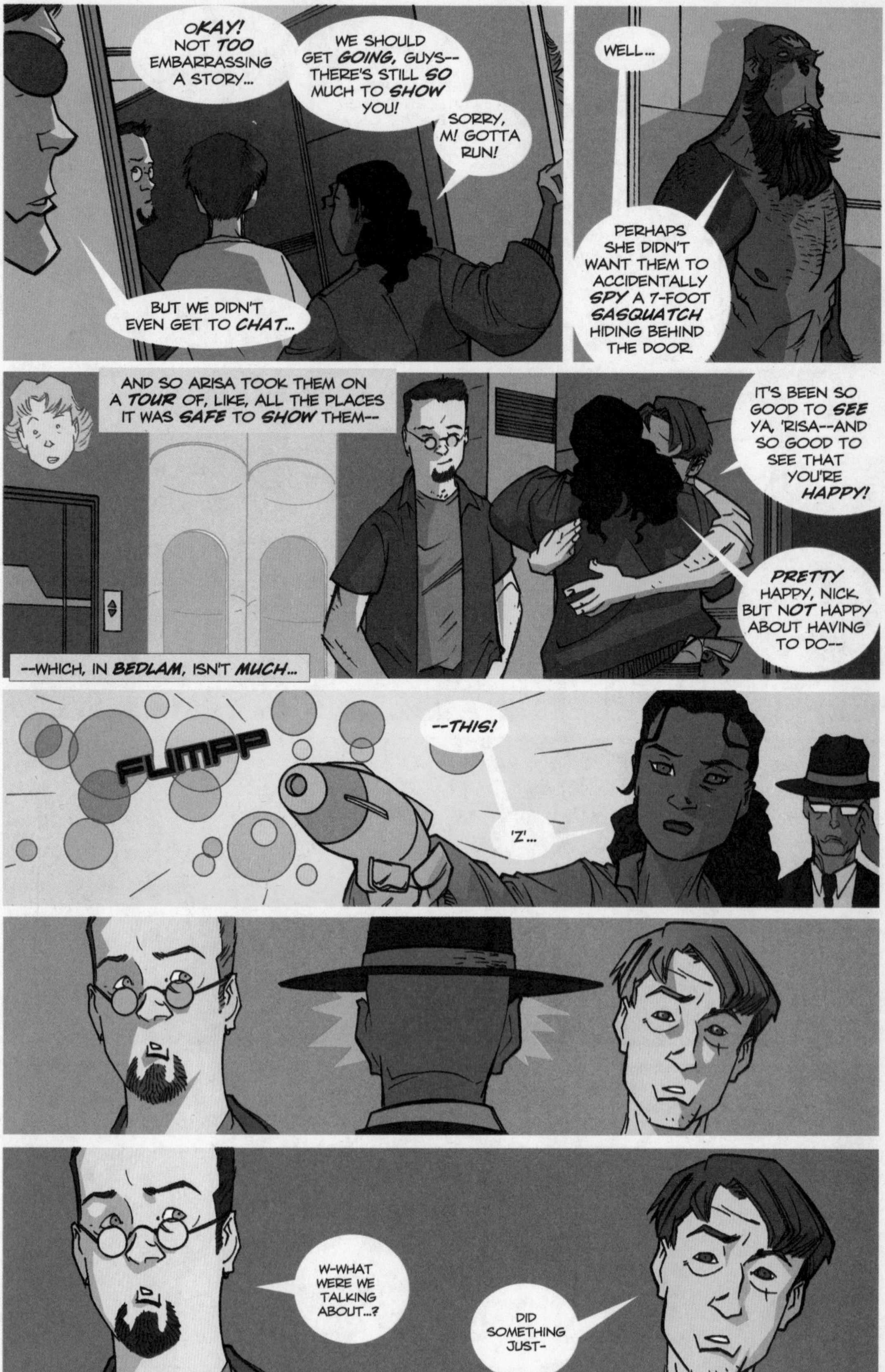
OKAY! NOT TOO EMBARRASSING A STORY...
WE SHOULD GET GOING, GUYS-- THERE'S STILL SO MUCH TO SHOW YOU!
SORRY, M! GOTTA RUN!
BUT WE DIDN'T EVEN GET TO CHAT...
WELL...
PERHAPS SHE DIDN'T WANT THEM TO ACCIDENTALLY SPY A 7-FOOT SASQUATCH HIDING BEHIND THE DOOR.
AND SO ARISA TOOK THEM ON A TOUR OF, LIKE, ALL THE PLACES IT WAS SAFE TO SHOW THEM--
--WHICH, IN BEDLAM, ISN'T MUCH...
IT'S BEEN SO GOOD TO SEE YA, 'RISA--AND SO GOOD TO SEE THAT YOU'RE HAPPY!
PRETTY HAPPY, NICK. BUT NOT HAPPY ABOUT HAVING TO DO--
FUMPP
--THIS!
'Z'...
W-WHAT WERE WE TALKING ABOUT...?
DID SOMETHING JUST-

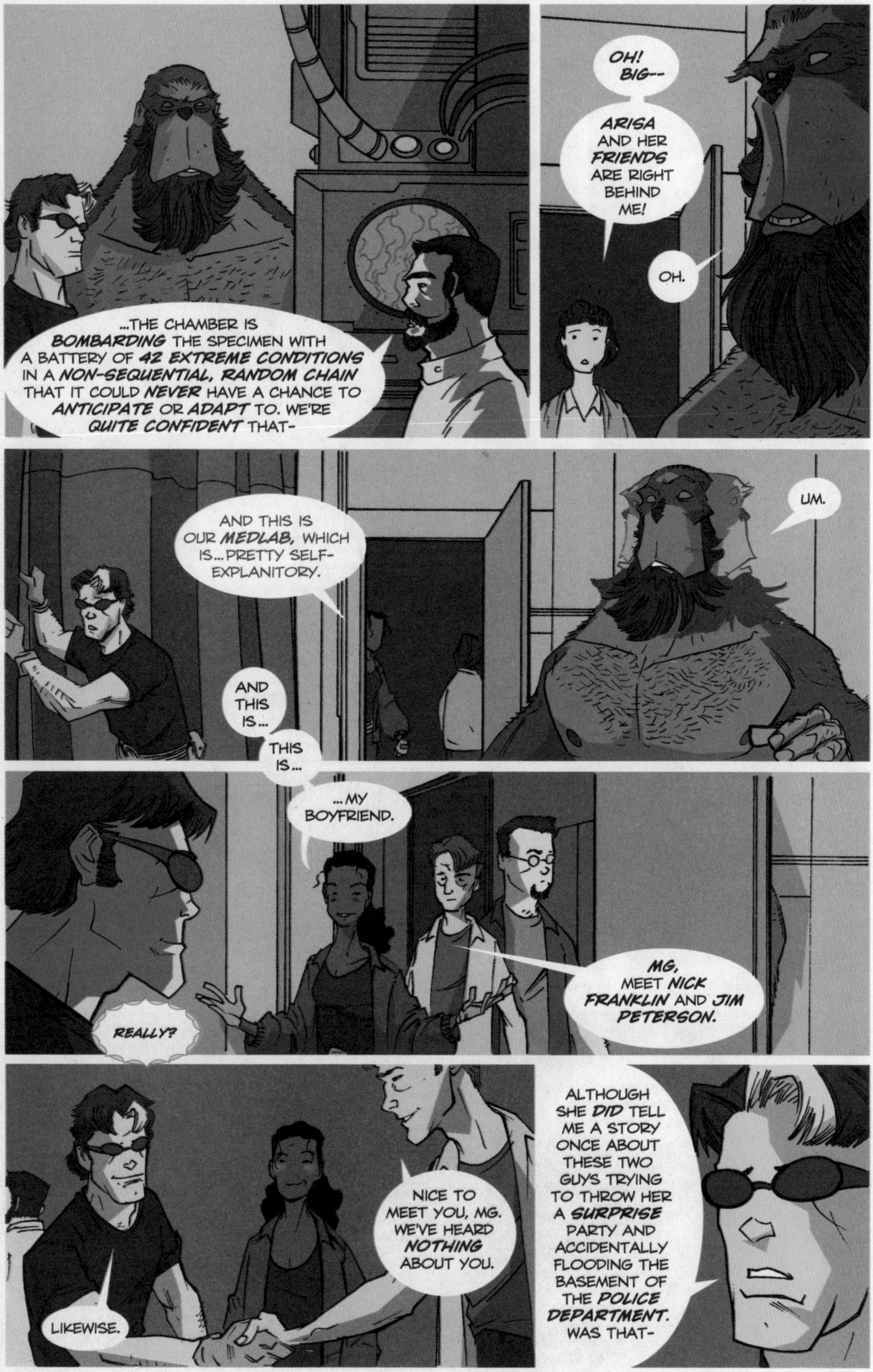
...THE CHAMBER IS BOMBARDING THE SPECIMEN WITH A BATTERY OF 42 EXTREME CONDITIONS IN A NON-SEQUENTIAL, RANDOM CHAIN THAT IT COULD NEVER HAVE A CHANCE TO ANTICIPATE OR ADAPT TO. WE'RE QUITE CONFIDENT THAT-
OH! BIG--
ARISA AND HER FRIENDS ARE RIGHT BEHIND ME!
OH.
AND THIS IS OUR MEDLAB, WHICH IS...PRETTY SELF-EXPLANITORY.
UM.
AND THIS IS...
THIS IS...
...MY BOYFRIEND.
REALLY?
MG, MEET NICK FRANKLIN AND JIM PETERSON.
NICE TO MEET YOU, MG. WE'VE HEARD NOTHING ABOUT YOU.
LIKEWISE.
ALTHOUGH SHE DID TELL ME A STORY ONCE ABOUT THESE TWO GUYS TRYING TO THROW HER A SURPRISE PARTY AND ACCIDENTALLY FLOODING THE BASEMENT OF THE POLICE DEPARTMENT. WAS THAT-

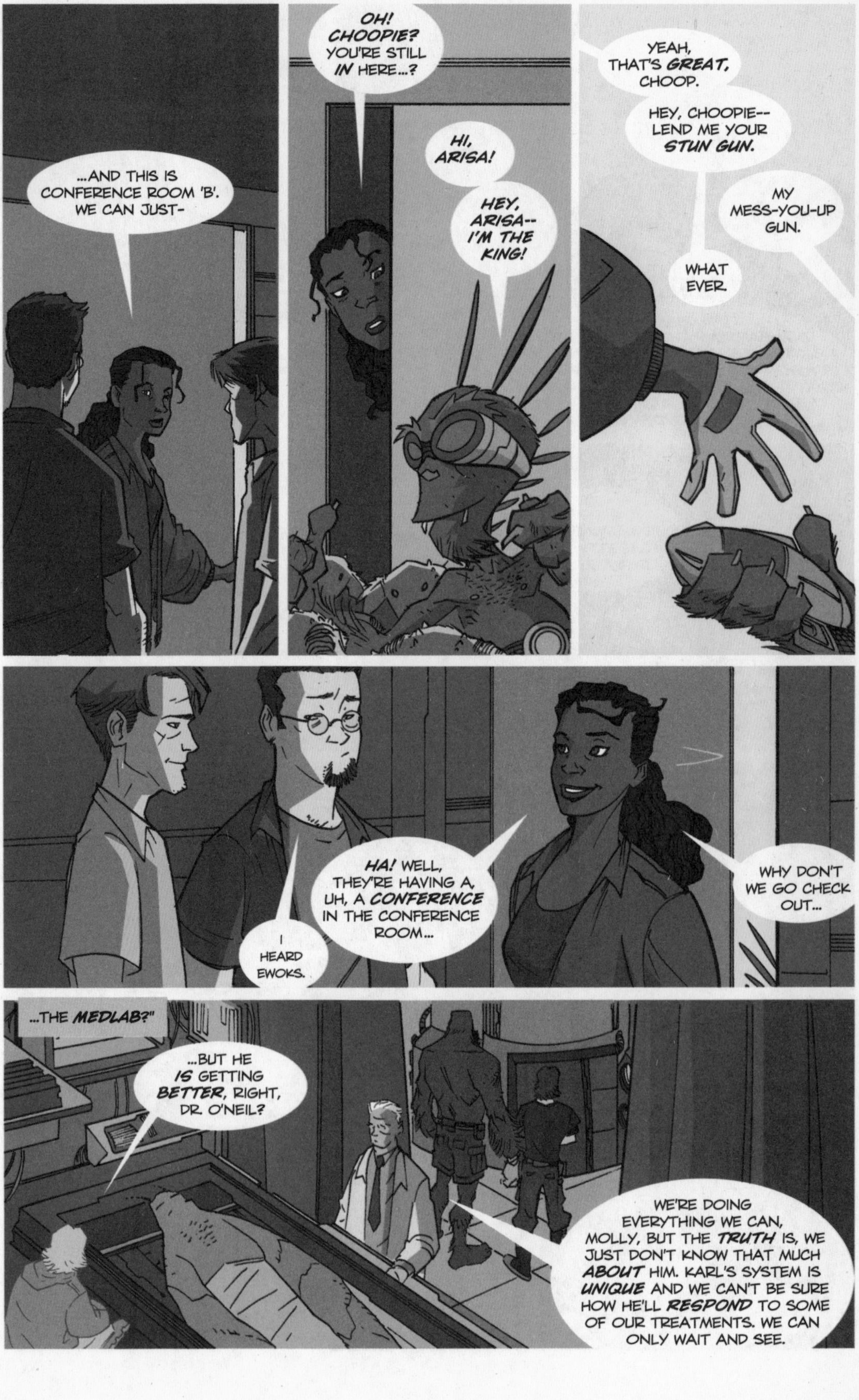
...AND THIS IS CONFERENCE ROOM 'B'. WE CAN JUST-
OH! CHOOPIE? YOU'RE STILL IN HERE...?
HI, ARISA!
HEY, ARISA-- I'M THE KING!
YEAH, THAT'S GREAT, CHOOP.
HEY, CHOOPIE-- LEND ME YOUR STUN GUN.
MY MESS-YOU-UP GUN.
WHAT EVER.
I HEARD EWOKS.
HA! WELL, THEY'RE HAVING A, UH, A CONFERENCE IN THE CONFERENCE ROOM...
WHY DON'T WE GO CHECK OUT...
...THE MEDLAB?"
...BUT HE IS GETTING BETTER, RIGHT, DR. O'NEIL?
WE'RE DOING EVERYTHING WE CAN, MOLLY, BUT THE TRUTH IS, WE JUST DON'T KNOW THAT MUCH ABOUT HIM. KARL'S SYSTEM IS UNIQUE AND WE CAN'T BE SURE HOW HE'LL RESPOND TO SOME OF OUR TREATMENTS. WE CAN ONLY WAIT AND SEE.

"The OTHER ARISA"

words by todd dezago
illustrations by richard case

MG's Journal-
July 19

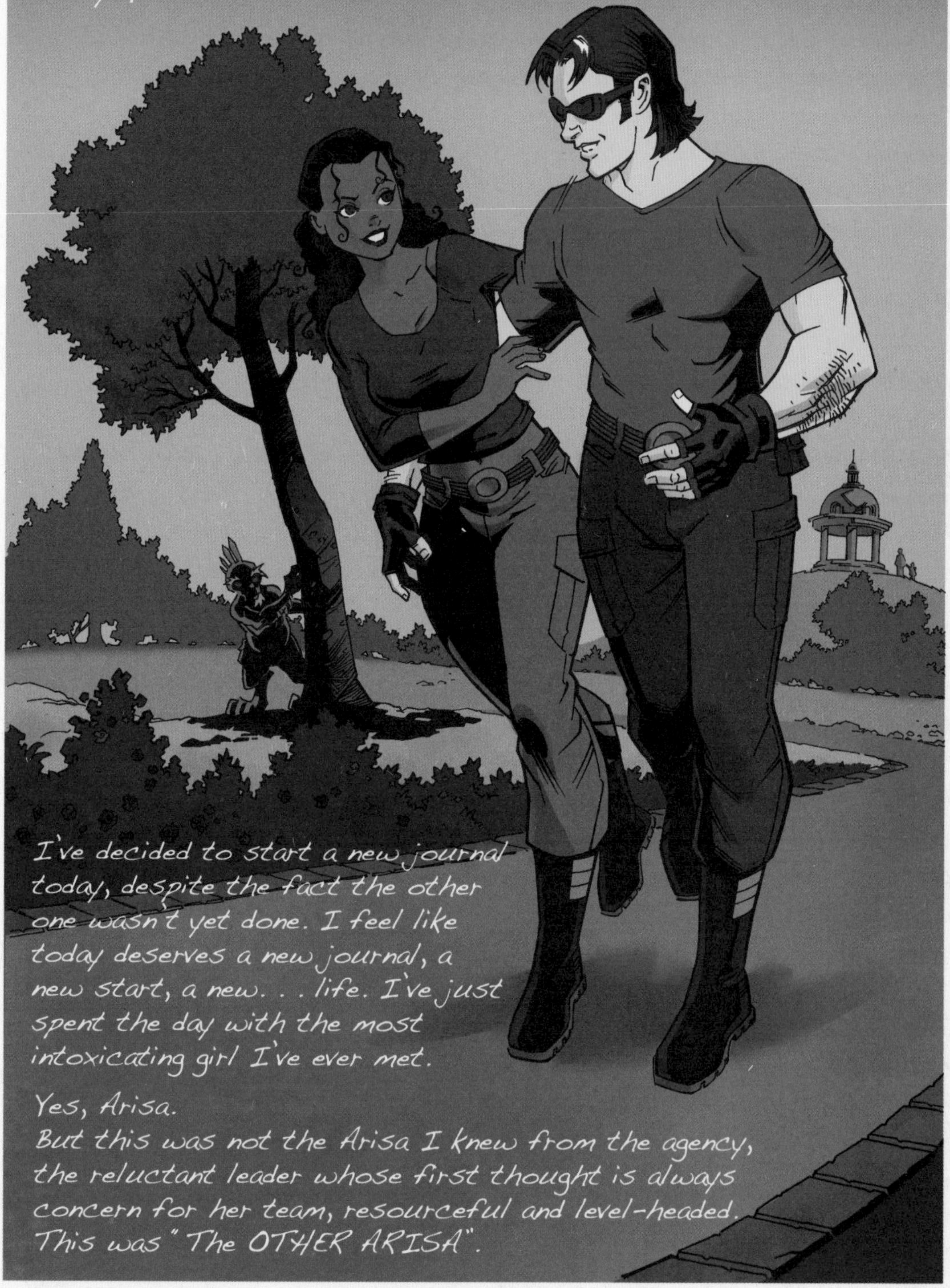

I've decided to start a new journal today, despite the fact the other one wasn't yet done. I feel like today deserves a new journal, a new start, a new. . . life. I've just spent the day with the most intoxicating girl I've ever met.

Yes, Arisa.
But this was not the Arisa I knew from the agency, the reluctant leader whose first thought is always concern for her team, resourceful and level-headed. This was "The OTHER ARISA".

I met her almost the moment she stepped into the car, away from BEDLAM, away from monsters and magic and the weight of responsibility. I watched it slip away from her in an instant and suddenly was faced with a girl I had only glimpsed at odd moments in the field; a playful, bubbly, mischievous girl, flirtatious and funny, beautiful beyond words.

I had, of course, been guarded around her since the day we met. She a telepath and I . . . well, keeper of so many secrets. It took being around her for several months before I let down my defenses around her, finally trusting that she wasn't the type to pry. My attraction, however, was there from the start and something, I know now, was wonderfully mutual. Finally, our fondness and flirtations grew until we decided to have a day out together. A date.

Her smile was what she gave me first as she got in the car; a bright, beautiful, radiant smile that I had never seen before and that immediately inspired one of my own. She glowed, sitting there in the passenger seat as I drove down the highway, stealing as many glances as I could without wrecking us. She beamed and somehow made me feel that it was because of me, because she was happy to be with me. And I felt that way all day long.

She chatted and teased and babbled and laughed--God, that laugh! She summed up our short, adventure-laden history together in a matter of miles and soon we were driving into the small town she had picked as our destination for that day. We walked around the town, looking into shop windows, stopping into a few, and I watched as she saw things in a much different way than she does when we're "working", seeing life and joy in everything.

There was a conspiracy between us now; an intimacy established from the moment we set out. An understanding. We would hold hands. There seemed an open invitation to touch one another whenever we could. She nudged me and punched me and played with my hair. I played with hers.

In the diner, she sat as close as she could, leaning into the table, over it, to whisper to me, joke with me. No shyness here, no tentative gestures, she was comfortable in " us ", oblivious of the other customers, of the rest of the world. We split a sandwich, neither one of us very hungry.

There was one of those small juke boxes perched right there in the booth, Arisa flipped the knob-- flack, flack, flack --and soon announced that all the selections were old. I slid her a few quarters and we allowed our knees to rest against one another as we mused over which tunes to play. I played Glenn Miller, she played someone called 50 Cent.

Her eyes flashed.

" Let's pretend we're spies!" she whispered to me, conspiratorially. " We've never met before, but we've been assigned together to pose as a married couple in order to track down a mysterious double-agent!" Her eyes twinkled." We'll have to learn everything we can about each other in case we're stopped!"

" Okay," I agreed, pulling her close to me so that I could whisper in her ear, "but I'll only do it if we have to speak with Russian accents."

" Vedy Good." she said, sounding nothing like Natasha from an old Bullwinkle cartoon." Only you most be choosing for me, a name. . ."

She was Natalia, I was Sven.

" Isn't Sven more of a . . . Nordic name?" I asked, my own accent sounding nothing like Boris Badenov. I had thought that Ivan or Mikhail would have better fit the bill.

" Your mother was from there. Is all part of your cover."

We laughed and tried our accents out on each other, falling into this funny fantasy, this impromptu role play. We were playing.

We chose the waitress as our target, watching her over the tops of our menus in turns and reporting back to the other. She was, we could see, very openly passing top secret documents to various spies and counter-spies (these were the " spies" actually seated at the counter. . .) each time she delivered a bill. She was, of course, a criminal mastermind.

We tipped her well for her part.

We laughed.

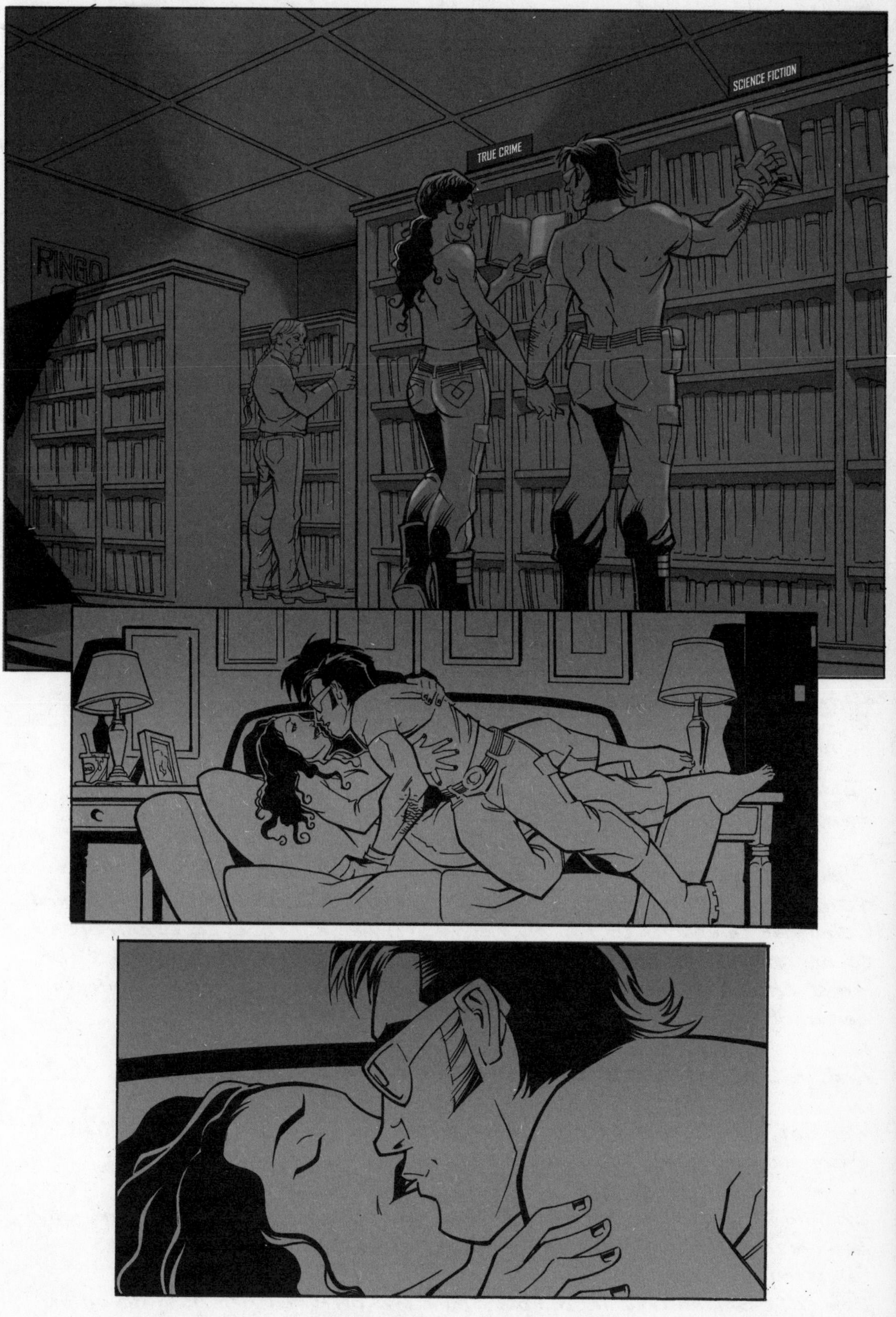
SCIENCE FICTION
TRUE CRIME
RINGO

On the sidewalk,' Risa sidled up close to me." I like being spies with you." she said. I did too.

In an oblong bookstore, she held my hand across the aisle, even as we looked at different books, not wanting to let go. . .

I told her that I was having a wonderful day.

We kissed there, for the first time, a long, telling, tender, and passionate promise, not caring who saw us. . .

The rest of the afternoon was more walking and talking, soaking in both the sun and each other. We sat on a bench by a pond and soon Arisa was down at the water's edge, twirling a reed just so to get the frogs to jump at it.

This was the day. The day they talk about, when two people discover each other, immerse themselves in each other. . . fall in love with each other.

There was more kissing and talking, in the car, in her driveway, on her sofa, in front of the tv. Questions and queries as we tried to drink each other up. She poured herself out to me and I felt guilty as I found myself, even then, holding back.
For just a moment.

" I don't want to know your secrets, MG. That's not what we're doing here. I just want to know you."

She touched my head then, placing her fingers gently on my brow, gazing deep into my eyes as she did so--and she stepped into my mind, using her telepathy to fill my head with her essence, to open herself to me and let ME feel HER feelings--her emotions for emotions for me at that very moment! I was enveloped in her joy, in her thrill, in her unbridled excitement about me! About ME!

And, in that moment, I opened myself to her-- and matched it.

Her smile broadened, if that were truly possible, and a tear spilled from each eye and rolled down her perfect cheeks.

She didn't press me then to go further, to learn more about me with her amazing power, to delve into what I'm sure is a treasure as tempting as Pandora's Box. . .
She just smiled that incredible smile and brushed her hand down my face, that smile assuring me that this was just a beginning. . .

No pressure. No rushing. In time.

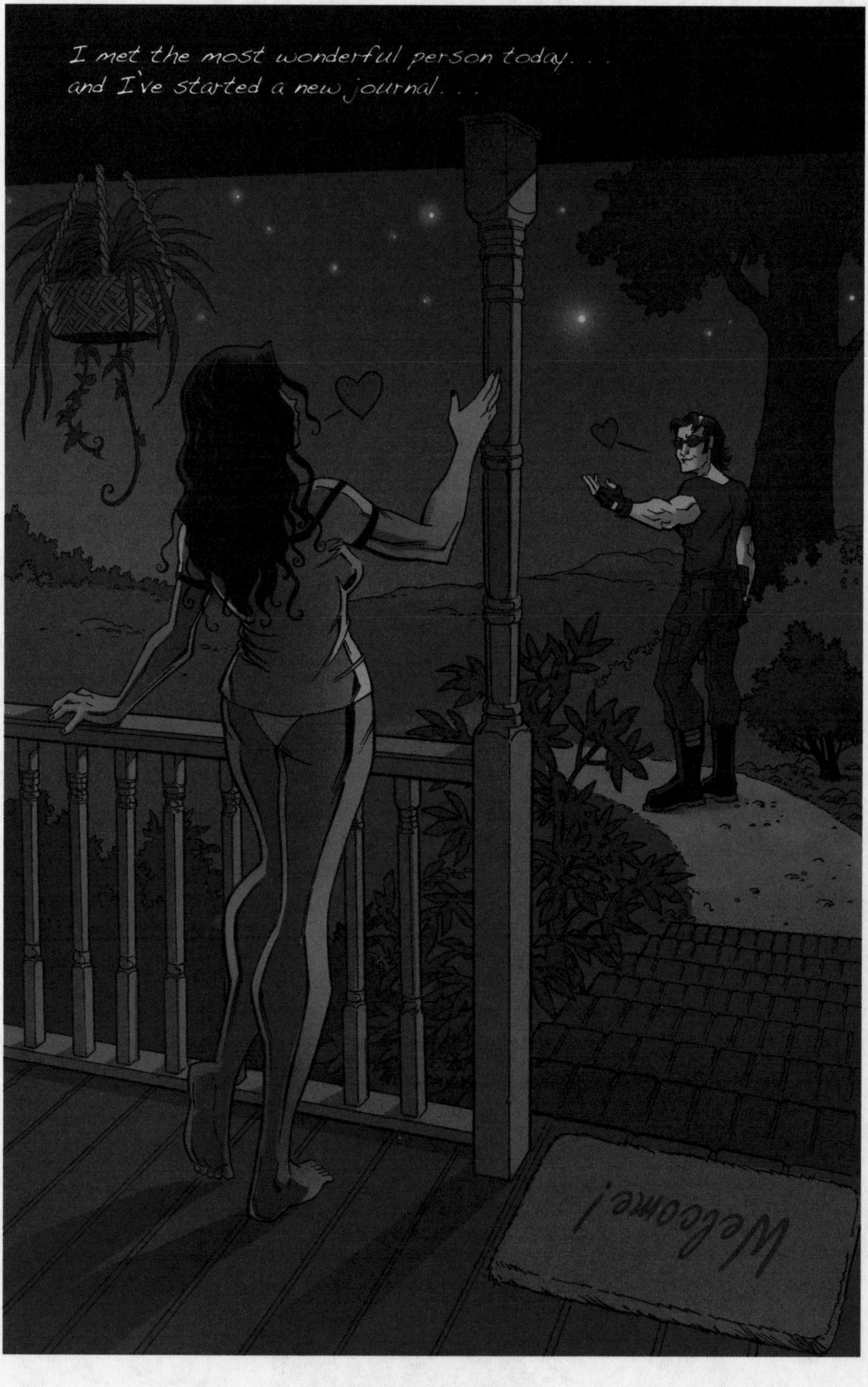
I met the most wonderful person today...
and I've started a new journal...
Welcome!

perhapanauts 3

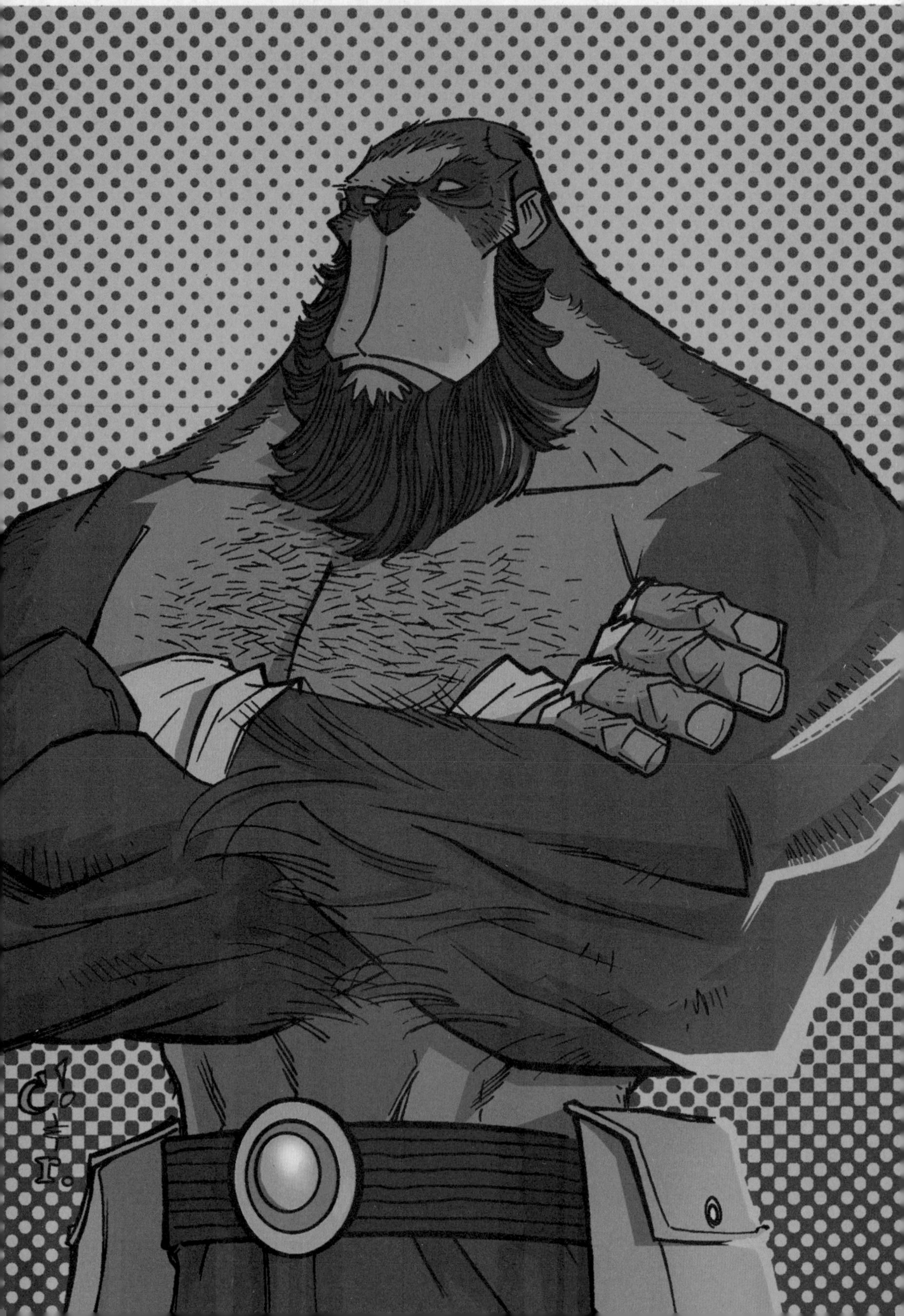

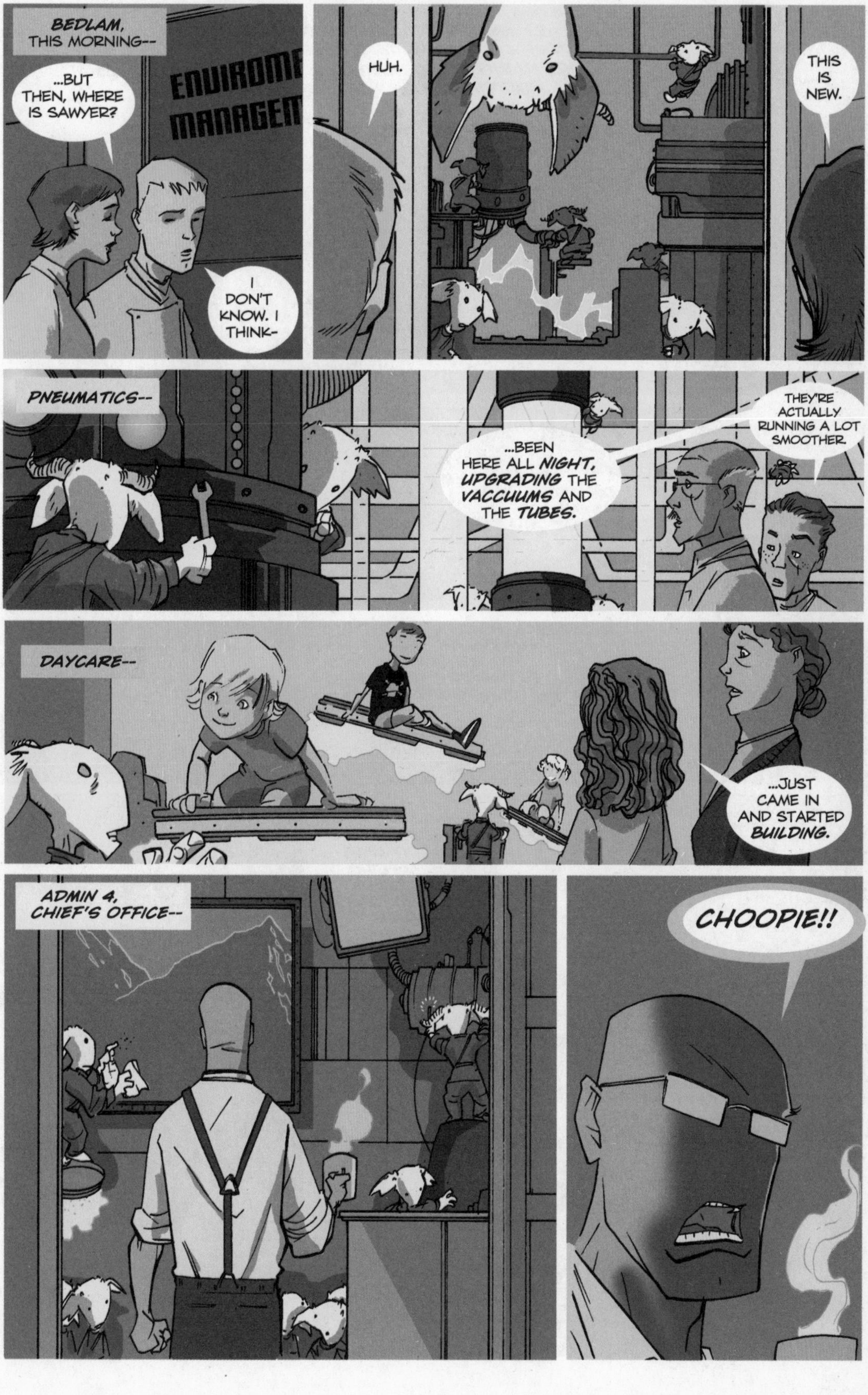
BEDLAM, THIS MORNING--
...BUT THEN, WHERE IS SAWYER?
I DON'T KNOW. I THINK-
HUH.
THIS IS NEW.
PNEUMATICS--
...BEEN HERE ALL NIGHT, UPGRADING THE VACCUUMS AND THE TUBES.
THEY'RE ACTUALLY RUNNING A LOT SMOOTHER.
DAYCARE--
...JUST CAME IN AND STARTED BUILDING.
ADMIN 4, CHIEF'S OFFICE--
CHOOPIE!!

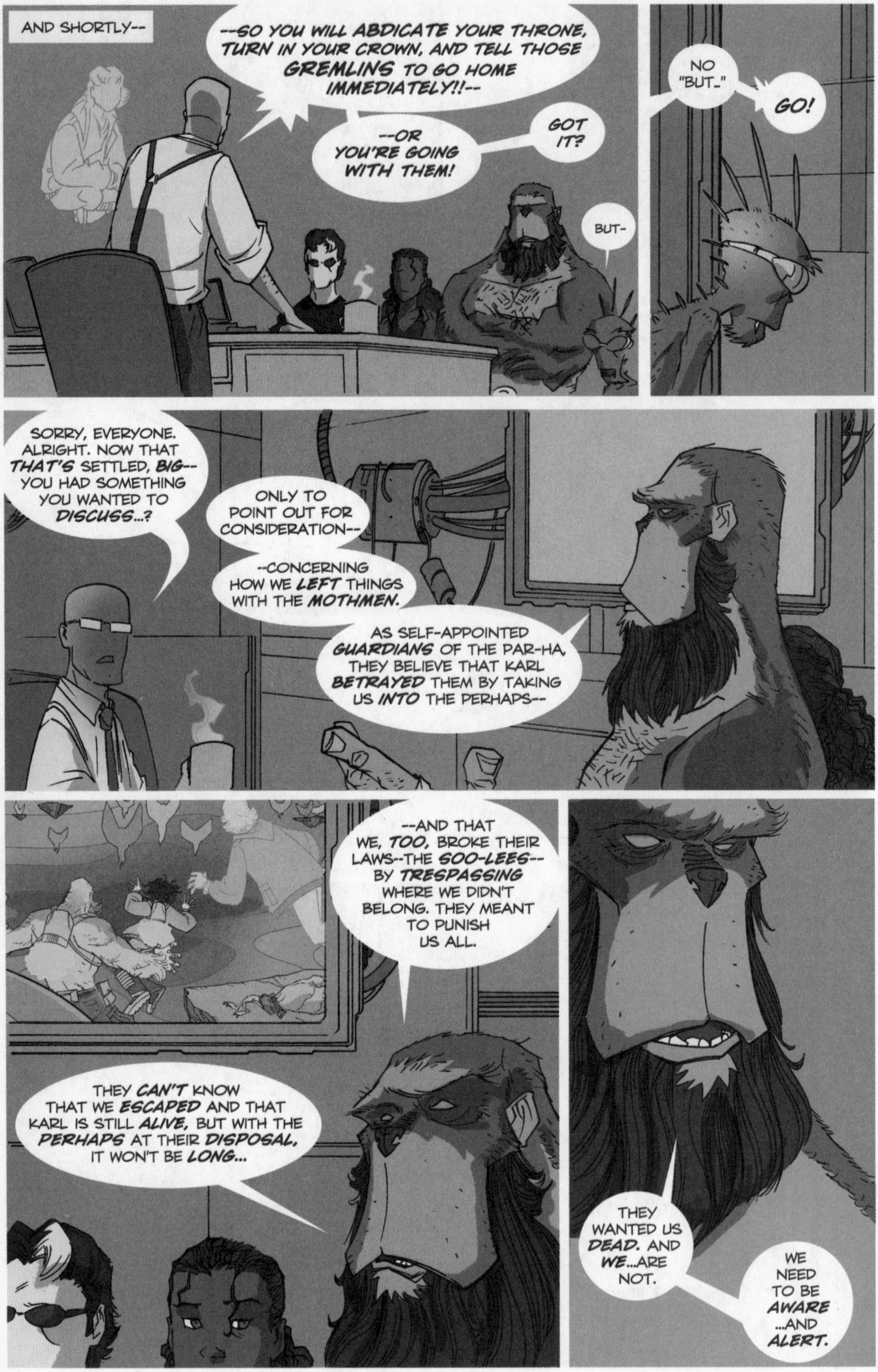
AND SHORTLY--
--SO YOU WILL ABDICATE YOUR THRONE, TURN IN YOUR CROWN, AND TELL THOSE GREMLINS TO GO HOME IMMEDIATELY!!--
--OR YOU'RE GOING WITH THEM!
GOT IT?
BUT-
NO "BUT-"
GO!
SORRY, EVERYONE. ALRIGHT. NOW THAT THAT'S SETTLED, BIG-- YOU HAD SOMETHING YOU WANTED TO DISCUSS...?
ONLY TO POINT OUT FOR CONSIDERATION--
--CONCERNING HOW WE LEFT THINGS WITH THE MOTHMEN.
AS SELF-APPOINTED GUARDIANS OF THE PAR-HA, THEY BELIEVE THAT KARL BETRAYED THEM BY TAKING US INTO THE PERHAPS--
--AND THAT WE, TOO, BROKE THEIR LAWS--THE SOO-LEES-- BY TRESPASSING WHERE WE DIDN'T BELONG. THEY MEANT TO PUNISH US ALL.
THEY CAN'T KNOW THAT WE ESCAPED AND THAT KARL IS STILL ALIVE, BUT WITH THE PERHAPS AT THEIR DISPOSAL, IT WON'T BE LONG...
THEY WANTED US DEAD. AND WE...ARE NOT.
WE NEED TO BE AWARE ...AND ALERT.

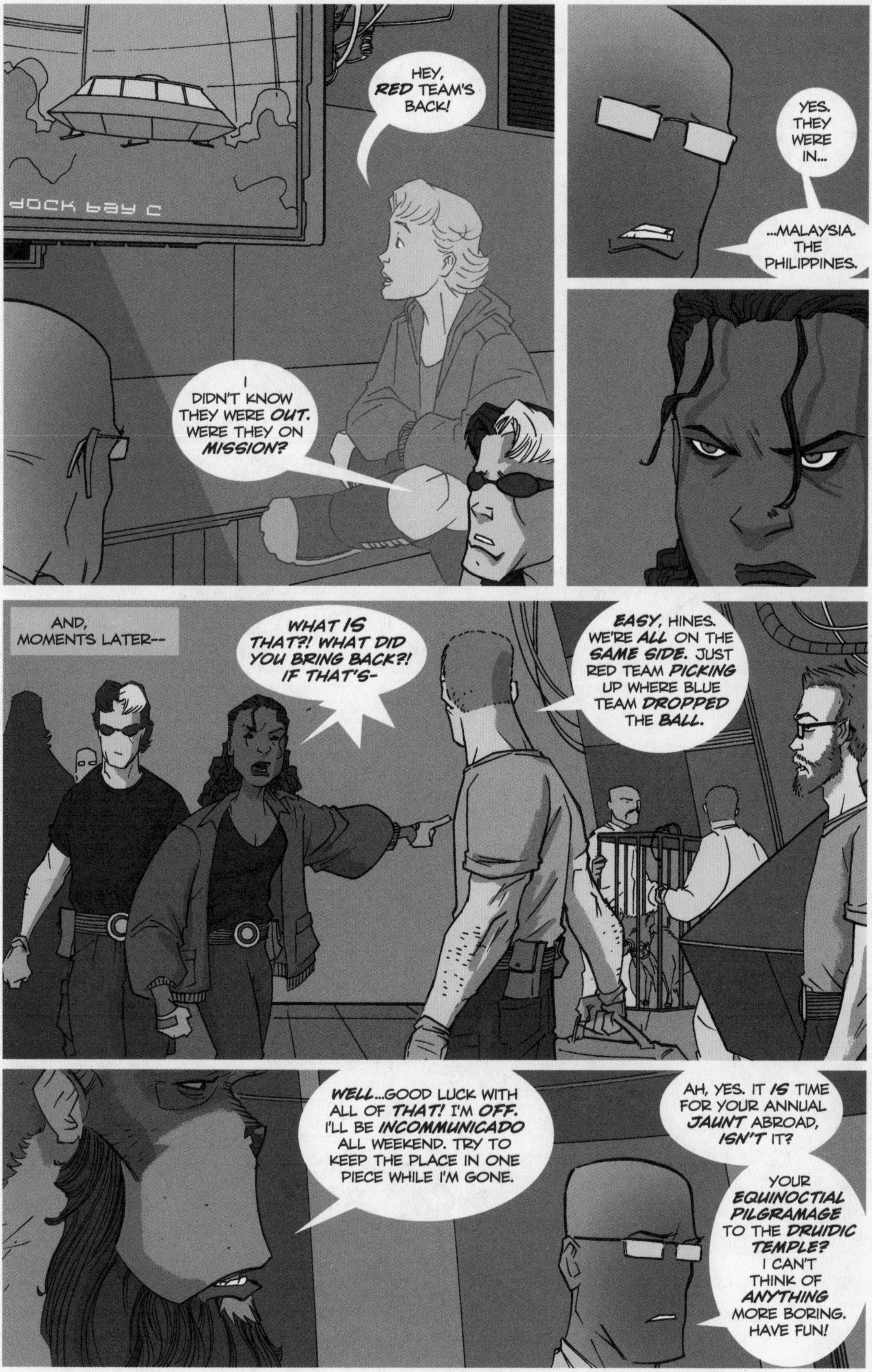
DOCK BAY C
HEY, RED TEAM'S BACK!
I DIDN'T KNOW THEY WERE OUT. WERE THEY ON MISSION?
YES. THEY WERE IN...
...MALAYSIA. THE PHILIPPINES.
AND, MOMENTS LATER--
WHAT IS THAT?! WHAT DID YOU BRING BACK?! IF THAT'S-
EASY, HINES. WE'RE ALL ON THE SAME SIDE. JUST RED TEAM PICKING UP WHERE BLUE TEAM DROPPED THE BALL.
WELL...GOOD LUCK WITH ALL OF THAT! I'M OFF. I'LL BE INCOMMUNICADO ALL WEEKEND. TRY TO KEEP THE PLACE IN ONE PIECE WHILE I'M GONE.
AH, YES. IT IS TIME FOR YOUR ANNUAL JAUNT ABROAD, ISN'T IT?
YOUR EQUINOCTIAL PILGRAMAGE TO THE DRUIDIC TEMPLE? I CAN'T THINK OF ANYTHING MORE BORING. HAVE FUN!

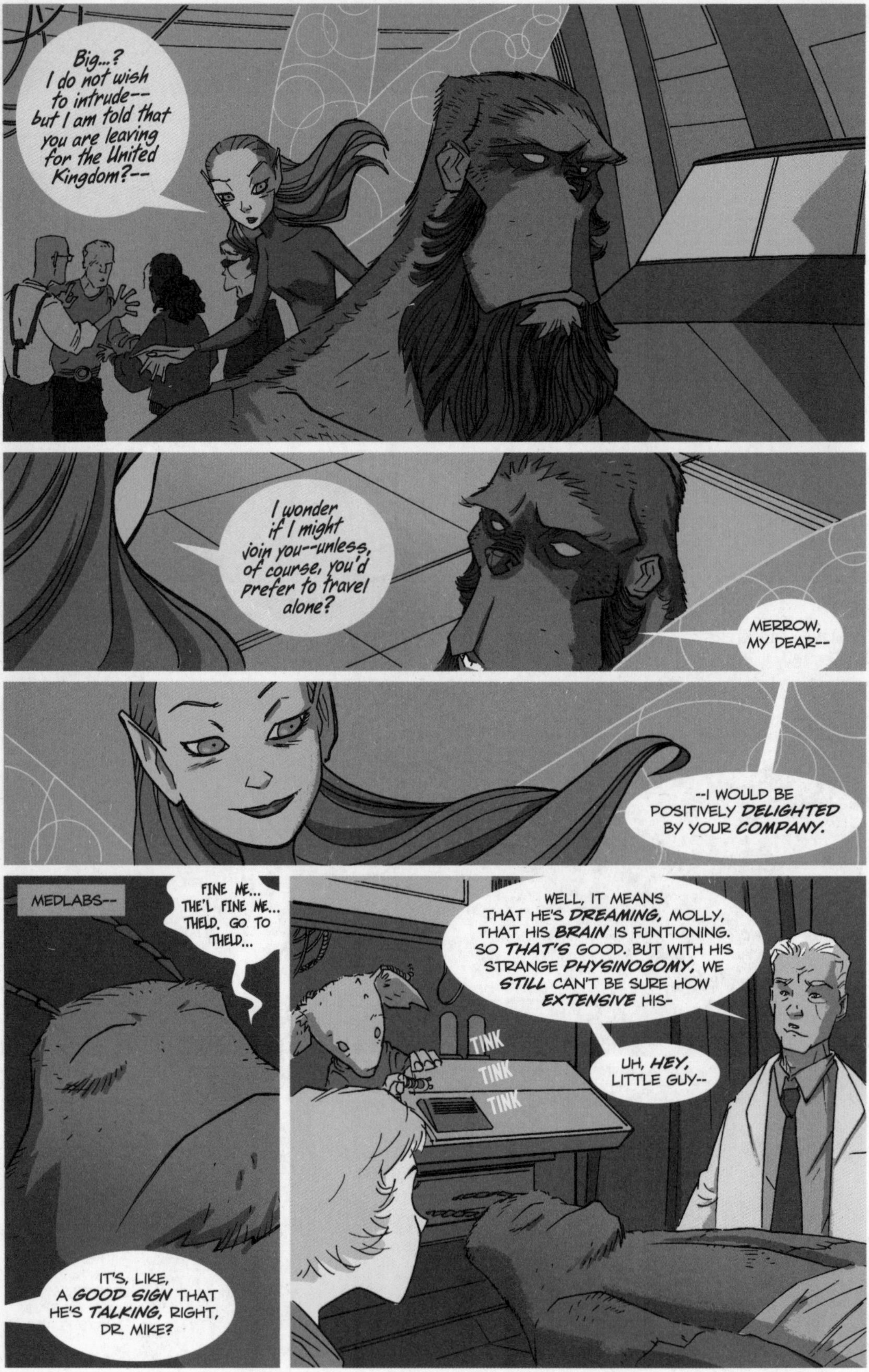
Big...? I do not wish to intrude-- but I am told that you are leaving for the United Kingdom?--
I wonder if I might join you--unless, of course, you'd prefer to travel alone?
MERROW, MY DEAR--
--I WOULD BE POSITIVELY DELIGHTED BY YOUR COMPANY.
MEDLABS--
FINE ME... THE'L FINE ME... THELD. GO TO THELD...
IT'S, LIKE, A GOOD SIGN THAT HE'S TALKING, RIGHT, DR. MIKE?
WELL, IT MEANS THAT HE'S DREAMING, MOLLY, THAT HIS BRAIN IS FUNTIONING. SO THAT'S GOOD. BUT WITH HIS STRANGE PHYSINOGOMY, WE STILL CAN'T BE SURE HOW EXTENSIVE HIS-
TINK
TINK
TINK
UH, HEY, LITTLE GUY--

--YOU PROBABLY SHOULDN'T BE *MONKEYING* WITH THAT. I'M SURE YOU HAVE THE BEST *INTENTIONS,* BUT THIS IS A VERY *DELICATE* SITUATION...

...YOU DON'T KNOW *WHAT* KIND OF DAMAGE YOU MIGHT DO!

SKIPPER B CLEARED FOR LAUNCH. AT YOUR DISCRETION, DOCTOR

THANK YOU, TRACI. MERROW--ARE YOU *ALRIGHT?* YOU SEEM A BIT ...*STIFF?*

I am sorry, Big. It is my faerie nature. I am not always comfortable with man's technology.

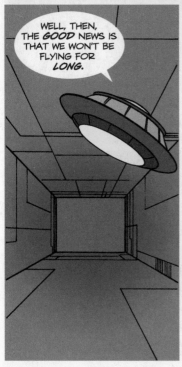

WELL, THEN, THE *GOOD* NEWS IS THAT WE WON'T BE FLYING FOR *LONG.*

I'VE LINED UP SEVERAL *WORMHOLES* SO THAT OUR ETA TO *SCOTLAND* SHOULD BE JUST UNDER *47* MINUTES.

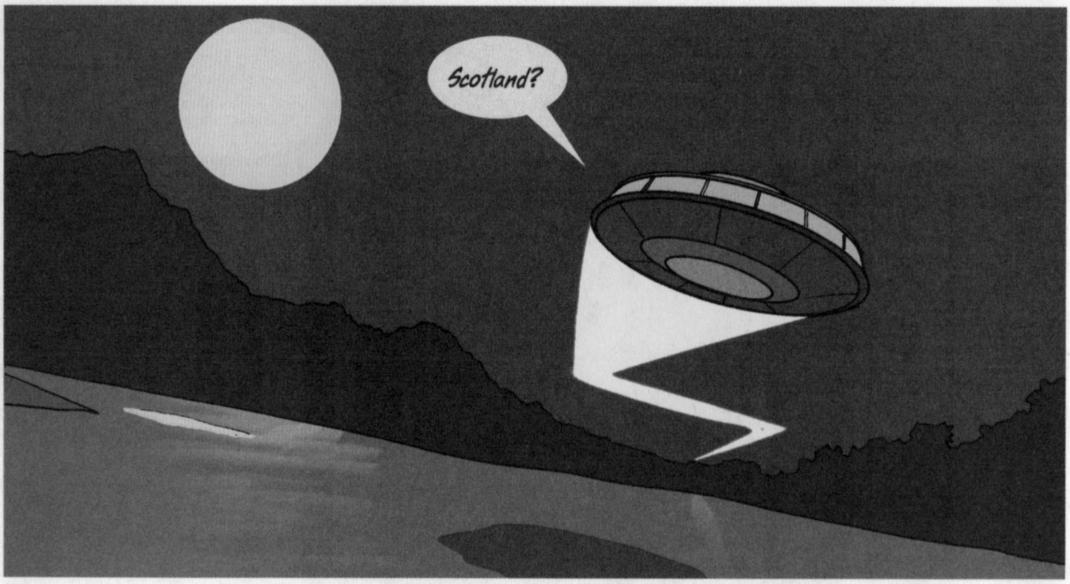
Scotland?

THE Perhapanauts — TODD AND CRAIG'S

in

"BIG SECRETS..."

TRIANGLE PART 3

STORY BY TODD ART BY CRAIG
COLORS BY RICO
2K8

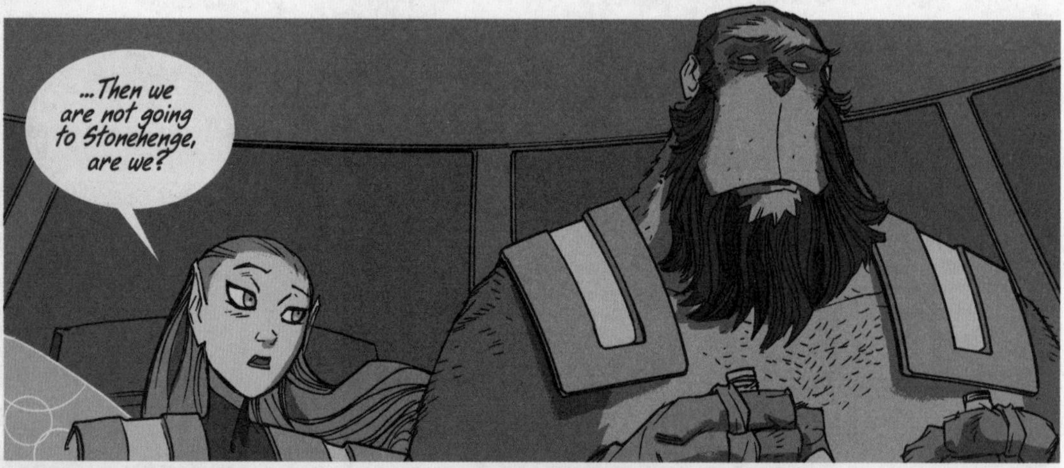
...Then we are not going to Stonehenge, are we?

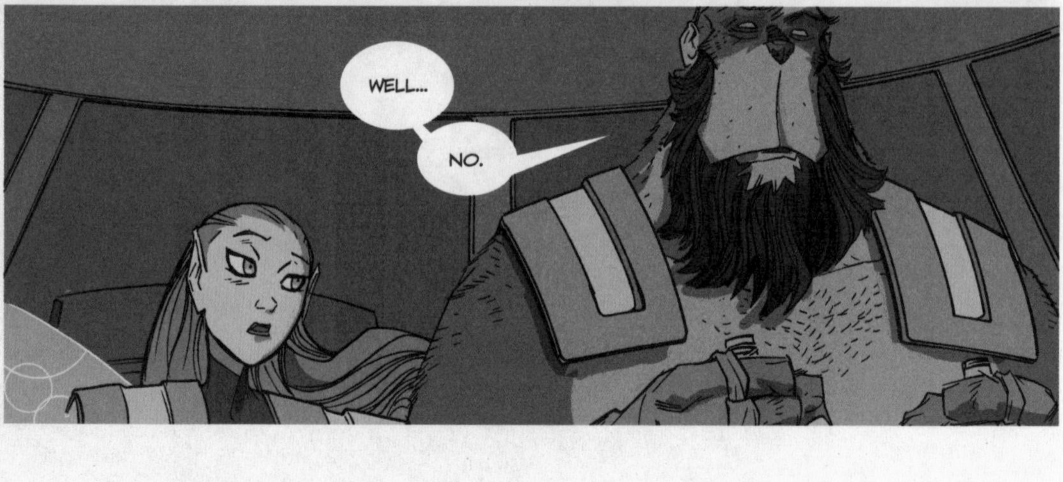
WELL...
NO.

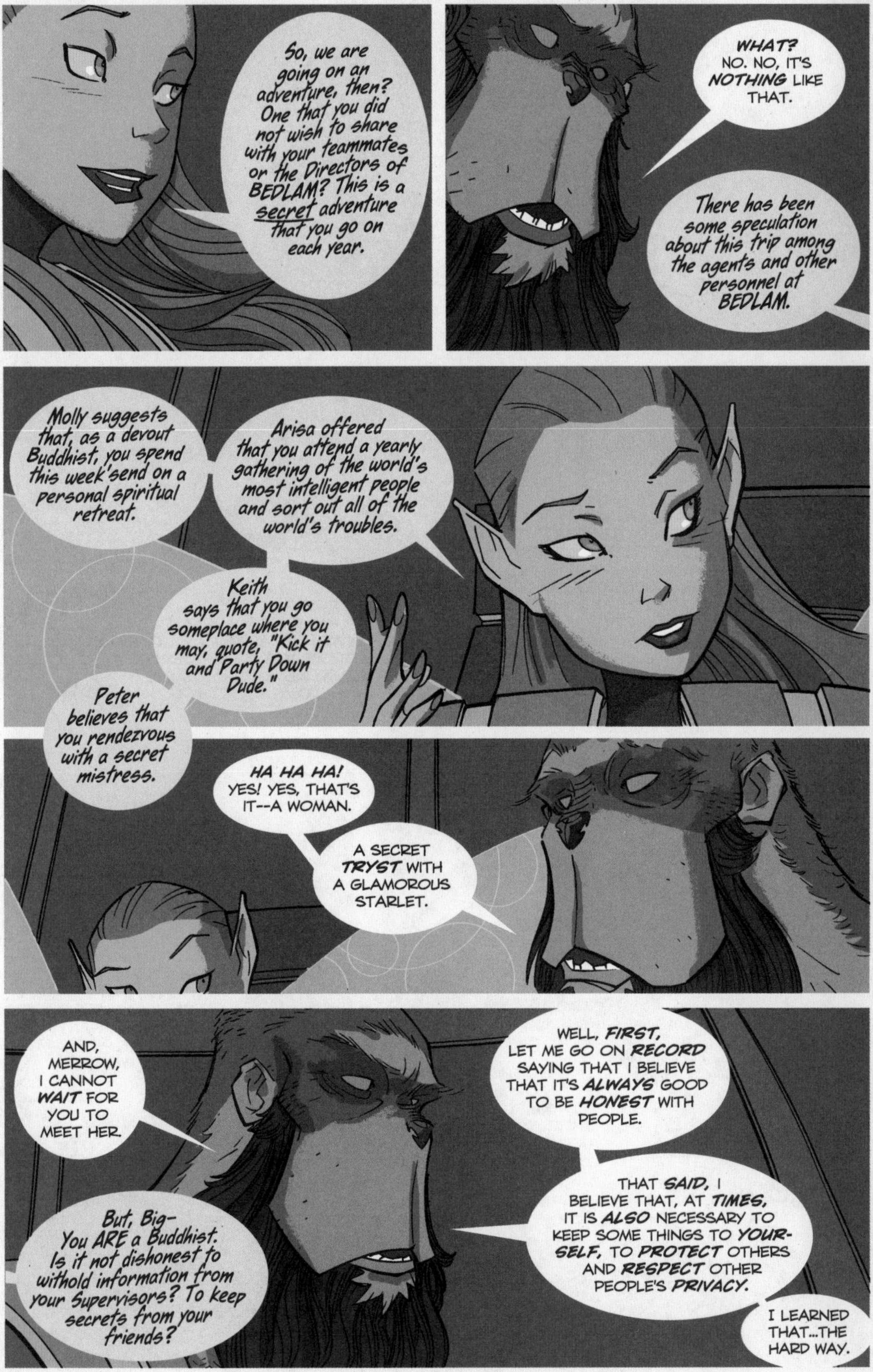
So, we are going on an adventure, then? One that you did not wish to share with your teammates or the Directors of BEDLAM? This is a secret adventure that you go on each year.
WHAT? NO. NO, IT'S NOTHING LIKE THAT.
There has been some speculation about this trip among the agents and other personnel at BEDLAM.
Molly suggests that, as a devout Buddhist, you spend this week'send on a personal spiritual retreat.
Arisa offered that you attend a yearly gathering of the world's most intelligent people and sort out all of the world's troubles.
Keith says that you go someplace where you may, quote, "Kick it and Party Down Dude."
Peter believes that you rendezvous with a secret mistress.
HA HA HA! YES! YES, THAT'S IT--A WOMAN.
A SECRET TRYST WITH A GLAMOROUS STARLET.
AND, MERROW, I CANNOT WAIT FOR YOU TO MEET HER.
But, Big- You ARE a Buddhist. Is it not dishonest to withold information from your Supervisors? To keep secrets from your friends?
WELL, FIRST, LET ME GO ON RECORD SAYING THAT I BELIEVE THAT IT'S ALWAYS GOOD TO BE HONEST WITH PEOPLE.
THAT SAID, I BELIEVE THAT, AT TIMES, IT IS ALSO NECESSARY TO KEEP SOME THINGS TO YOURSELF, TO PROTECT OTHERS AND RESPECT OTHER PEOPLE'S PRIVACY.
I LEARNED THAT...THE HARD WAY.

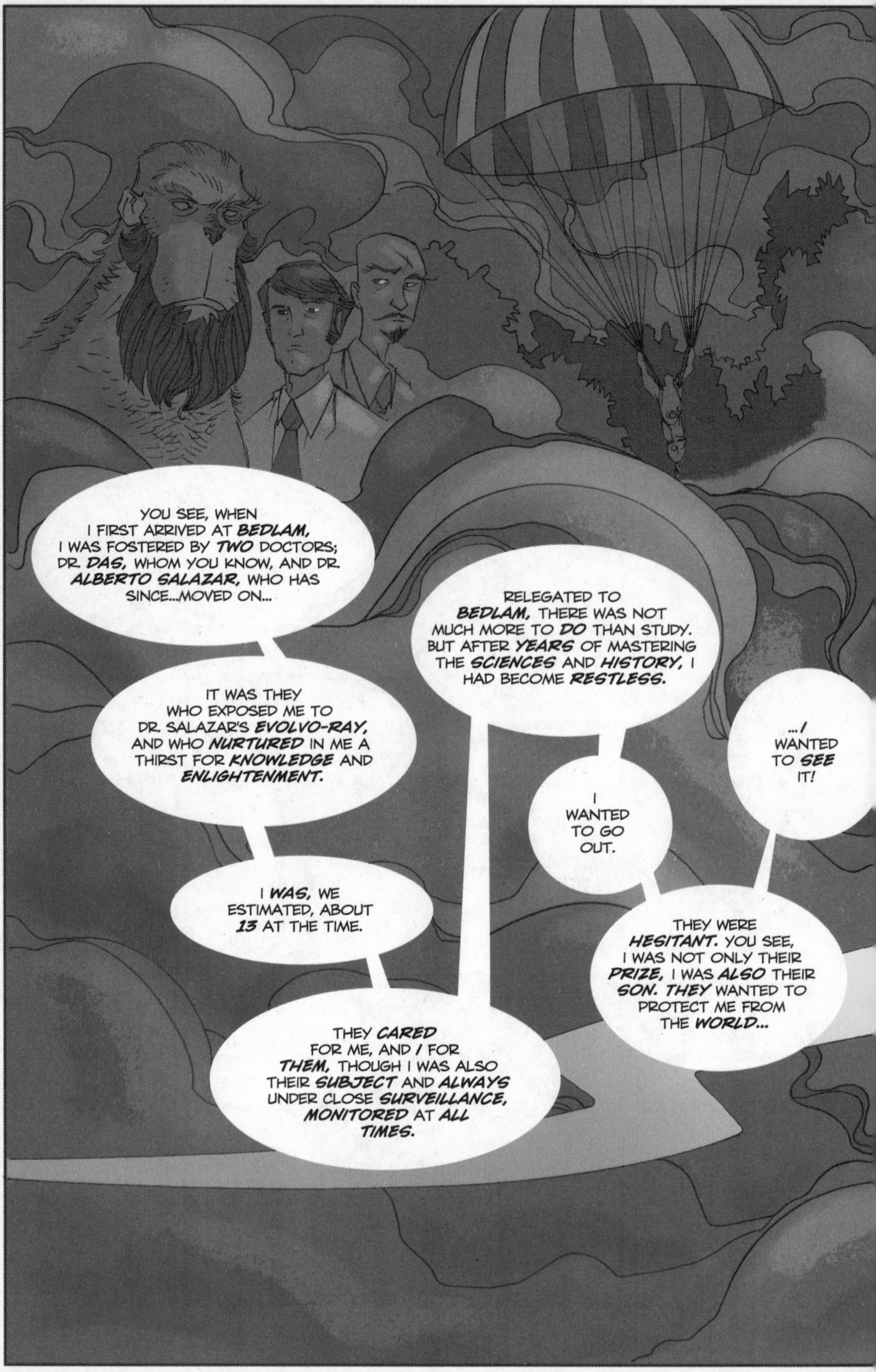
YOU SEE, WHEN I FIRST ARRIVED AT BEDLAM, I WAS FOSTERED BY TWO DOCTORS; DR. DAS, WHOM YOU KNOW, AND DR. ALBERTO SALAZAR, WHO HAS SINCE...MOVED ON...
IT WAS THEY WHO EXPOSED ME TO DR. SALAZAR'S EVOLVO-RAY, AND WHO NURTURED IN ME A THIRST FOR KNOWLEDGE AND ENLIGHTENMENT.
I WAS, WE ESTIMATED, ABOUT 13 AT THE TIME.
THEY CARED FOR ME, AND I FOR THEM, THOUGH I WAS ALSO THEIR SUBJECT AND ALWAYS UNDER CLOSE SURVEILLANCE, MONITORED AT ALL TIMES.
RELEGATED TO BEDLAM, THERE WAS NOT MUCH MORE TO DO THAN STUDY. BUT AFTER YEARS OF MASTERING THE SCIENCES AND HISTORY, I HAD BECOME RESTLESS.
I WANTED TO GO OUT.
THEY WERE HESITANT. YOU SEE, I WAS NOT ONLY THEIR PRIZE, I WAS ALSO THEIR SON. THEY WANTED TO PROTECT ME FROM THE WORLD...
...I WANTED TO SEE IT!

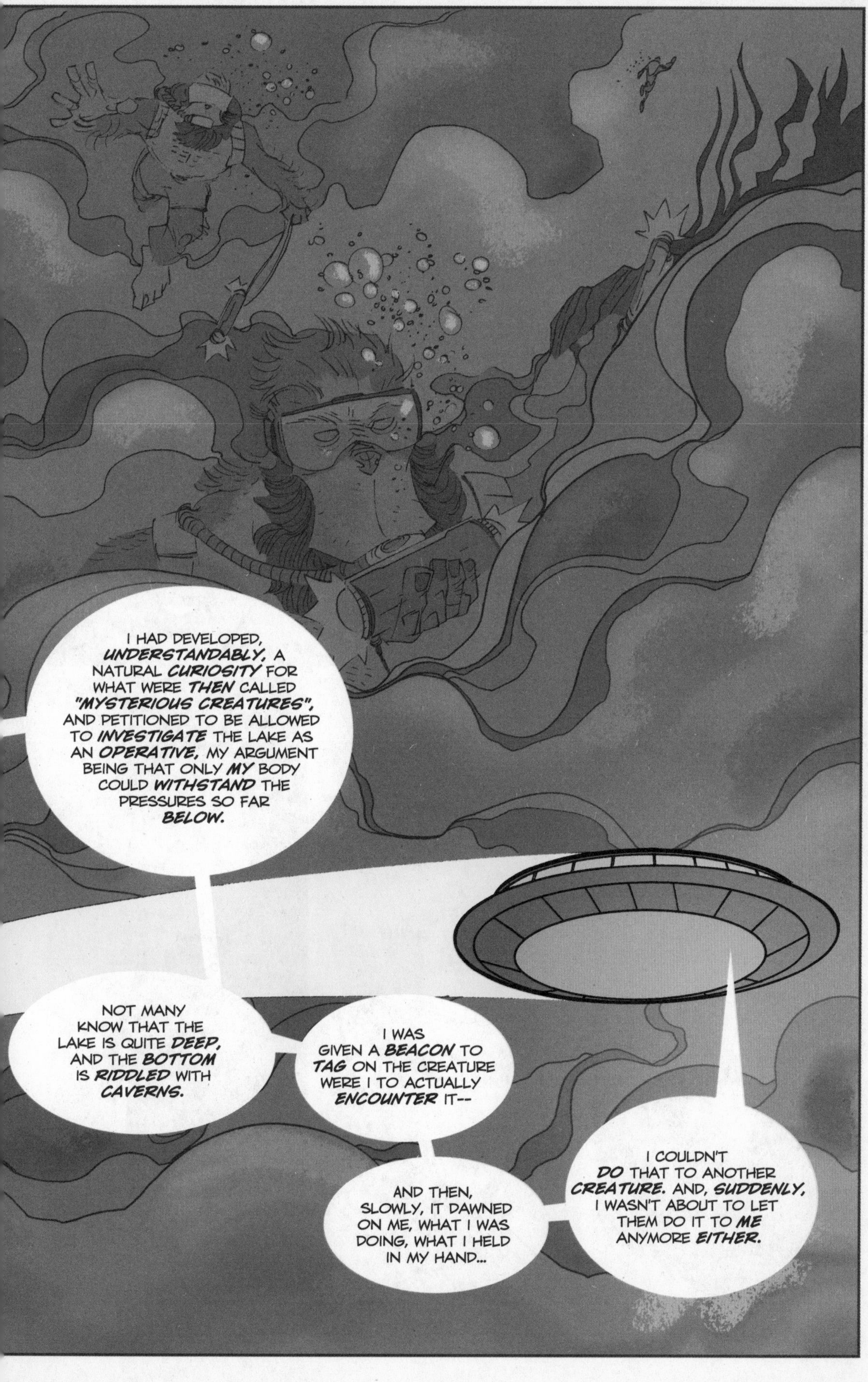

I HAD DEVELOPED, UNDERSTANDABLY, A NATURAL CURIOSITY FOR WHAT WERE THEN CALLED "MYSTERIOUS CREATURES", AND PETITIONED TO BE ALLOWED TO INVESTIGATE THE LAKE AS AN OPERATIVE, MY ARGUMENT BEING THAT ONLY MY BODY COULD WITHSTAND THE PRESSURES SO FAR BELOW.
NOT MANY KNOW THAT THE LAKE IS QUITE DEEP, AND THE BOTTOM IS RIDDLED WITH CAVERNS.
I WAS GIVEN A BEACON TO TAG ON THE CREATURE WERE I TO ACTUALLY ENCOUNTER IT--
AND THEN, SLOWLY, IT DAWNED ON ME, WHAT I WAS DOING, WHAT I HELD IN MY HAND...
I COULDN'T DO THAT TO ANOTHER CREATURE. AND, SUDDENLY, I WASN'T ABOUT TO LET THEM DO IT TO ME ANYMORE EITHER.

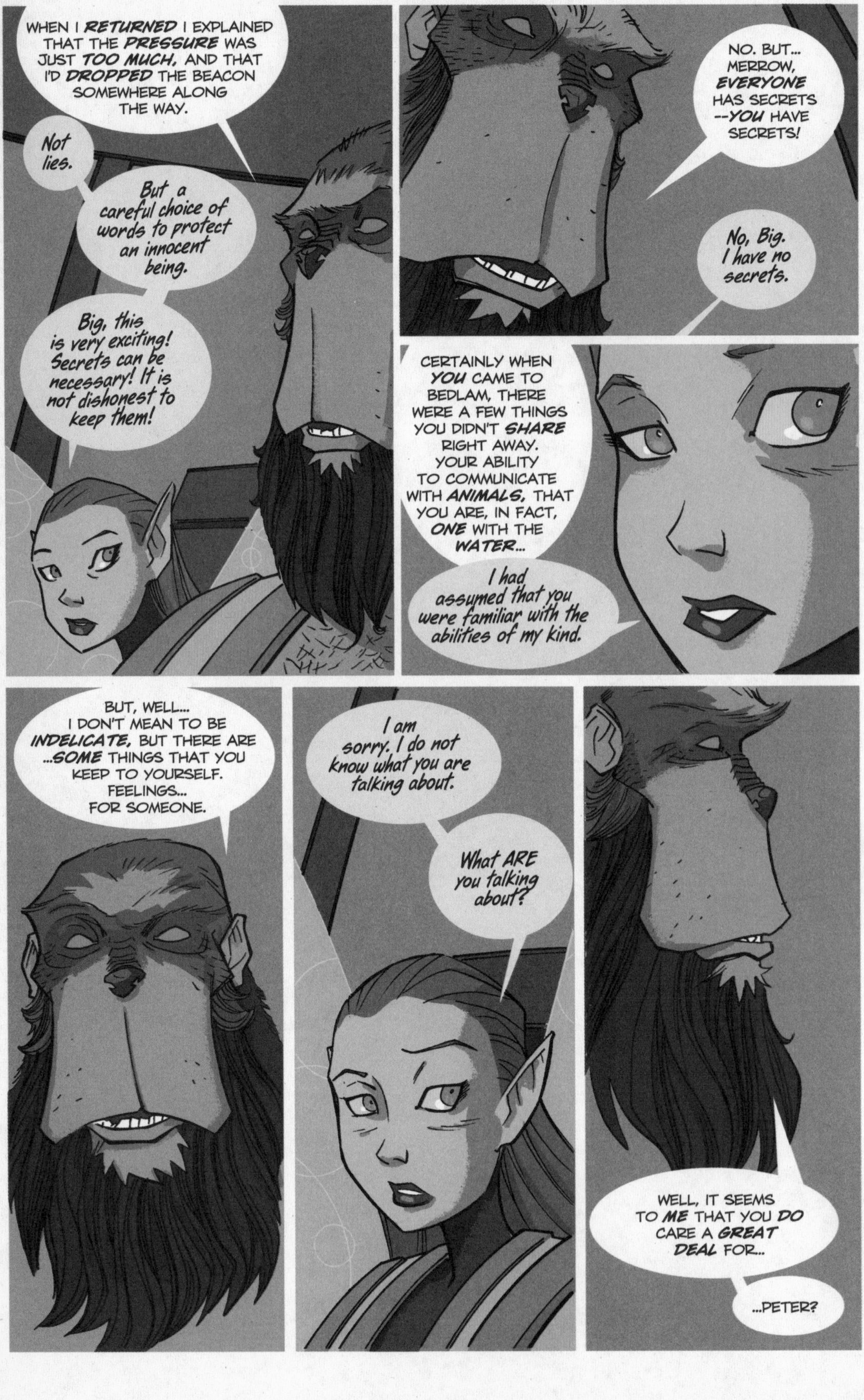
WHEN I RETURNED I EXPLAINED THAT THE PRESSURE WAS JUST TOO MUCH, AND THAT I'D DROPPED THE BEACON SOMEWHERE ALONG THE WAY.
Not lies.
But a careful choice of words to protect an innocent being.
Big, this is very exciting! Secrets can be necessary! It is not dishonest to keep them!
NO. BUT... MERROW, EVERYONE HAS SECRETS --YOU HAVE SECRETS!
No, Big. I have no secrets.
CERTAINLY WHEN YOU CAME TO BEDLAM, THERE WERE A FEW THINGS YOU DIDN'T SHARE RIGHT AWAY. YOUR ABILITY TO COMMUNICATE WITH ANIMALS, THAT YOU ARE, IN FACT, ONE WITH THE WATER...
I had assumed that you were familiar with the abilities of my kind.
BUT, WELL... I DON'T MEAN TO BE INDELICATE, BUT THERE ARE ...SOME THINGS THAT YOU KEEP TO YOURSELF. FEELINGS... FOR SOMEONE.
I am sorry. I do not know what you are talking about.
What ARE you talking about?
WELL, IT SEEMS TO ME THAT YOU DO CARE A GREAT DEAL FOR...
...PETER?

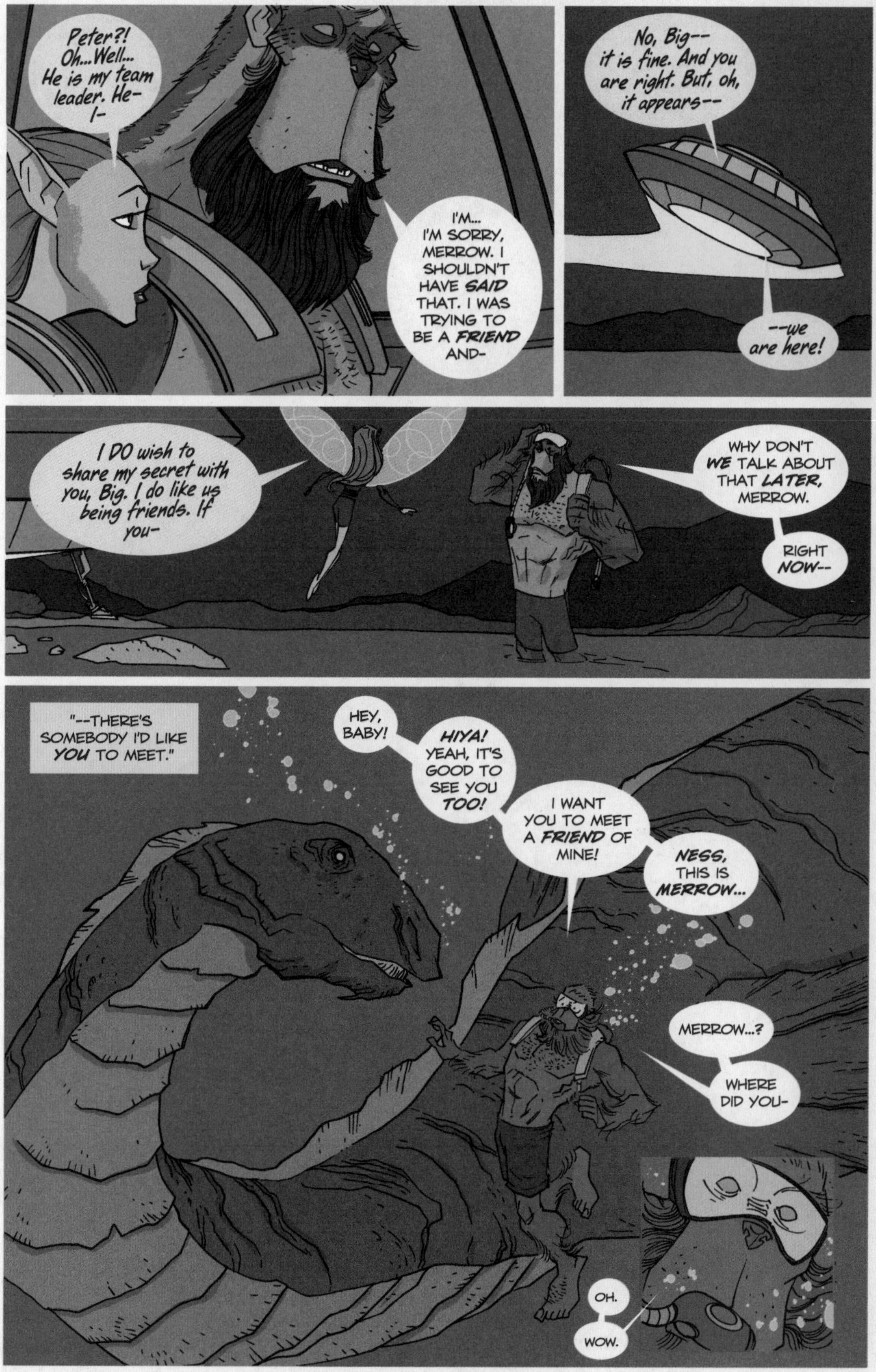
Peter?! Oh...Well... He is my team leader. He- I-
I'M... I'M SORRY, MERROW. I SHOULDN'T HAVE SAID THAT. I WAS TRYING TO BE A FRIEND AND-
No, Big-- it is fine. And you are right. But, oh, it appears--
--we are here!
I DO wish to share my secret with you, Big. I do like us being friends. If you-
WHY DON'T WE TALK ABOUT THAT LATER, MERROW.
RIGHT NOW--
"--THERE'S SOMEBODY I'D LIKE YOU TO MEET."
HEY, BABY!
HIYA! YEAH, IT'S GOOD TO SEE YOU TOO!
I WANT YOU TO MEET A FRIEND OF MINE!
NESS, THIS IS MERROW...
MERROW...?
WHERE DID YOU-
OH.
WOW.

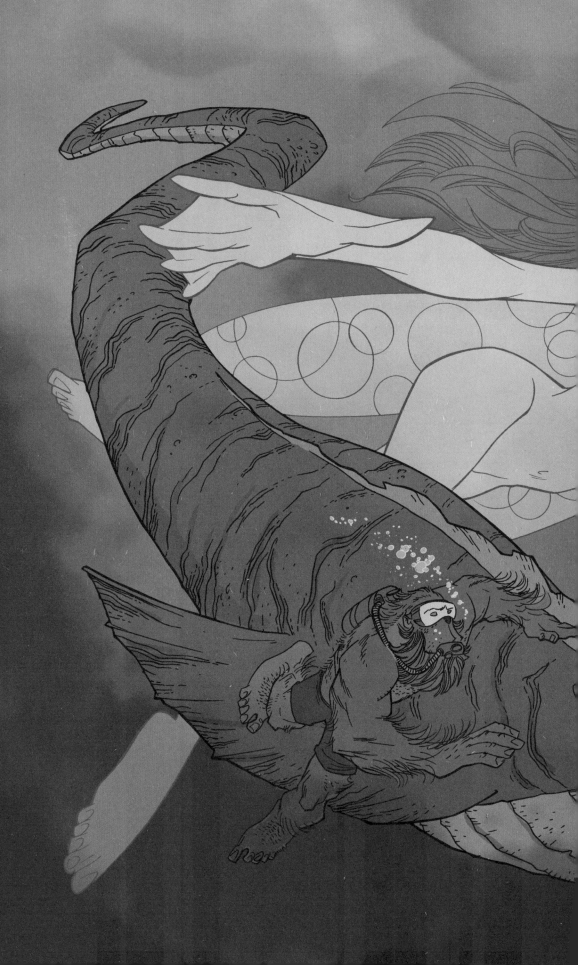

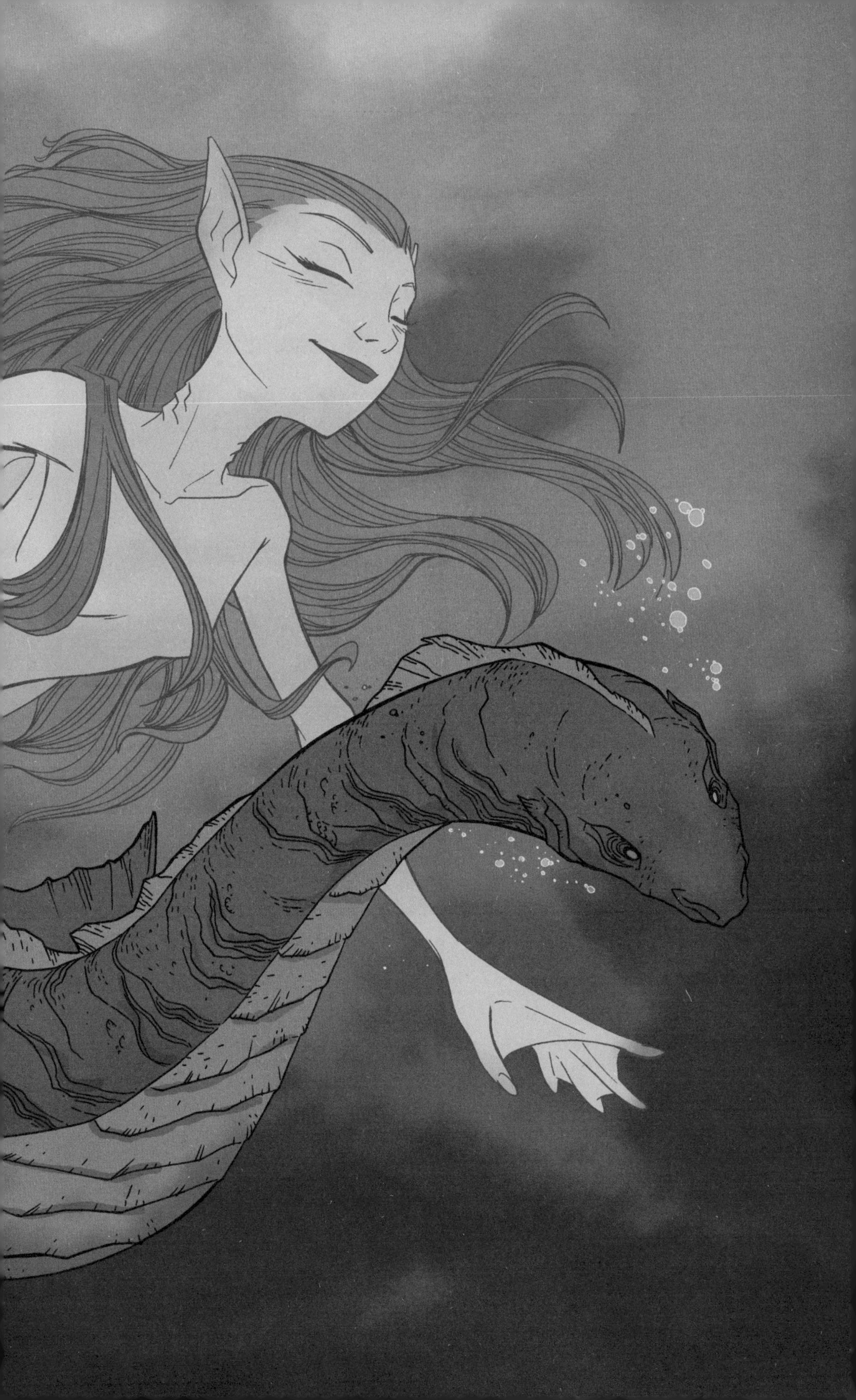

E P I L O G U E

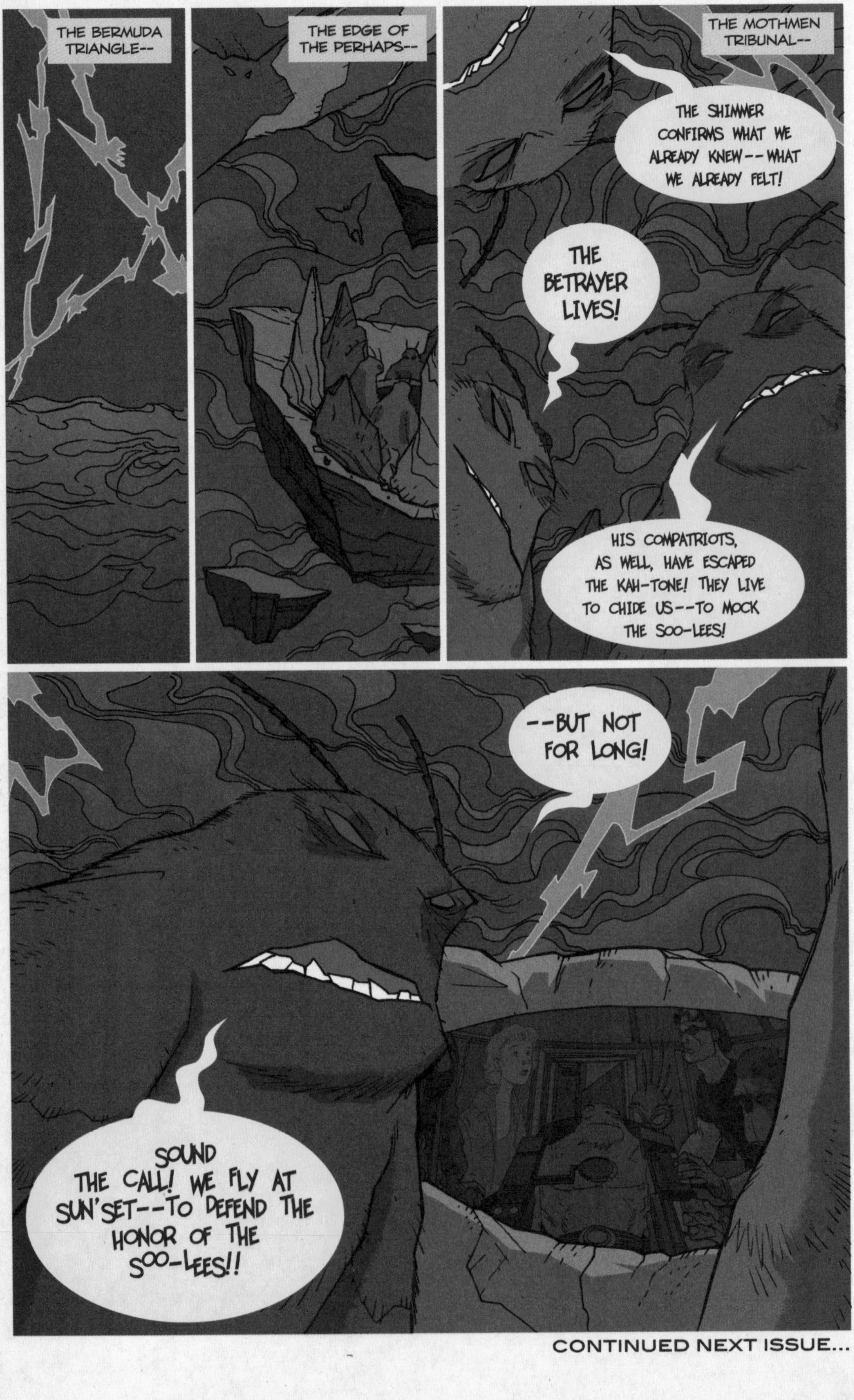

THE BERMUDA TRIANGLE--
THE EDGE OF THE PERHAPS--
THE MOTHMEN TRIBUNAL--
THE SHIMMER CONFIRMS WHAT WE ALREADY KNEW--WHAT WE ALREADY FELT!
THE BETRAYER LIVES!
HIS COMPATRIOTS, AS WELL, HAVE ESCAPED THE KAH-TONE! THEY LIVE TO CHIDE US--TO MOCK THE SOO-LEES!
--BUT NOT FOR LONG!
SOUND THE CALL! WE FLY AT SUN'SET--TO DEFEND THE HONOR OF THE SOO-LEES!!

CONTINUED NEXT ISSUE...

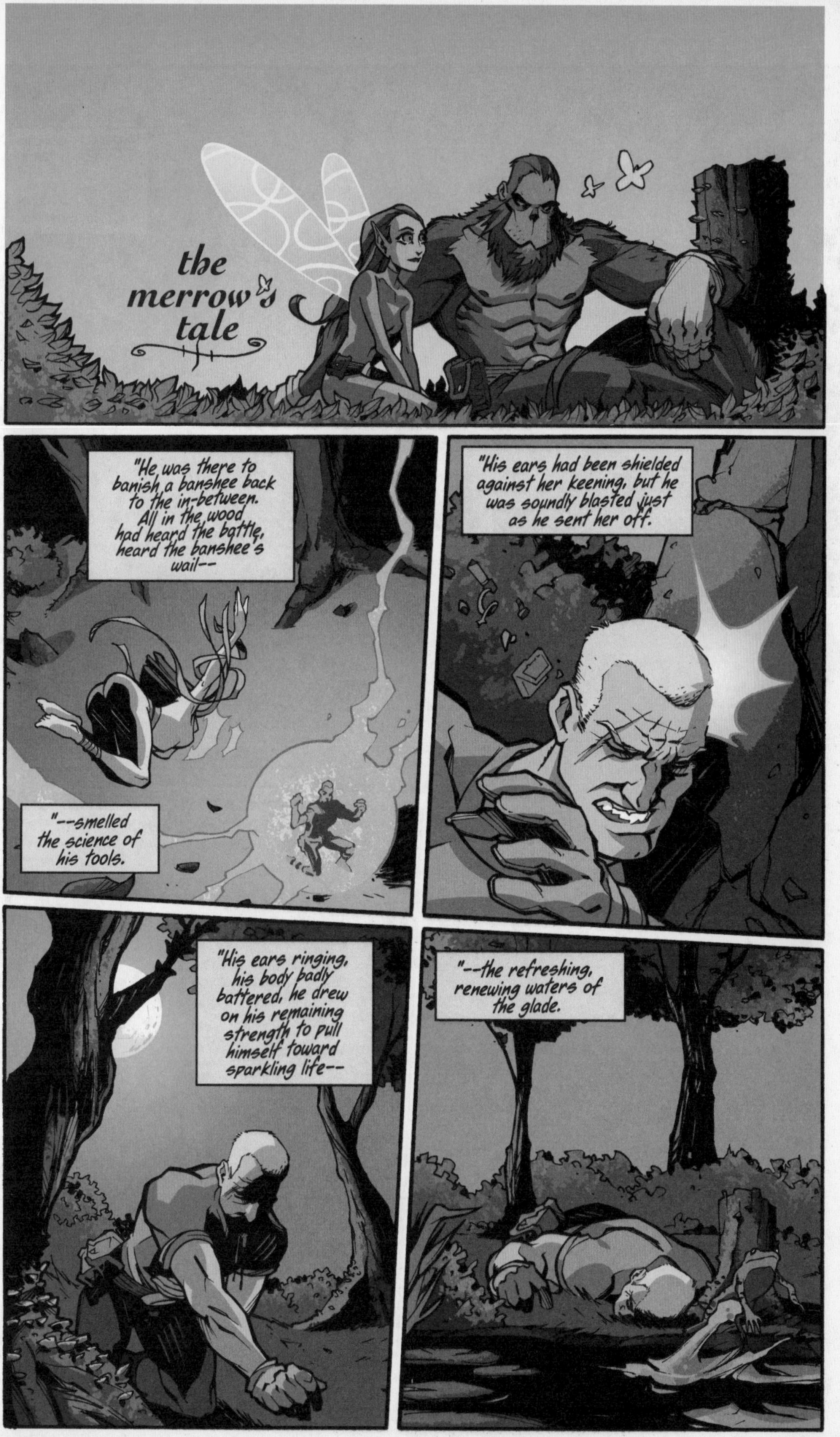
the merrow's tale
"He was there to banish a banshee back to the in-between. All in the wood had heard the battle, heard the banshee's wail--
"--smelled the science of his tools.
"His ears had been shielded against her keening, but he was soundly blasted just as he sent her off.
"His ears ringing, his body badly battered, he drew on his remaining strength to pull himself toward sparkling life--
"--the refreshing, renewing waters of the glade.

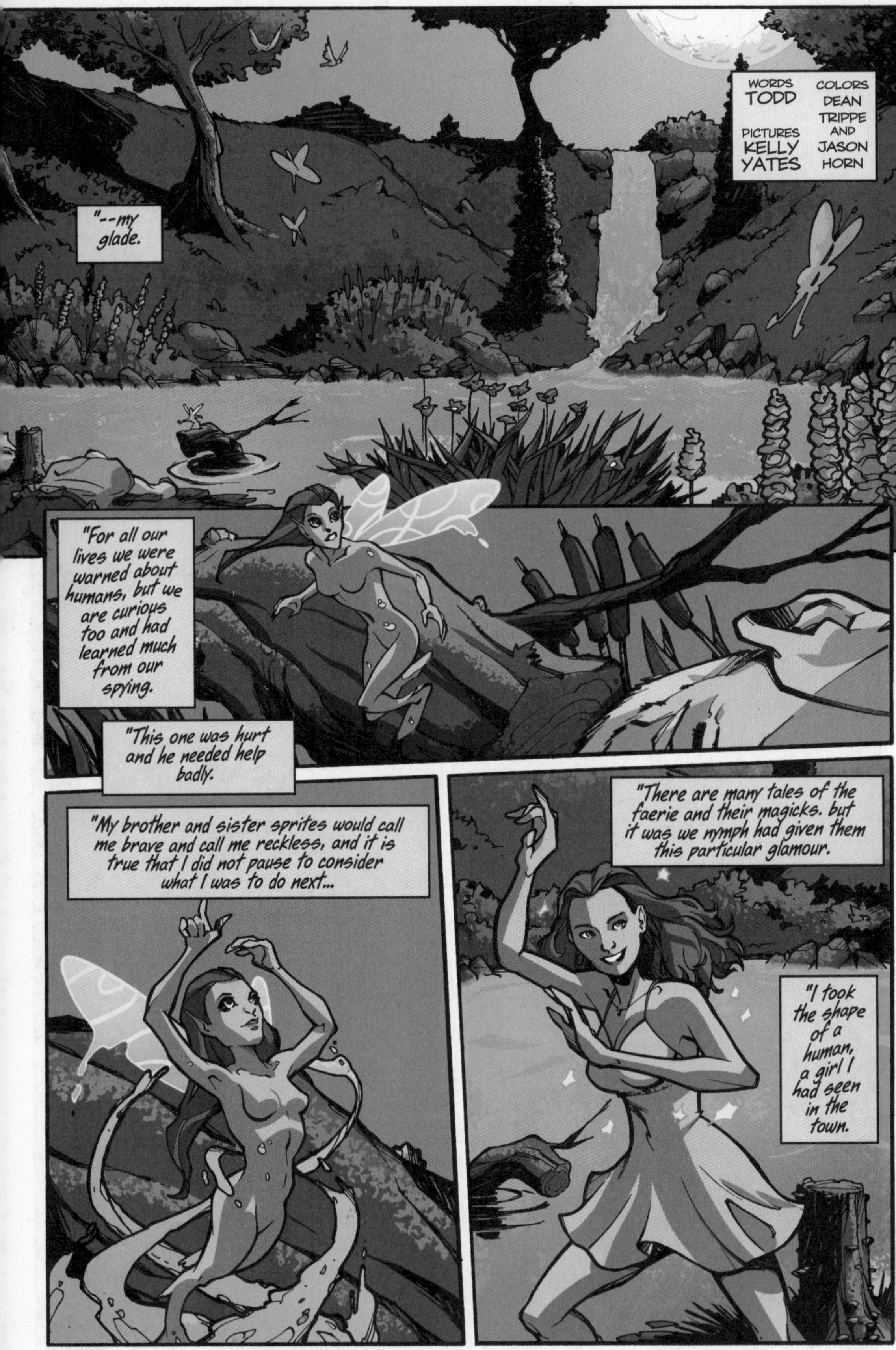
WORDS
TODD
PICTURES
KELLY
YATES
COLORS
DEAN
TRIPPE
AND
JASON
HORN
"--my glade.
"For all our lives we were warned about humans, but we are curious too and had learned much from our spying.
"This one was hurt and he needed help badly.
"My brother and sister sprites would call me brave and call me reckless, and it is true that I did not pause to consider what I was to do next...
"There are many tales of the faerie and their magicks. but it was we nymph had given them this particular glamour.
"I took the shape of a human, a girl I had seen in the town.

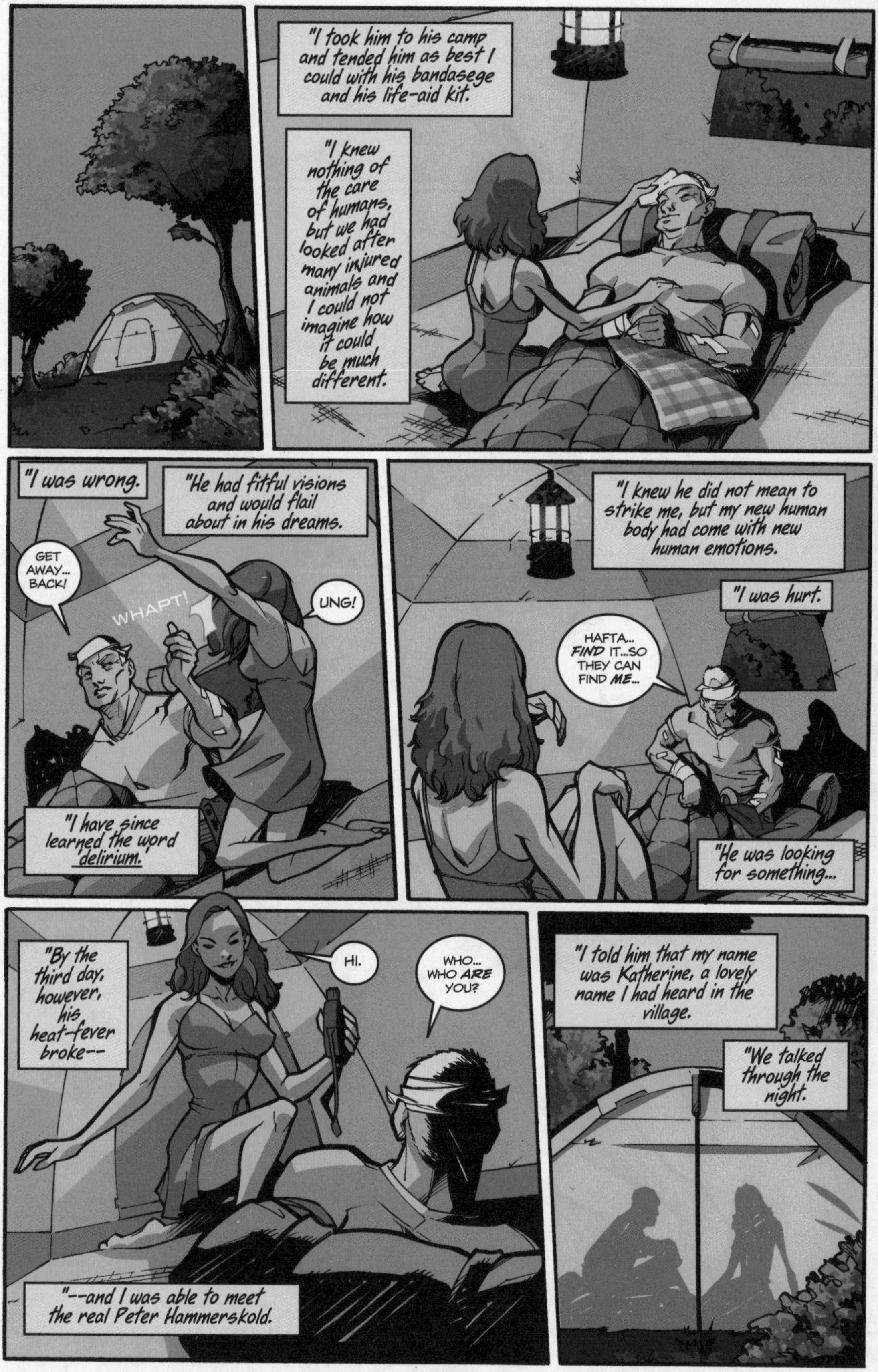
"I took him to his camp and tended him as best I could with his bandasege and his life-aid kit.
"I knew nothing of the care of humans, but we had looked after many injured animals and I could not imagine how it could be much different.
"I was wrong.
"He had fitful visions and would flail about in his dreams.
GET AWAY... BACK!
WHAPT!
UNG!
"I have since learned the word delirium.
"I knew he did not mean to strike me, but my new human body had come with new human emotions.
"I was hurt.
HAFTA... FIND IT...SO THEY CAN FIND ME...
"He was looking for something...
"By the third day, however, his heat-fever broke--
HI.
WHO... WHO ARE YOU?
"--and I was able to meet the real Peter Hammerskold.
"I told him that my name was Katherine, a lovely name I had heard in the village.
"We talked through the night.

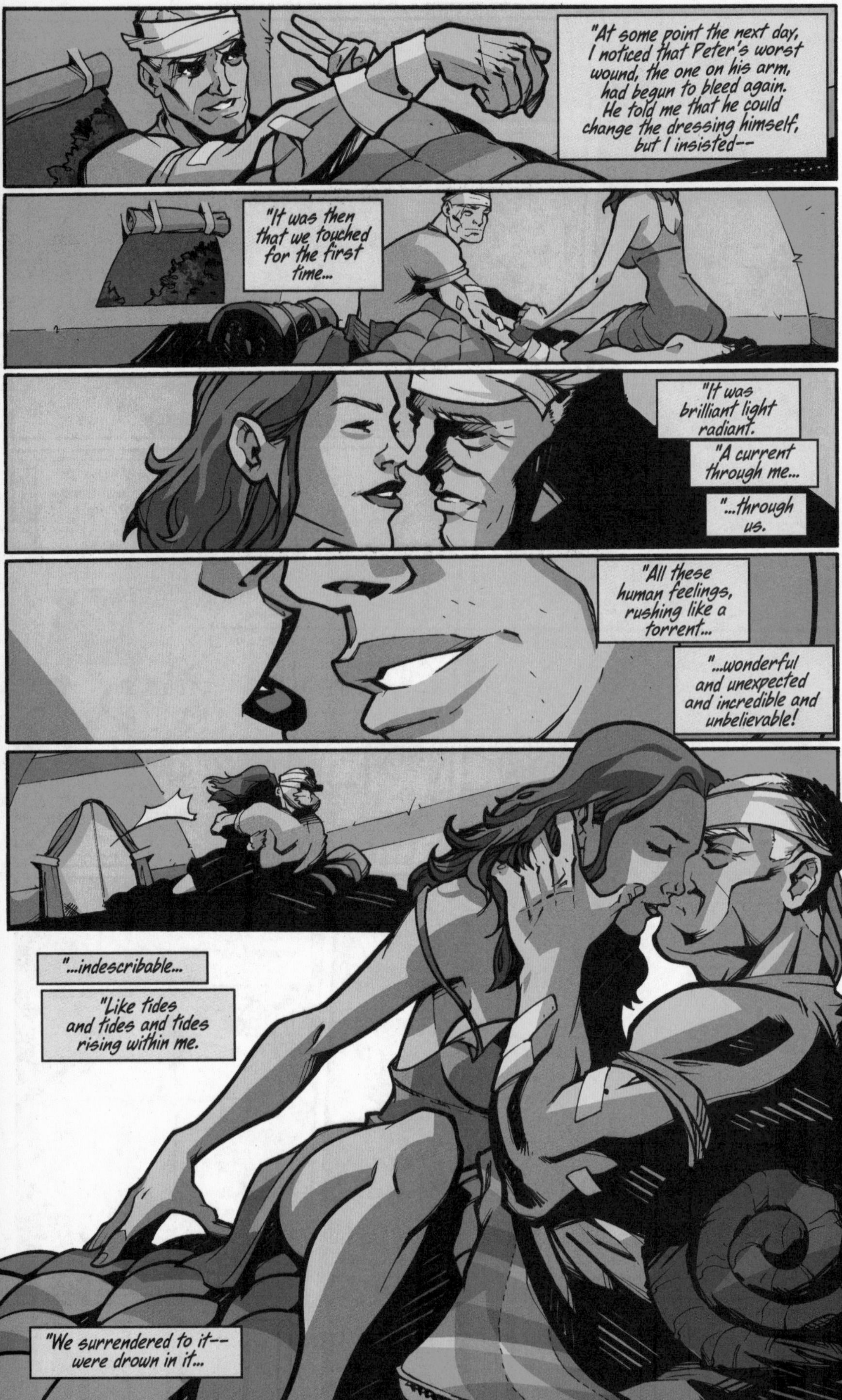
"At some point the next day, I noticed that Peter's worst wound, the one on his arm, had begun to bleed again. He told me that he could change the dressing himself, but I insisted--
"It was then that we touched for the first time...
"It was brilliant light radiant.
"A current through me...
"...through us.
"All these human feelings, rushing like a torrent...
"...wonderful and unexpected and incredible and unbelievable!
"...indescribable...
"Like tides and tides and tides rising within me.
"We surrendered to it-- were drown in it...

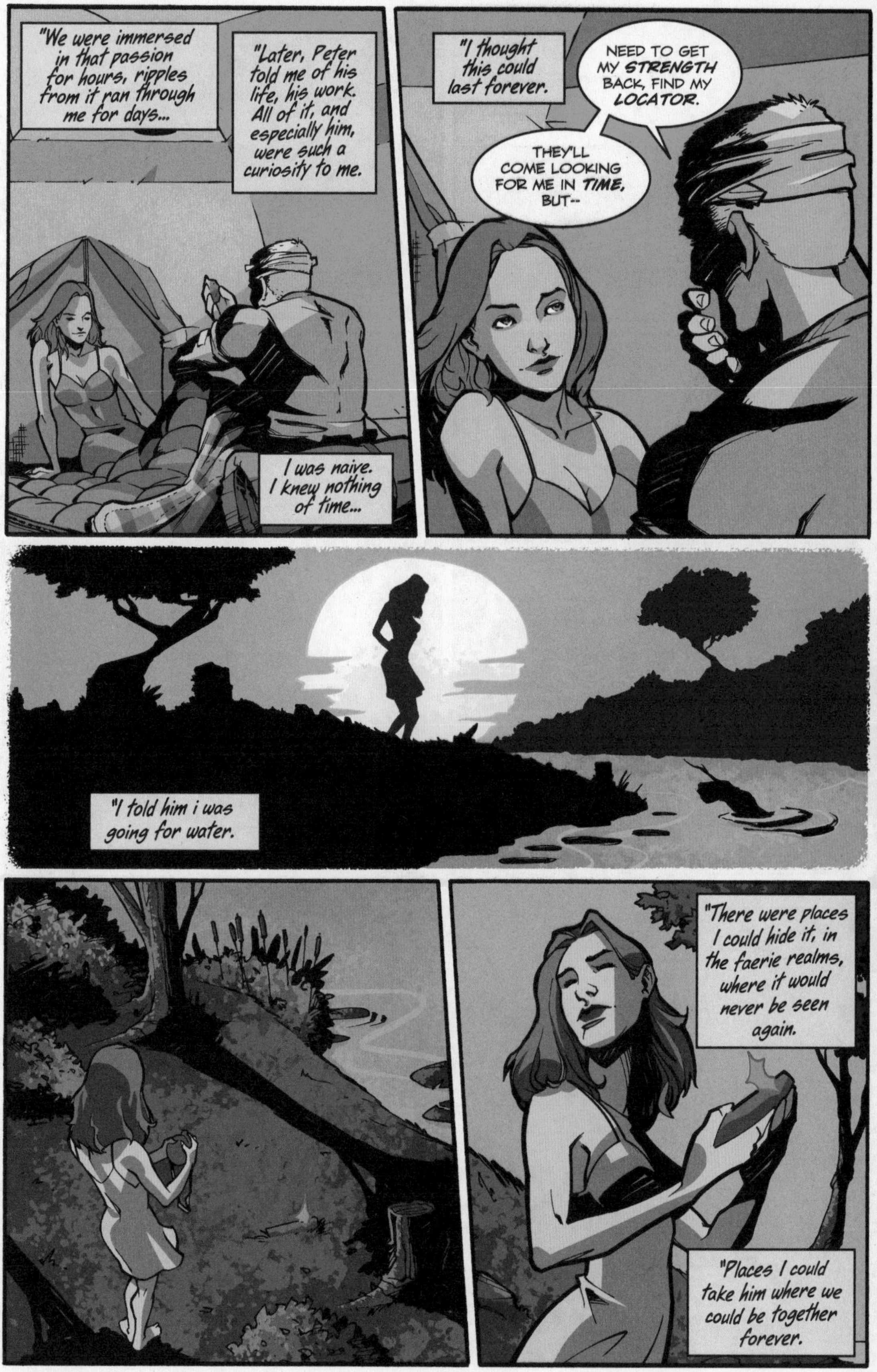
"We were immersed in that passion for hours, ripples from it ran through me for days...
"Later, Peter told me of his life, his work. All of it, and especially him, were such a curiosity to me.
I was naive. I knew nothing of time...
"I thought this could last forever.
NEED TO GET MY STRENGTH BACK, FIND MY LOCATOR.
THEY'LL COME LOOKING FOR ME IN TIME, BUT--
"I told him i was going for water.
"There were places I could hide it, in the faerie realms, where it would never be seen again.
"Places I could take him where we could be together forever.

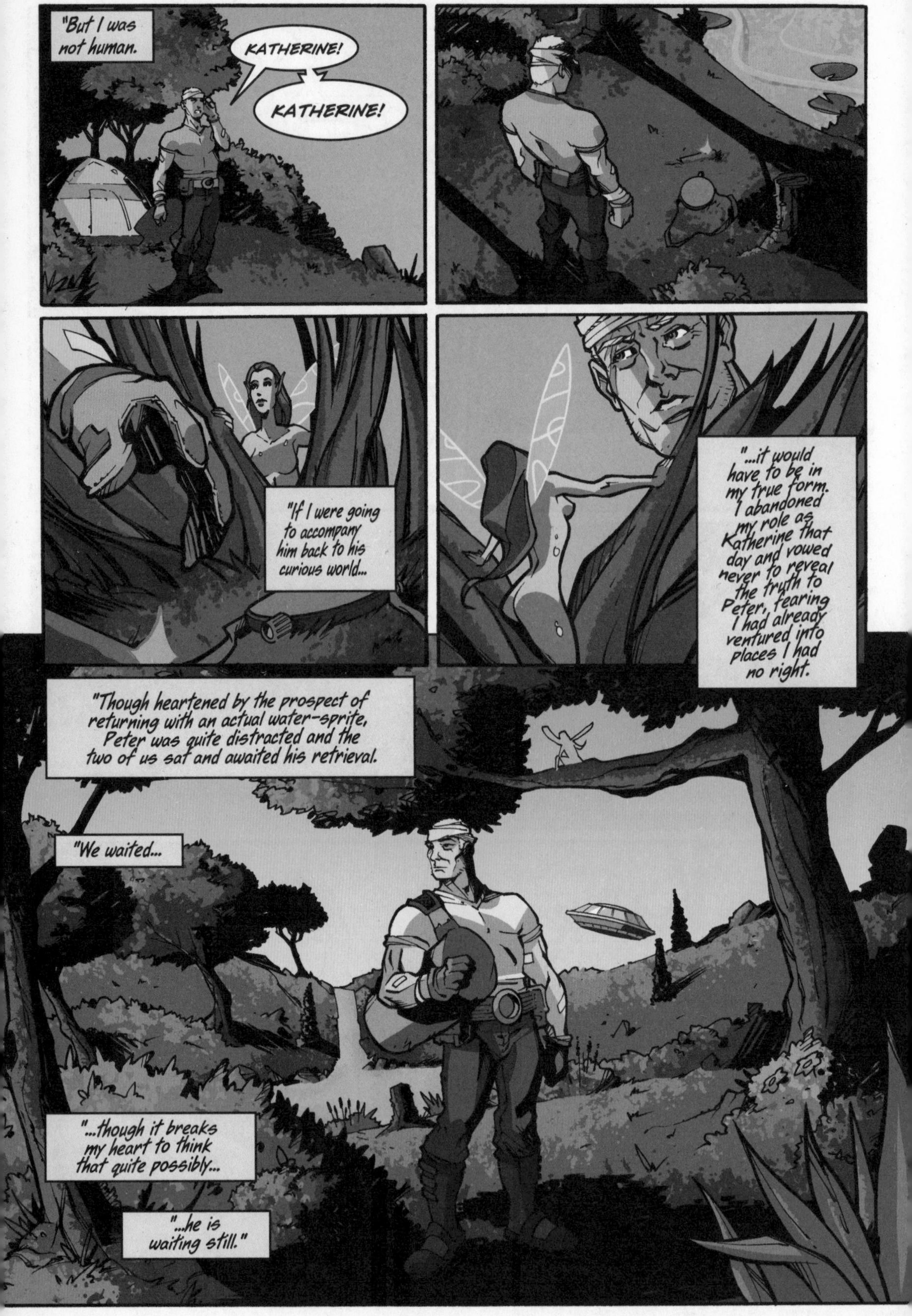
"But I was not human.
KATHERINE!
KATHERINE!
"If I were going to accompany him back to his curious world...
"...it would have to be in my true form. I abandoned my role as Katherine that day and vowed never to reveal the truth to Peter, fearing I had already ventured into places I had no right.
"Though heartened by the prospect of returning with an actual water-sprite, Peter was quite distracted and the two of us sat and awaited his retrieval.
"We waited...
"...though it breaks my heart to think that quite possibly...
"...he is waiting still."

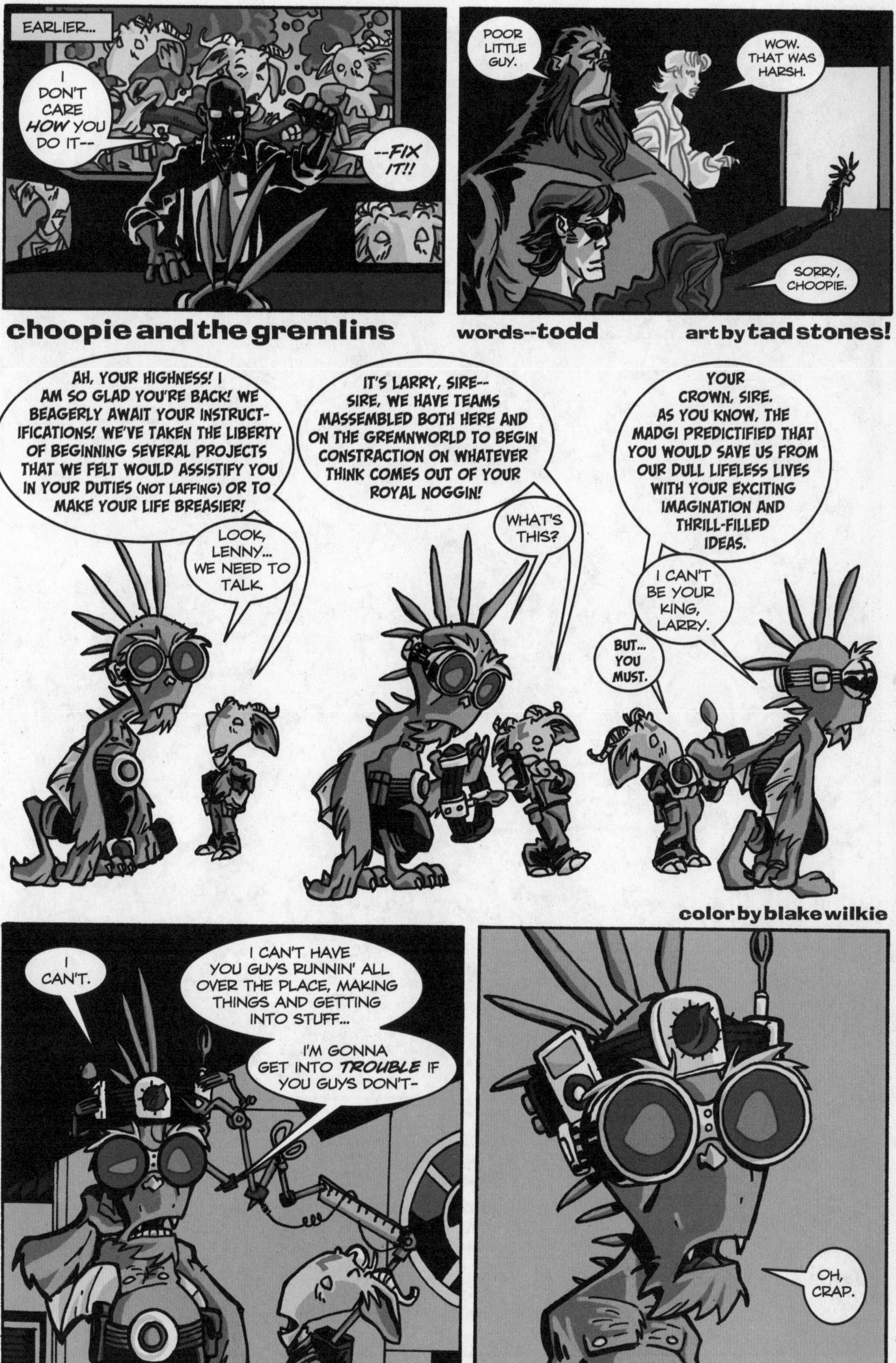
EARLIER...
I DON'T CARE HOW YOU DO IT--
--FIX IT!!
POOR LITTLE GUY.
WOW. THAT WAS HARSH.
SORRY, CHOOPIE.
choopie and the gremlins
words--todd
art by tad stones!
AH, YOUR HIGHNESS! I AM SO GLAD YOU'RE BACK! WE BEAGERLY AWAIT YOUR INSTRUCT-IFICATIONS! WE'VE TAKEN THE LIBERTY OF BEGINNING SEVERAL PROJECTS THAT WE FELT WOULD ASSISTIFY YOU IN YOUR DUTIES (NOT LAFFING) OR TO MAKE YOUR LIFE BREASIER!
LOOK, LENNY... WE NEED TO TALK.
IT'S LARRY, SIRE-- SIRE, WE HAVE TEAMS MASSEMBLED BOTH HERE AND ON THE GREMNWORLD TO BEGIN CONSTRACTION ON WHATEVER THINK COMES OUT OF YOUR ROYAL NOGGIN!
WHAT'S THIS?
YOUR CROWN, SIRE. AS YOU KNOW, THE MADGI PREDICTIFIED THAT YOU WOULD SAVE US FROM OUR DULL LIFELESS LIVES WITH YOUR EXCITING IMAGINATION AND THRILL-FILLED IDEAS.
I CAN'T BE YOUR KING, LARRY.
BUT... YOU MUST.
color by blake wilkie
I CAN'T.
I CAN'T HAVE YOU GUYS RUNNIN' ALL OVER THE PLACE, MAKING THINGS AND GETTING INTO STUFF...
I'M GONNA GET INTO TROUBLE IF YOU GUYS DON'T-
OH, CRAP.

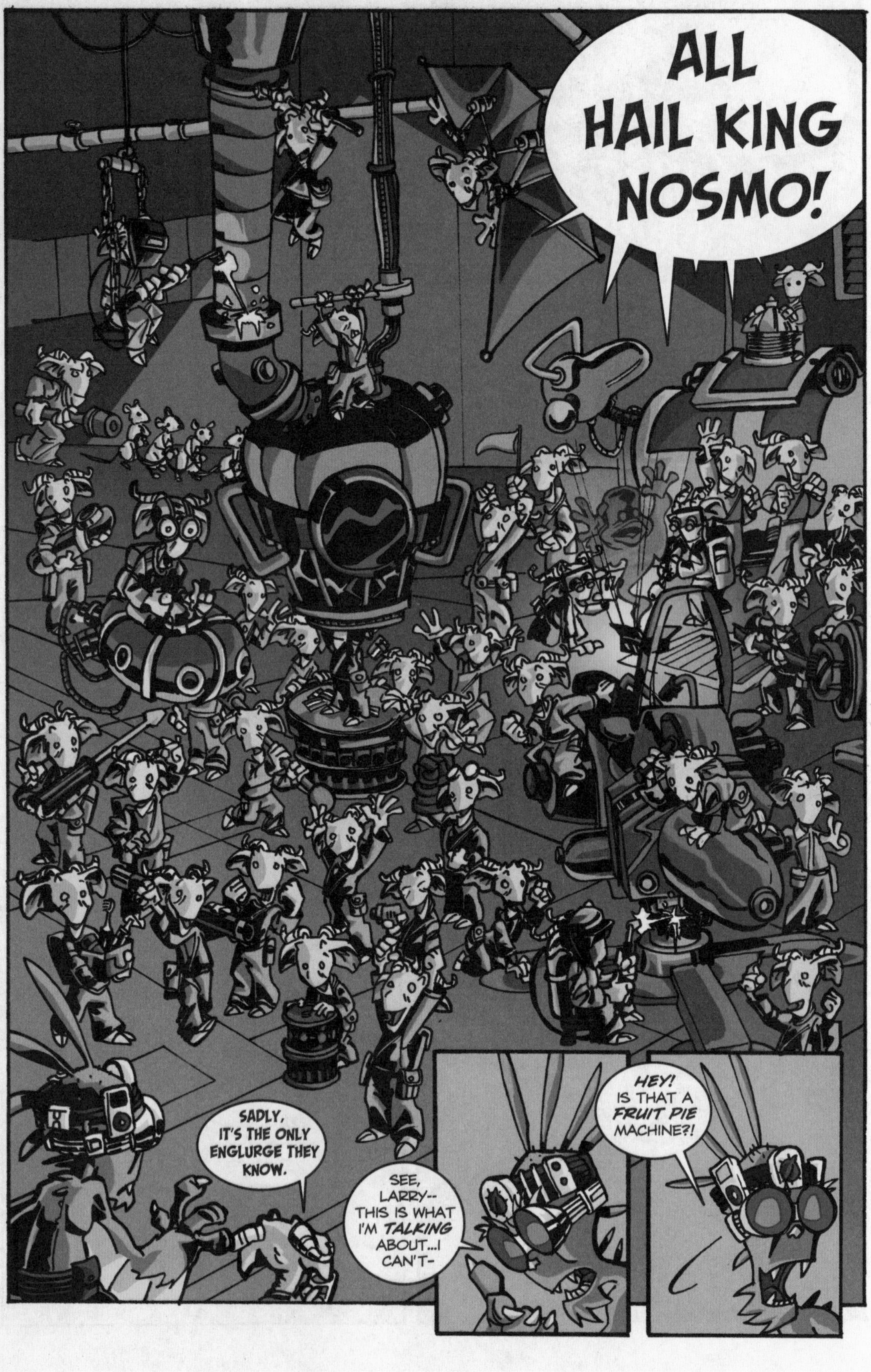

ALL HAIL KING NOSMO!
SADLY, IT'S THE ONLY ENGLURGE THEY KNOW.
SEE, LARRY-- THIS IS WHAT I'M TALKING ABOUT...I CAN'T-
HEY! IS THAT A FRUIT PIE MACHINE?!

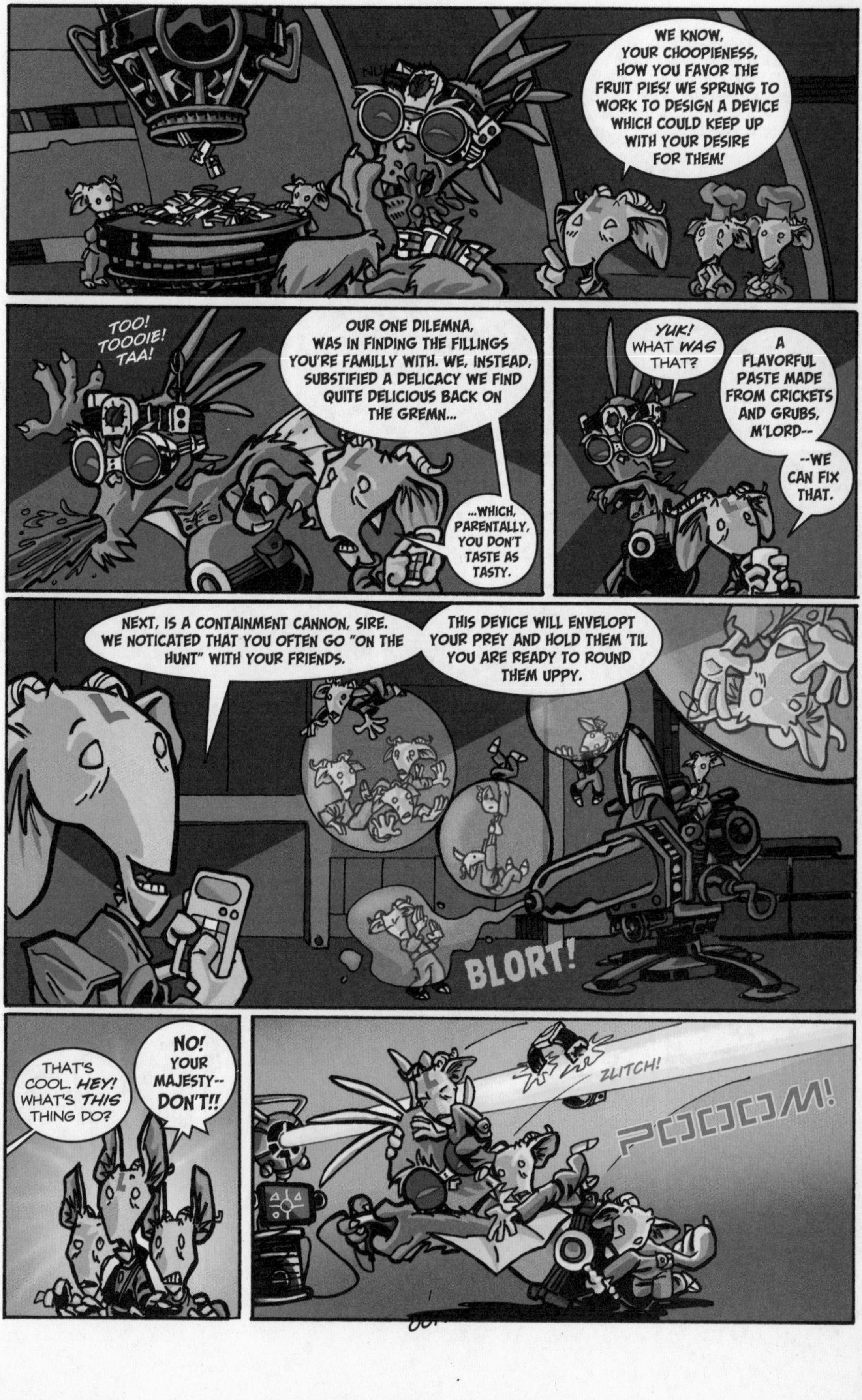
WE KNOW, YOUR CHOOPIENESS, HOW YOU FAVOR THE FRUIT PIES! WE SPRUNG TO WORK TO DESIGN A DEVICE WHICH COULD KEEP UP WITH YOUR DESIRE FOR THEM!
TOO! TOOOIE! TAA!
OUR ONE DILEMNA, WAS IN FINDING THE FILLINGS YOU'RE FAMILLY WITH. WE, INSTEAD, SUBSTIFIED A DELICACY WE FIND QUITE DELICIOUS BACK ON THE GREMN...
...WHICH, PARENTALLY, YOU DON'T TASTE AS TASTY.
YUK! WHAT WAS THAT?
A FLAVORFUL PASTE MADE FROM CRICKETS AND GRUBS, M'LORD--
--WE CAN FIX THAT.
NEXT, IS A CONTAINMENT CANNON, SIRE. WE NOTICATED THAT YOU OFTEN GO "ON THE HUNT" WITH YOUR FRIENDS.
THIS DEVICE WILL ENVELOPT YOUR PREY AND HOLD THEM 'TIL YOU ARE READY TO ROUND THEM UPPY.
BLORT!
THAT'S COOL. HEY! WHAT'S THIS THING DO?
NO! YOUR MAJESTY-- DON'T!!
ZLITCH!
POOOM!

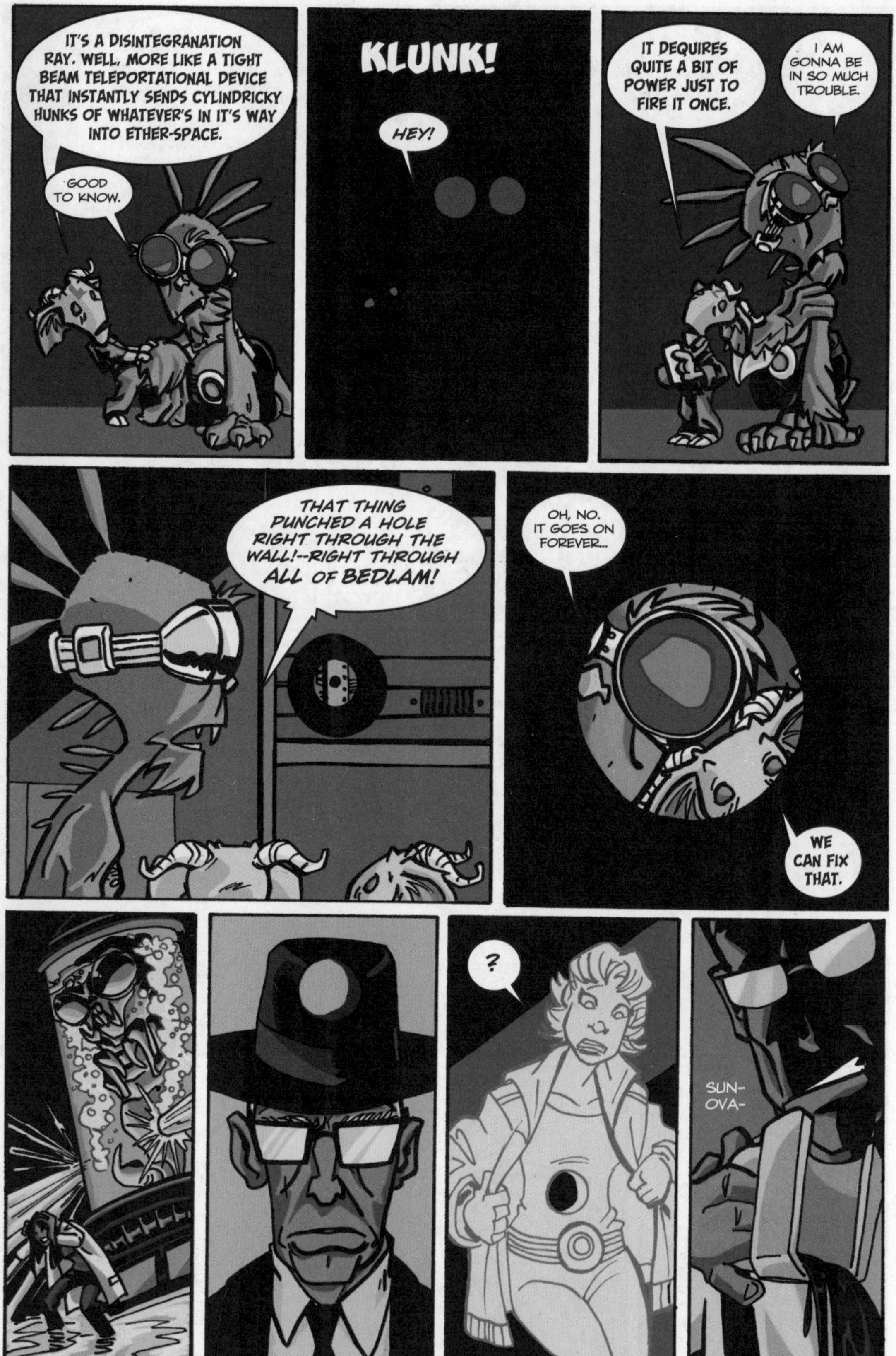
IT'S A DISINTEGRANATION RAY. WELL, MORE LIKE A TIGHT BEAM TELEPORTATIONAL DEVICE THAT INSTANTLY SENDS CYLINDRICKY HUNKS OF WHATEVER'S IN IT'S WAY INTO ETHER-SPACE.
GOOD TO KNOW.
KLUNK!
HEY!
IT DEQUIRES QUITE A BIT OF POWER JUST TO FIRE IT ONCE.
I AM GONNA BE IN SO MUCH TROUBLE.
THAT THING PUNCHED A HOLE RIGHT THROUGH THE WALL!--RIGHT THROUGH ALL OF BEDLAM!
OH, NO. IT GOES ON FOREVER...
WE CAN FIX THAT.
?
SUN-
OVA-

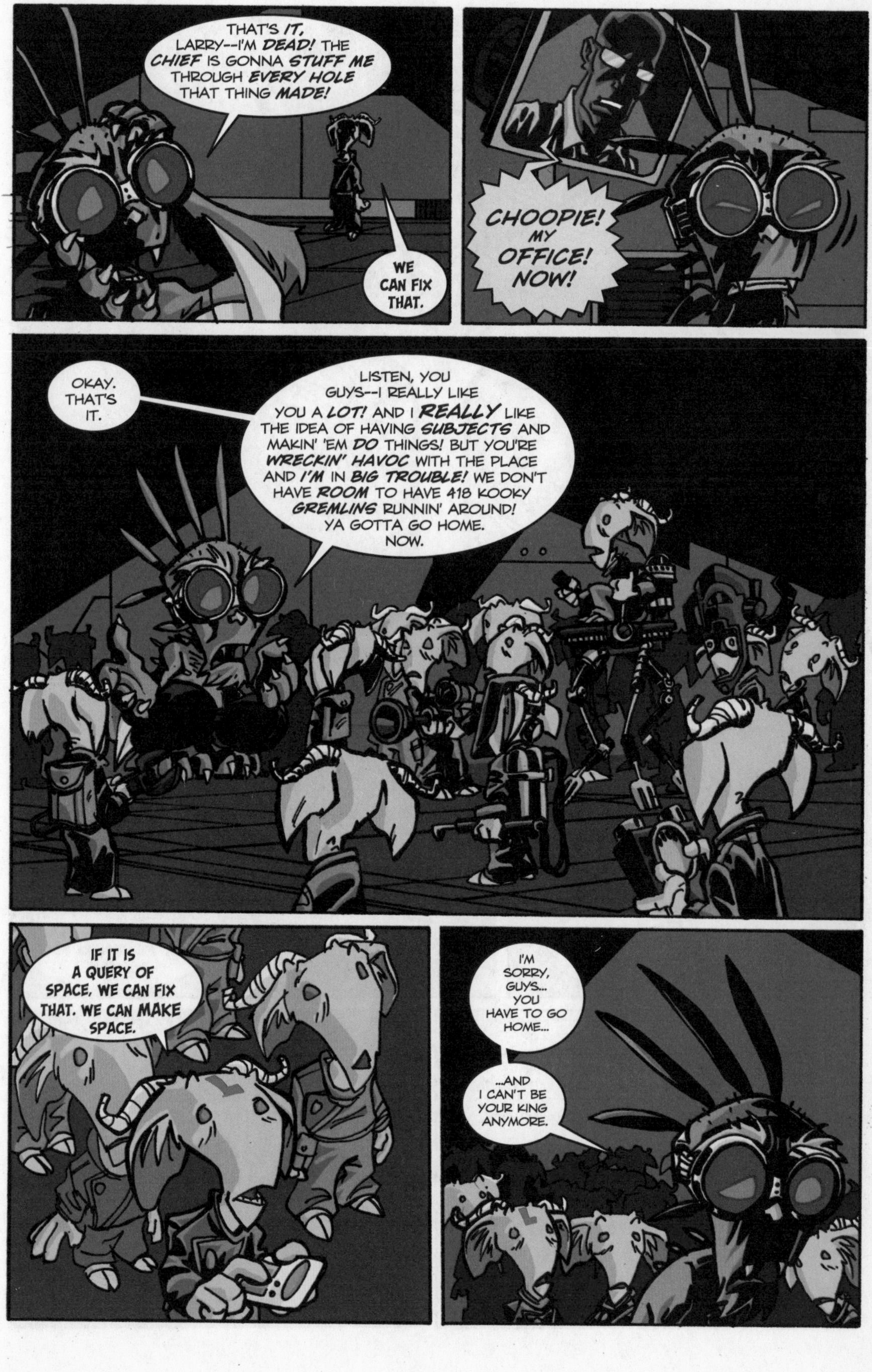
THAT'S IT, LARRY--I'M DEAD! THE CHIEF IS GONNA STUFF ME THROUGH EVERY HOLE THAT THING MADE!
WE CAN FIX THAT.
CHOOPIE! MY OFFICE! NOW!
OKAY. THAT'S IT.
LISTEN, YOU GUYS--I REALLY LIKE YOU A LOT! AND I REALLY LIKE THE IDEA OF HAVING SUBJECTS AND MAKIN' 'EM DO THINGS! BUT YOU'RE WRECKIN' HAVOC WITH THE PLACE AND I'M IN BIG TROUBLE! WE DON'T HAVE ROOM TO HAVE 418 KOOKY GREMLINS RUNNIN' AROUND! YA GOTTA GO HOME. NOW.
IF IT IS A QUERY OF SPACE, WE CAN FIX THAT. WE CAN MAKE SPACE.
I'M SORRY, GUYS... YOU HAVE TO GO HOME...
...AND I CAN'T BE YOUR KING ANYMORE.

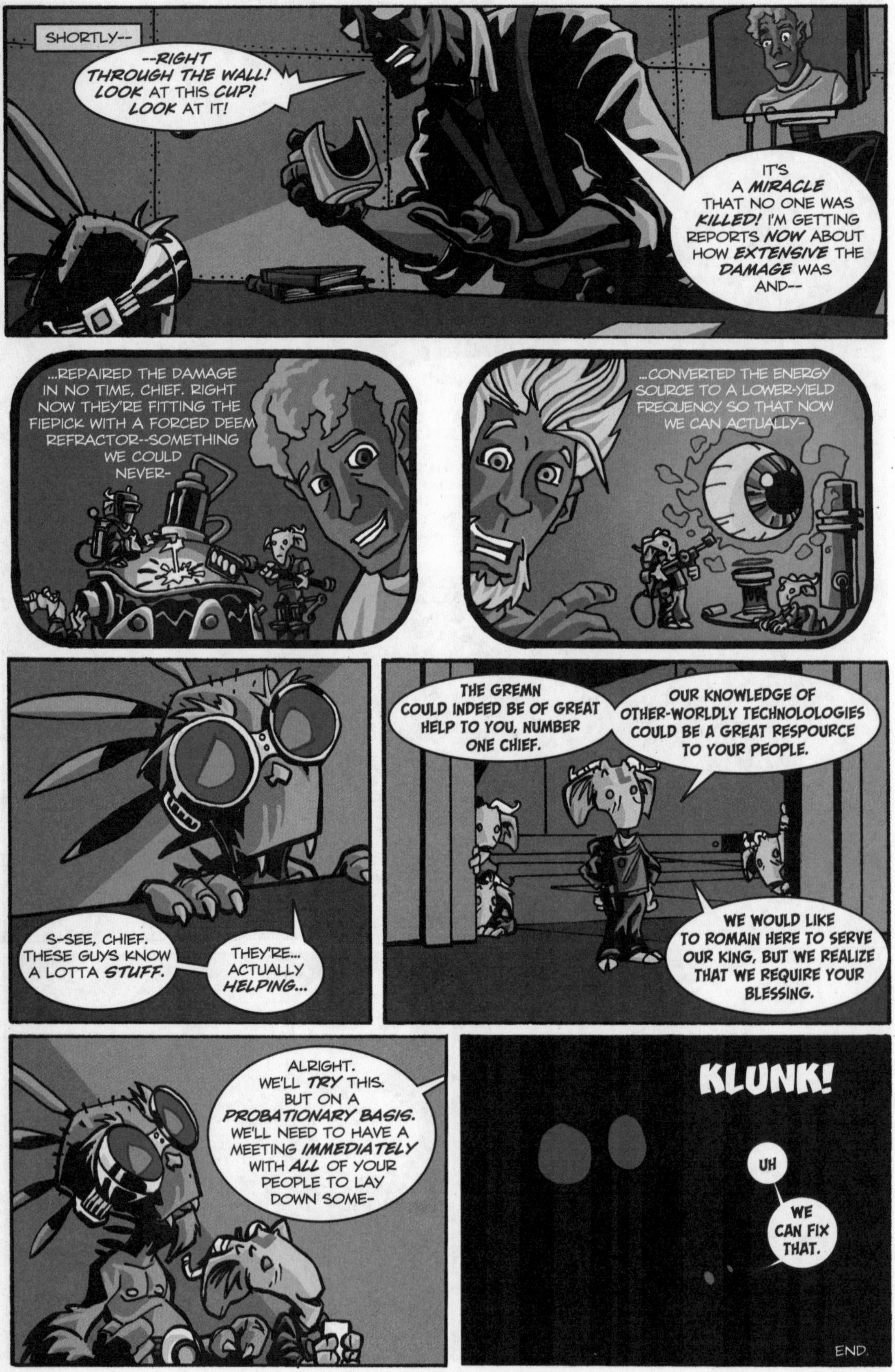
SHORTLY--
--RIGHT THROUGH THE WALL! LOOK AT THIS CUP! LOOK AT IT!
IT'S A MIRACLE THAT NO ONE WAS KILLED! I'M GETTING REPORTS NOW ABOUT HOW EXTENSIVE THE DAMAGE WAS AND--
...REPAIRED THE DAMAGE IN NO TIME, CHIEF. RIGHT NOW THEY'RE FITTING THE FIEPICK WITH A FORCED DEEM REFRACTOR--SOMETHING WE COULD NEVER-
...CONVERTED THE ENERGY SOURCE TO A LOWER-YIELD FREQUENCY SO THAT NOW WE CAN ACTUALLY-
S-SEE, CHIEF. THESE GUYS KNOW A LOTTA STUFF.
THEY'RE... ACTUALLY HELPING...
THE GREMN COULD INDEED BE OF GREAT HELP TO YOU, NUMBER ONE CHIEF.
OUR KNOWLEDGE OF OTHER-WORLDLY TECHNOLOGIES COULD BE A GREAT RESPOURCE TO YOUR PEOPLE.
WE WOULD LIKE TO ROMAIN HERE TO SERVE OUR KING, BUT WE REALIZE THAT WE REQUIRE YOUR BLESSING.
ALRIGHT. WE'LL TRY THIS. BUT ON A PROBATIONARY BASIS. WE'LL NEED TO HAVE A MEETING IMMEDIATELY WITH ALL OF YOUR PEOPLE TO LAY DOWN SOME-
KLUNK!
UH
WE CAN FIX THAT.
END.

random stuff

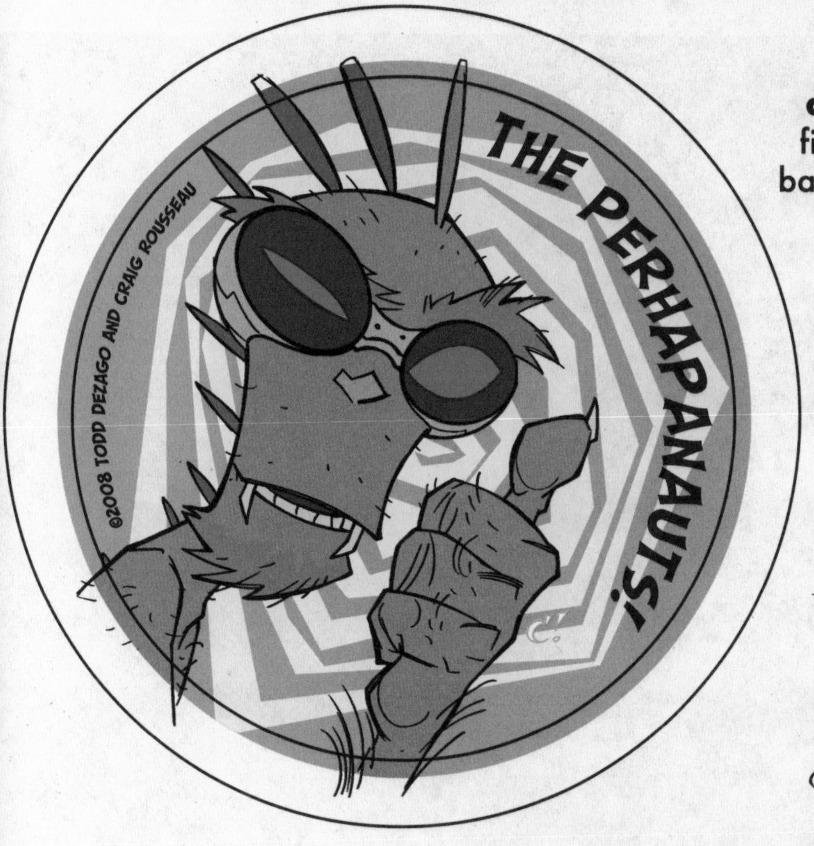
THE PERHAPANAUTS!
©2008 TODD DEZAGO AND CRAIG ROUSSEAU

choopie button
first available at
baltimore comicon
2008

PERHAPANAUTS PIN

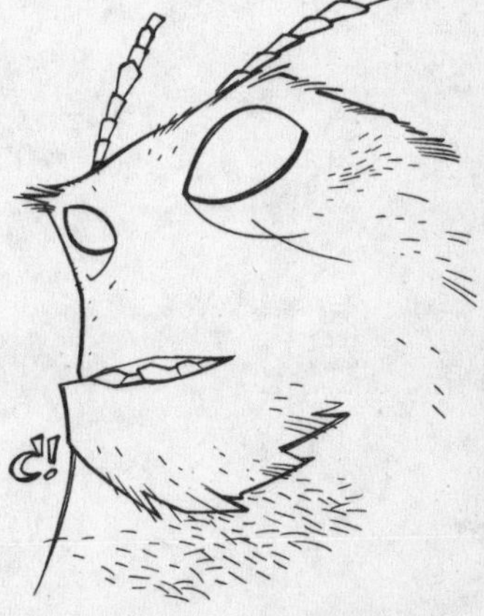

line art for karl (mothman) button

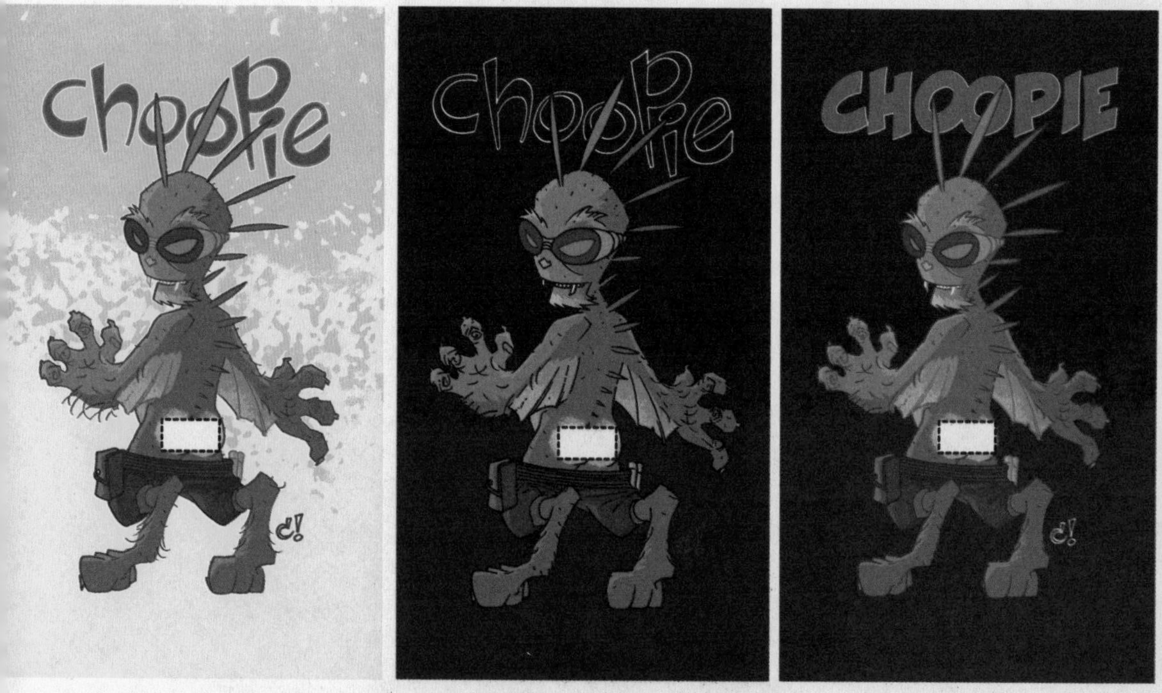
choopie
choopie
CHOOPIE

the infamous choopie butt card

perhapanauts 4

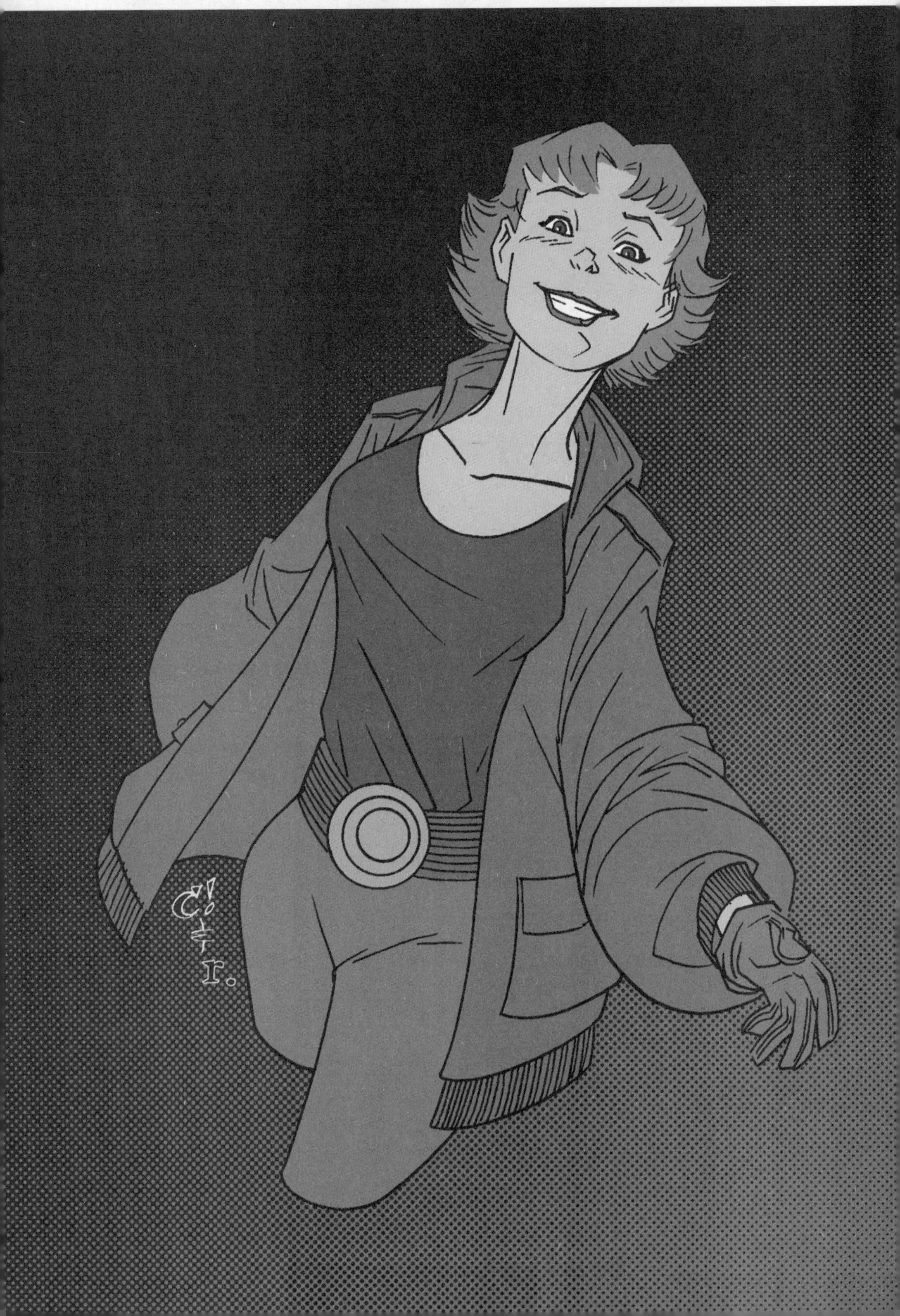

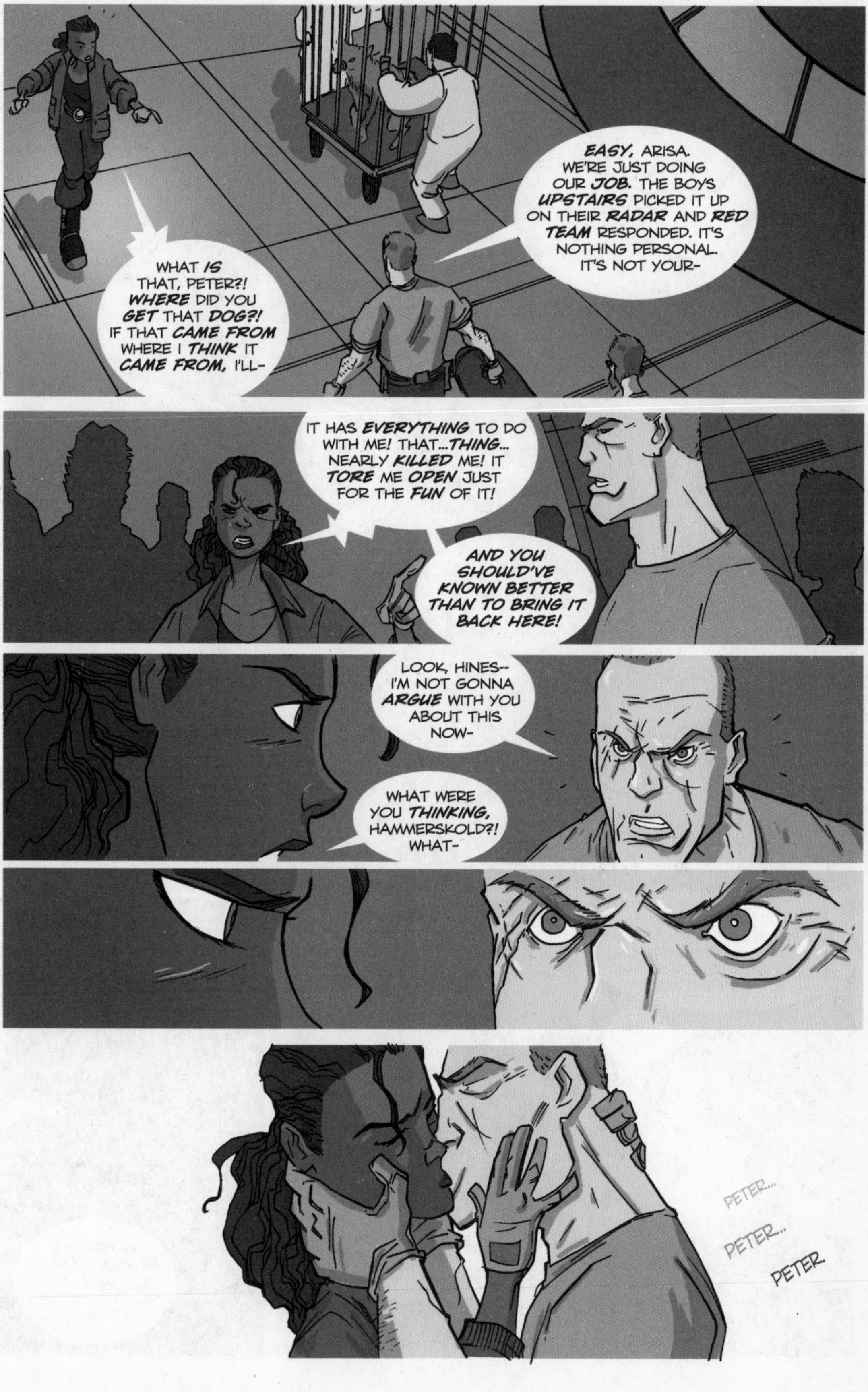
WHAT IS THAT, PETER?! WHERE DID YOU GET THAT DOG?! IF THAT CAME FROM WHERE I THINK IT CAME FROM, I'LL-
EASY, ARISA. WE'RE JUST DOING OUR JOB. THE BOYS UPSTAIRS PICKED IT UP ON THEIR RADAR AND RED TEAM RESPONDED. IT'S NOTHING PERSONAL. IT'S NOT YOUR-
IT HAS EVERYTHING TO DO WITH ME! THAT...THING... NEARLY KILLED ME! IT TORE ME OPEN JUST FOR THE FUN OF IT!
AND YOU SHOULD'VE KNOWN BETTER THAN TO BRING IT BACK HERE!
LOOK, HINES-- I'M NOT GONNA ARGUE WITH YOU ABOUT THIS NOW-
WHAT WERE YOU THINKING, HAMMERSKOLD?! WHAT-
PETER...
PETER...
PETER.

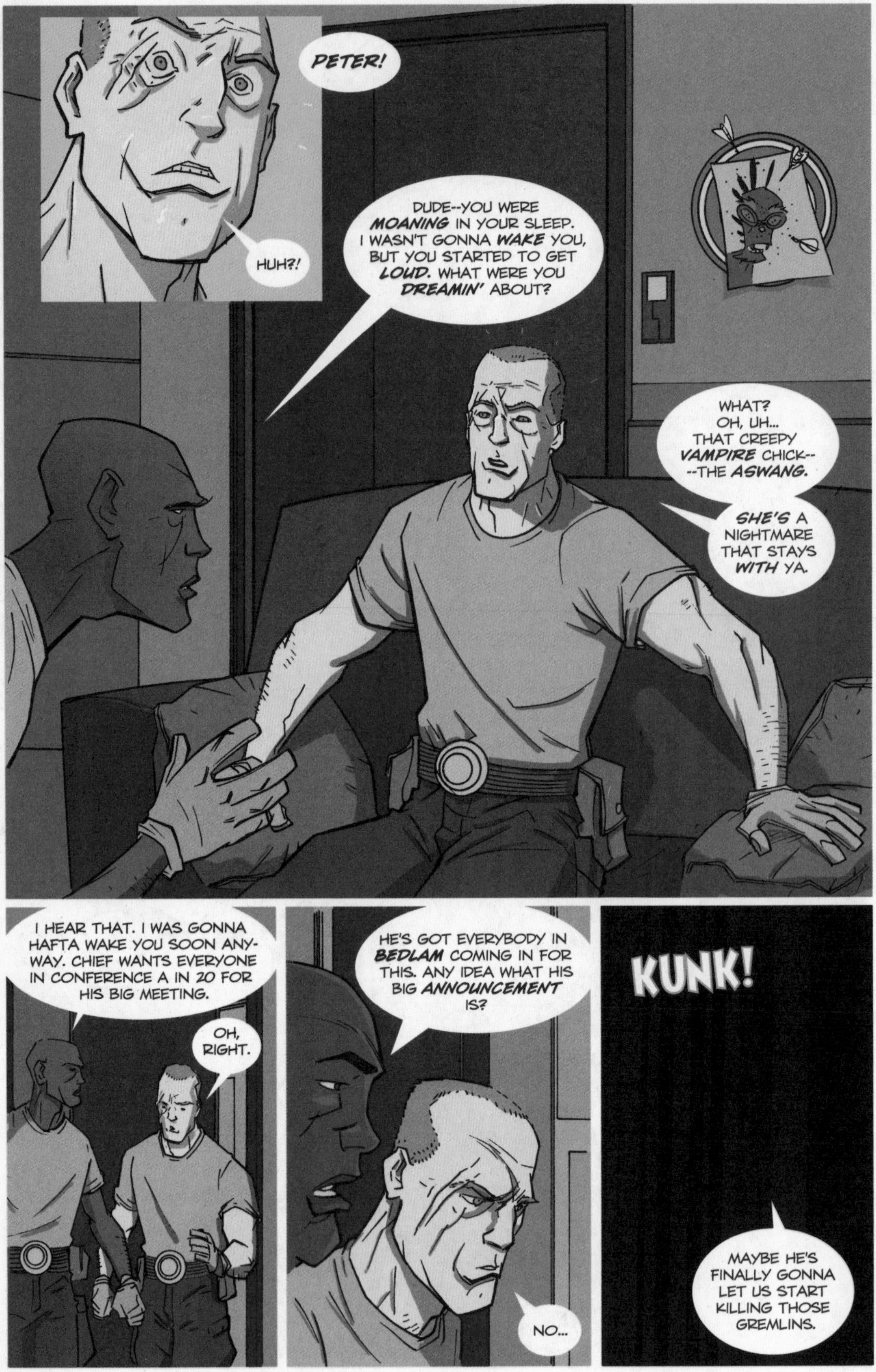
PETER!
HUH?!
DUDE--YOU WERE MOANING IN YOUR SLEEP. I WASN'T GONNA WAKE YOU, BUT YOU STARTED TO GET LOUD. WHAT WERE YOU DREAMIN' ABOUT?
WHAT? OH, UH... THAT CREEPY VAMPIRE CHICK-- --THE ASWANG.
SHE'S A NIGHTMARE THAT STAYS WITH YA.
I HEAR THAT. I WAS GONNA HAFTA WAKE YOU SOON ANY-WAY. CHIEF WANTS EVERYONE IN CONFERENCE A IN 20 FOR HIS BIG MEETING.
OH, RIGHT.
HE'S GOT EVERYBODY IN BEDLAM COMING IN FOR THIS. ANY IDEA WHAT HIS BIG ANNOUNCEMENT IS?
NO...
KUNK!
MAYBE HE'S FINALLY GONNA LET US START KILLING THOSE GREMLINS.

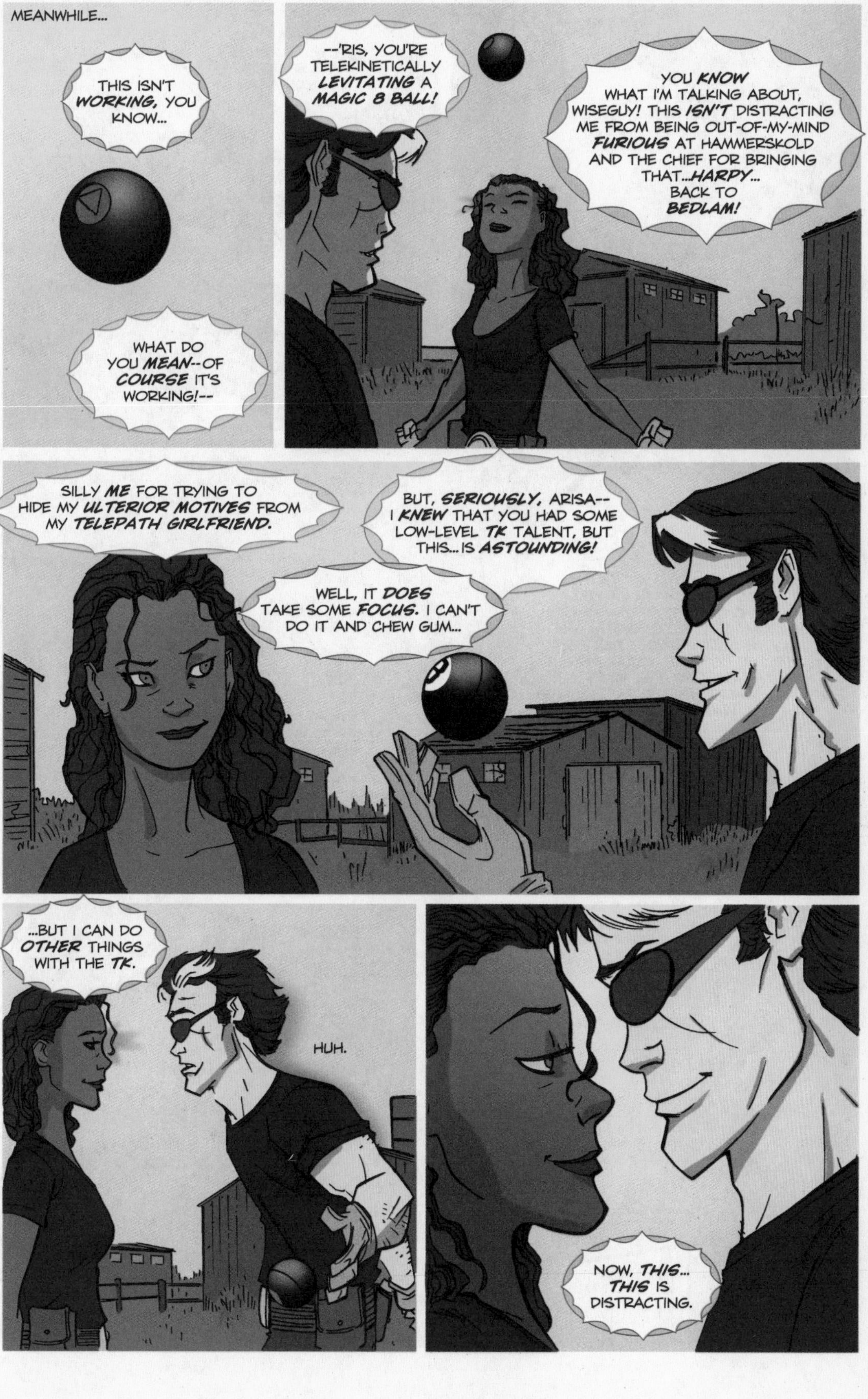
MEANWHILE...
THIS ISN'T WORKING, YOU KNOW...
WHAT DO YOU MEAN--OF COURSE IT'S WORKING!--
--'RIS, YOU'RE TELEKINETICALLY LEVITATING A MAGIC 8 BALL!
YOU KNOW WHAT I'M TALKING ABOUT, WISEGUY! THIS ISN'T DISTRACTING ME FROM BEING OUT-OF-MY-MIND FURIOUS AT HAMMERSKOLD AND THE CHIEF FOR BRINGING THAT...HARPY... BACK TO BEDLAM!
SILLY ME FOR TRYING TO HIDE MY ULTERIOR MOTIVES FROM MY TELEPATH GIRLFRIEND.
BUT, SERIOUSLY, ARISA-- I KNEW THAT YOU HAD SOME LOW-LEVEL TK TALENT, BUT THIS... IS ASTOUNDING!
WELL, IT DOES TAKE SOME FOCUS. I CAN'T DO IT AND CHEW GUM...
...BUT I CAN DO OTHER THINGS WITH THE TK.
HUH.
NOW, THIS... THIS IS DISTRACTING.

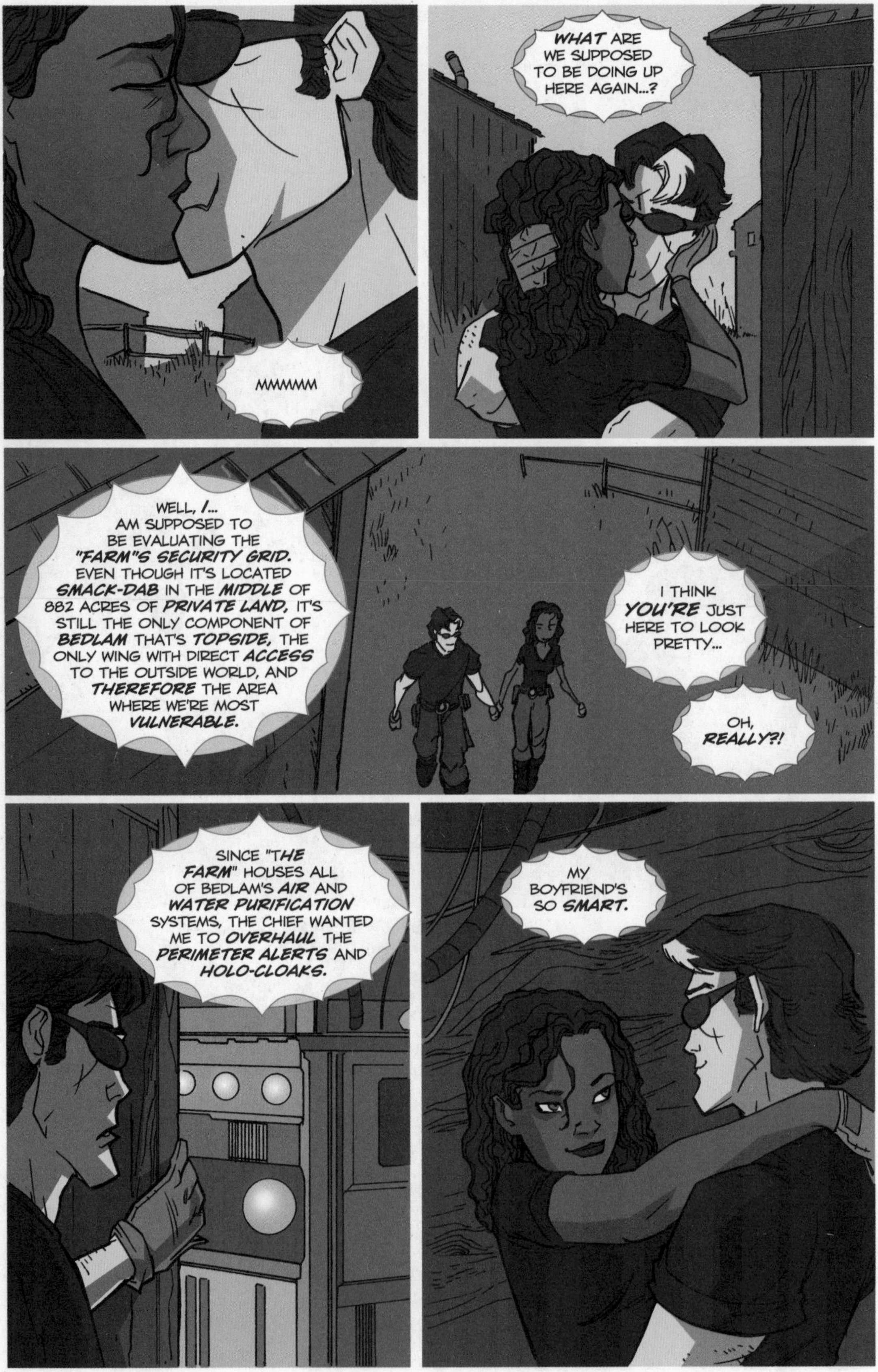
MMMMMM
WHAT ARE WE SUPPOSED TO BE DOING UP HERE AGAIN...?
WELL, I... AM SUPPOSED TO BE EVALUATING THE "FARM"'S SECURITY GRID. EVEN THOUGH IT'S LOCATED SMACK-DAB IN THE MIDDLE OF 882 ACRES OF PRIVATE LAND, IT'S STILL THE ONLY COMPONENT OF BEDLAM THAT'S TOPSIDE, THE ONLY WING WITH DIRECT ACCESS TO THE OUTSIDE WORLD, AND THEREFORE THE AREA WHERE WE'RE MOST VULNERABLE.
I THINK YOU'RE JUST HERE TO LOOK PRETTY...
OH, REALLY?!
SINCE "THE FARM" HOUSES ALL OF BEDLAM'S AIR AND WATER PURIFICATION SYSTEMS, THE CHIEF WANTED ME TO OVERHAUL THE PERIMETER ALERTS AND HOLO-CLOAKS.
MY BOYFRIEND'S SO SMART.

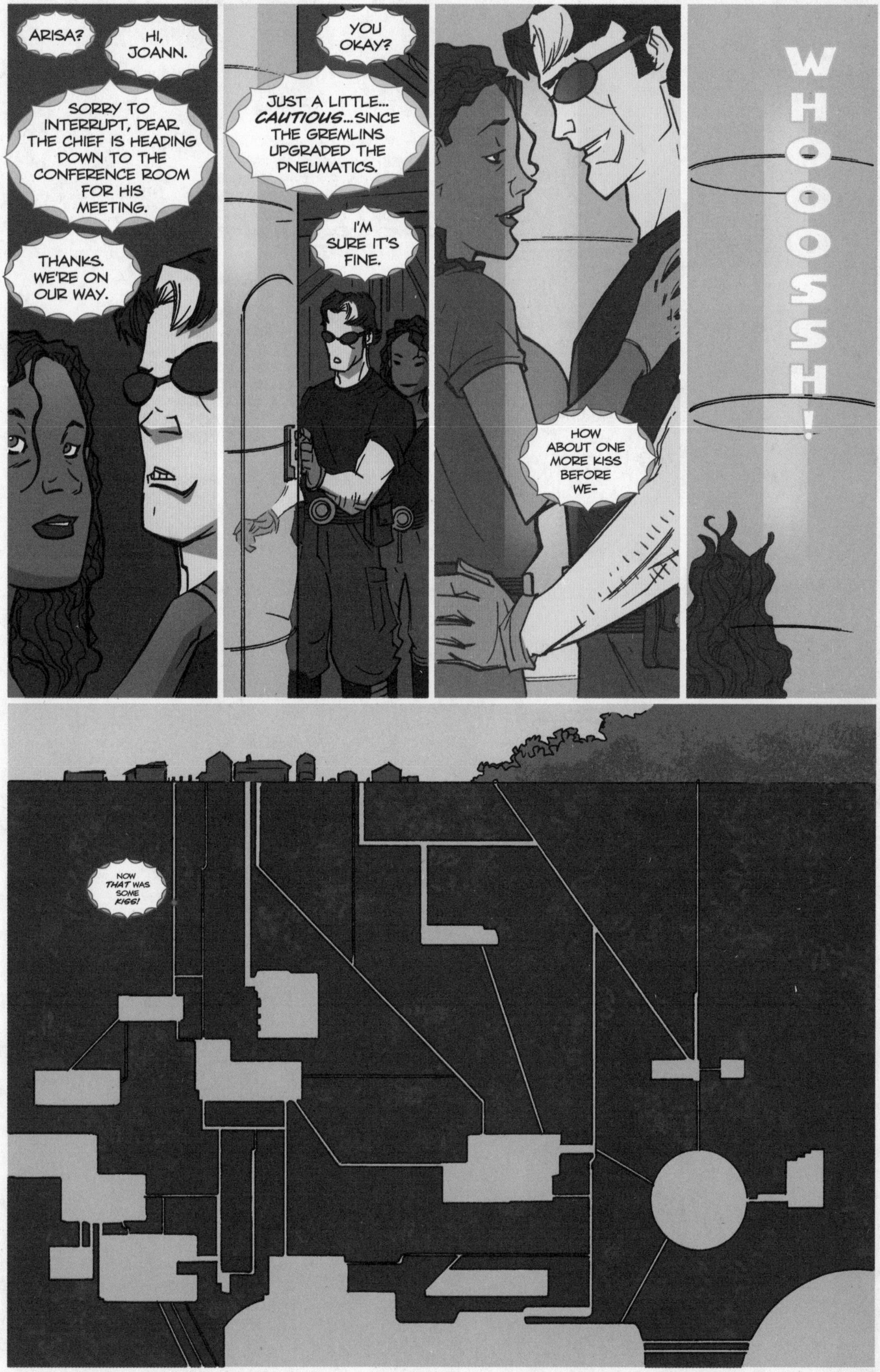
ARISA?
HI, JOANN.
SORRY TO INTERRUPT, DEAR. THE CHIEF IS HEADING DOWN TO THE CONFERENCE ROOM FOR HIS MEETING.
THANKS. WE'RE ON OUR WAY.
YOU OKAY?
JUST A LITTLE... *CAUTIOUS*...SINCE THE GREMLINS UPGRADED THE PNEUMATICS.
I'M SURE IT'S FINE.
HOW ABOUT ONE MORE KISS BEFORE WE-
WHOOOSSH!
NOW *THAT* WAS SOME *KISS!*

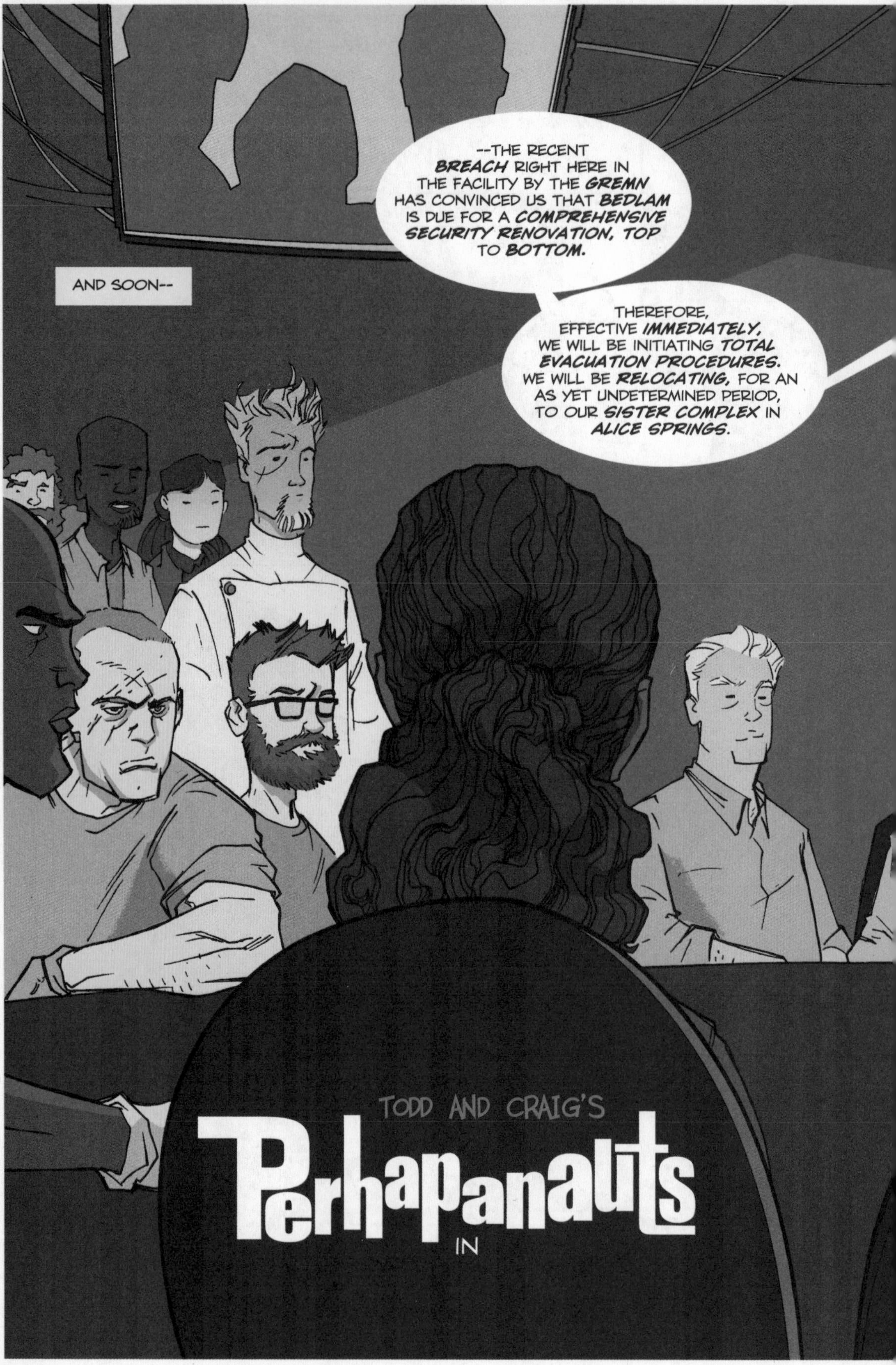
--THE RECENT BREACH RIGHT HERE IN THE FACILITY BY THE GREMN HAS CONVINCED US THAT BEDLAM IS DUE FOR A COMPREHENSIVE SECURITY RENOVATION, TOP TO BOTTOM.
AND SOON--
THEREFORE, EFFECTIVE IMMEDIATELY, WE WILL BE INITIATING TOTAL EVACUATION PROCEDURES. WE WILL BE RELOCATING, FOR AN AS YET UNDETERMINED PERIOD, TO OUR SISTER COMPLEX IN ALICE SPRINGS.
TODD AND CRAIG'S
Perhapanauts
IN

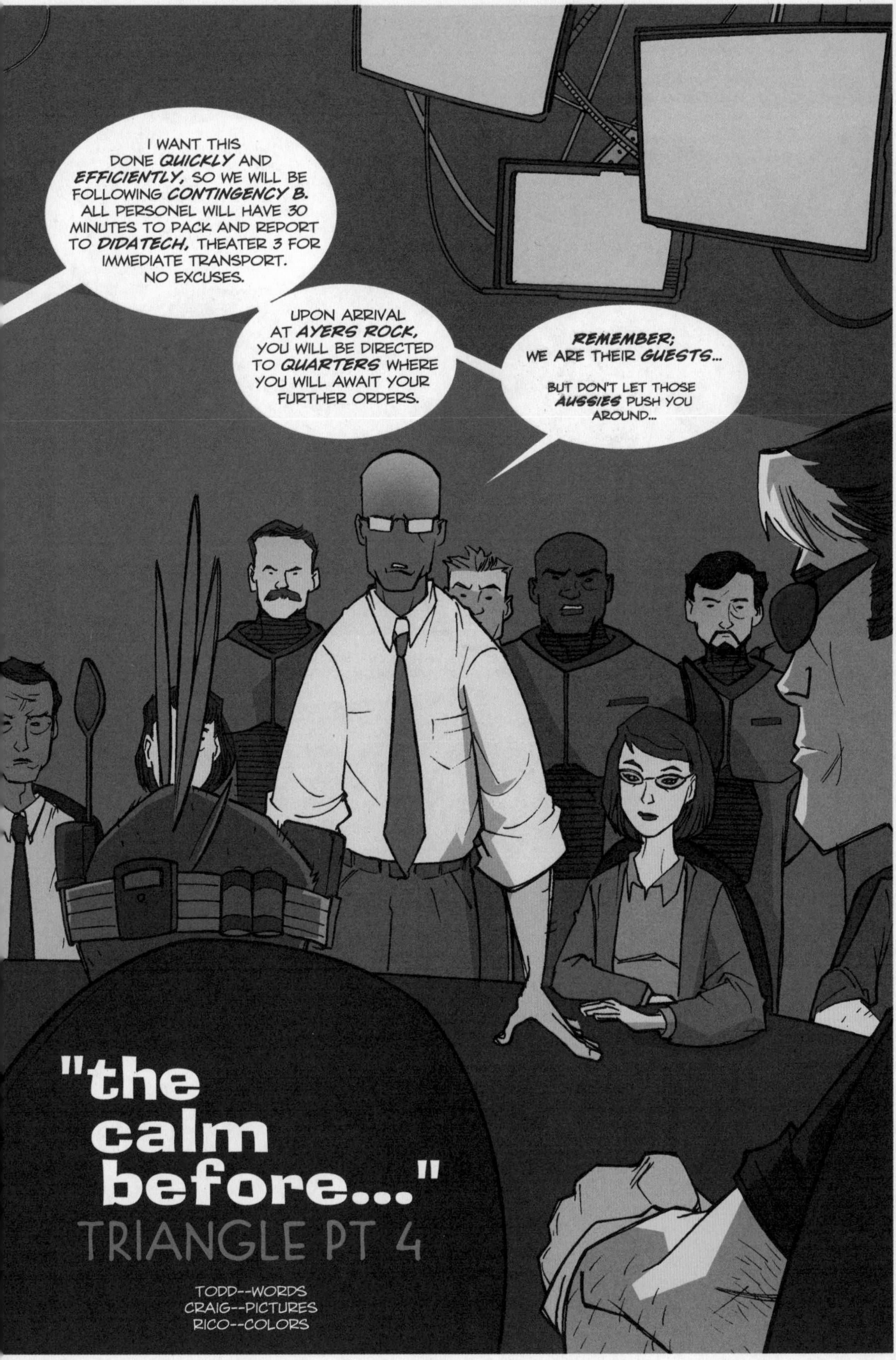
I WANT THIS DONE QUICKLY AND EFFICIENTLY, SO WE WILL BE FOLLOWING CONTINGENCY B. ALL PERSONEL WILL HAVE 30 MINUTES TO PACK AND REPORT TO DIDATECH, THEATER 3 FOR IMMEDIATE TRANSPORT. NO EXCUSES.
UPON ARRIVAL AT AYERS ROCK, YOU WILL BE DIRECTED TO QUARTERS WHERE YOU WILL AWAIT YOUR FURTHER ORDERS.
REMEMBER; WE ARE THEIR GUESTS...
BUT DON'T LET THOSE AUSSIES PUSH YOU AROUND...
"the calm before..."
TRIANGLE PT 4
TODD--WORDS
CRAIG--PICTURES
RICO--COLORS

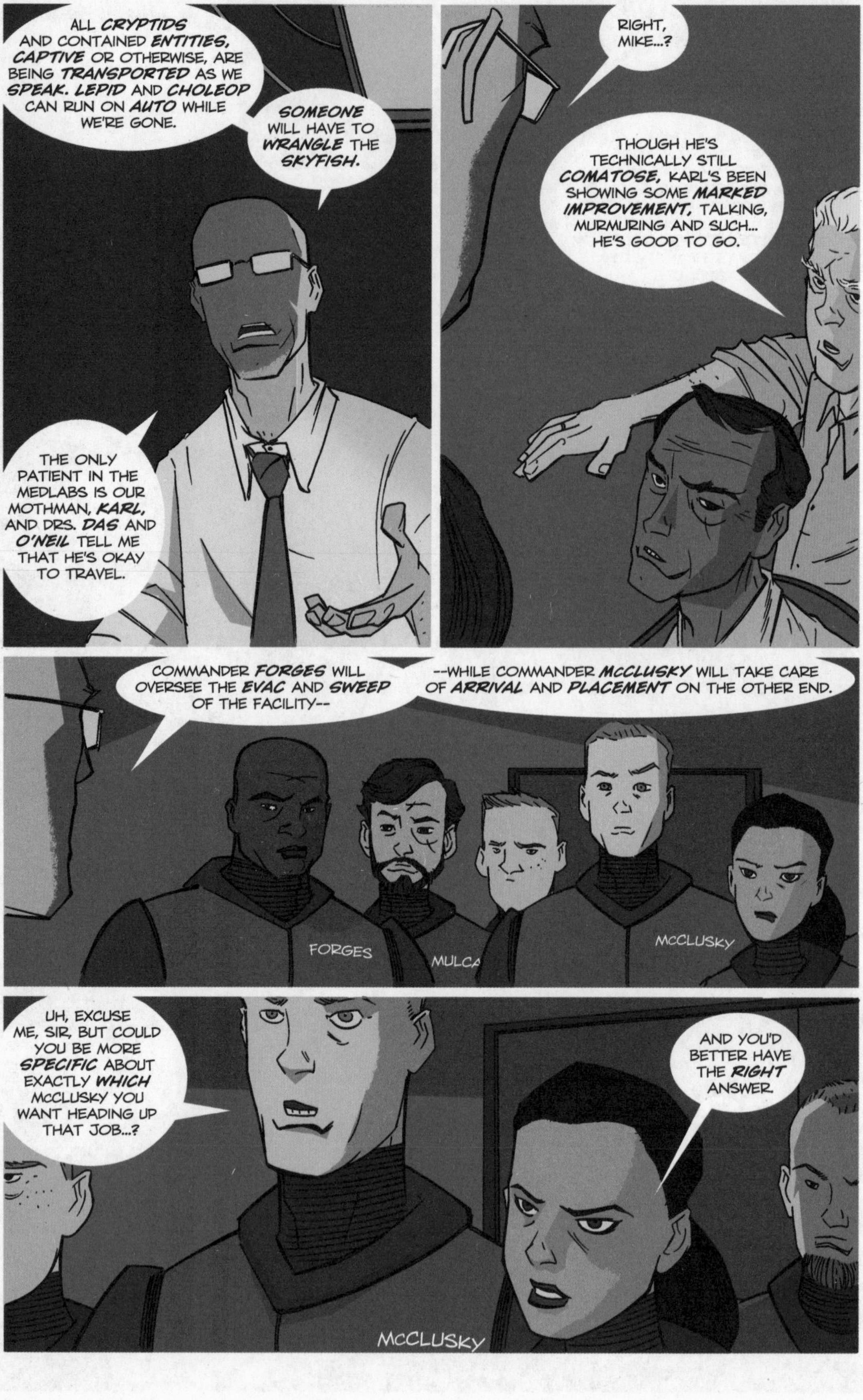
ALL CRYPTIDS AND CONTAINED ENTITIES, CAPTIVE OR OTHERWISE, ARE BEING TRANSPORTED AS WE SPEAK. LEPID AND CHOLEOP CAN RUN ON AUTO WHILE WE'RE GONE.
SOMEONE WILL HAVE TO WRANGLE THE SKYFISH.
THE ONLY PATIENT IN THE MEDLABS IS OUR MOTHMAN, KARL, AND DRS. DAS AND O'NEIL TELL ME THAT HE'S OKAY TO TRAVEL.
RIGHT, MIKE...?
THOUGH HE'S TECHNICALLY STILL COMATOSE, KARL'S BEEN SHOWING SOME MARKED IMPROVEMENT, TALKING, MURMURING AND SUCH... HE'S GOOD TO GO.
COMMANDER FORGES WILL OVERSEE THE EVAC AND SWEEP OF THE FACILITY--
--WHILE COMMANDER McCLUSKY WILL TAKE CARE OF ARRIVAL AND PLACEMENT ON THE OTHER END.
FORGES
MULCA
McCLUSKY
UH, EXCUSE ME, SIR, BUT COULD YOU BE MORE SPECIFIC ABOUT EXACTLY WHICH McCLUSKY YOU WANT HEADING UP THAT JOB...?
AND YOU'D BETTER HAVE THE RIGHT ANSWER.
McCLUSKY

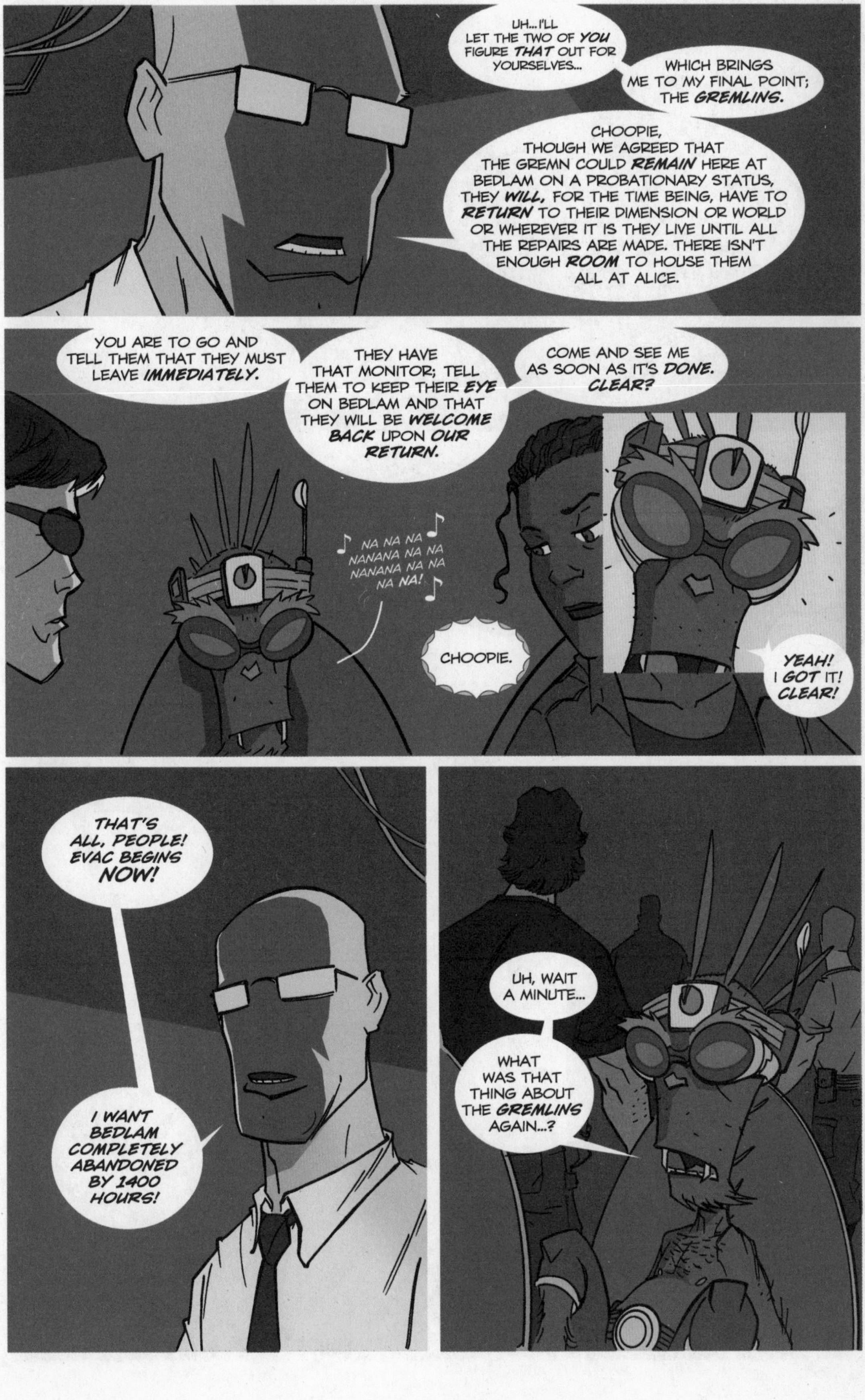

UH... I'LL LET THE TWO OF *YOU* FIGURE *THAT* OUT FOR YOURSELVES...
WHICH BRINGS ME TO MY FINAL POINT; THE *GREMLINS.*
CHOOPIE, THOUGH WE AGREED THAT THE GREMN COULD *REMAIN* HERE AT BEDLAM ON A PROBATIONARY STATUS, THEY *WILL,* FOR THE TIME BEING, HAVE TO *RETURN* TO THEIR DIMENSION OR WORLD OR WHEREVER IT IS THEY LIVE UNTIL ALL THE REPAIRS ARE MADE. THERE ISN'T ENOUGH *ROOM* TO HOUSE THEM ALL AT ALICE.
YOU ARE TO GO AND TELL THEM THAT THEY MUST LEAVE *IMMEDIATELY.*
THEY HAVE THAT MONITOR; TELL THEM TO KEEP THEIR *EYE* ON BEDLAM AND THAT THEY WILL BE *WELCOME BACK* UPON *OUR RETURN.*
COME AND SEE ME AS SOON AS IT'S *DONE. CLEAR?*
♪ NA NA NA ♪ NANANA NA NA NANANA NA NA NA *NA!* ♪
CHOOPIE.
YEAH! I *GOT* IT! *CLEAR!*
THAT'S ALL, PEOPLE! EVAC BEGINS NOW!
I WANT BEDLAM COMPLETELY ABANDONED BY 1400 HOURS!
UH, WAIT A MINUTE...
WHAT WAS THAT THING ABOUT THE *GREMLINS* AGAIN...?

SOMEWHERE IN IRELAND...

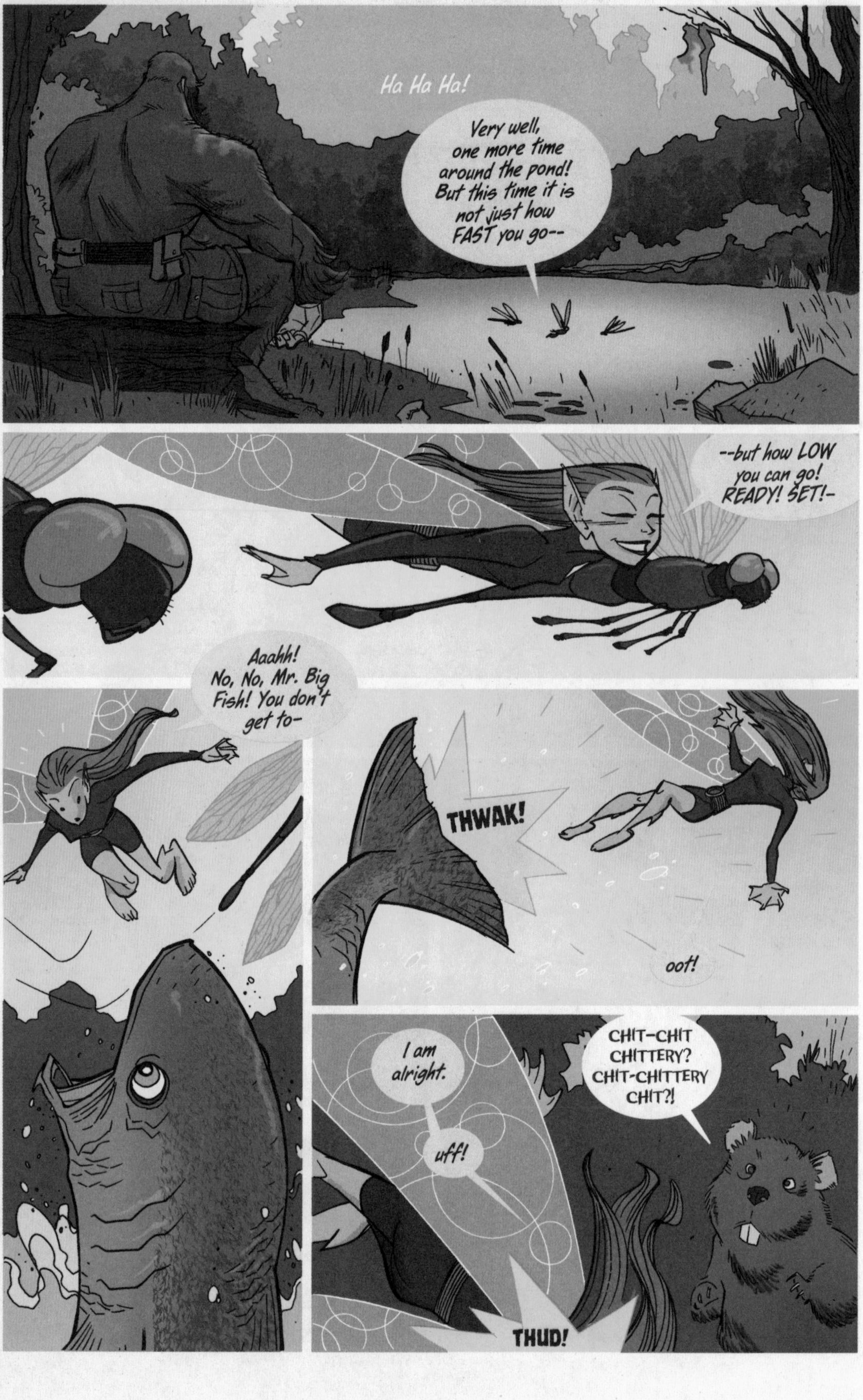
Ha Ha Ha!
Very well, one more time around the pond! But this time it is not just how FAST you go--
--but how LOW you can go! READY! SET!-
Aaahh! No, No, Mr. Big Fish! You don't get to-
THWAK!
oof!
I am alright.
uff!
CHIT-CHIT CHITTERY? CHIT-CHITTERY CHIT?!
THUD!

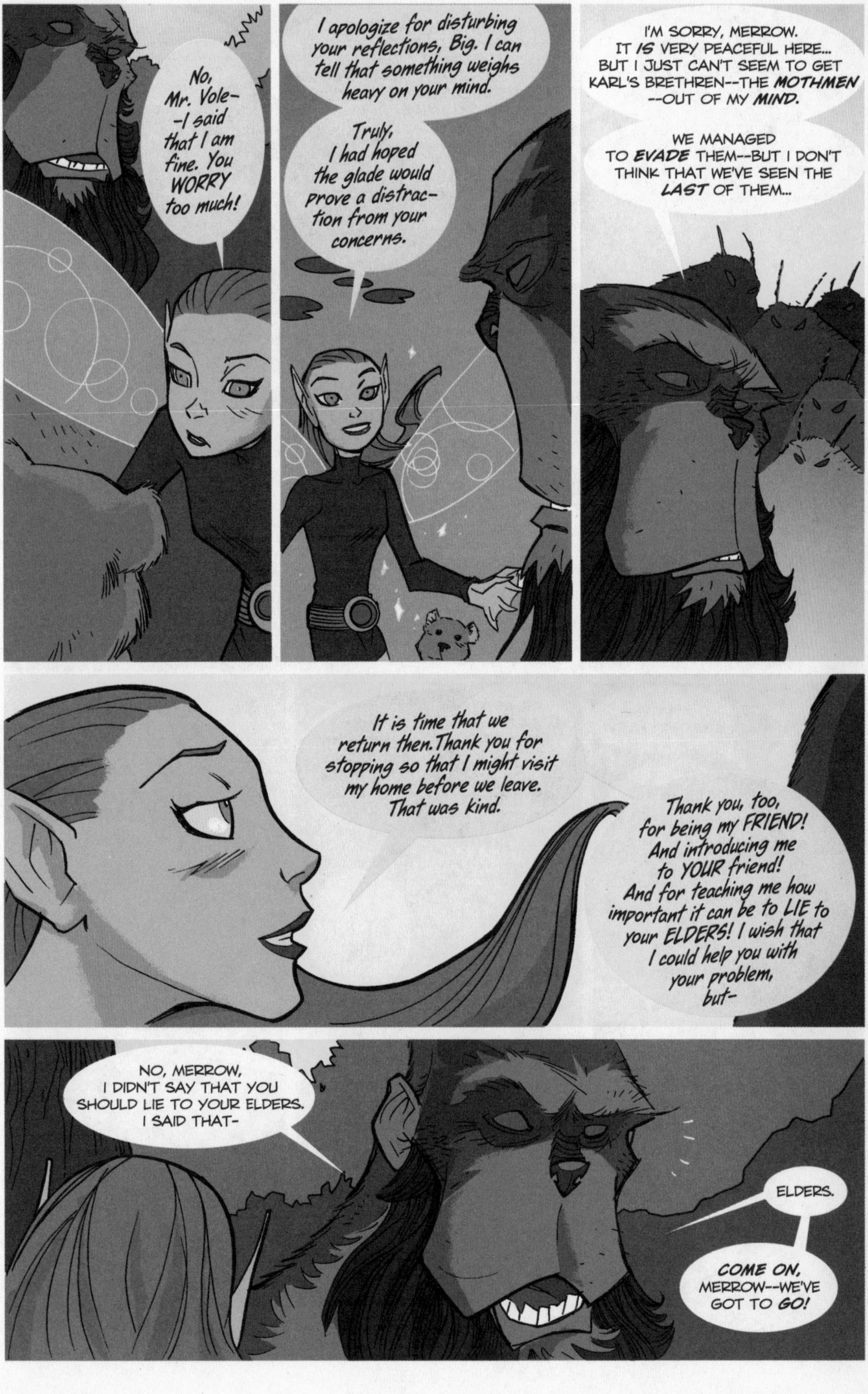
No, Mr. Vole--I said that I am fine. You WORRY too much!
I apologize for disturbing your reflections, Big. I can tell that something weighs heavy on your mind.
Truly, I had hoped the glade would prove a distraction from your concerns.
I'M SORRY, MERROW. IT IS VERY PEACEFUL HERE... BUT I JUST CAN'T SEEM TO GET KARL'S BRETHREN--THE MOTHMEN --OUT OF MY MIND.
WE MANAGED TO EVADE THEM--BUT I DON'T THINK THAT WE'VE SEEN THE LAST OF THEM...
It is time that we return then. Thank you for stopping so that I might visit my home before we leave. That was kind.
Thank you, too, for being my FRIEND! And introducing me to YOUR friend! And for teaching me how important it can be to LIE to your ELDERS! I wish that I could help you with your problem, but-
NO, MERROW, I DIDN'T SAY THAT YOU SHOULD LIE TO YOUR ELDERS. I SAID THAT-
ELDERS.
COME ON, MERROW--WE'VE GOT TO GO!

20 MINUTES LATER--

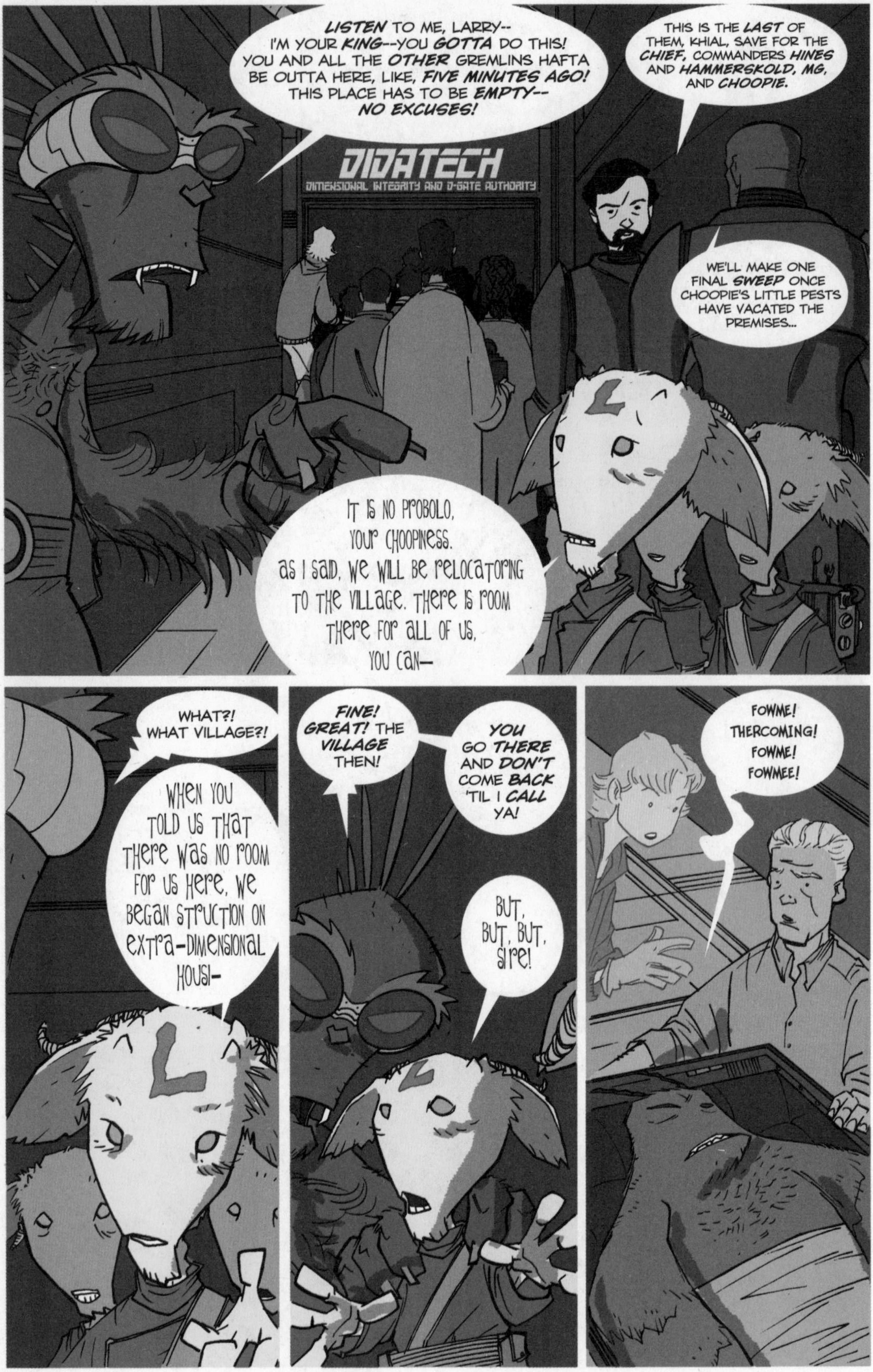
LISTEN TO ME, LARRY-- I'M YOUR KING--YOU GOTTA DO THIS! YOU AND ALL THE OTHER GREMLINS HAFTA BE OUTTA HERE, LIKE, FIVE MINUTES AGO! THIS PLACE HAS TO BE EMPTY-- NO EXCUSES!
THIS IS THE LAST OF THEM, KHIAL, SAVE FOR THE CHIEF, COMMANDERS HINES AND HAMMERSKOLD, MG, AND CHOOPIE.
DIDATECH
DIMENSIONAL INTEGRITY AND D-GATE AUTHORITY
WE'LL MAKE ONE FINAL SWEEP ONCE CHOOPIE'S LITTLE PESTS HAVE VACATED THE PREMISES...
IT IS NO PROBOLO, YOUR CHOOPINESS. AS I SAID, WE WILL BE RELOCATORING TO THE VILLAGE. THERE IS ROOM THERE FOR ALL OF US, YOU CAN—
WHAT?! WHAT VILLAGE?!
WHEN YOU TOLD US THAT THERE WAS NO ROOM FOR US HERE, WE BEGAN STRUCTION ON EXTRA-DIMENSIONAL HOUSI-
FINE! GREAT! THE VILLAGE THEN!
YOU GO THERE AND DON'T COME BACK 'TIL I CALL YA!
BUT, BUT, BUT, SIRE!
FOWME! THERCOMING! FOWME! FOWMEE!

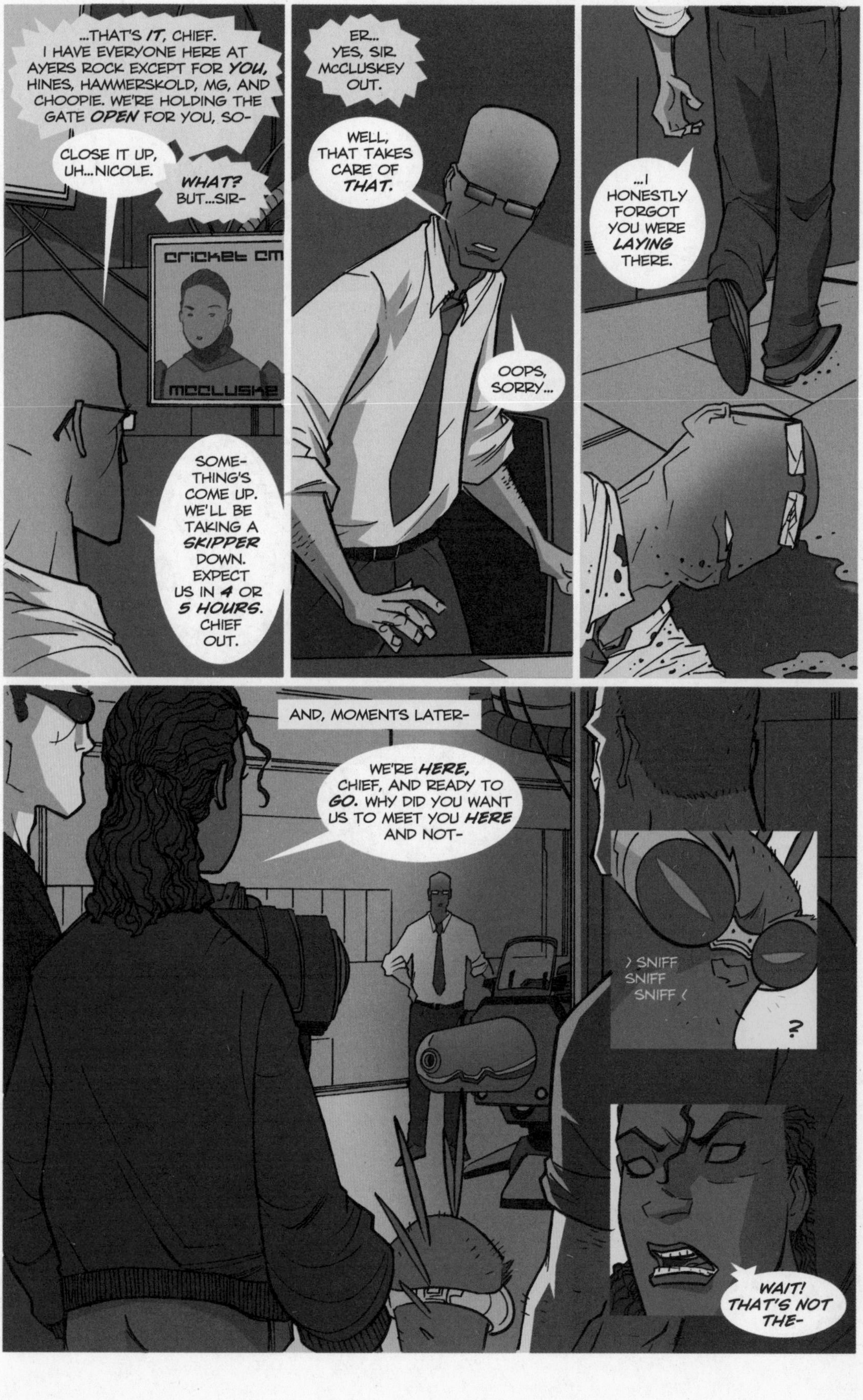
...THAT'S IT, CHIEF. I HAVE EVERYONE HERE AT AYERS ROCK EXCEPT FOR YOU, HINES, HAMMERSKOLD, MG, AND CHOOPIE. WE'RE HOLDING THE GATE OPEN FOR YOU, SO-
CLOSE IT UP, UH...NICOLE.
WHAT? BUT...SIR-
CRICKET CM
MCCLUSKE
SOME-THING'S COME UP. WE'LL BE TAKING A SKIPPER DOWN. EXPECT US IN 4 OR 5 HOURS. CHIEF OUT.
ER... YES, SIR. McCLUSKEY OUT.
WELL, THAT TAKES CARE OF THAT.
OOPS, SORRY...
...I HONESTLY FORGOT YOU WERE LAYING THERE.
AND, MOMENTS LATER-
WE'RE HERE, CHIEF, AND READY TO GO. WHY DID YOU WANT US TO MEET YOU HERE AND NOT-
› SNIFF SNIFF SNIFF ‹
?
WAIT! THAT'S NOT THE-

BLORT! BLORT! BLORT!

IMPRESSIVE, WITCH! YOU FOUND ME OUT *FAR* QUICKER THAN I'D *ANTICIPATED!* NO MATTER THOUGH!

AREN'T *GREMLIN-MADE* WEAPONS THE *BEST?!*

WHAT- WHO THE-?

OOPS! MISSED ONE!

NO PROBLEM. I'LL JUST-

AAAAH AAAAHH AAAAAHHH! YOU B-

SECURITY BREACH RIMETER AIRSPACE INCOMING ENTIFIED ALERT

THIS... BRAIN. C-CAN'T PRO...PROTECT IT...IN...THIS... FORM...

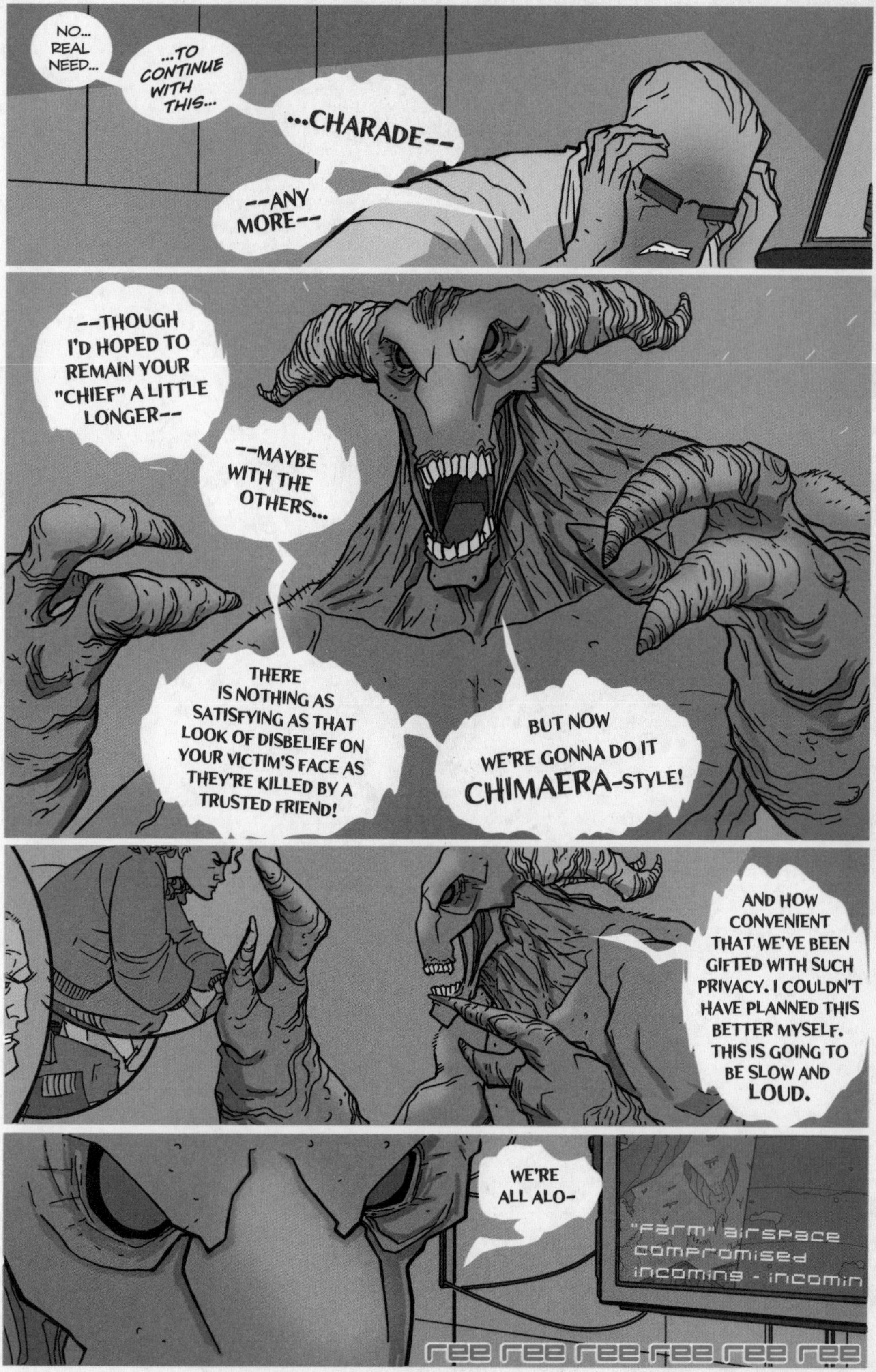
NO... REAL NEED...
...TO CONTINUE WITH THIS...
...CHARADE--
--ANY MORE--
--THOUGH I'D HOPED TO REMAIN YOUR "CHIEF" A LITTLE LONGER--
--MAYBE WITH THE OTHERS...
THERE IS NOTHING AS SATISFYING AS THAT LOOK OF DISBELIEF ON YOUR VICTIM'S FACE AS THEY'RE KILLED BY A TRUSTED FRIEND!
BUT NOW WE'RE GONNA DO IT CHIMAERA-STYLE!
AND HOW CONVENIENT THAT WE'VE BEEN GIFTED WITH SUCH PRIVACY. I COULDN'T HAVE PLANNED THIS BETTER MYSELF. THIS IS GOING TO BE SLOW AND LOUD.
WE'RE ALL ALO-
"farm" airspace
compromised
incoming - incomin
ree ree ree ree ree ree

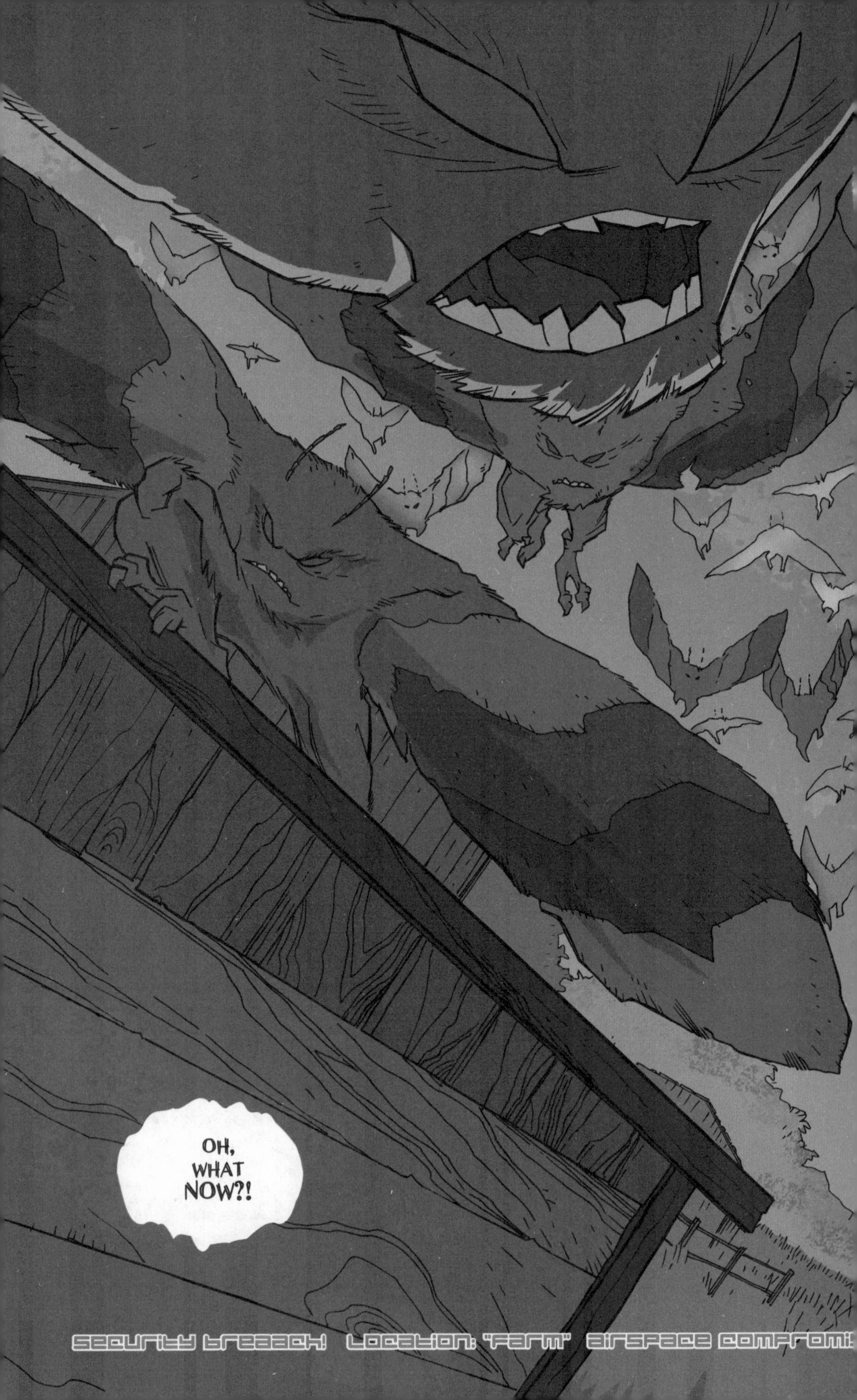
OH, WHAT NOW?!
security breaach! location: "farm" airspace compromi:

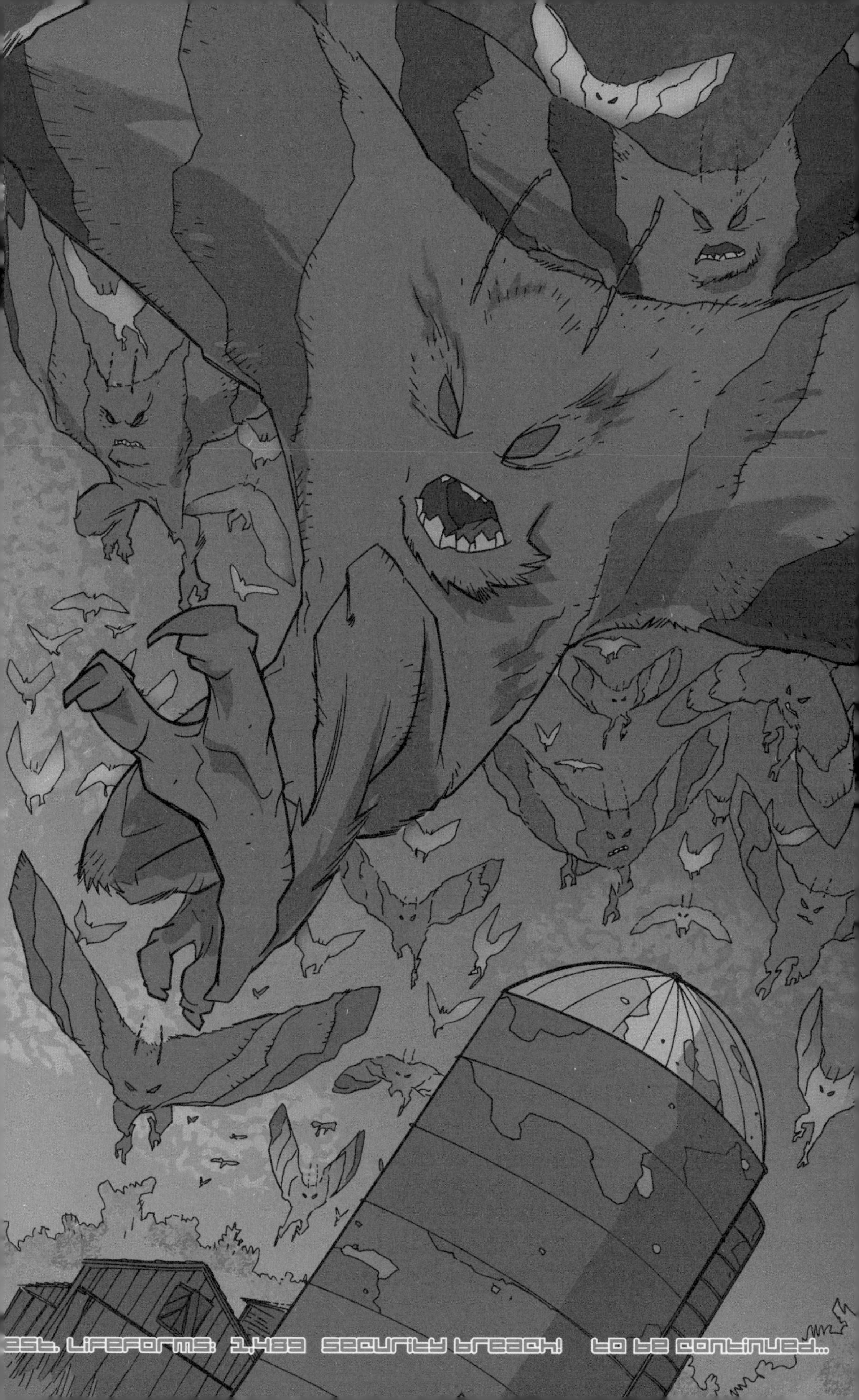
est. lifeforms: 1,489
security breach!
to be continued...

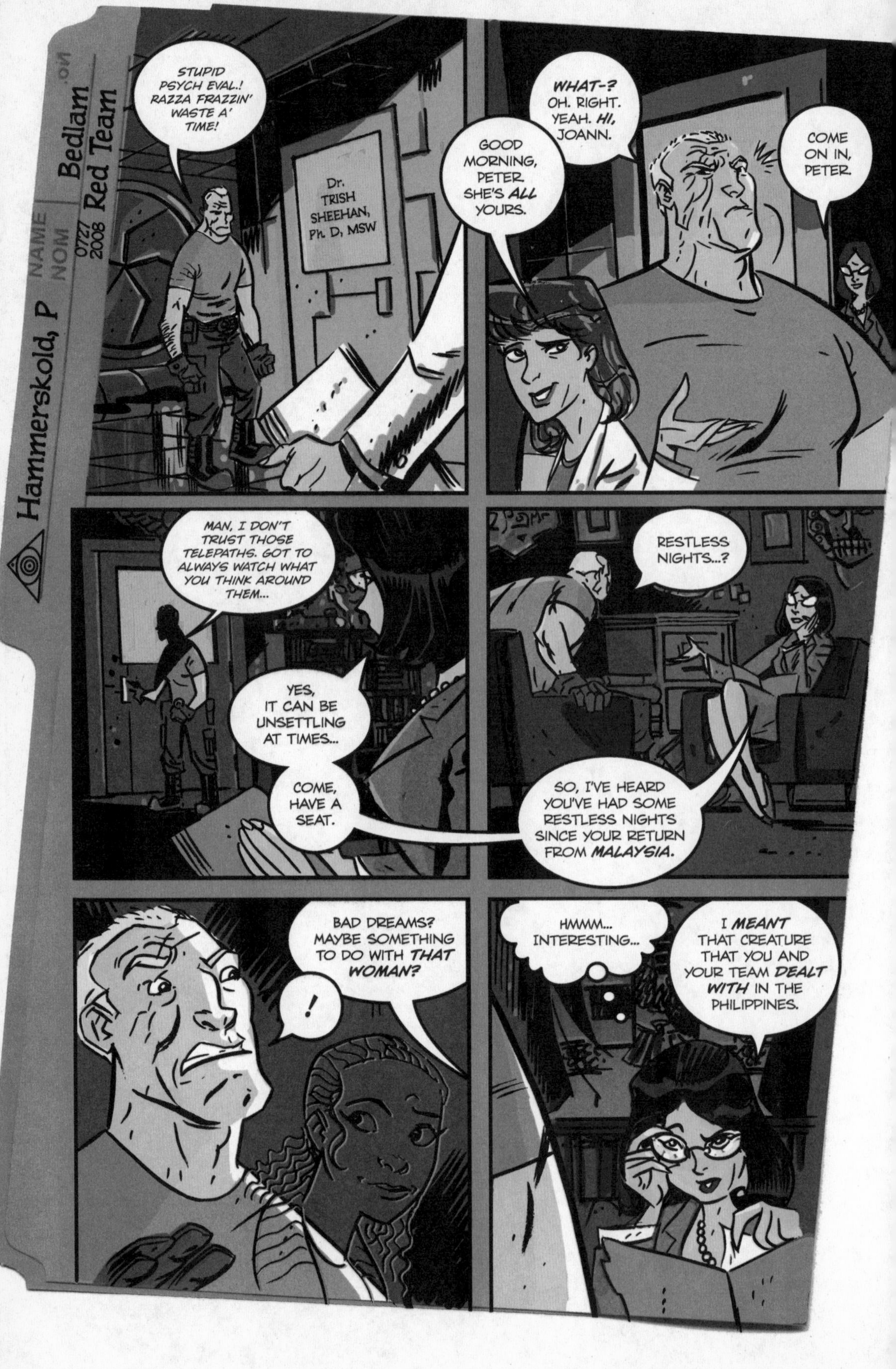
Hammerskold, P
NAME NOM
0727 2008
Bedlam
Red Team
STUPID PSYCH EVAL.! RAZZA FRAZZIN' WASTE A' TIME!
Dr. TRISH SHEEHAN, Ph. D, MSW
GOOD MORNING, PETER SHE'S ALL YOURS.
WHAT-? OH. RIGHT. YEAH. HI, JOANN.
COME ON IN, PETER.
MAN, I DON'T TRUST THOSE TELEPATHS. GOT TO ALWAYS WATCH WHAT YOU THINK AROUND THEM...
YES, IT CAN BE UNSETTLING AT TIMES...
COME, HAVE A SEAT.
RESTLESS NIGHTS...?
SO, I'VE HEARD YOU'VE HAD SOME RESTLESS NIGHTS SINCE YOUR RETURN FROM MALAYSIA.
BAD DREAMS? MAYBE SOMETHING TO DO WITH THAT WOMAN?
!
HMMM... INTERESTING...
I MEANT THAT CREATURE THAT YOU AND YOUR TEAM DEALT WITH IN THE PHILIPPINES.

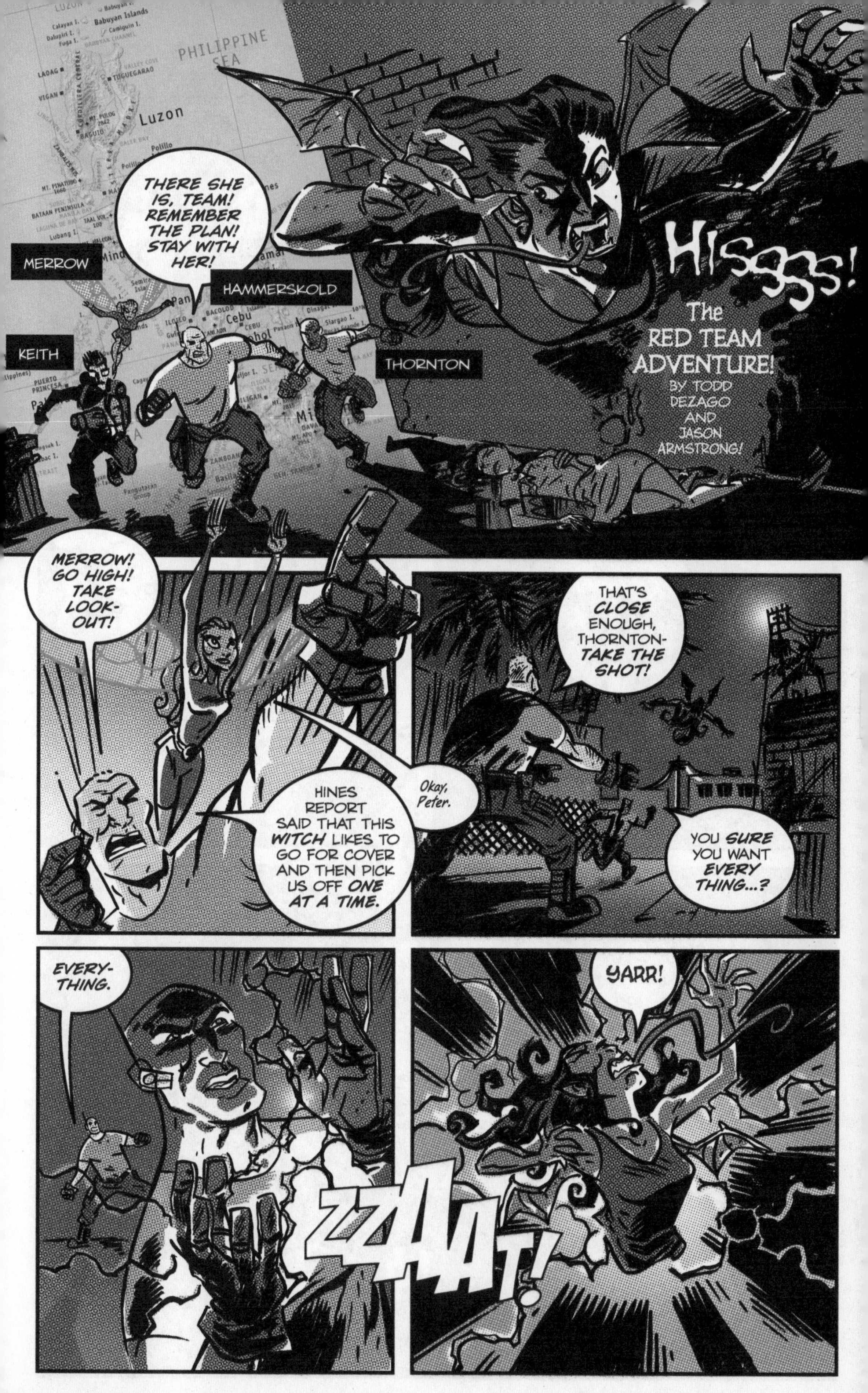
THERE SHE IS, TEAM! REMEMBER THE PLAN! STAY WITH HER!
MERROW
HAMMERSKOLD
KEITH
THORNTON
HISSSS!
The RED TEAM ADVENTURE!
BY TODD DEZAGO AND JASON ARMSTRONG!
MERROW! GO HIGH! TAKE LOOK-OUT!
HINES REPORT SAID THAT THIS WITCH LIKES TO GO FOR COVER AND THEN PICK US OFF ONE AT A TIME.
Okay, Peter.
THAT'S CLOSE ENOUGH, THORNTON- TAKE THE SHOT!
YOU SURE YOU WANT EVERY THING...?
EVERY-THING.
YARR!
ZZAAAT!

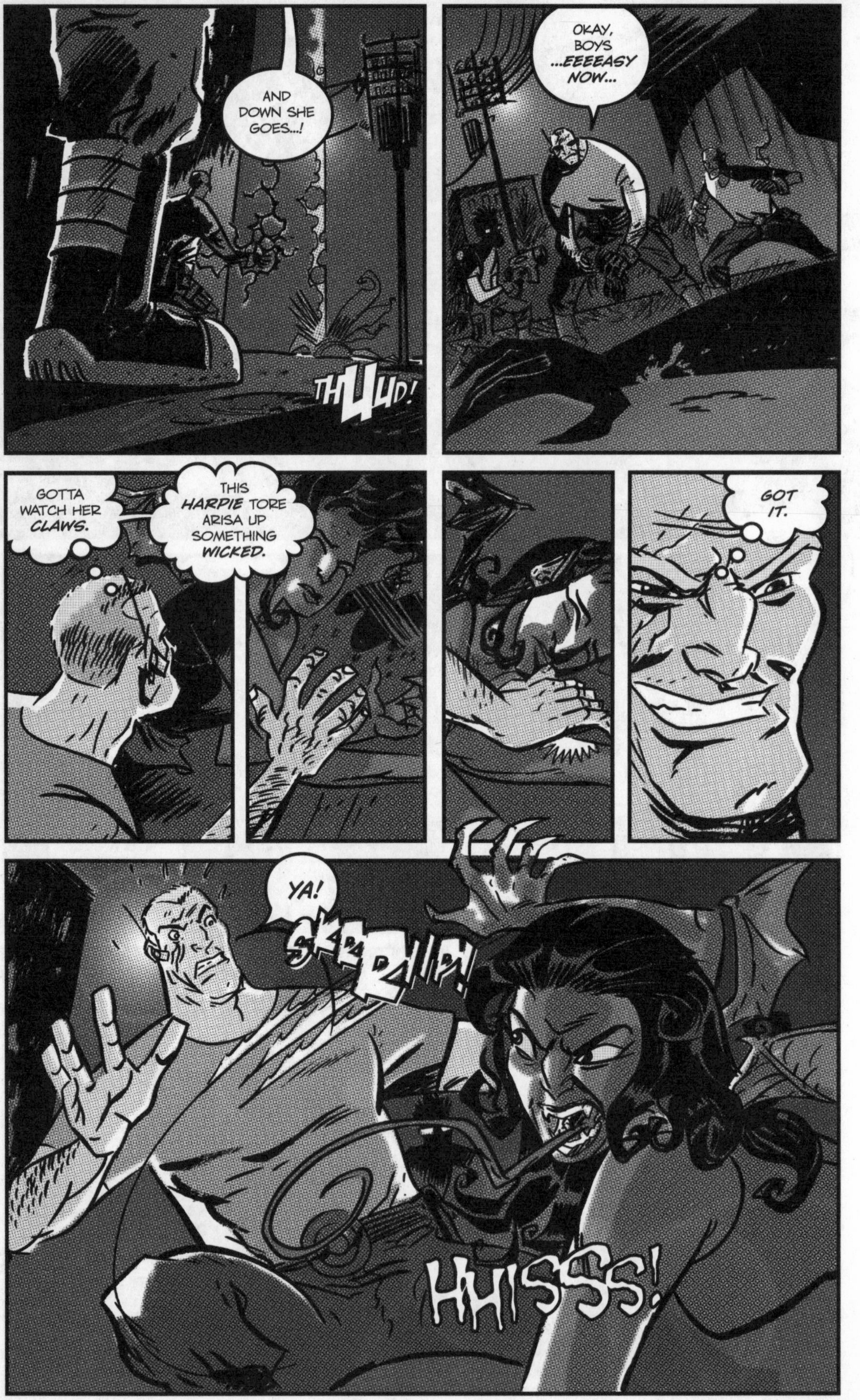
AND DOWN SHE GOES...!
THHUUD!
OKAY, BOYS ...EEEEASY NOW...
GOTTA WATCH HER CLAWS.
THIS HARPIE TORE ARISA UP SOMETHING WICKED.
GOT IT.
YA!
SKRAARIIP!
HHISSS!

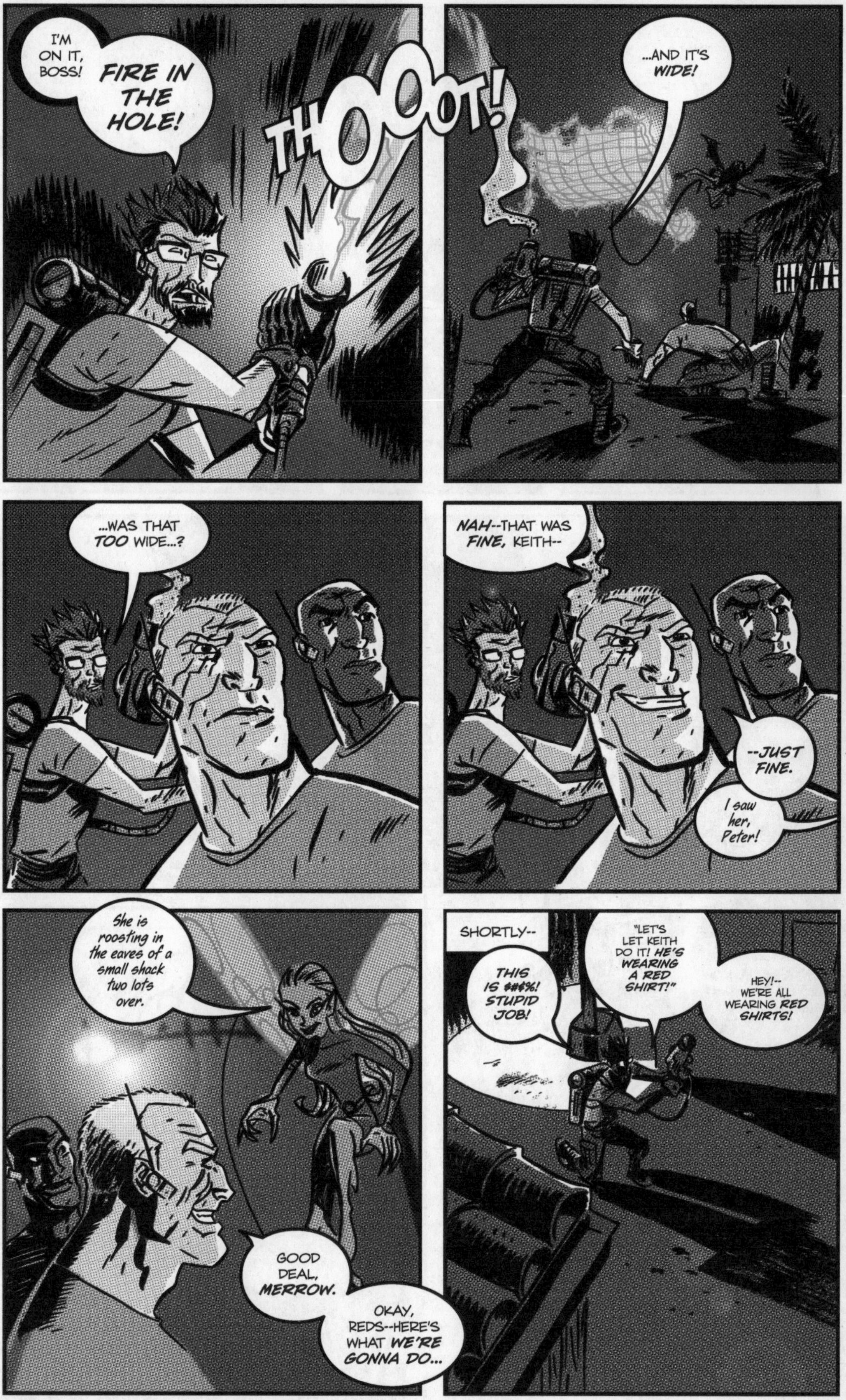
I'M ON IT, BOSS!
FIRE IN THE HOLE!
THOOOT!
...AND IT'S WIDE!
...WAS THAT TOO WIDE...?
NAH--THAT WAS FINE, KEITH--
--JUST FINE.
I saw her, Peter!
She is roosting in the eaves of a small shack two lots over.
GOOD DEAL, MERROW.
OKAY, REDS--HERE'S WHAT WE'RE GONNA DO...
SHORTLY--
THIS IS $#$%! STUPID JOB!
"LET'S LET KEITH DO IT! HE'S WEARING A RED SHIRT!"
HEY!--WE'RE ALL WEARING RED SHIRTS!

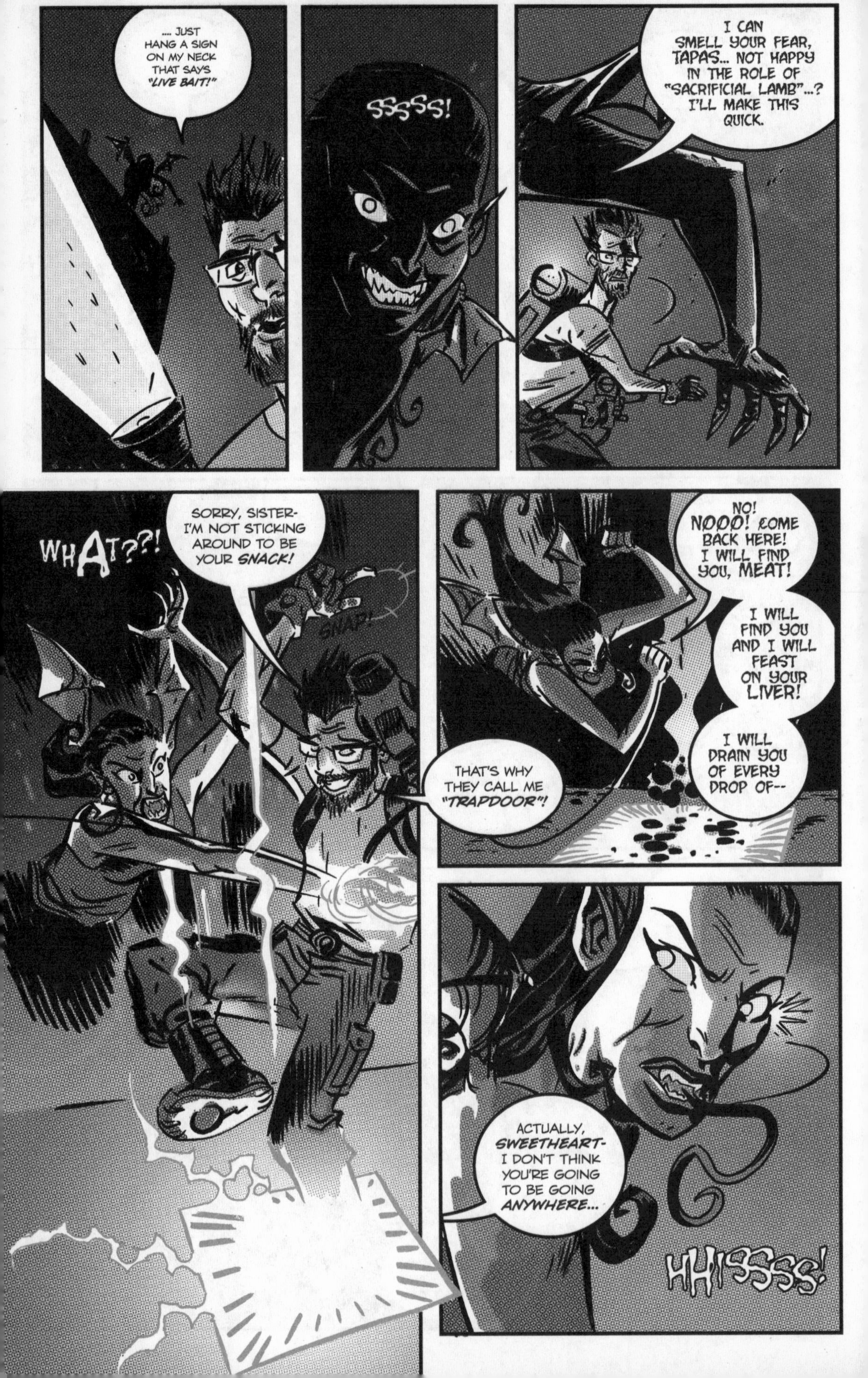
... JUST HANG A SIGN ON MY NECK THAT SAYS "LIVE BAIT!"
SSSSS!
I CAN SMELL YOUR FEAR, TAPAS... NOT HAPPY IN THE ROLE OF "SACRIFICIAL LAMB"...? I'LL MAKE THIS QUICK.
WHAT??!
SORRY, SISTER- I'M NOT STICKING AROUND TO BE YOUR SNACK!
SNAP!
THAT'S WHY THEY CALL ME "TRAPDOOR"!
NO! NOOO! COME BACK HERE! I WILL FIND YOU, MEAT!
I WILL FIND YOU AND I WILL FEAST ON YOUR LIVER!
I WILL DRAIN YOU OF EVERY DROP OF--
ACTUALLY, SWEETHEART- I DON'T THINK YOU'RE GOING TO BE GOING ANYWHERE...
HHISSSS!

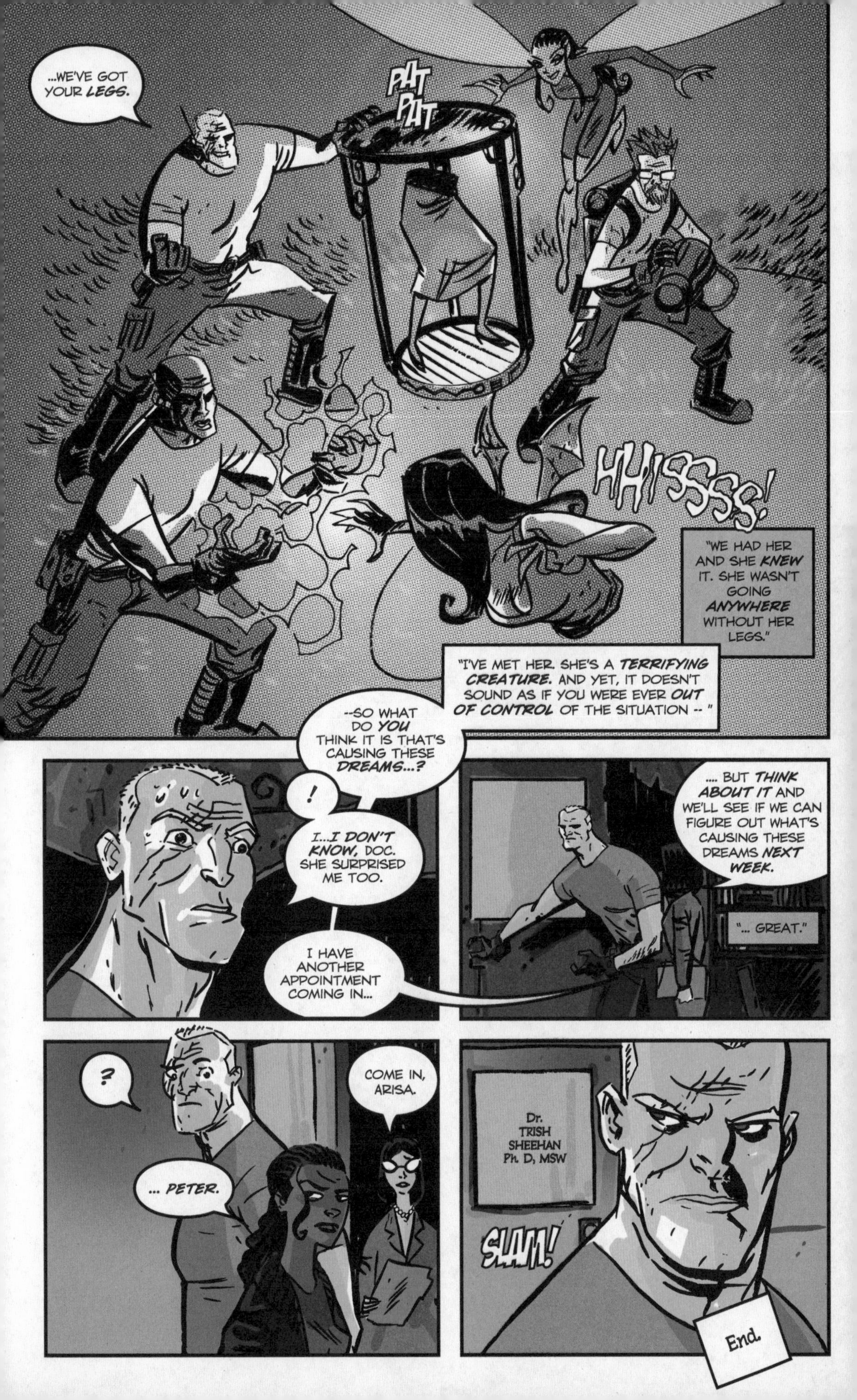
...WE'VE GOT YOUR LEGS.
PHT PHT
HHISSSS!
"WE HAD HER AND SHE KNEW IT. SHE WASN'T GOING ANYWHERE WITHOUT HER LEGS."
"I'VE MET HER. SHE'S A TERRIFYING CREATURE. AND YET, IT DOESN'T SOUND AS IF YOU WERE EVER OUT OF CONTROL OF THE SITUATION -- "
--SO WHAT DO YOU THINK IT IS THAT'S CAUSING THESE DREAMS...?
!
I...I DON'T KNOW, DOC. SHE SURPRISED ME TOO.
I HAVE ANOTHER APPOINTMENT COMING IN...
.... BUT THINK ABOUT IT AND WE'LL SEE IF WE CAN FIGURE OUT WHAT'S CAUSING THESE DREAMS NEXT WEEK.
"... GREAT."
?
COME IN, ARISA.
... PETER.
Dr. TRISH SHEEHAN Ph. D, MSW
SLAM!
End.

perhapanauts 5

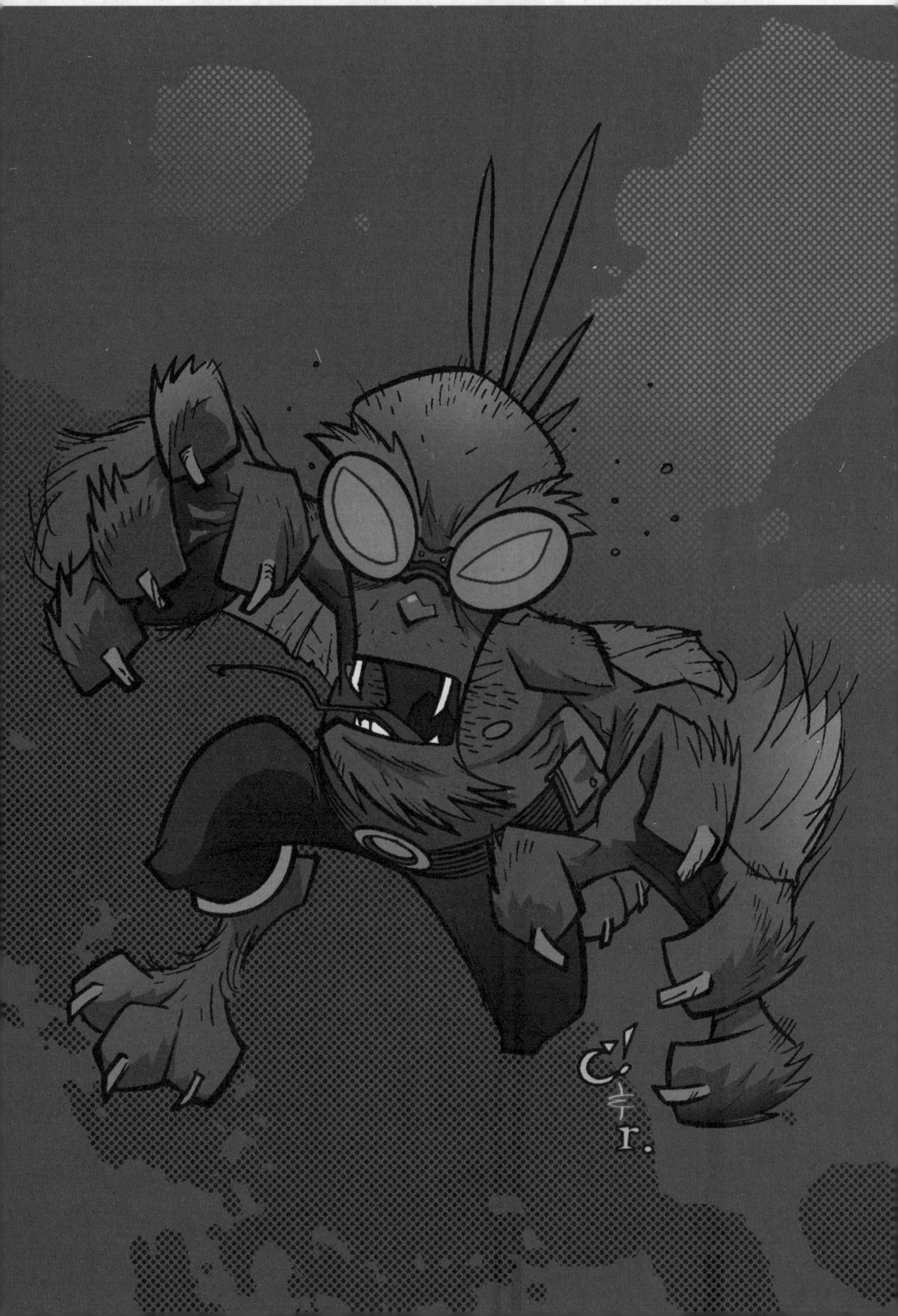

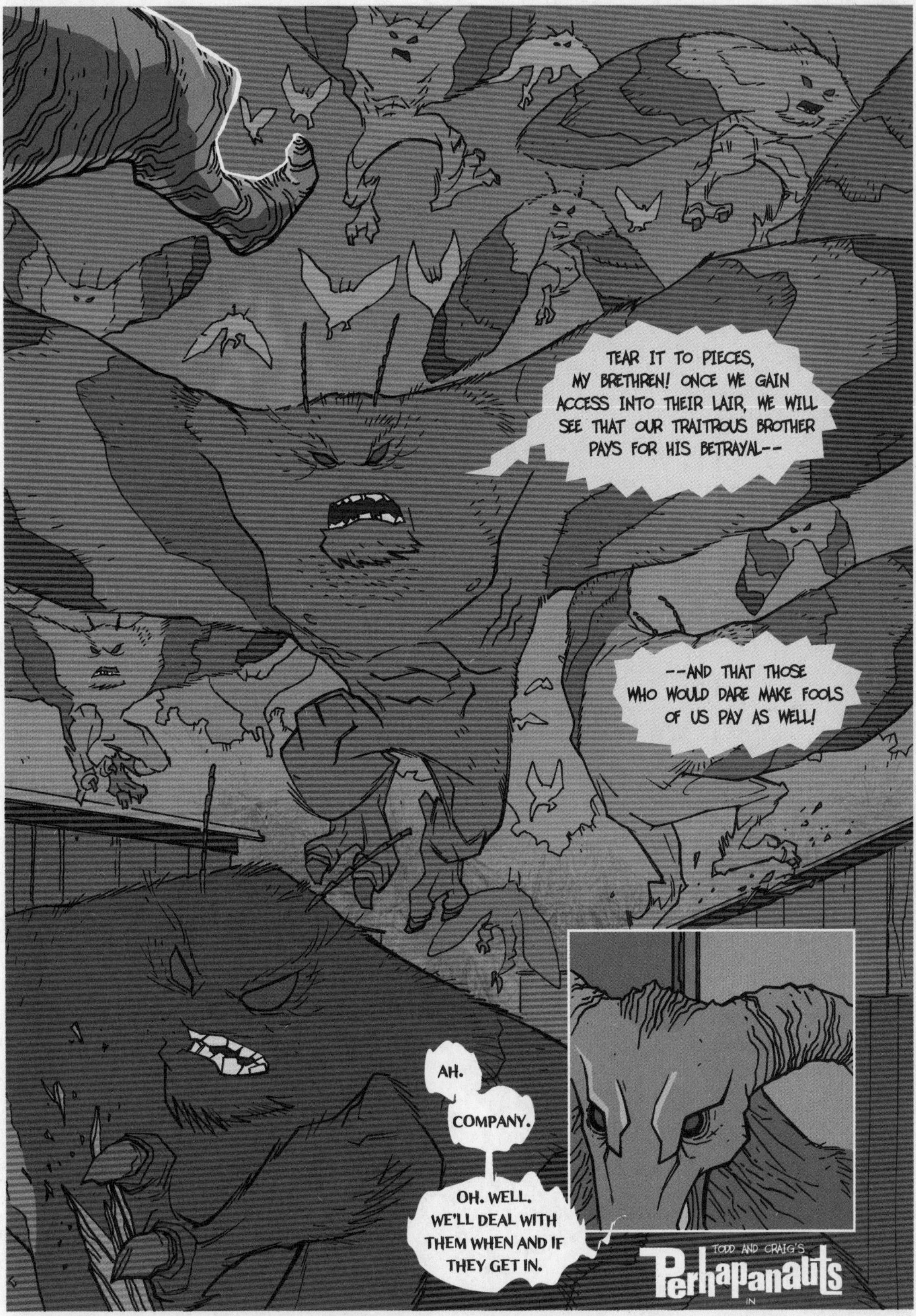
TEAR IT TO PIECES, MY BRETHREN! ONCE WE GAIN ACCESS INTO THEIR LAIR, WE WILL SEE THAT OUR TRAITROUS BROTHER PAYS FOR HIS BETRAYAL--
--AND THAT THOSE WHO WOULD DARE MAKE FOOLS OF US PAY AS WELL!
AH.
COMPANY.
OH. WELL. WE'LL DEAL WITH THEM WHEN AND IF THEY GET IN.
TODD AND CRAIG'S
Perhapanauts
IN

"DIVIDED WE FALL"

TRIANGLE PART 5

TODD--WORDS CRAIG--PICTURES RICO--COLORS

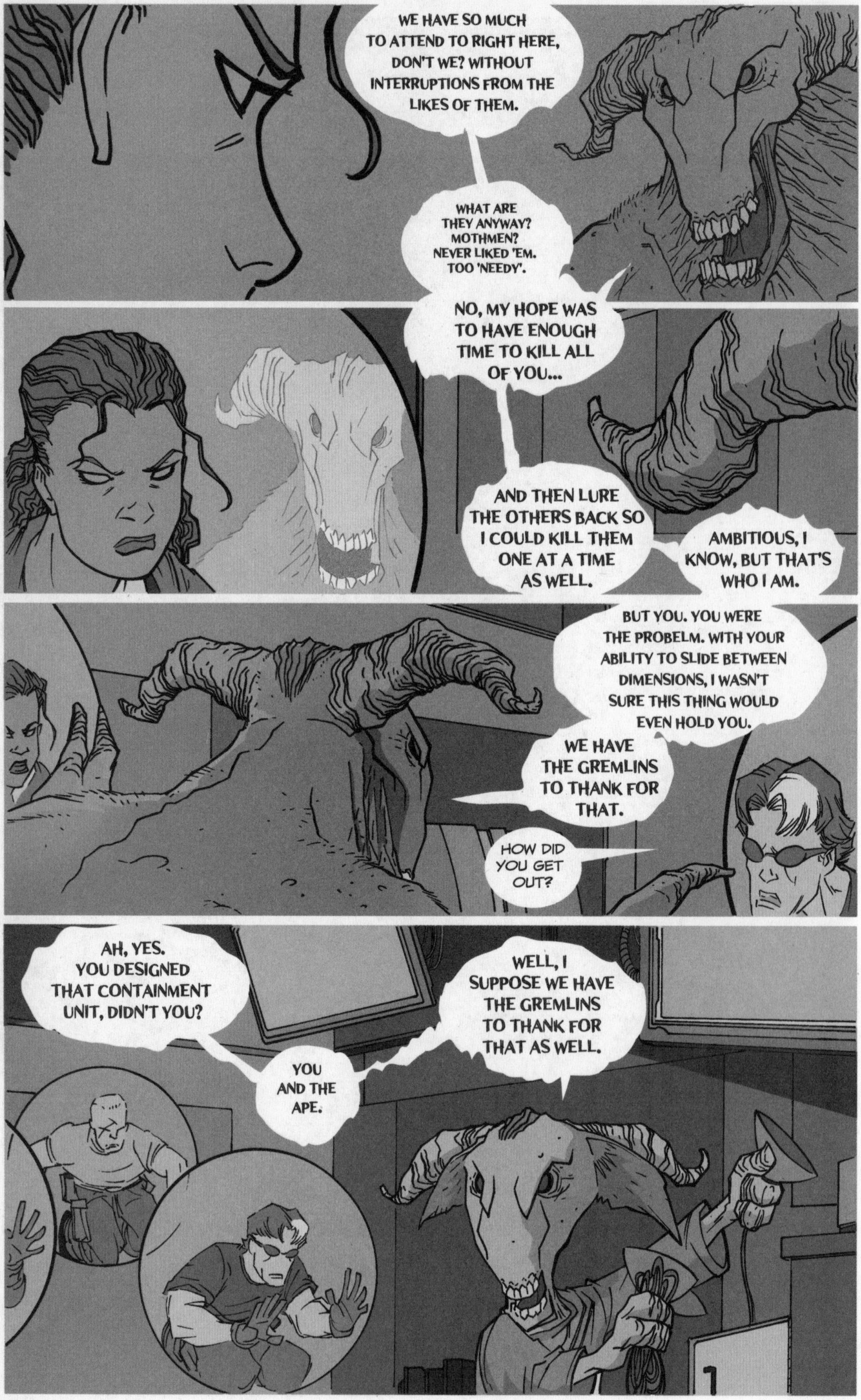
WE HAVE SO MUCH TO ATTEND TO RIGHT HERE, DON'T WE? WITHOUT INTERRUPTIONS FROM THE LIKES OF THEM.
WHAT ARE THEY ANYWAY? MOTHMEN? NEVER LIKED 'EM. TOO 'NEEDY'.
NO, MY HOPE WAS TO HAVE ENOUGH TIME TO KILL ALL OF YOU...
AND THEN LURE THE OTHERS BACK SO I COULD KILL THEM ONE AT A TIME AS WELL.
AMBITIOUS, I KNOW, BUT THAT'S WHO I AM.
BUT YOU. YOU WERE THE PROBELM. WITH YOUR ABILITY TO SLIDE BETWEEN DIMENSIONS, I WASN'T SURE THIS THING WOULD EVEN HOLD YOU.
WE HAVE THE GREMLINS TO THANK FOR THAT.
HOW DID YOU GET OUT?
AH, YES. YOU DESIGNED THAT CONTAINMENT UNIT, DIDN'T YOU?
YOU AND THE APE.
WELL, I SUPPOSE WE HAVE THE GREMLINS TO THANK FOR THAT AS WELL.

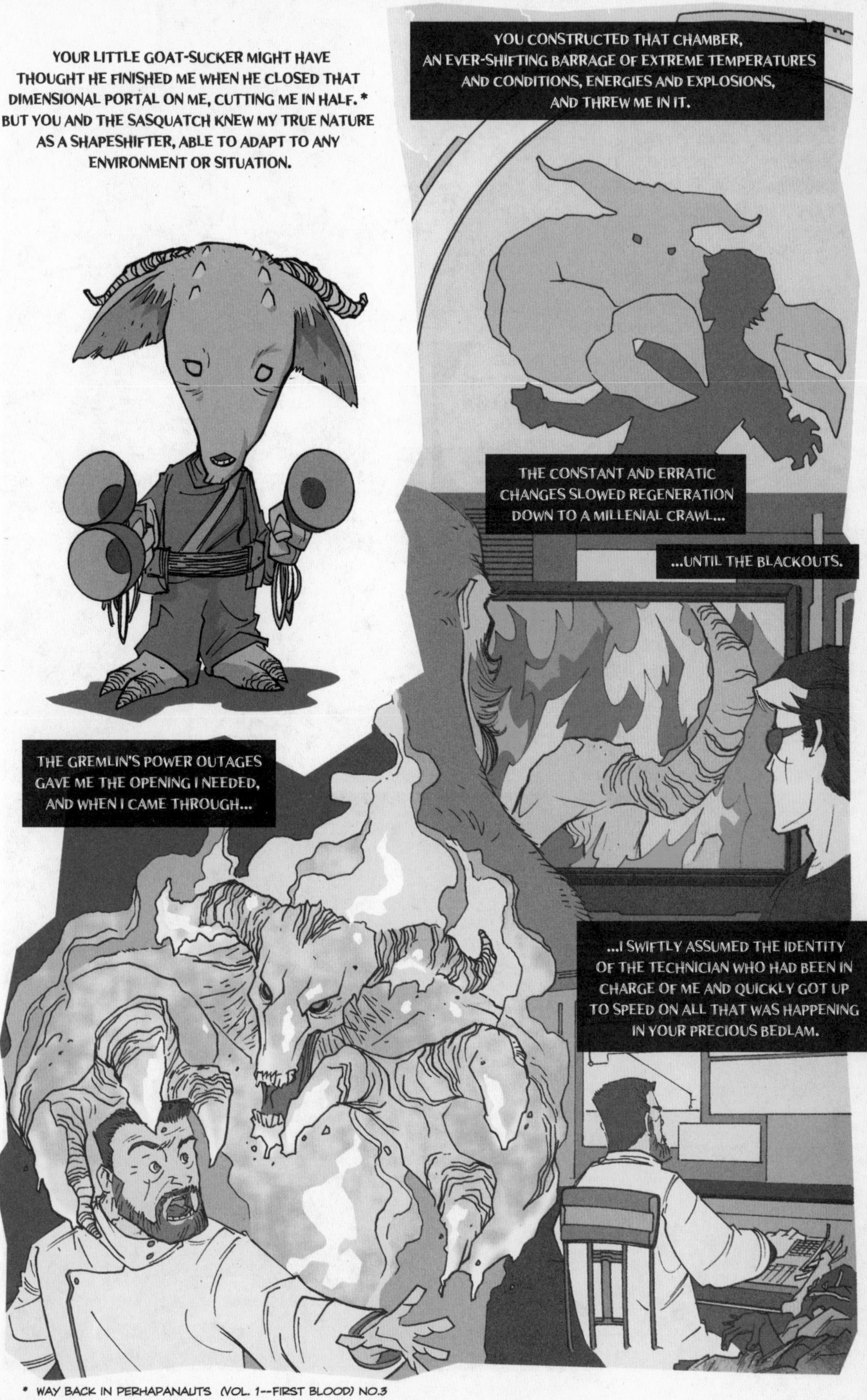
YOUR LITTLE GOAT-SUCKER MIGHT HAVE THOUGHT HE FINISHED ME WHEN HE CLOSED THAT DIMENSIONAL PORTAL ON ME, CUTTING ME IN HALF. * BUT YOU AND THE SASQUATCH KNEW MY TRUE NATURE AS A SHAPESHIFTER, ABLE TO ADAPT TO ANY ENVIRONMENT OR SITUATION.
YOU CONSTRUCTED THAT CHAMBER, AN EVER-SHIFTING BARRAGE OF EXTREME TEMPERATURES AND CONDITIONS, ENERGIES AND EXPLOSIONS, AND THREW ME IN IT.
THE CONSTANT AND ERRATIC CHANGES SLOWED REGENERATION DOWN TO A MILLENIAL CRAWL...
...UNTIL THE BLACKOUTS.
THE GREMLIN'S POWER OUTAGES GAVE ME THE OPENING I NEEDED, AND WHEN I CAME THROUGH...
...I SWIFTLY ASSUMED THE IDENTITY OF THE TECHNICIAN WHO HAD BEEN IN CHARGE OF ME AND QUICKLY GOT UP TO SPEED ON ALL THAT WAS HAPPENING IN YOUR PRECIOUS BEDLAM.

* WAY BACK IN PERHAPANAUTS (VOL. 1--FIRST BLOOD) NO.3

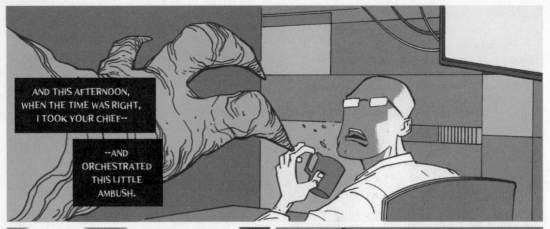

AND THIS AFTERNOON, WHEN THE TIME WAS RIGHT, I TOOK YOUR CHIEF--

--AND ORCHESTRATED THIS LITTLE AMBUSH.

BUT, STILL, YOU WERE THE PROBLEM... THE WILD CARD.

I KNOW WHAT YOU ARE, WHAT YOU CAN DO. THESE TWO WON'T BE A PROBLEM. BUT EVEN IF I LEFT YOU TO DIE OF STARVATION, DEHYDRATION, AXPHYXIATION -- NO GUARANTEE, YOU KNOW WHAT I MEAN?

SO HOW TO KILL MG...?

pok

HEH. WELL, WE HAVE THE GREMLINS TO THANK FOR THAT ONE, TOO!

#$%@!

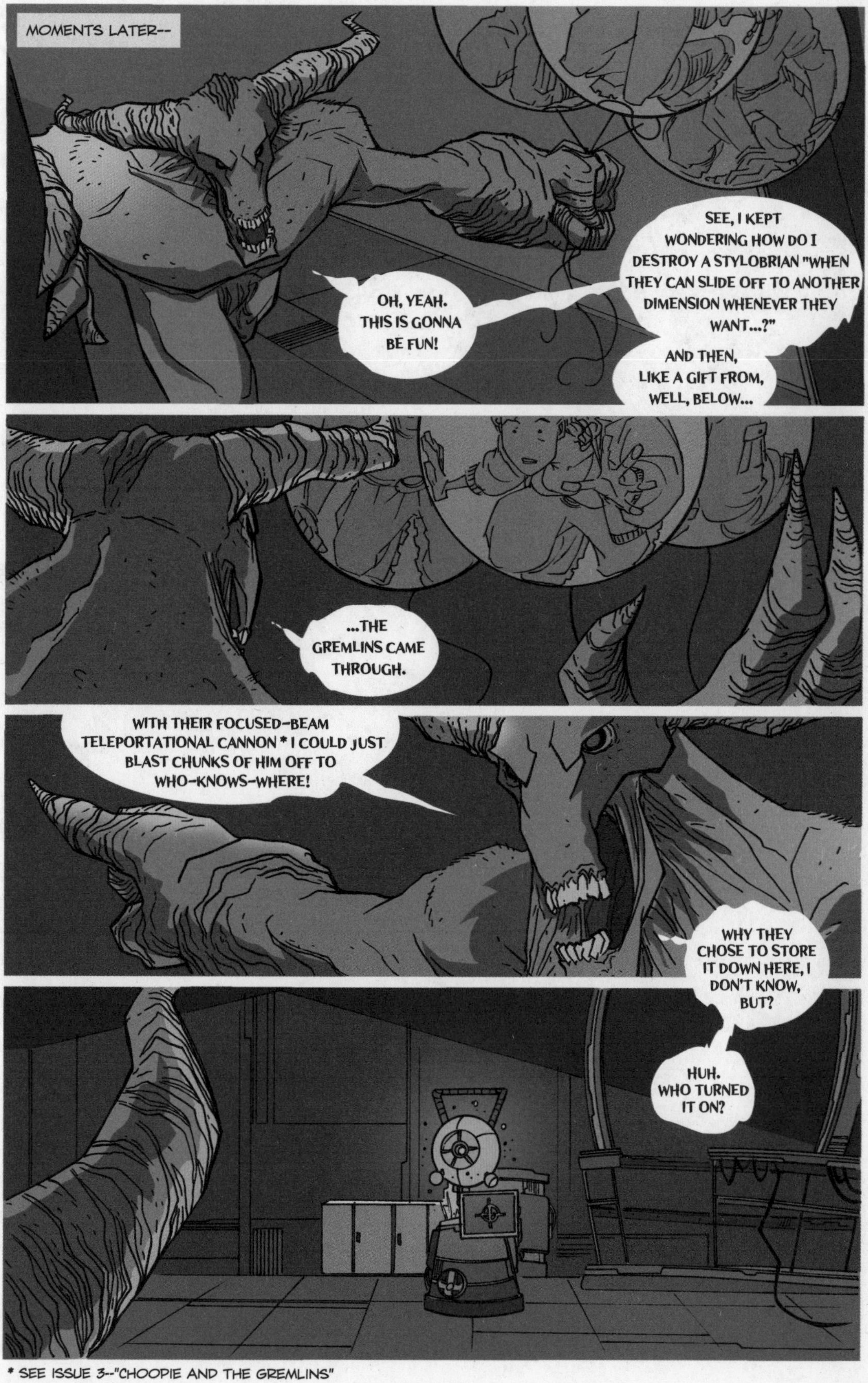
MOMENTS LATER--
OH, YEAH. THIS IS GONNA BE FUN!
SEE, I KEPT WONDERING HOW DO I DESTROY A STYLOBRIAN "WHEN THEY CAN SLIDE OFF TO ANOTHER DIMENSION WHENEVER THEY WANT...?"
AND THEN, LIKE A GIFT FROM, WELL, BELOW...
...THE GREMLINS CAME THROUGH.
WITH THEIR FOCUSED-BEAM TELEPORTATIONAL CANNON * I COULD JUST BLAST CHUNKS OF HIM OFF TO WHO-KNOWS-WHERE!
WHY THEY CHOSE TO STORE IT DOWN HERE, I DON'T KNOW, BUT?
HUH. WHO TURNED IT ON?

* SEE ISSUE 3--"CHOOPIE AND THE GREMLINS"

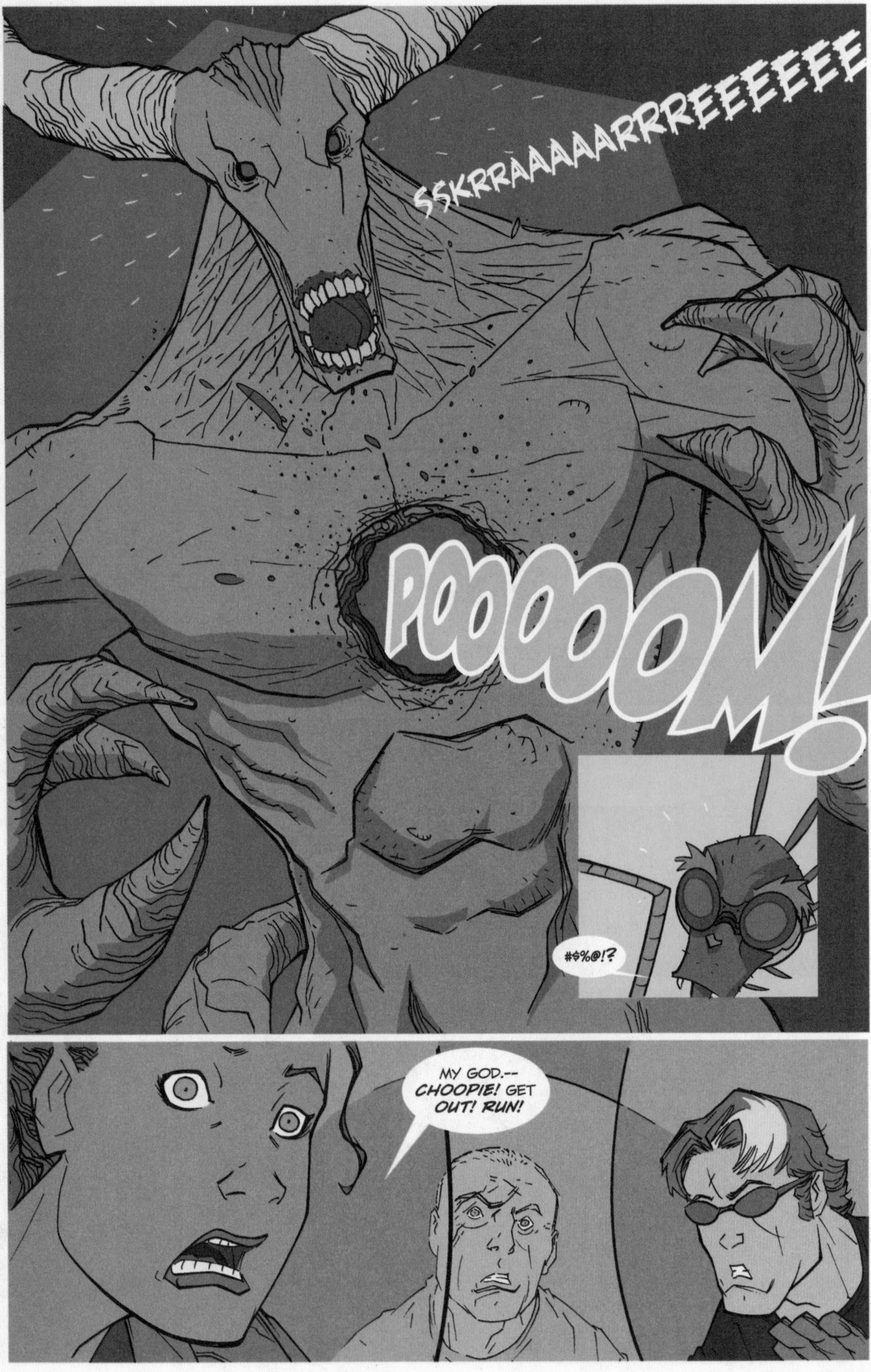
SSKRRAAAAARRREEEEEE
POOOOOM!
#$%@!?
MY GOD.-- CHOOPIE! GET OUT! RUN!

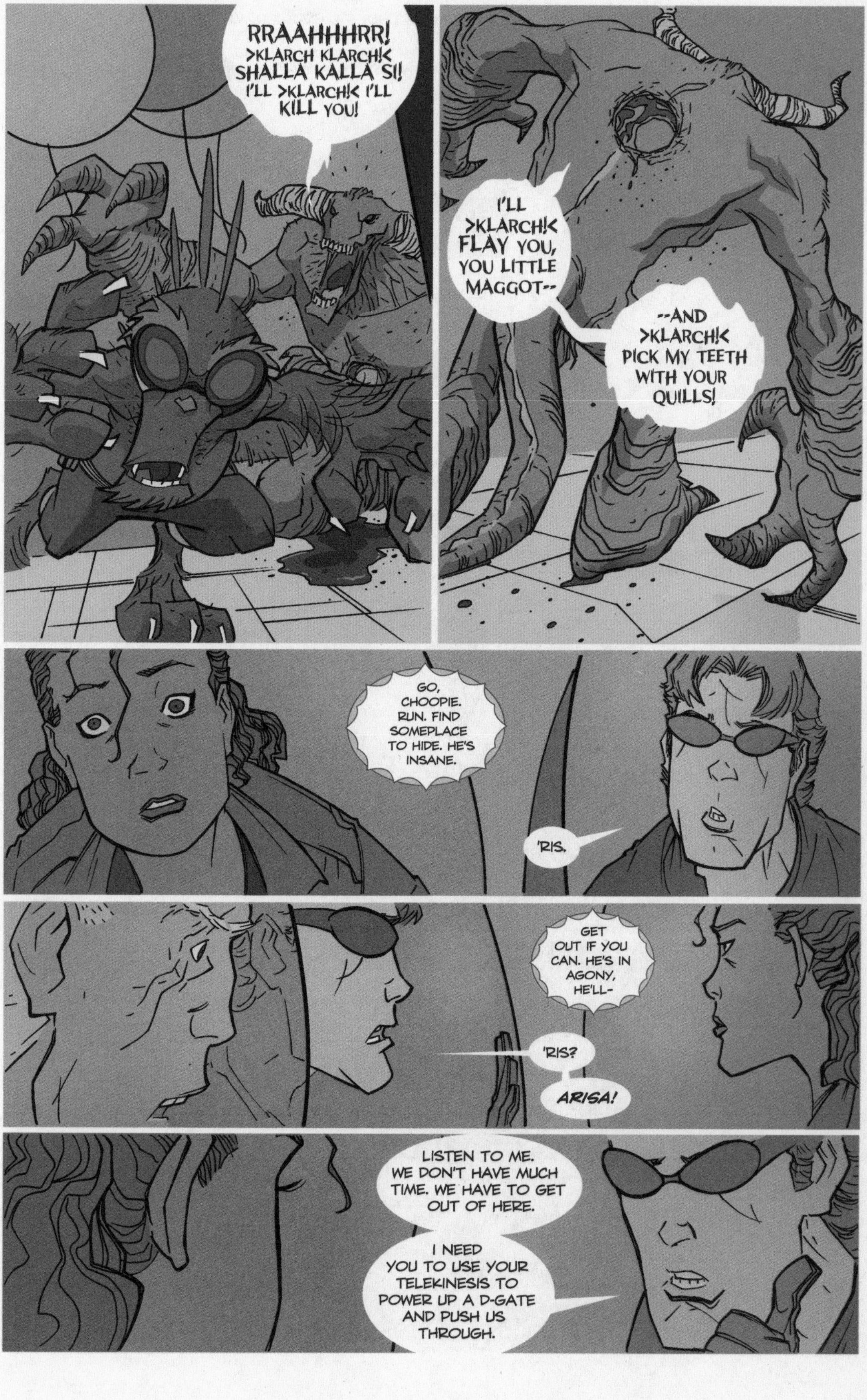
RRAAHHHRR! >KLARCH KLARCH!< SHALLA KALLA SI! I'LL >KLARCH!< I'LL KILL YOU!
I'LL >KLARCH!< FLAY YOU, YOU LITTLE MAGGOT--
--AND >KLARCH!< PICK MY TEETH WITH YOUR QUILLS!
GO, CHOOPIE. RUN. FIND SOMEPLACE TO HIDE. HE'S INSANE.
'RIS.
GET OUT IF YOU CAN. HE'S IN AGONY, HE'LL-
'RIS?
ARISA!
LISTEN TO ME. WE DON'T HAVE MUCH TIME. WE HAVE TO GET OUT OF HERE.
I NEED YOU TO USE YOUR TELEKINESIS TO POWER UP A D-GATE AND PUSH US THROUGH.

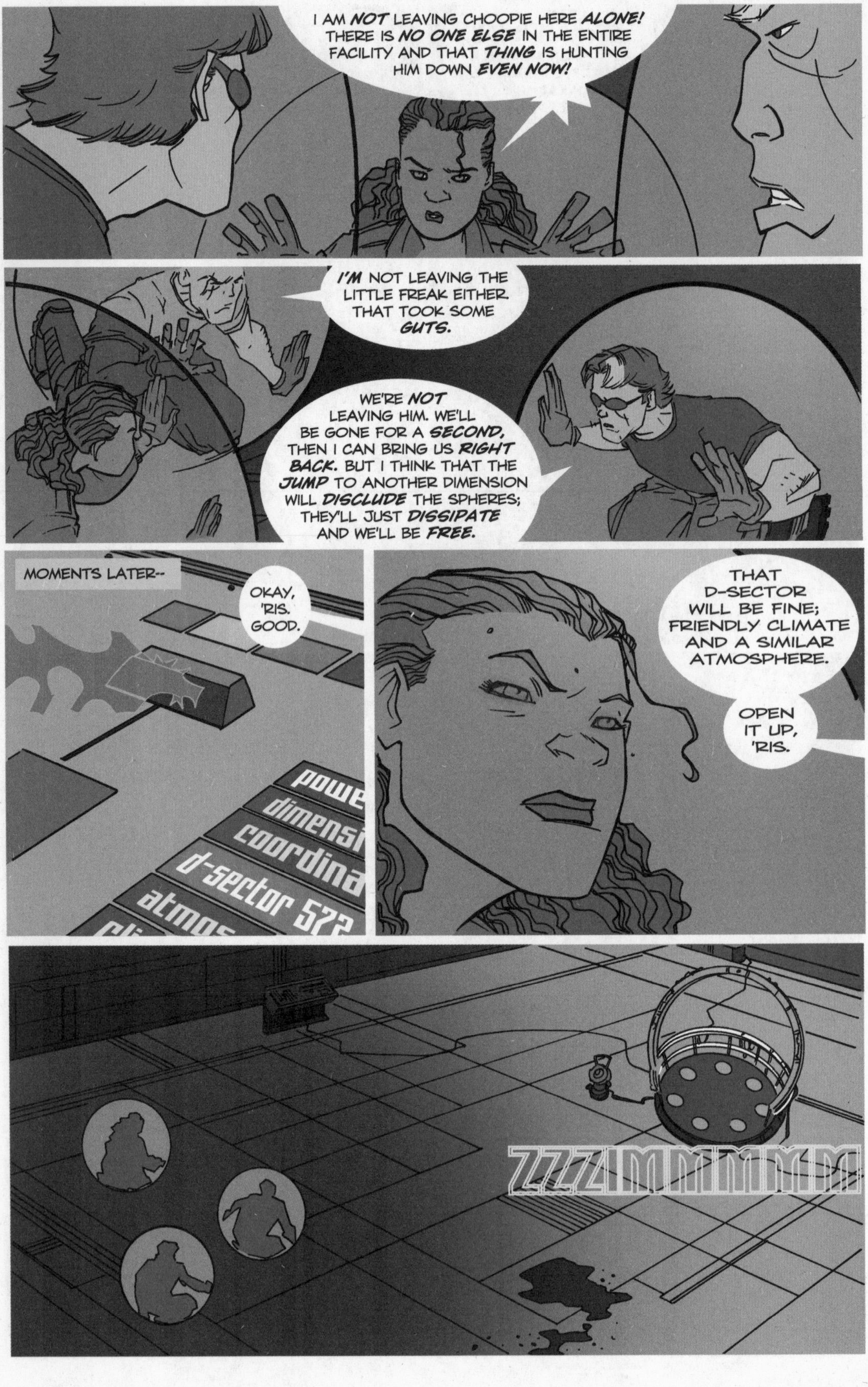
I AM NOT LEAVING CHOOPIE HERE ALONE! THERE IS NO ONE ELSE IN THE ENTIRE FACILITY AND THAT THING IS HUNTING HIM DOWN EVEN NOW!
I'M NOT LEAVING THE LITTLE FREAK EITHER. THAT TOOK SOME GUTS.
WE'RE NOT LEAVING HIM. WE'LL BE GONE FOR A SECOND, THEN I CAN BRING US RIGHT BACK. BUT I THINK THAT THE JUMP TO ANOTHER DIMENSION WILL DISCLUDE THE SPHERES; THEY'LL JUST DISSIPATE AND WE'LL BE FREE.
MOMENTS LATER--
OKAY, 'RIS. GOOD.
powe
dimensi
coordina
d-sector 572
atmos
THAT D-SECTOR WILL BE FINE; FRIENDLY CLIMATE AND A SIMILAR ATMOSPHERE.
OPEN IT UP, 'RIS.
ZZZIMMMMMM

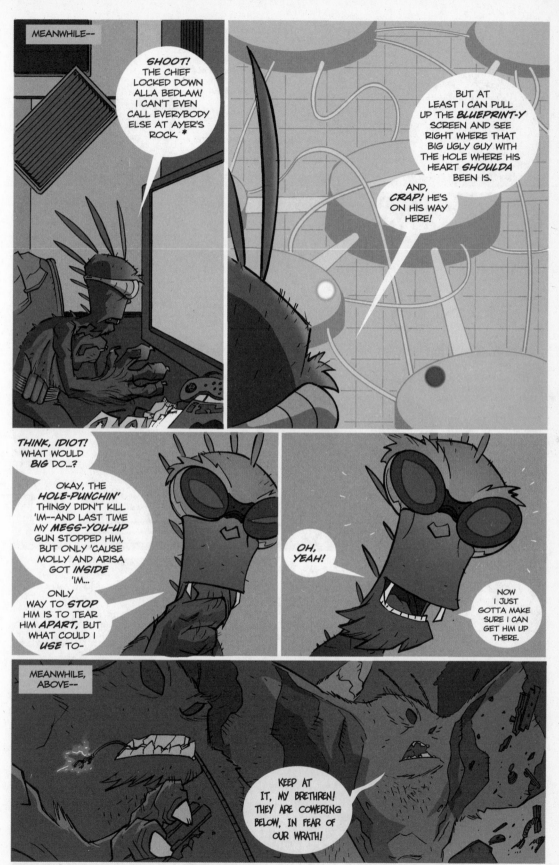

MEANWHILE--

SHOOT! THE CHIEF LOCKED DOWN ALLA BEDLAM! I CAN'T EVEN CALL EVERYBODY ELSE AT AYER'S ROCK. *

BUT AT LEAST I CAN PULL UP THE BLUEPRINT-Y SCREEN AND SEE RIGHT WHERE THAT BIG UGLY GUY WITH THE HOLE WHERE HIS HEART SHOULDA BEEN IS.

AND, CRAP! HE'S ON HIS WAY HERE!

THINK, IDIOT! WHAT WOULD BIG DO...?

OKAY, THE HOLE-PUNCHIN' THINGY DIDN'T KILL 'IM--AND LAST TIME MY MESS-YOU-UP GUN STOPPED HIM, BUT ONLY 'CAUSE MOLLY AND ARISA GOT INSIDE 'IM...

ONLY WAY TO STOP HIM IS TO TEAR HIM APART, BUT WHAT COULD I USE TO-

OH, YEAH!

NOW I JUST GOTTA MAKE SURE I CAN GET HIM UP THERE.

MEANWHILE, ABOVE--

KEEP AT IT, MY BRETHREN! THEY ARE COWERING BELOW, IN FEAR OF OUR WRATH!

* WHERE ALL THE REST OF BEDLAM CURRENTLY IS.

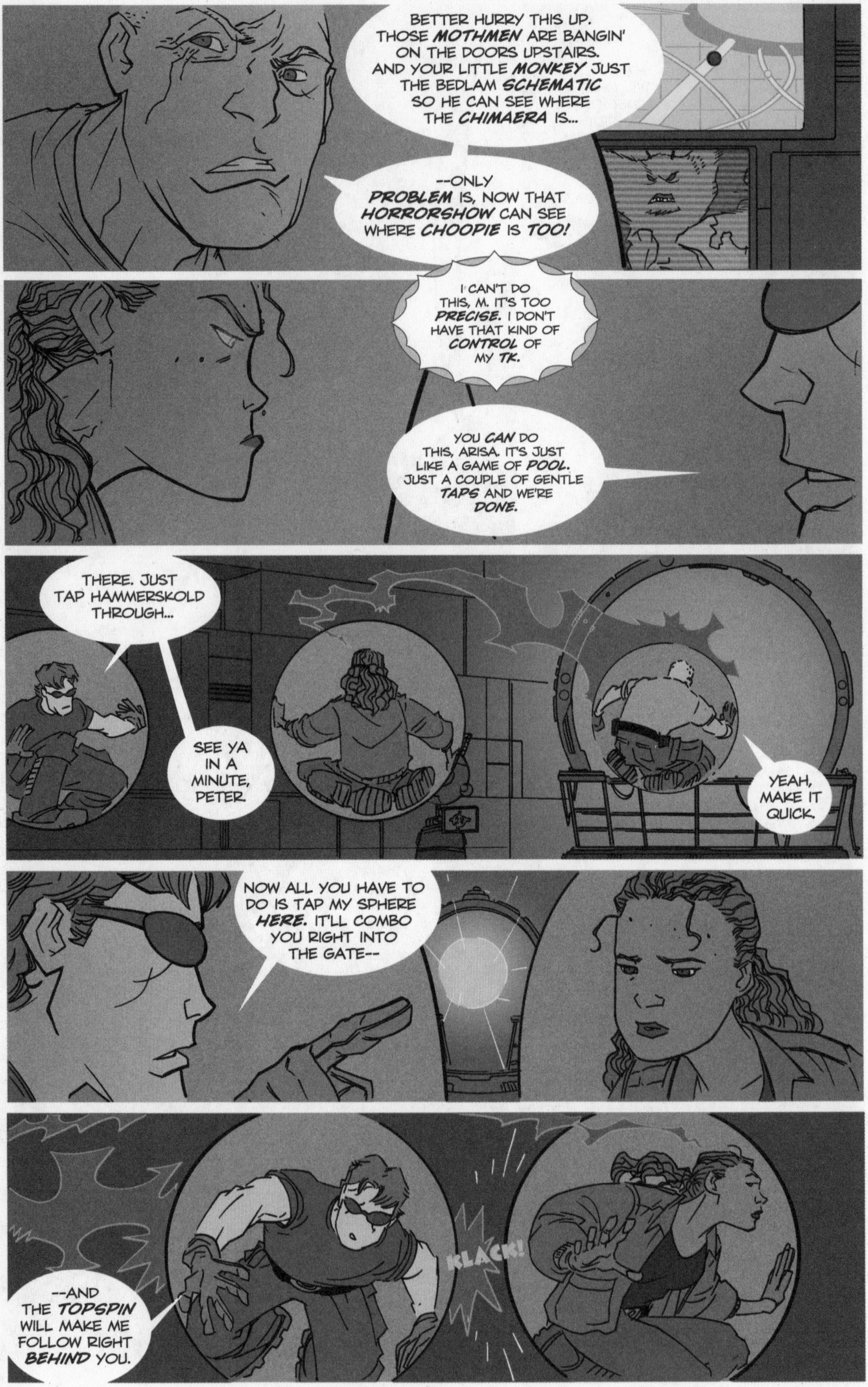

BETTER HURRY THIS UP. THOSE MOTHMEN ARE BANGIN' ON THE DOORS UPSTAIRS. AND YOUR LITTLE MONKEY JUST THE BEDLAM SCHEMATIC SO HE CAN SEE WHERE THE CHIMAERA IS...
--ONLY PROBLEM IS, NOW THAT HORRORSHOW CAN SEE WHERE CHOOPIE IS TOO!
I CAN'T DO THIS, M. IT'S TOO PRECISE. I DON'T HAVE THAT KIND OF CONTROL OF MY TK.
YOU CAN DO THIS, ARISA. IT'S JUST LIKE A GAME OF POOL. JUST A COUPLE OF GENTLE TAPS AND WE'RE DONE.
THERE. JUST TAP HAMMERSKOLD THROUGH...
SEE YA IN A MINUTE, PETER.
YEAH, MAKE IT QUICK.
NOW ALL YOU HAVE TO DO IS TAP MY SPHERE HERE. IT'LL COMBO YOU RIGHT INTO THE GATE--
KLACK!
--AND THE TOPSPIN WILL MAKE ME FOLLOW RIGHT BEHIND YOU.

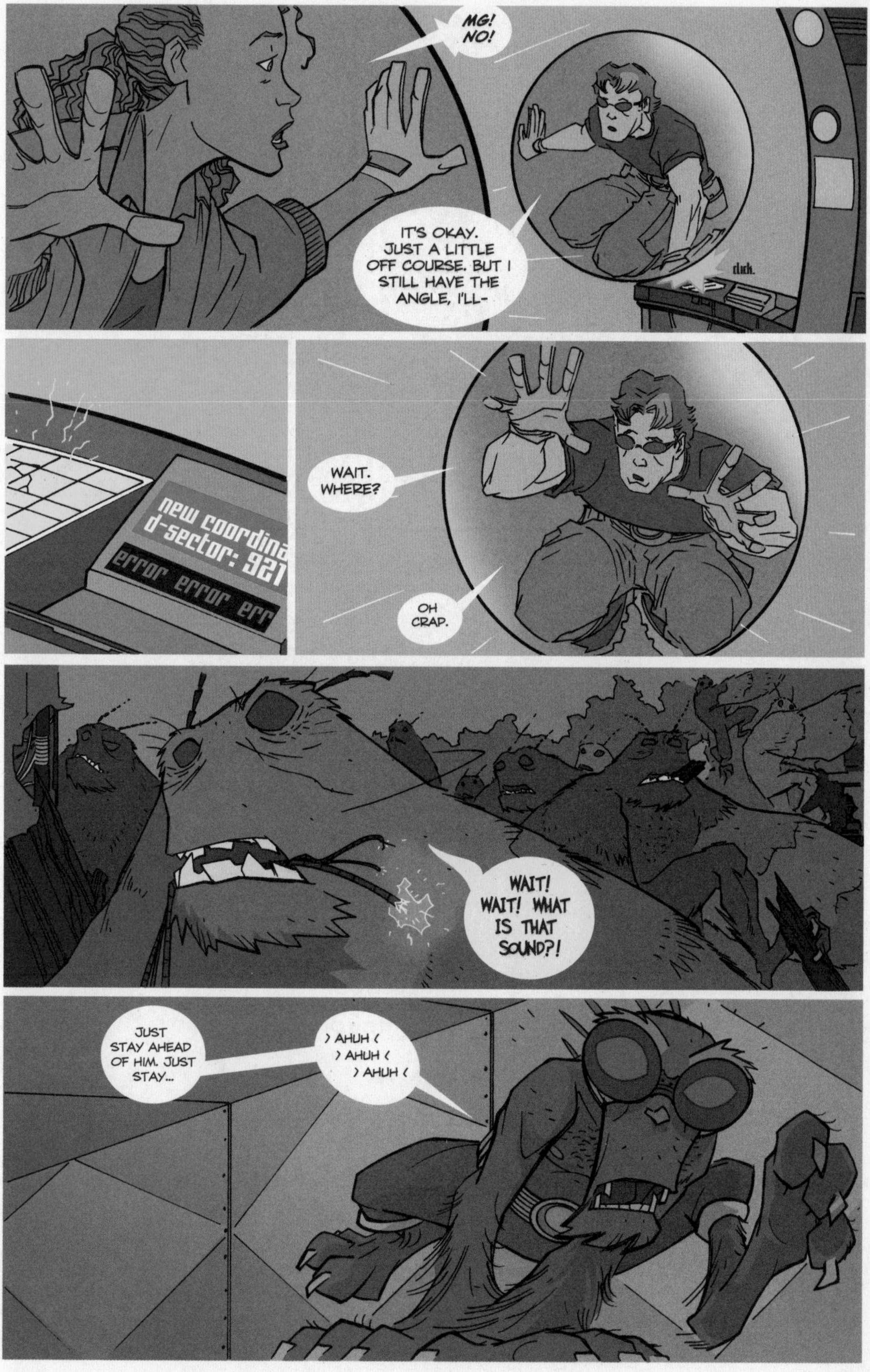
MG! NO!
IT'S OKAY. JUST A LITTLE OFF COURSE. BUT I STILL HAVE THE ANGLE, I'LL-
click.
new coordina
d-sector: 921
error error err
WAIT. WHERE?
OH CRAP.
WAIT! WAIT! WHAT IS THAT SOUND?!
JUST STAY AHEAD OF HIM. JUST STAY...
› AHUH ‹
› AHUH ‹
› AHUH ‹

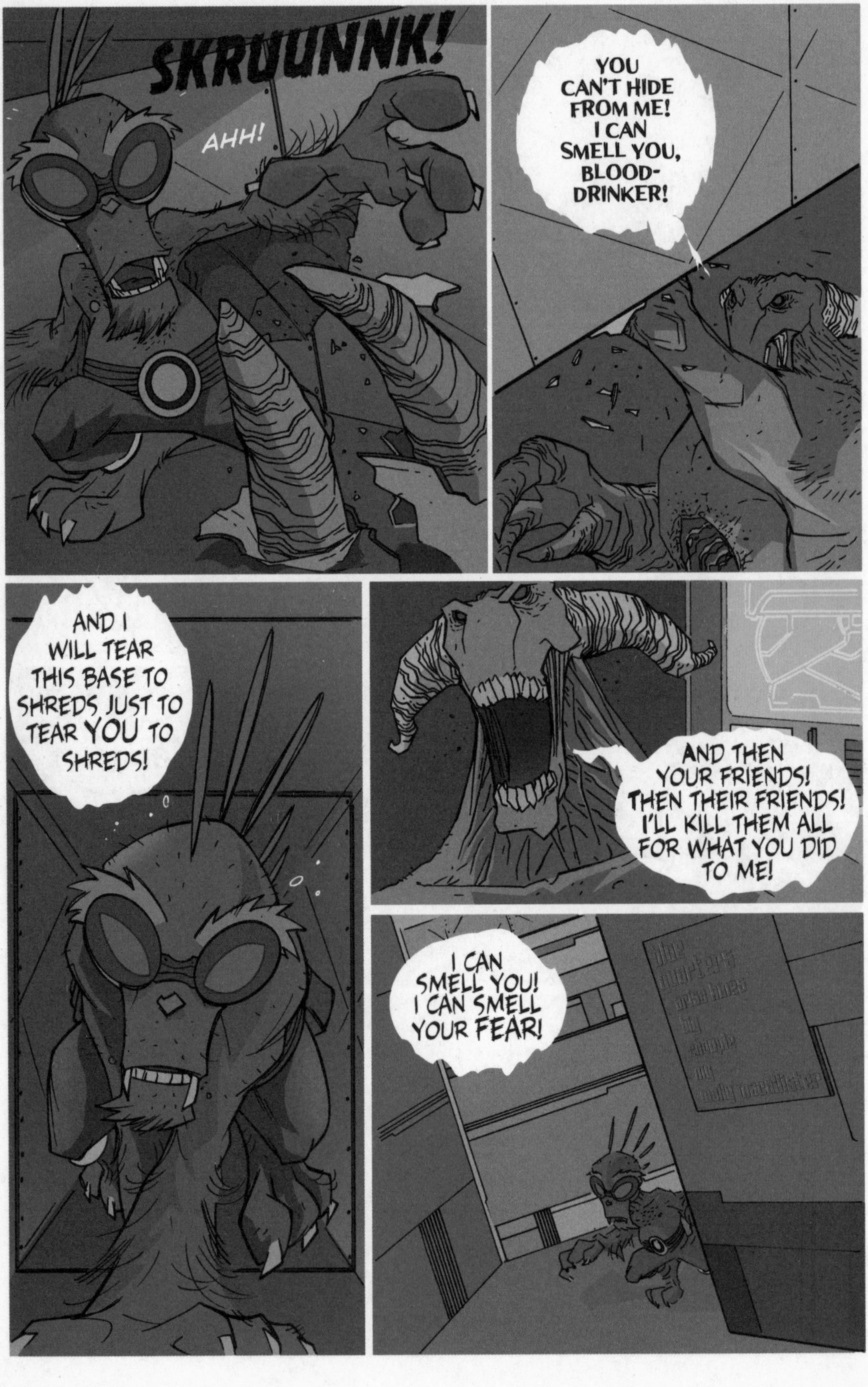
SKRUUNNK!
AHH!
YOU CAN'T HIDE FROM ME! I CAN SMELL YOU, BLOOD-DRINKER!
AND I WILL TEAR THIS BASE TO SHREDS JUST TO TEAR YOU TO SHREDS!
AND THEN YOUR FRIENDS! THEN THEIR FRIENDS! I'LL KILL THEM ALL FOR WHAT YOU DID TO ME!
I CAN SMELL YOU! I CAN SMELL YOUR FEAR!

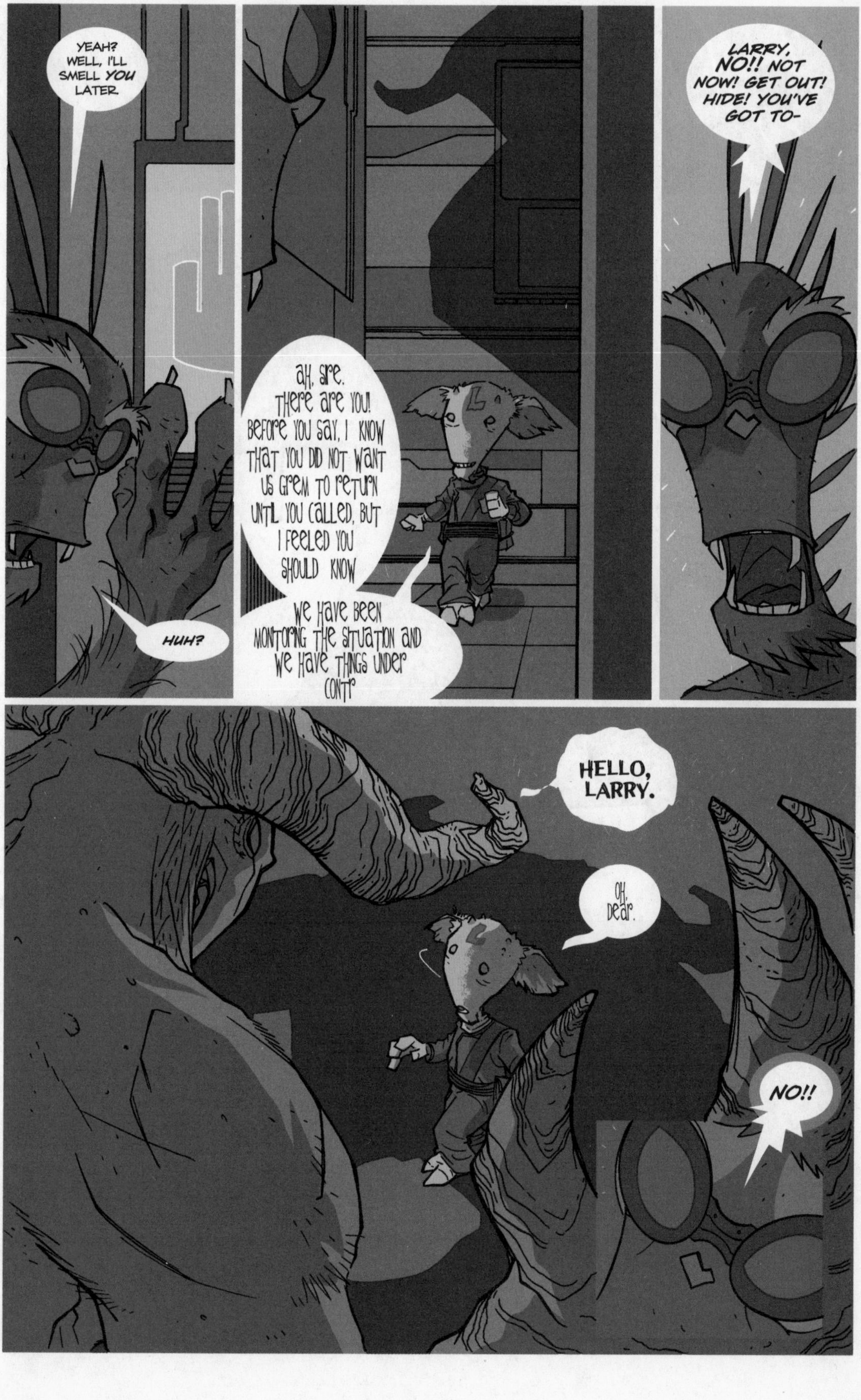
YEAH? WELL, I'LL SMELL YOU LATER.
HUH?
AH, SIRE. THERE ARE YOU! BEFORE YOU SAY, I KNOW THAT YOU DID NOT WANT US GREM TO RETURN UNTIL YOU CALLED, BUT I FEELED YOU SHOULD KNOW
WE HAVE BEEN MONITORING THE SITUATION AND WE HAVE THINGS UNDER CONTR
LARRY, NO!! NOT NOW! GET OUT! HIDE! YOU'VE GOT TO-
HELLO, LARRY.
OH, DEAR.
NO!!

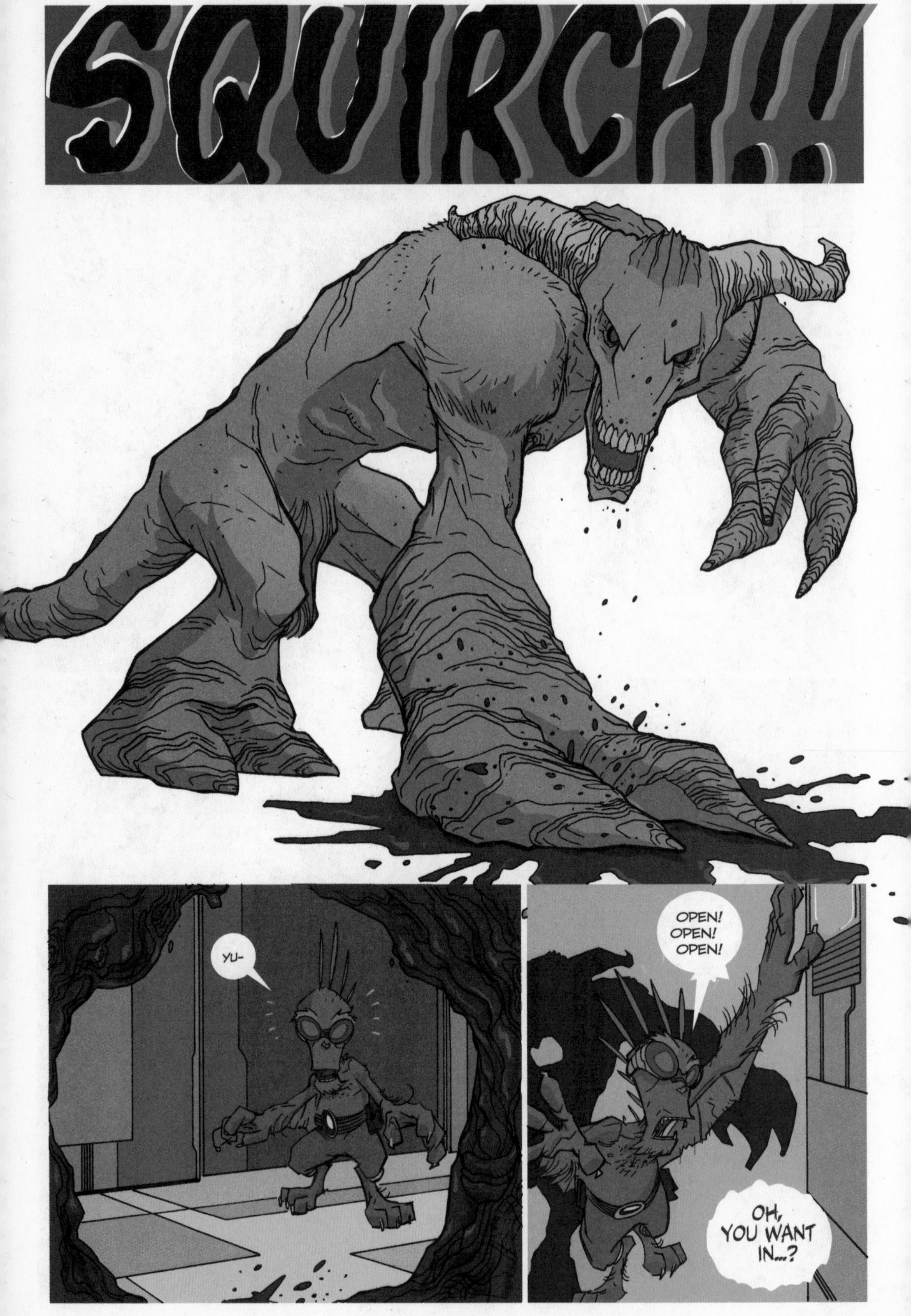
SQUIRCH!!
YU-
OPEN!
OPEN!
OPEN!
OH,
YOU WANT
IN...?

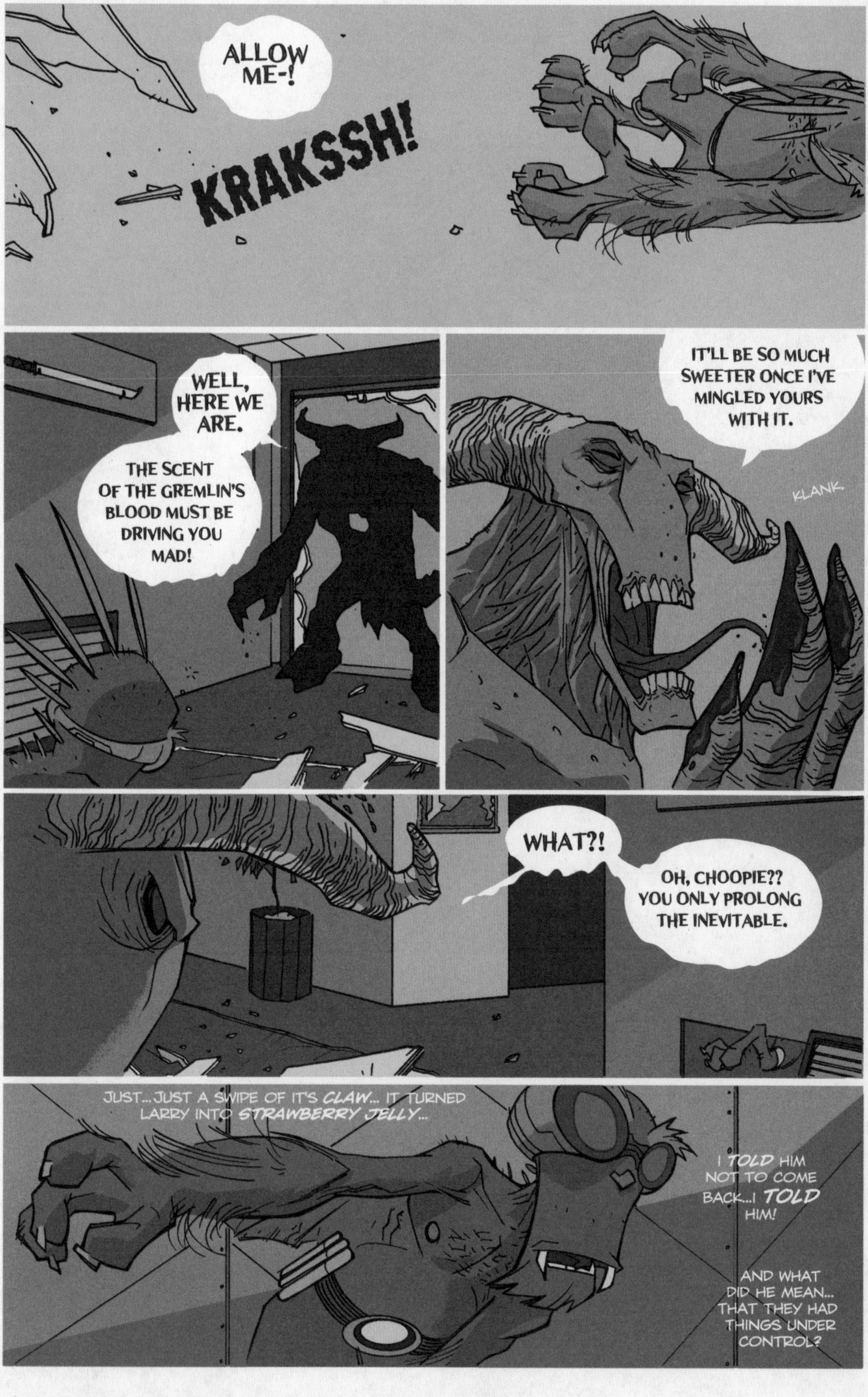
ALLOW ME-!
KRAKSSH!
WELL, HERE WE ARE.
THE SCENT OF THE GREMLIN'S BLOOD MUST BE DRIVING YOU MAD!
IT'LL BE SO MUCH SWEETER ONCE I'VE MINGLED YOURS WITH IT.
KLANK.
WHAT?!
OH, CHOOPIE?? YOU ONLY PROLONG THE INEVITABLE.
JUST...JUST A SWIPE OF IT'S CLAW... IT TURNED LARRY INTO STRAWBERRY JELLY...
I TOLD HIM NOT TO COME BACK...I TOLD HIM!
AND WHAT DID HE MEAN... THAT THEY HAD THINGS UNDER CONTROL?

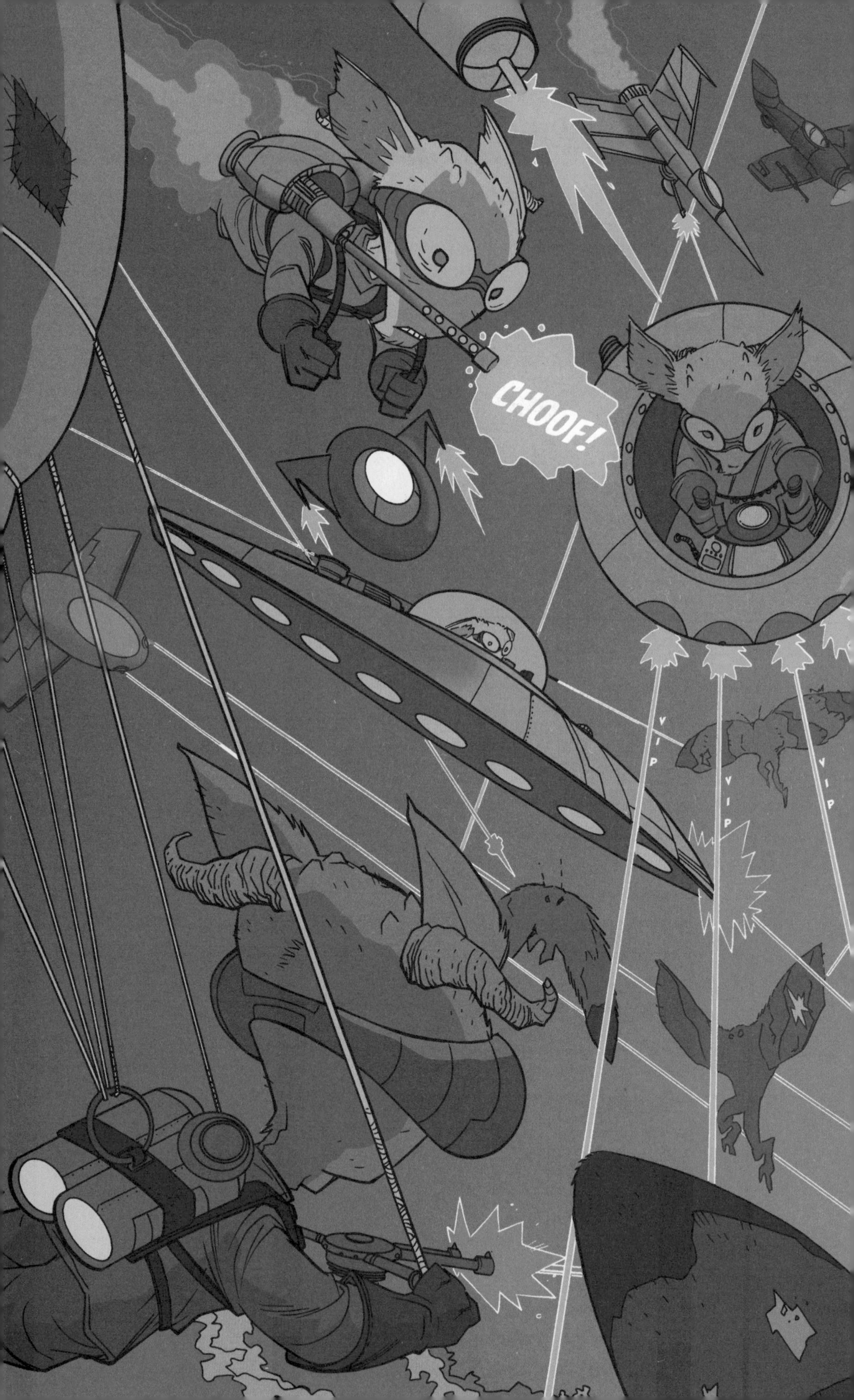

CHOOF!
VIP
VIP
VIP

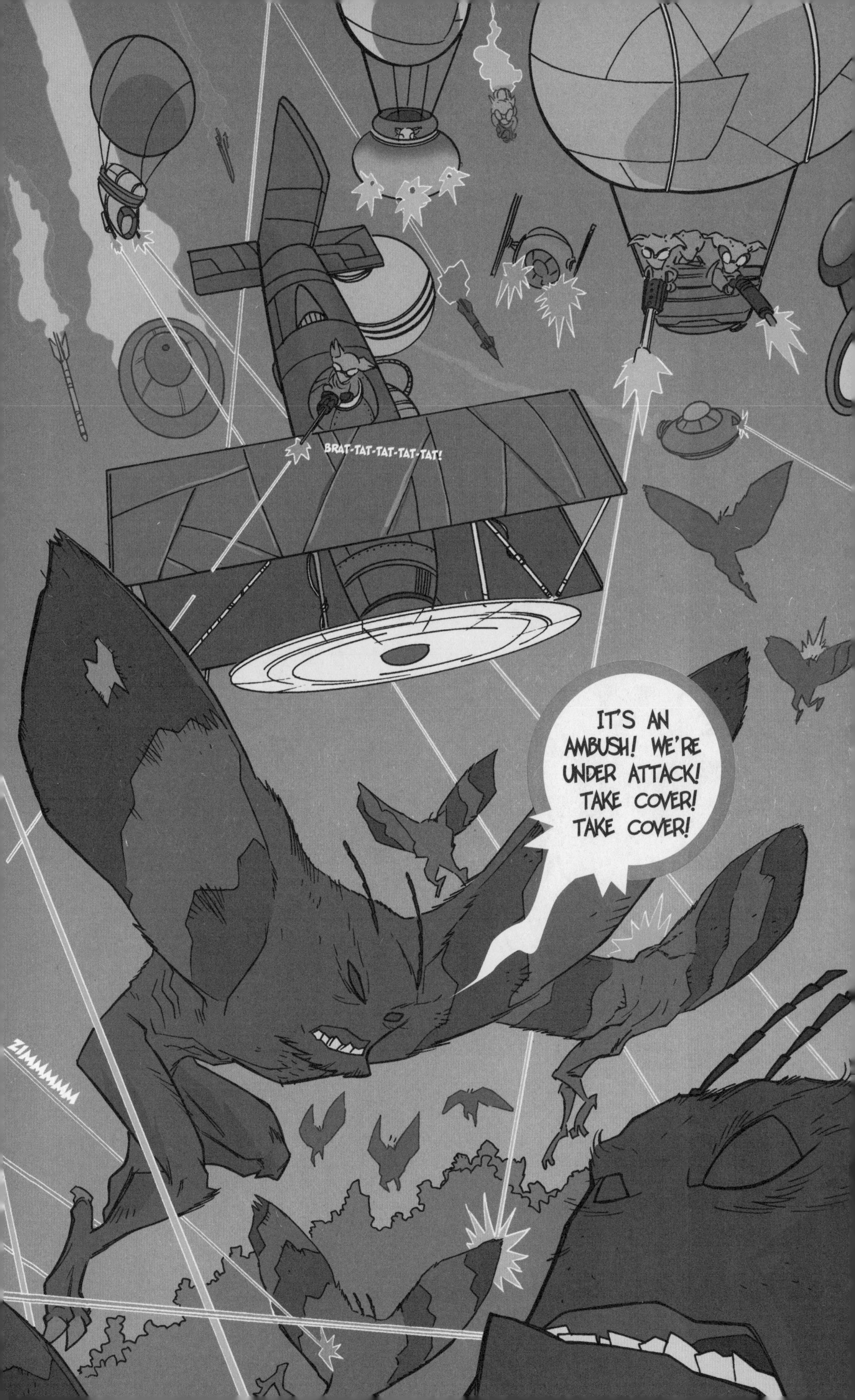
BRAT-TAT-TAT-TAT-TAT!
IT'S AN AMBUSH! WE'RE UNDER ATTACK! TAKE COVER! TAKE COVER!
ZIMMMMMM

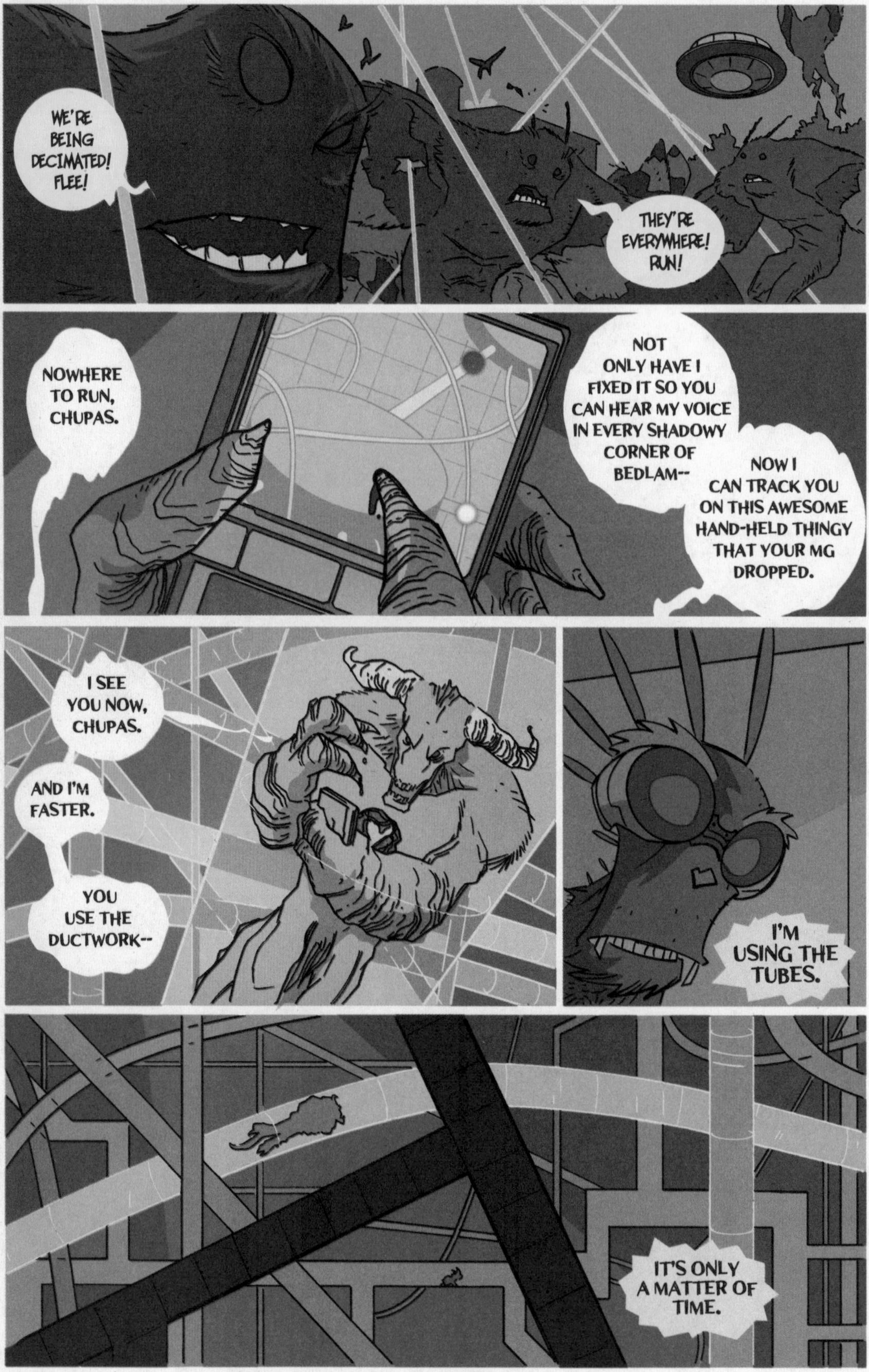
WE'RE BEING DECIMATED! FLEE!
THEY'RE EVERYWHERE! RUN!
NOWHERE TO RUN, CHUPAS.
NOT ONLY HAVE I FIXED IT SO YOU CAN HEAR MY VOICE IN EVERY SHADOWY CORNER OF BEDLAM--
NOW I CAN TRACK YOU ON THIS AWESOME HAND-HELD THINGY THAT YOUR MG DROPPED.
I SEE YOU NOW, CHUPAS.
AND I'M FASTER.
YOU USE THE DUCTWORK--
I'M USING THE TUBES.
IT'S ONLY A MATTER OF TIME.

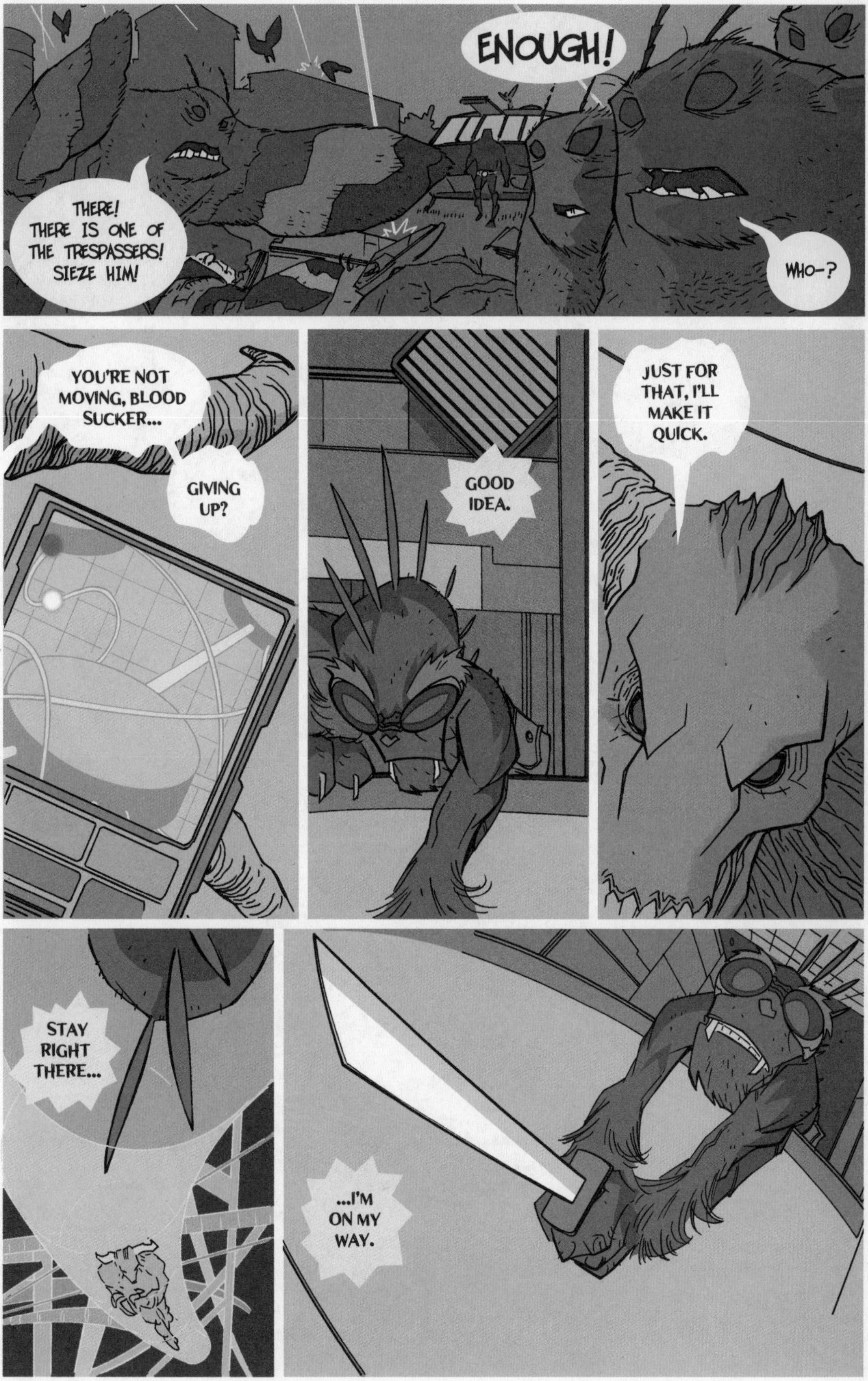
ENOUGH!
THERE! THERE IS ONE OF THE TRESPASSERS! SIEZE HIM!
WHO-?
YOU'RE NOT MOVING, BLOOD SUCKER...
GIVING UP?
GOOD IDEA.
JUST FOR THAT, I'LL MAKE IT QUICK.
STAY RIGHT THERE...
...I'M ON MY WAY.

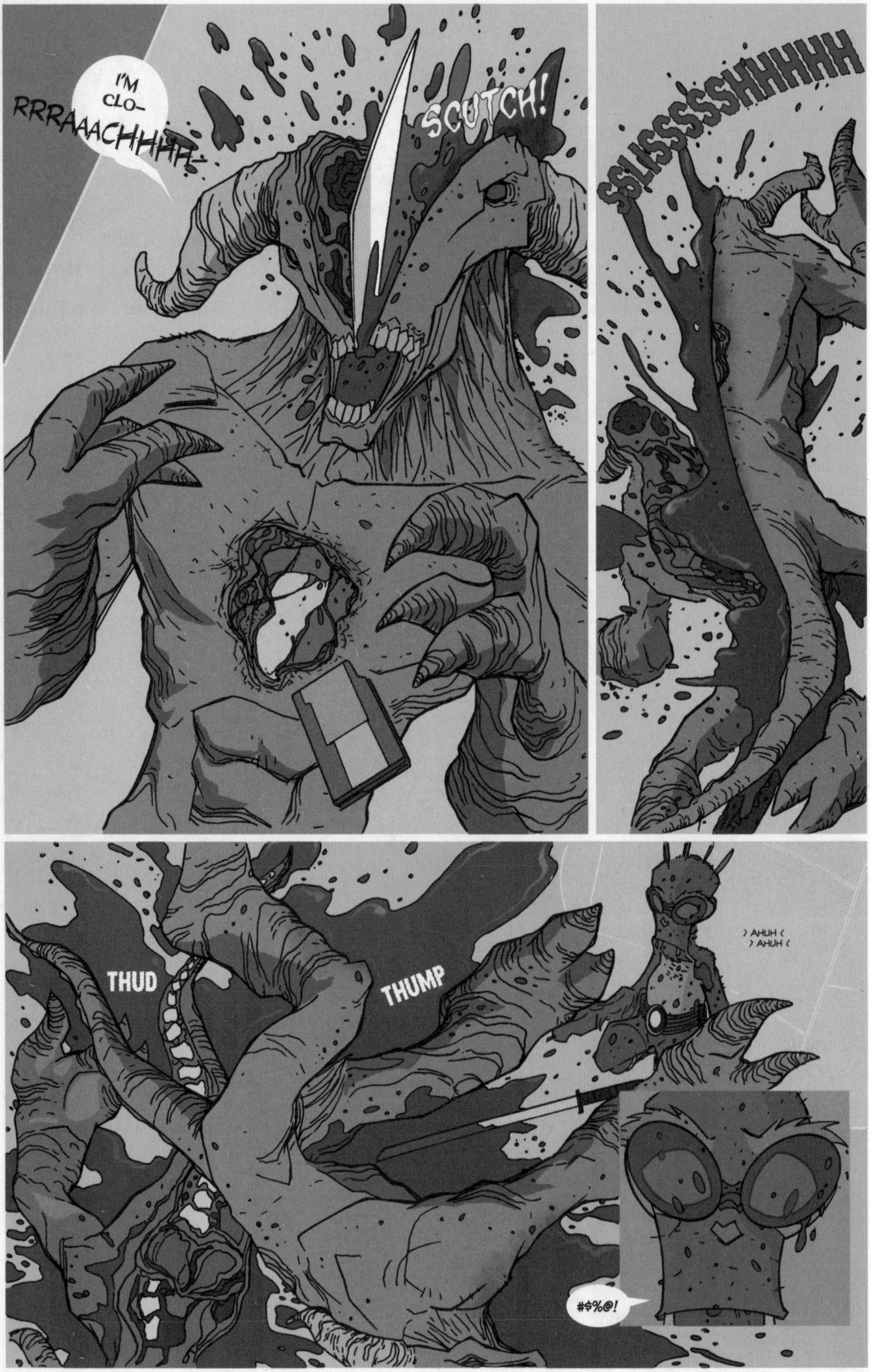
I'M CLO-
RRRAAACHHHH-
SCUTCH!
SSLISSSSSHHHHHH
THUD
THUMP
> AHUH <
> AHUH <
#$%@!

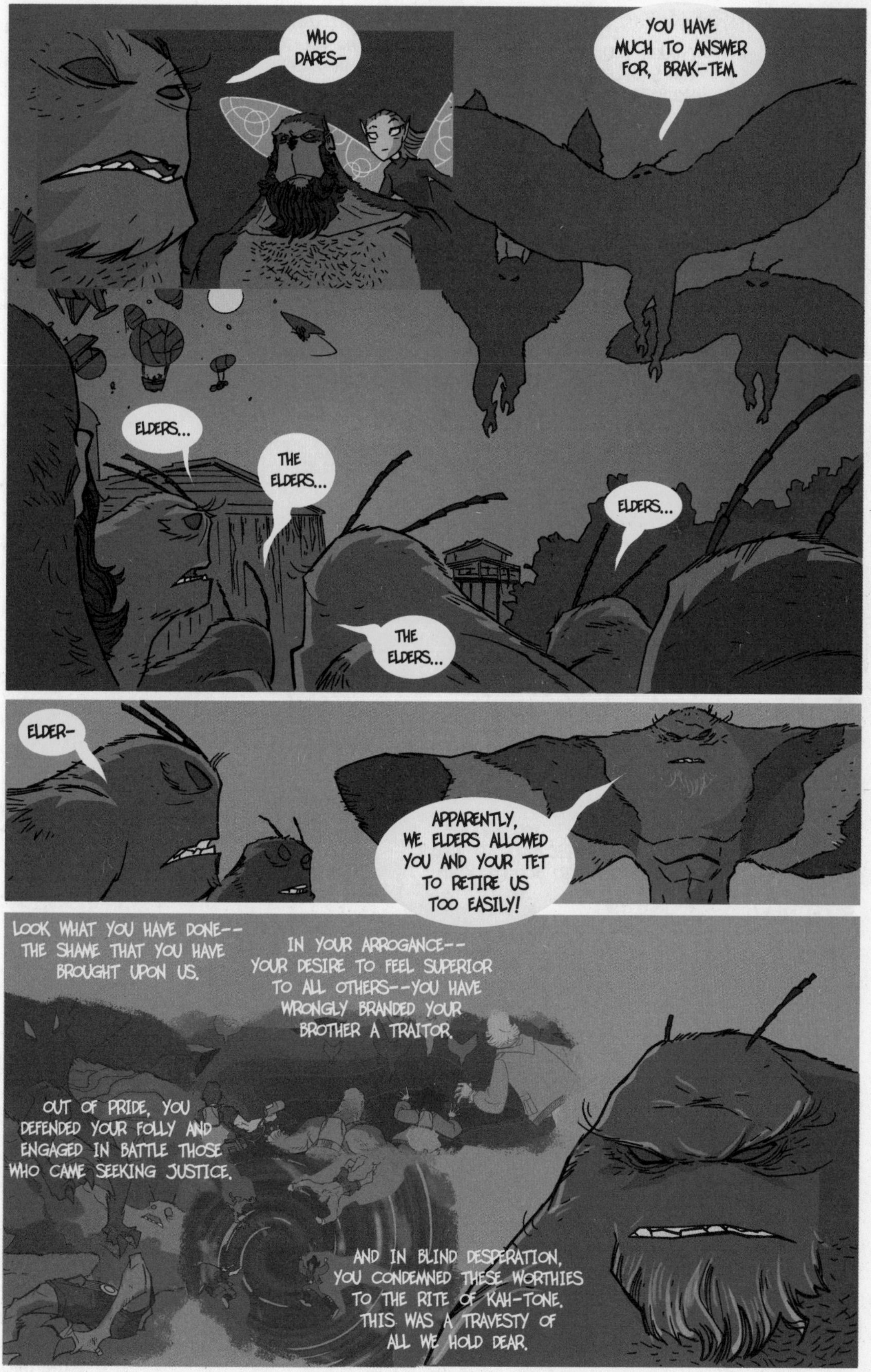
WHO DARES-
YOU HAVE MUCH TO ANSWER FOR, BRAK-TEM.
ELDERS...
THE ELDERS...
ELDERS...
THE ELDERS...
ELDER-
APPARENTLY, WE ELDERS ALLOWED YOU AND YOUR TET TO RETIRE US TOO EASILY!
LOOK WHAT YOU HAVE DONE-- THE SHAME THAT YOU HAVE BROUGHT UPON US.
IN YOUR ARROGANCE-- YOUR DESIRE TO FEEL SUPERIOR TO ALL OTHERS--YOU HAVE WRONGLY BRANDED YOUR BROTHER A TRAITOR.
OUT OF PRIDE, YOU DEFENDED YOUR FOLLY AND ENGAGED IN BATTLE THOSE WHO CAME SEEKING JUSTICE.
AND IN BLIND DESPERATION, YOU CONDEMNED THESE WORTHIES TO THE RITE OF KAH-TONE. THIS WAS A TRAVESTY OF ALL WE HOLD DEAR.

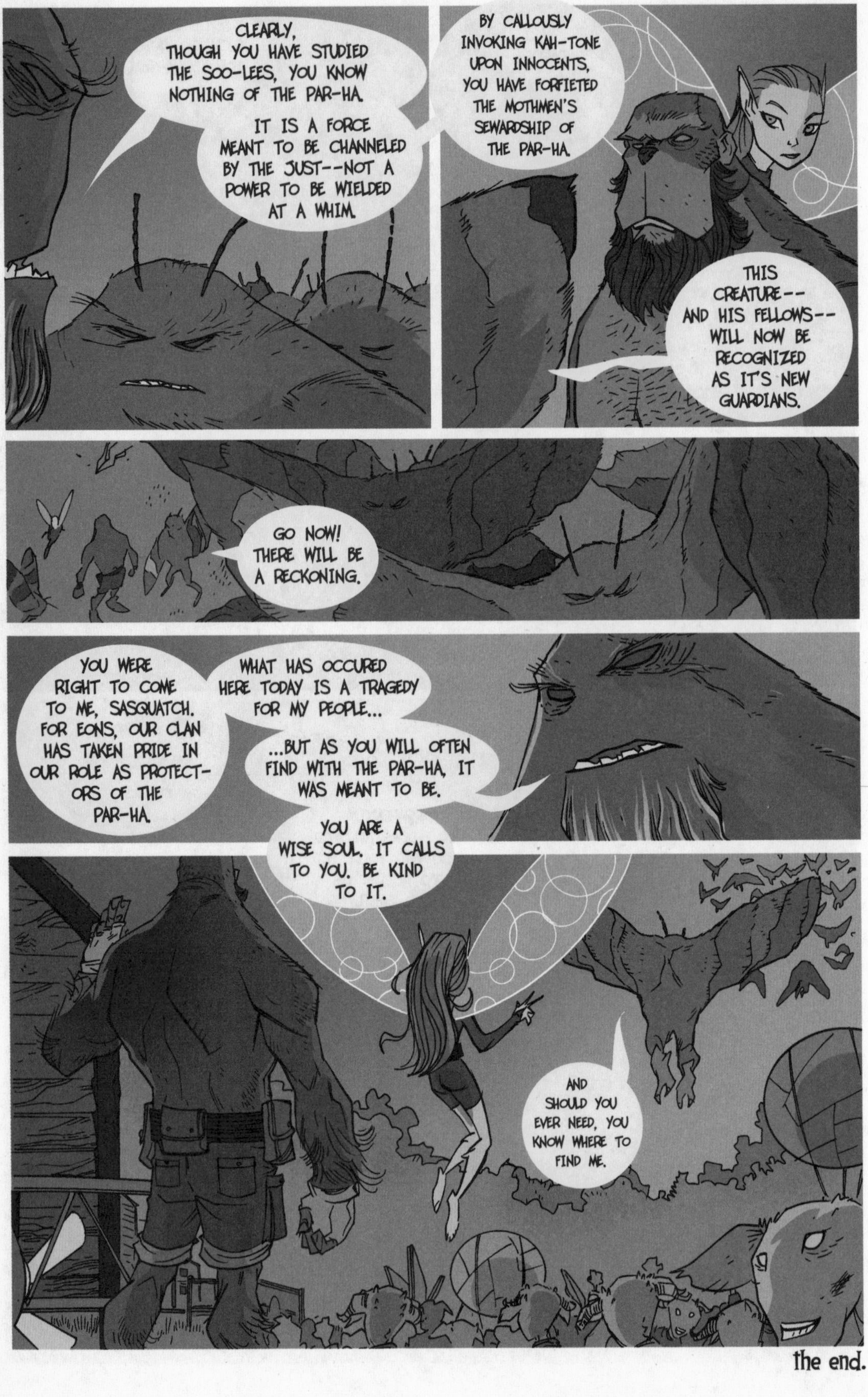
CLEARLY, THOUGH YOU HAVE STUDIED THE SOO-LEES, YOU KNOW NOTHING OF THE PAR-HA.
IT IS A FORCE MEANT TO BE CHANNELED BY THE JUST--NOT A POWER TO BE WIELDED AT A WHIM.
BY CALLOUSLY INVOKING KAH-TONE UPON INNOCENTS, YOU HAVE FORFIETED THE MOTHMEN'S SEWARDSHIP OF THE PAR-HA.
THIS CREATURE-- AND HIS FELLOWS-- WILL NOW BE RECOGNIZED AS IT'S NEW GUARDIANS.
GO NOW! THERE WILL BE A RECKONING.
YOU WERE RIGHT TO COME TO ME, SASQUATCH. FOR EONS, OUR CLAN HAS TAKEN PRIDE IN OUR ROLE AS PROTECT-ORS OF THE PAR-HA.
WHAT HAS OCCURED HERE TODAY IS A TRAGEDY FOR MY PEOPLE...
...BUT AS YOU WILL OFTEN FIND WITH THE PAR-HA, IT WAS MEANT TO BE.
YOU ARE A WISE SOUL. IT CALLS TO YOU. BE KIND TO IT.
AND SHOULD YOU EVER NEED, YOU KNOW WHERE TO FIND ME.

the end.

cover gallery

unused cover to perhapanauts no.3

"when we first threw around the idea of choopie being the gremlin king, nosmo, i couldn't get the image of conan on his throne outta my head and thought it would make a fun cover. as the story unfolded, however, things (as they often do) went in a different direction." - craig

HEAVY SITS THE CROWN
UPON THE BROW OF
THE GREMLIN KING

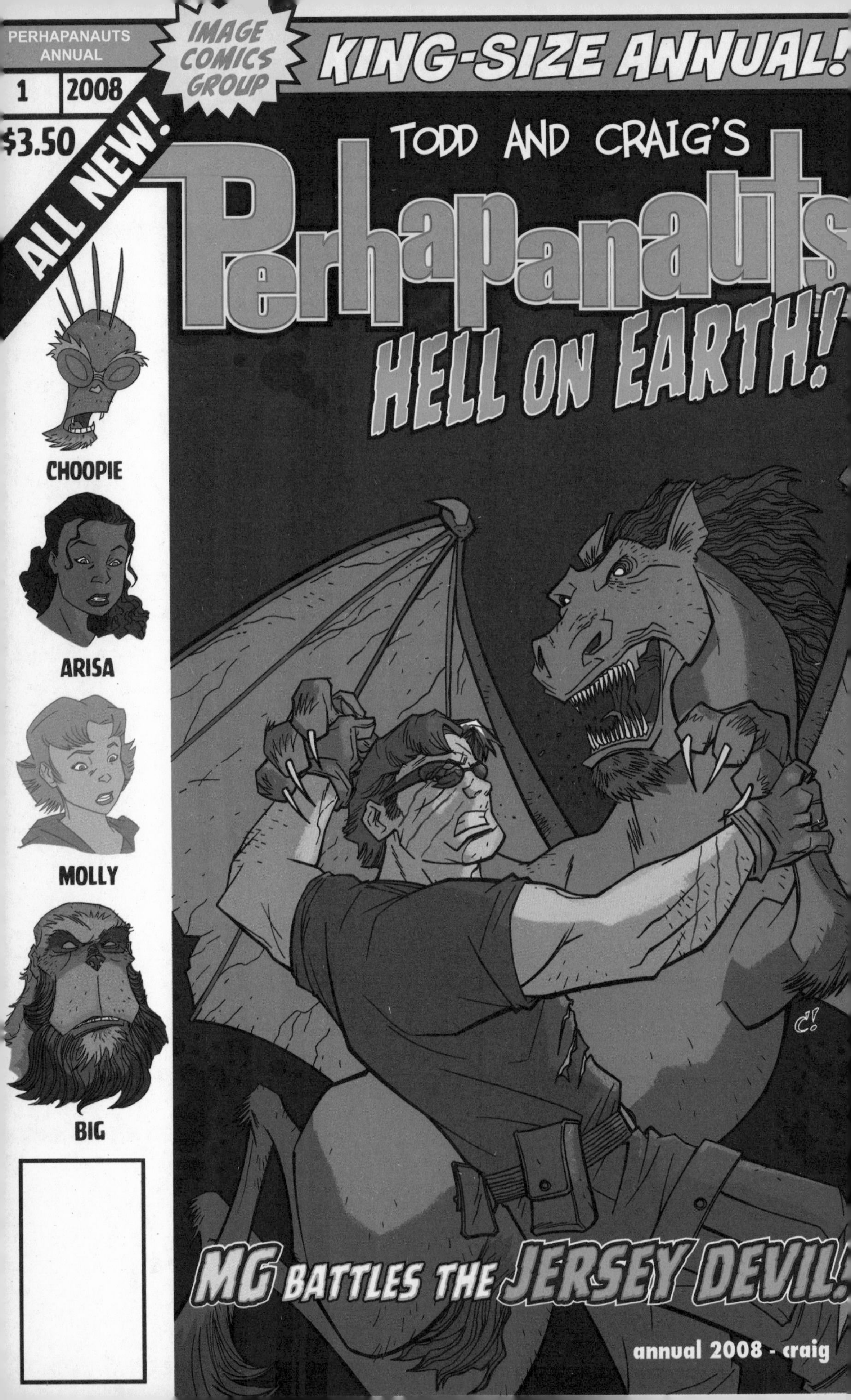

PERHAPANAUTS ANNUAL
1
2008
$3.50
IMAGE COMICS GROUP
KING-SIZE ANNUAL!
ALL NEW!
TODD AND CRAIG'S
Perhapanauts
HELL ON EARTH!
CHOOPIE
ARISA
MOLLY
BIG
MG BATTLES THE JERSEY DEVIL!
annual 2008 - craig

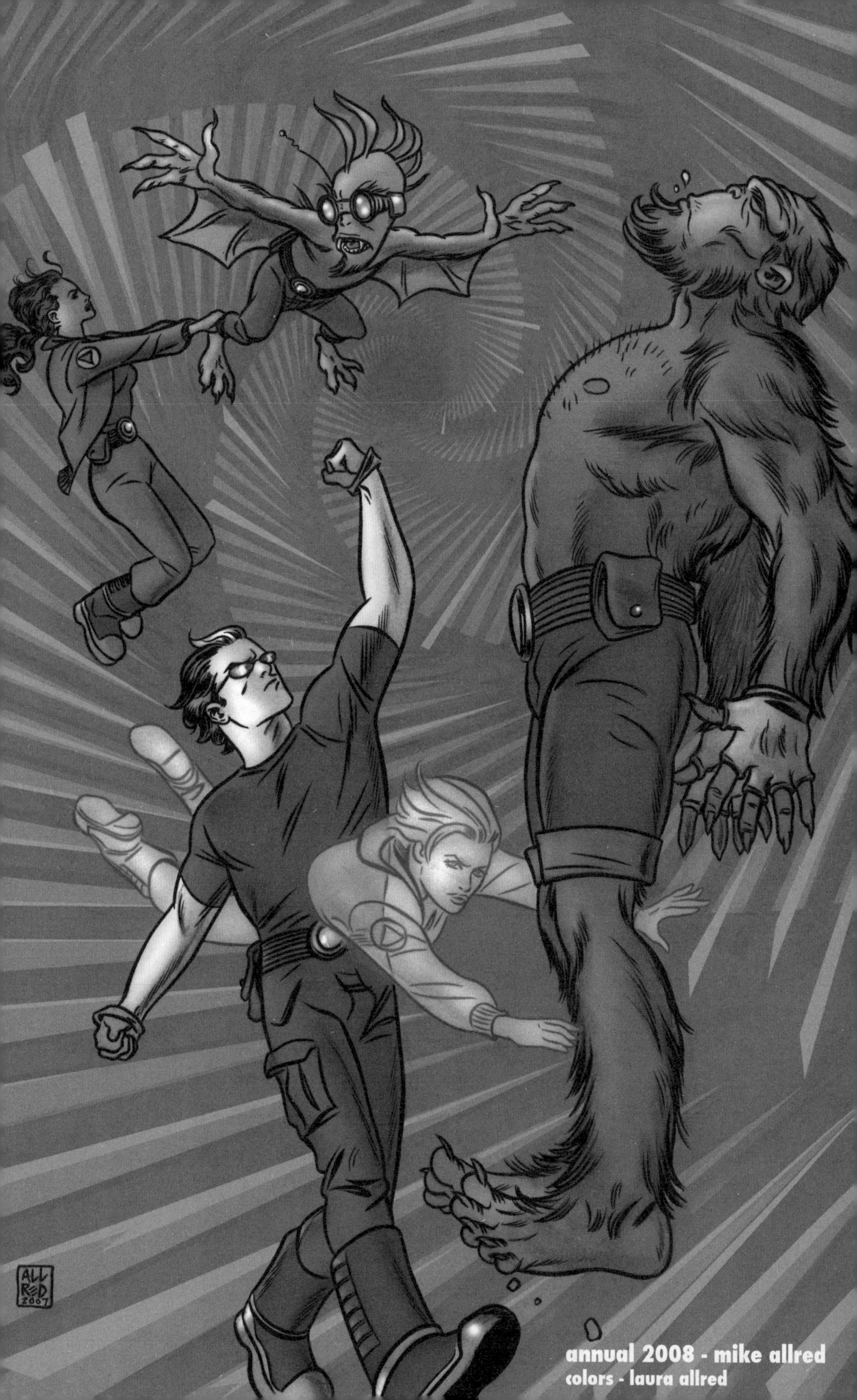
ALL
RED
2007
annual 2008 - mike allred
colors - laura allred

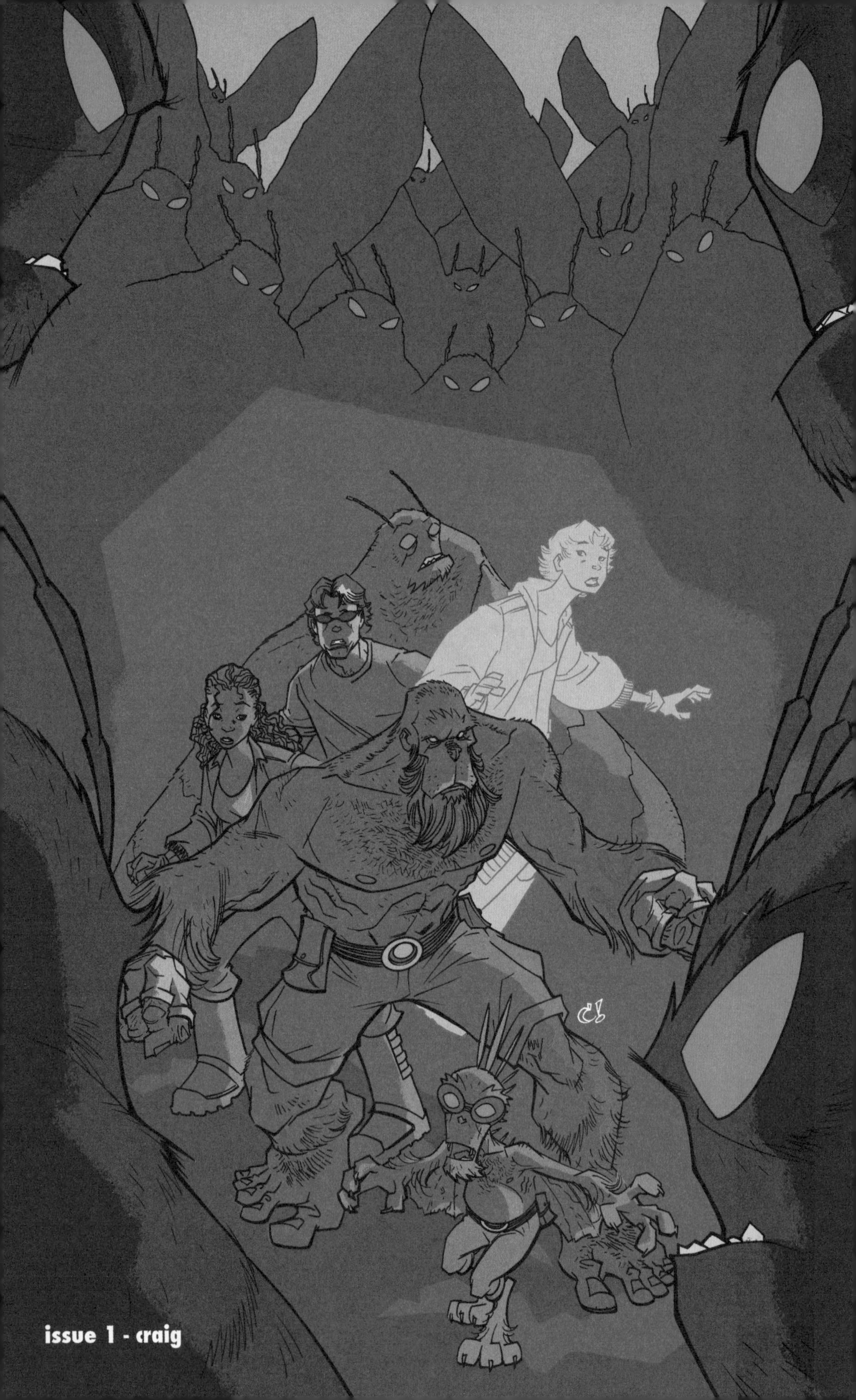
issue 1 - craig

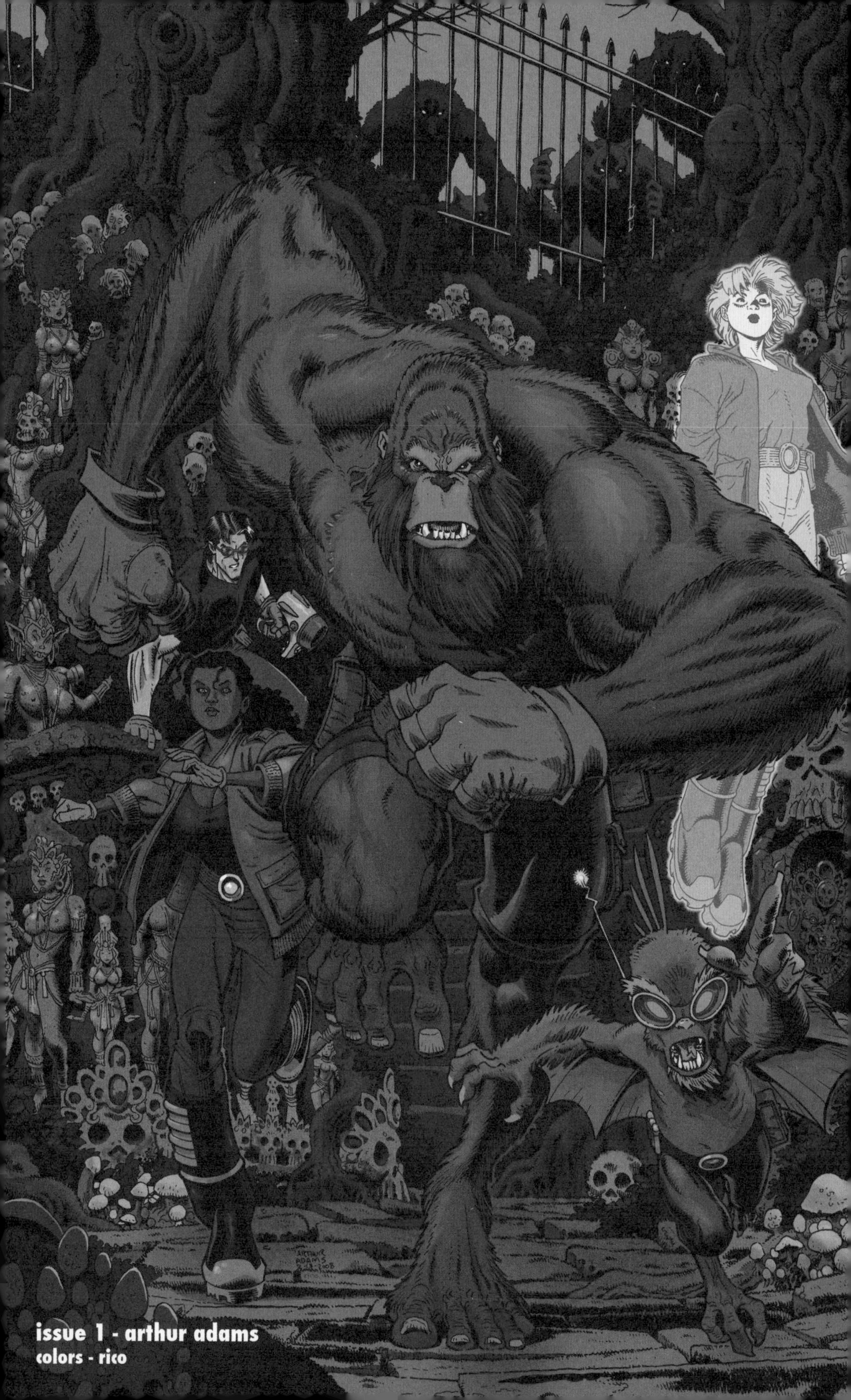

issue 1 - arthur adams
colors - rico

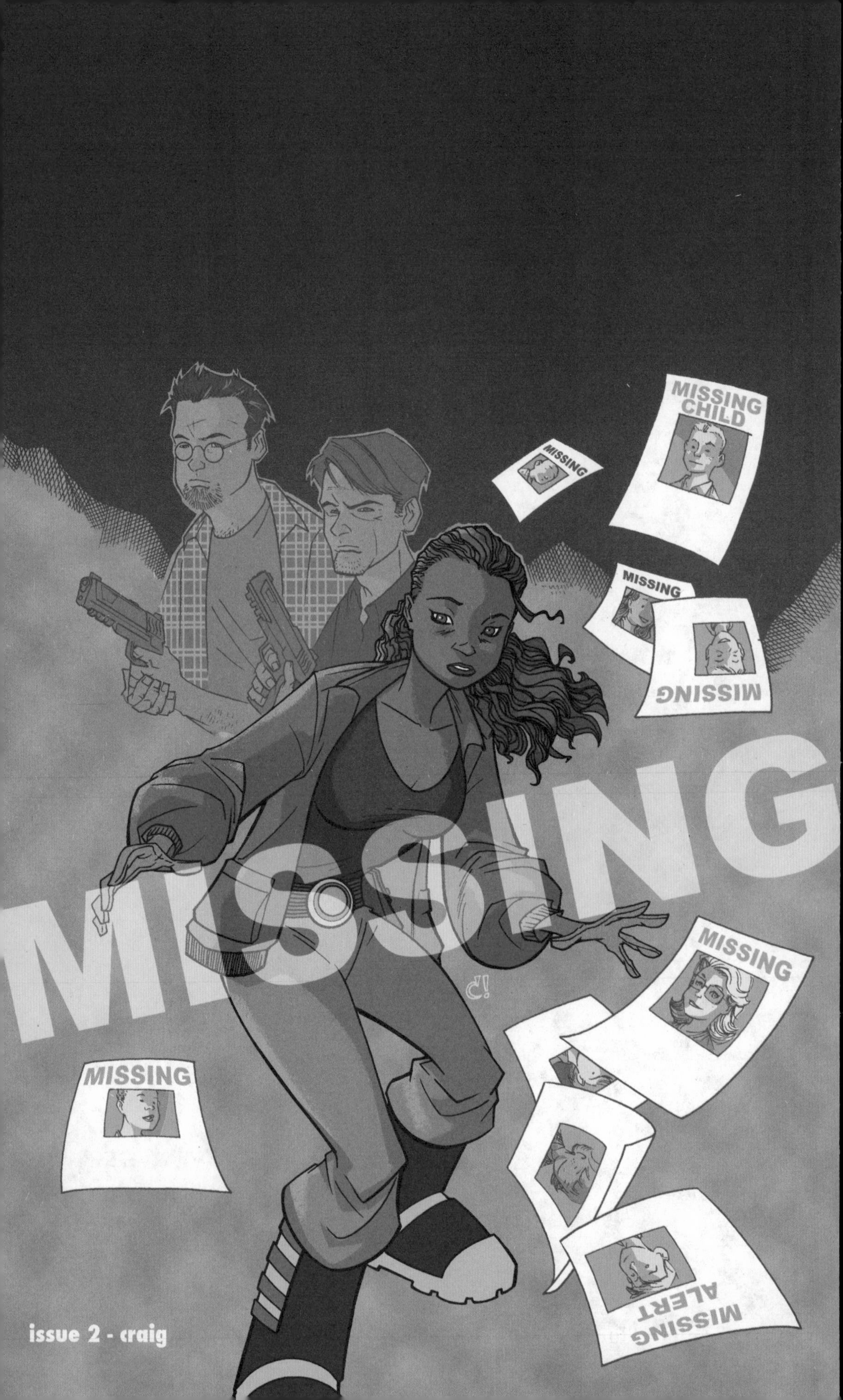
MISSING CHILD
MISSING
MISSING
MISSING
MISSING
MISSING
MISSING
MISSING ALERT
issue 2 - craig

NEXT ISSUE

"TRIANGLE Part 2"

ARISA'S PAST
catches up with her!

THE FATE OF KARL!

GREMLINS!

BACK UP STORY!
"The Other Arisa"
with artwork by Richard Case
(Doom Patrol, Sensational Spider-Man)

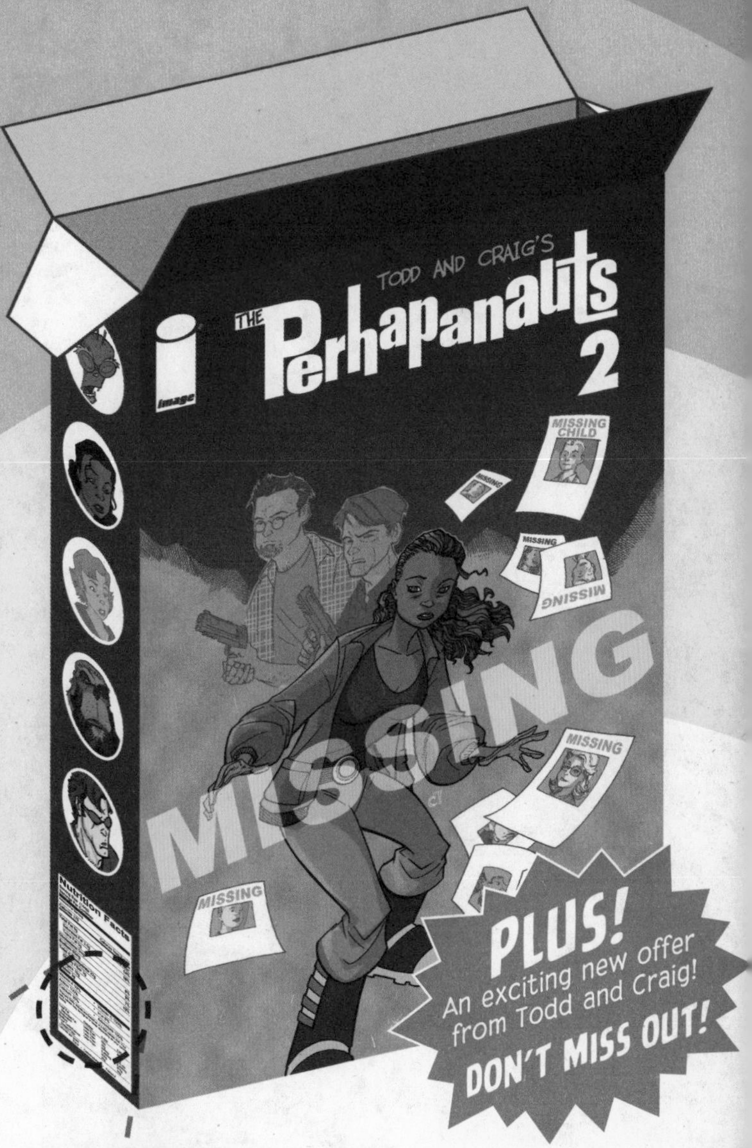

TODD AND CRAIG'S
THE Perhapanauts
2
image
MISSING CHILD
MISSING
MISSING
MISSING
MISSING
MISSING
MISSING
PLUS!
An exciting new offer from Todd and Craig!
DON'T MISS OUT!

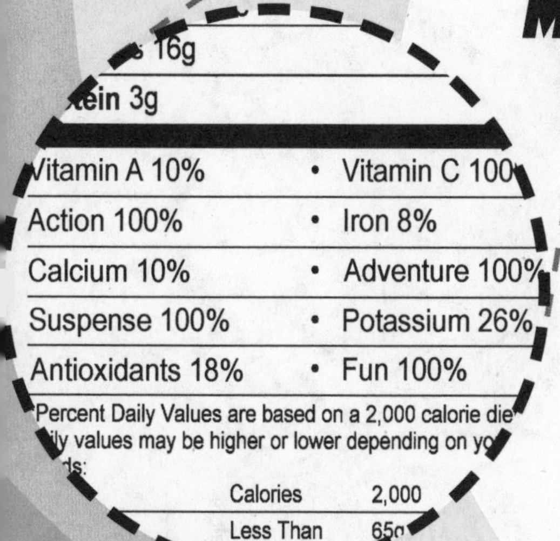

s 16g
tein 3g
Vitamin A 10% • Vitamin C 100
Action 100% • Iron 8%
Calcium 10% • Adventure 100%
Suspense 100% • Potassium 26%
Antioxidants 18% • Fun 100%
*Percent Daily Values are based on a 2,000 calorie die
ily values may be higher or lower depending on yo
ds:
Calories 2,000
Less Than 65g
Less Than

MAKE

TODD AND CRAIG'S THE PERHAPANAUTS

a part of your

NUTRITIOUS BREAKFAST!

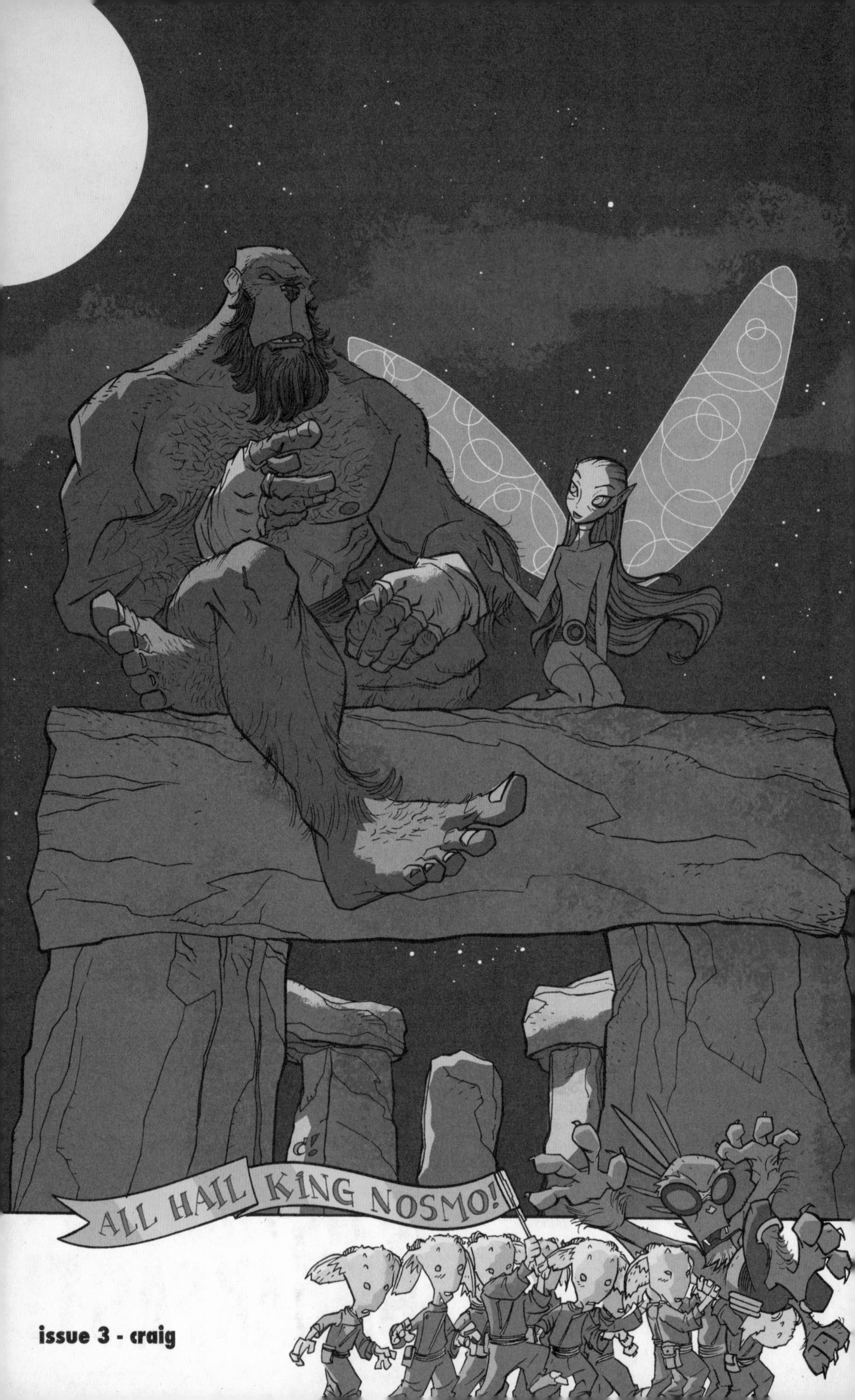
ALL HAIL KING NOSMO!

issue 3 - craig

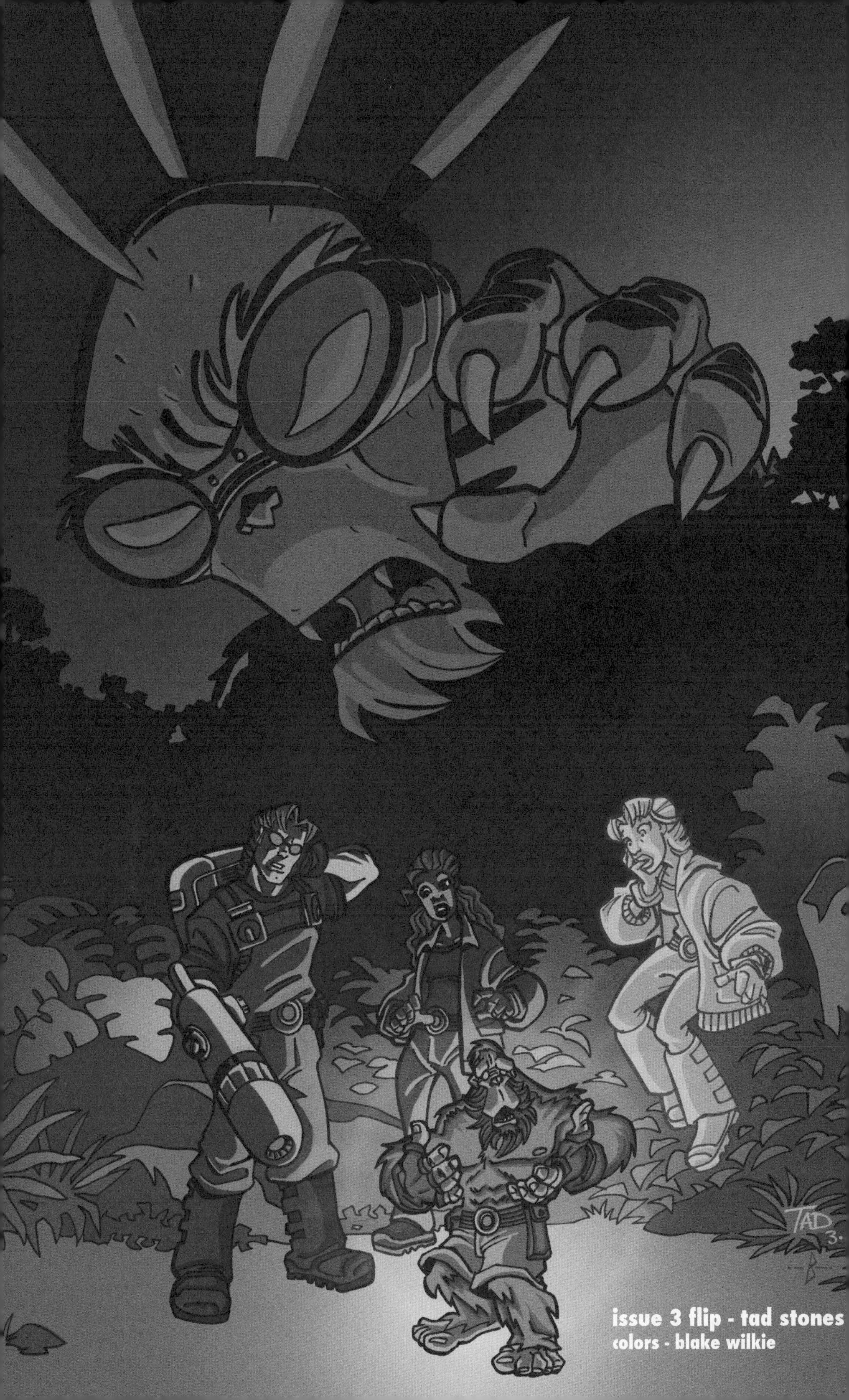

issue 3 flip - tad stones
colors - blake wilkie

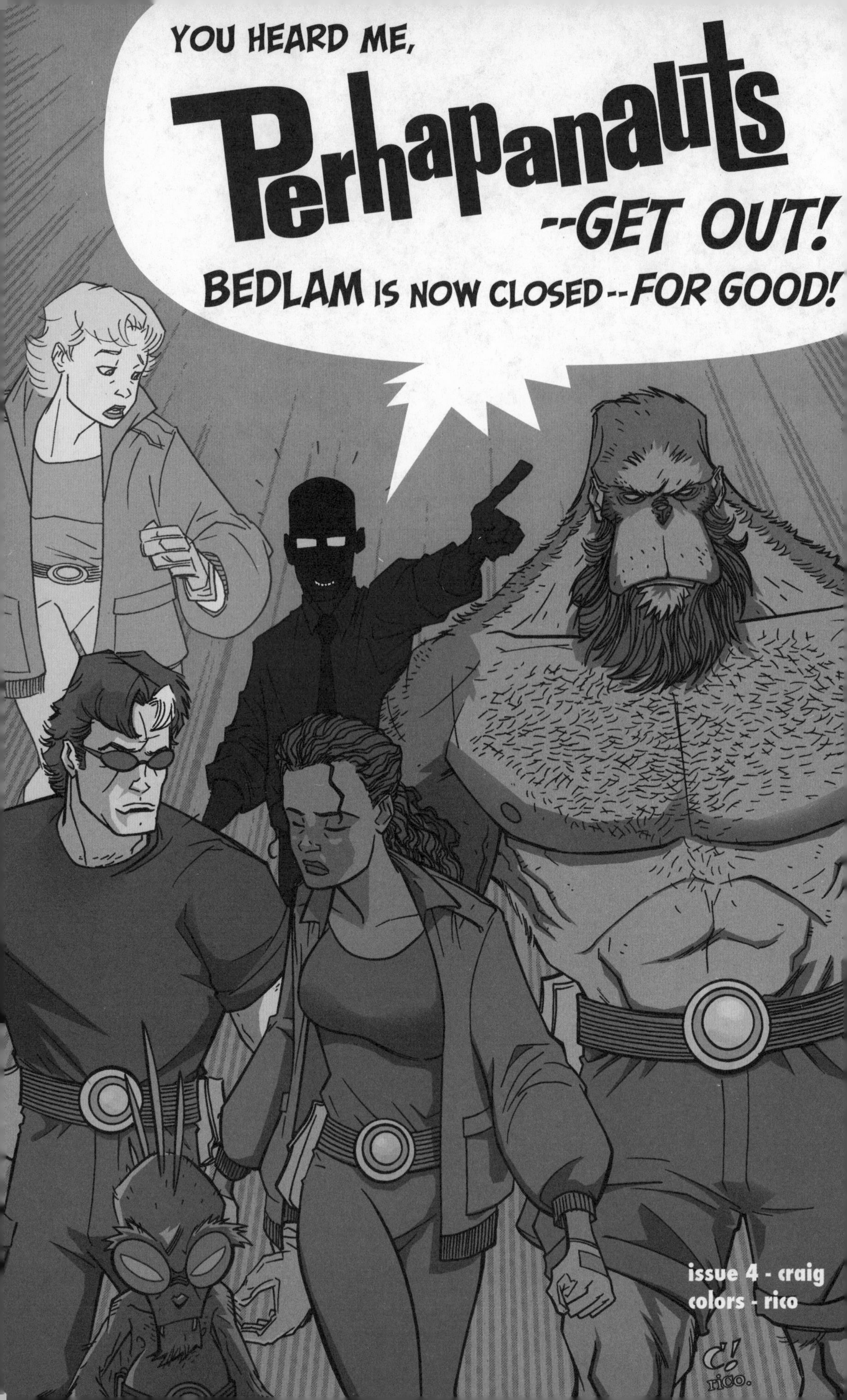
YOU HEARD ME,
Perhapanauts
--GET OUT!
BEDLAM IS NOW CLOSED--FOR GOOD!
issue 4 - craig
colors - rico

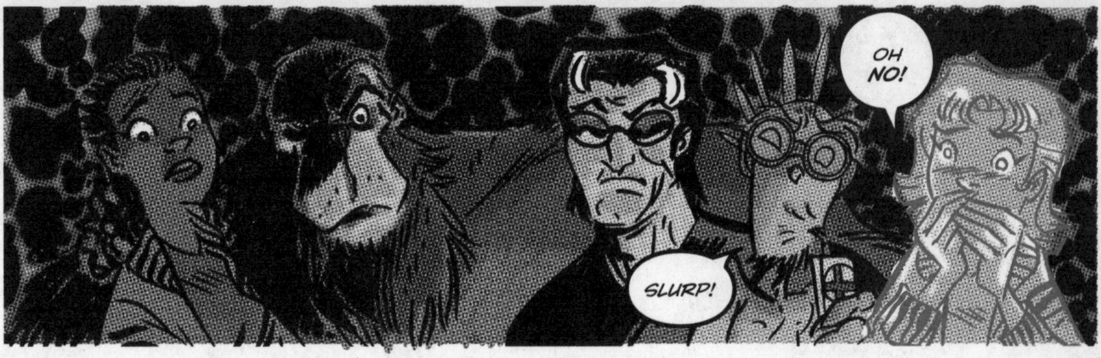
OH NO!
SLURP!

issue 4 flip - jason armstrong

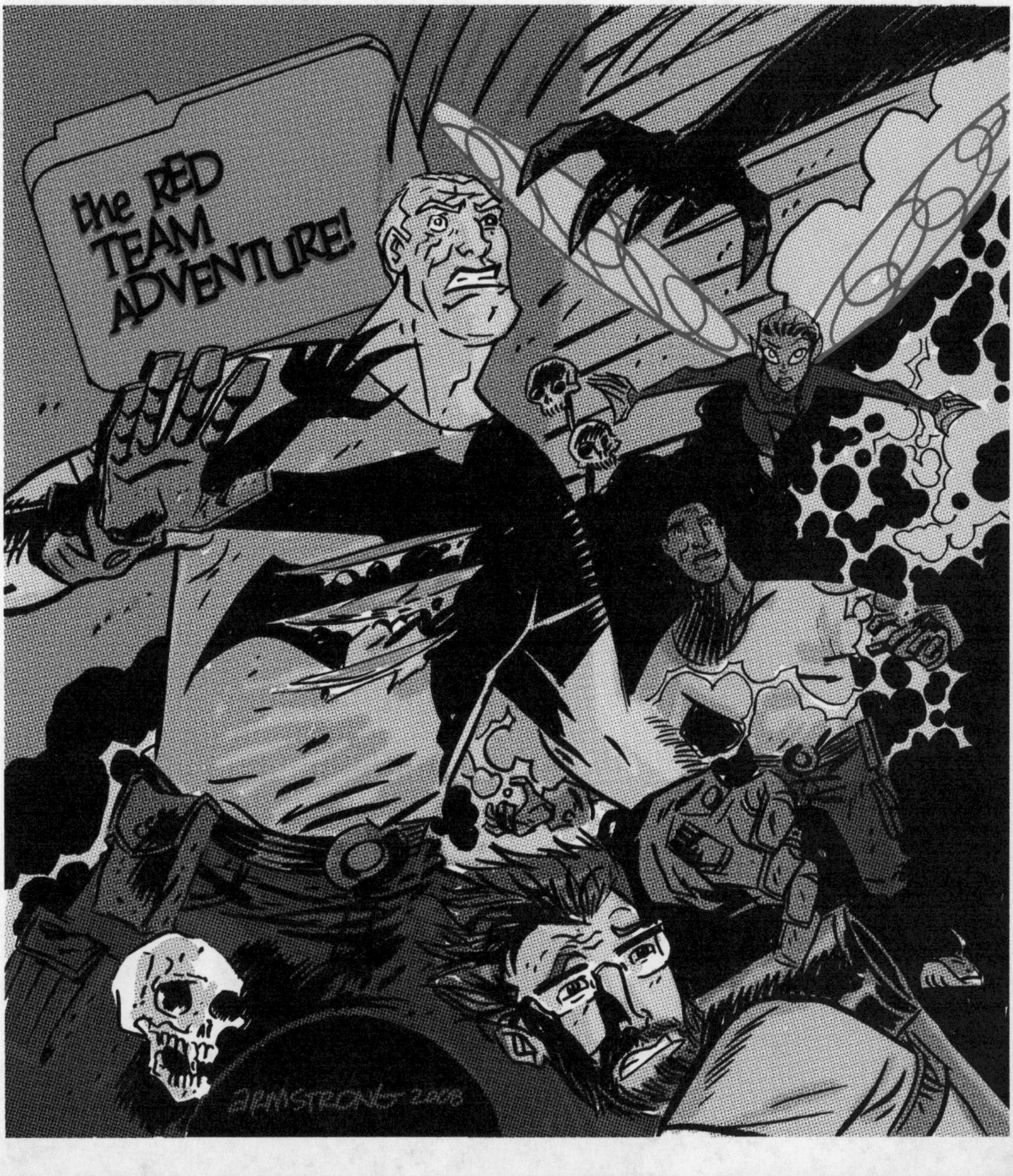
the RED TEAM ADVENTURE!
ARMSTRONG 2008

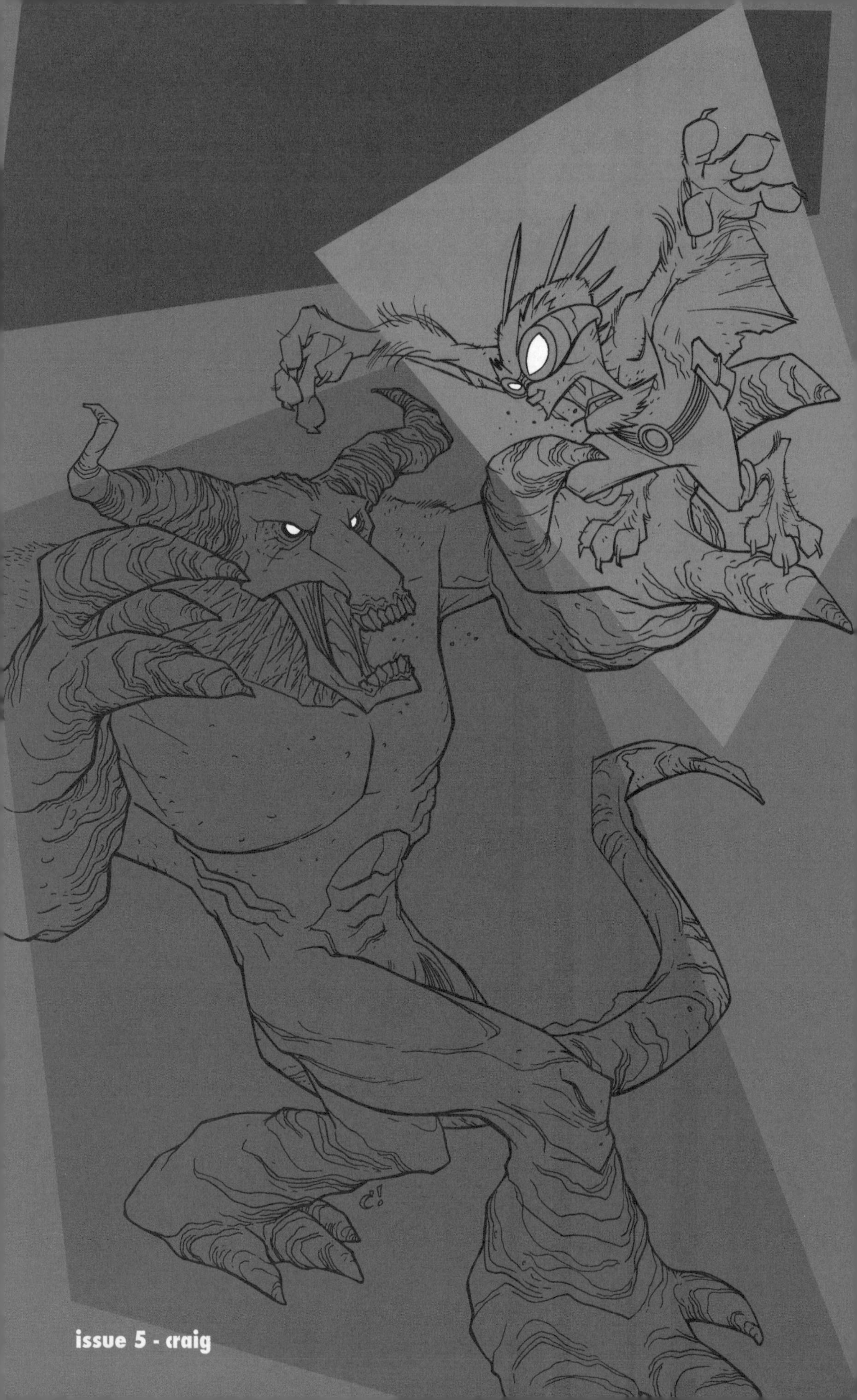

issue 5 - craig

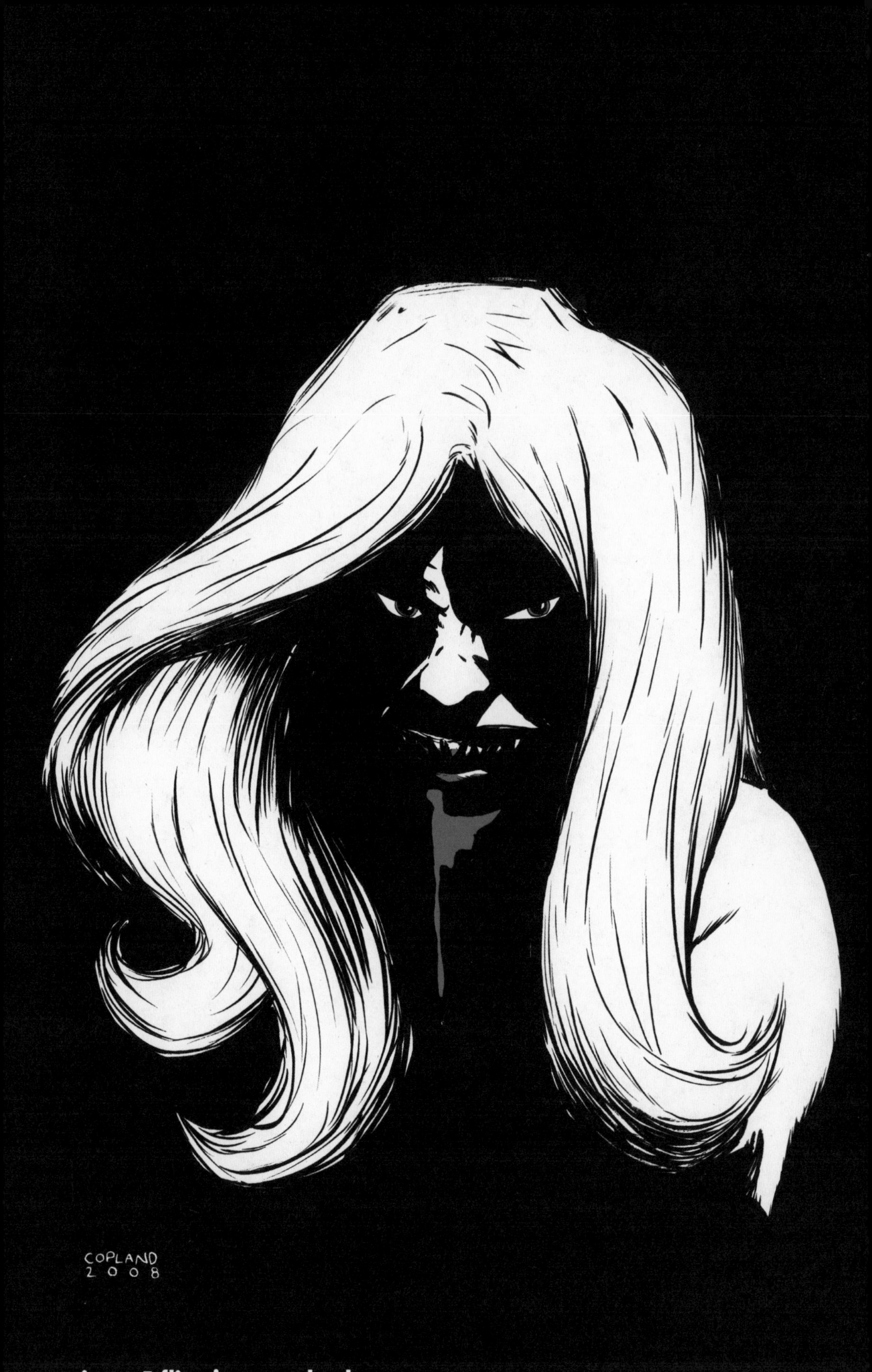
COPLAND
2008

issue 5 flip - jason copland

perhapa-pin-up gallery

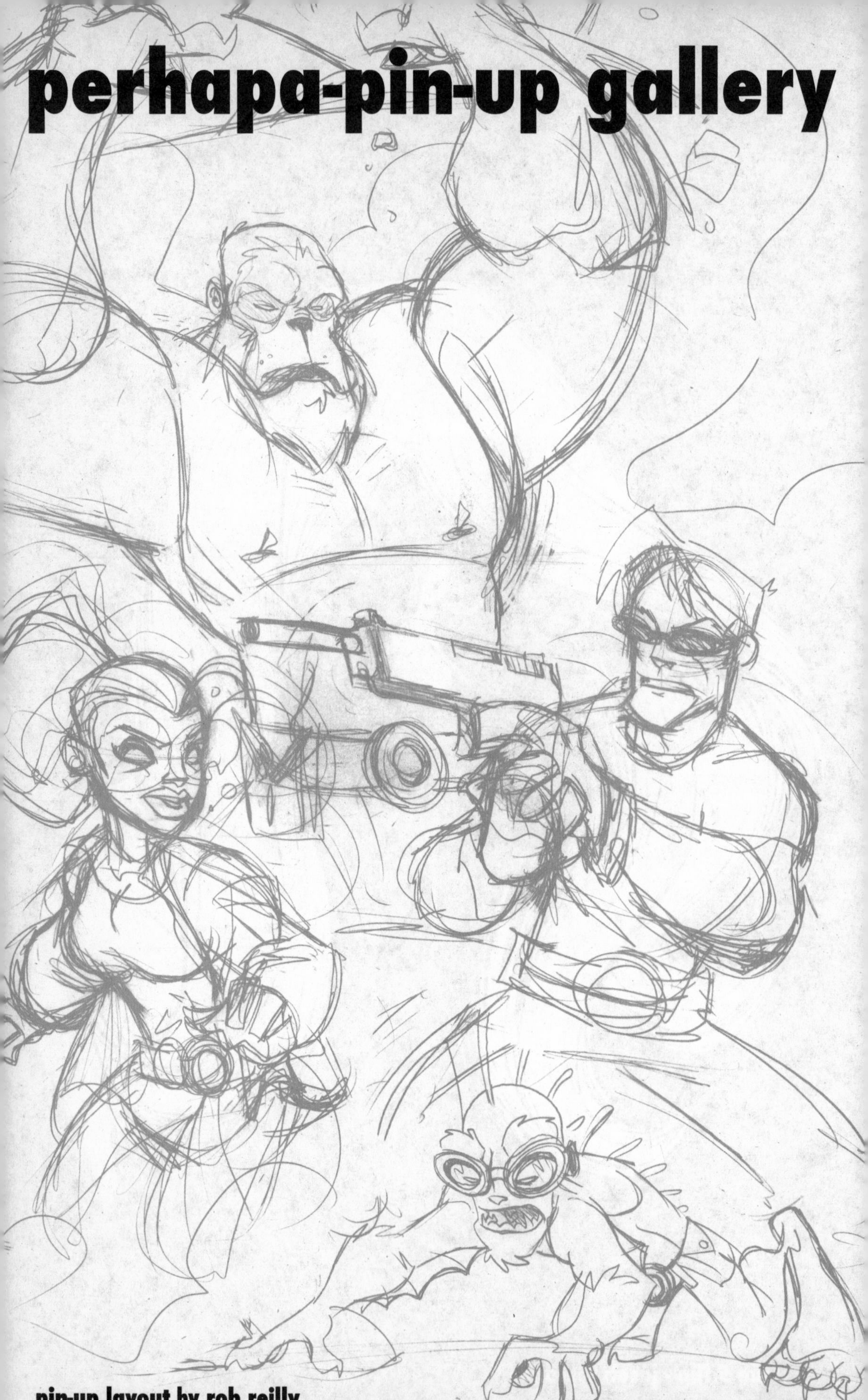

pin-up layout by rob reilly

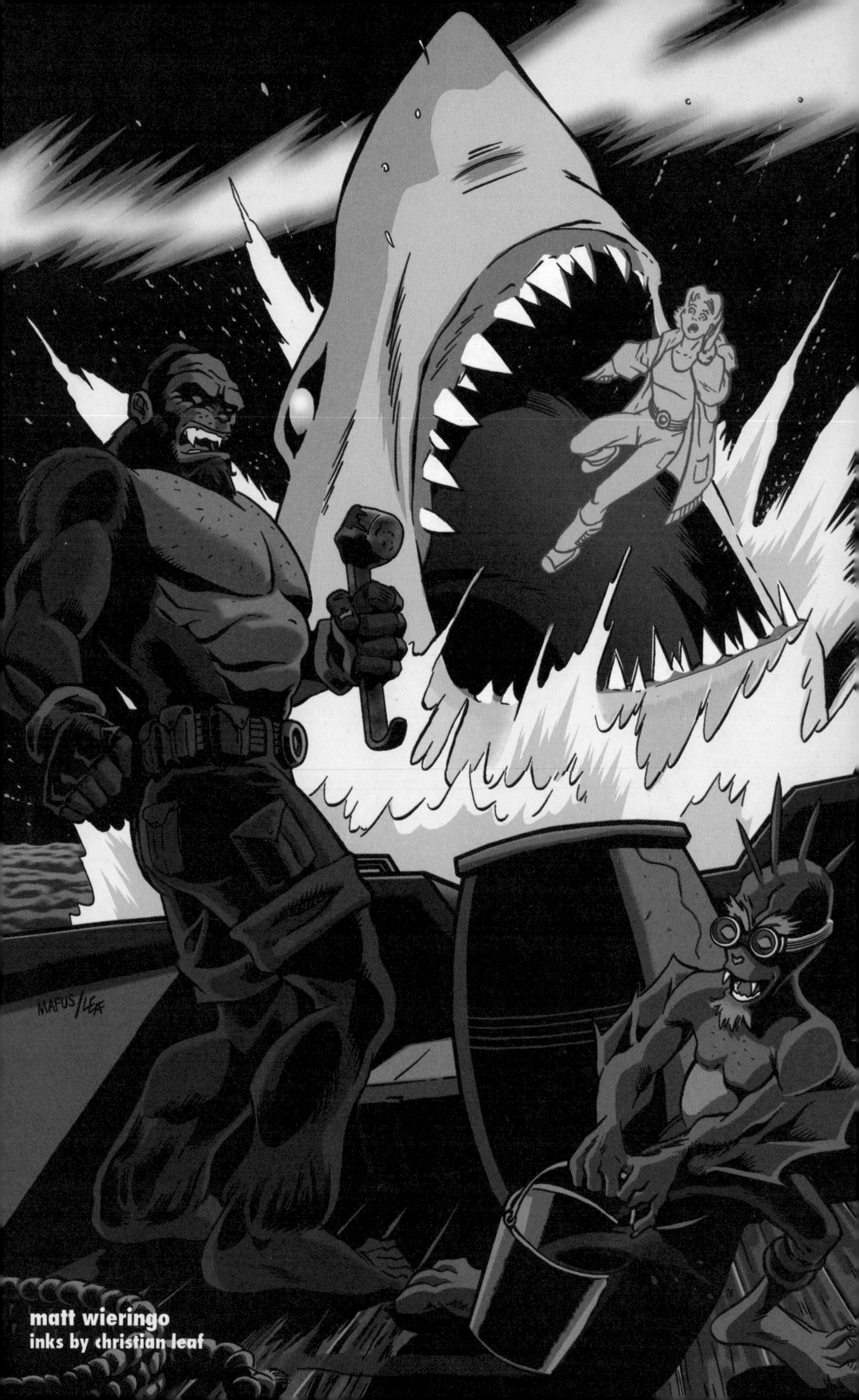

matt wieringo
inks by christian leaf

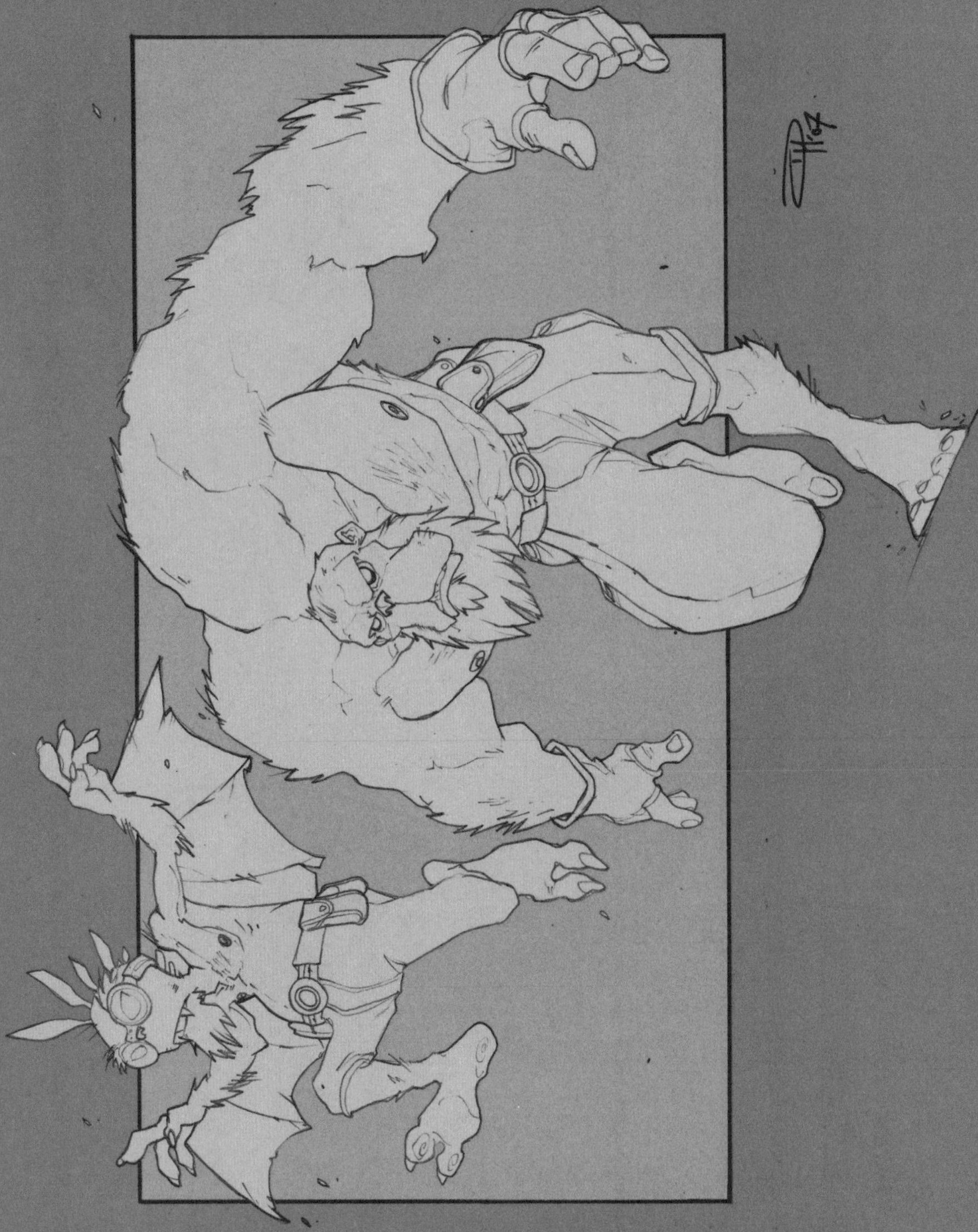

denis medri

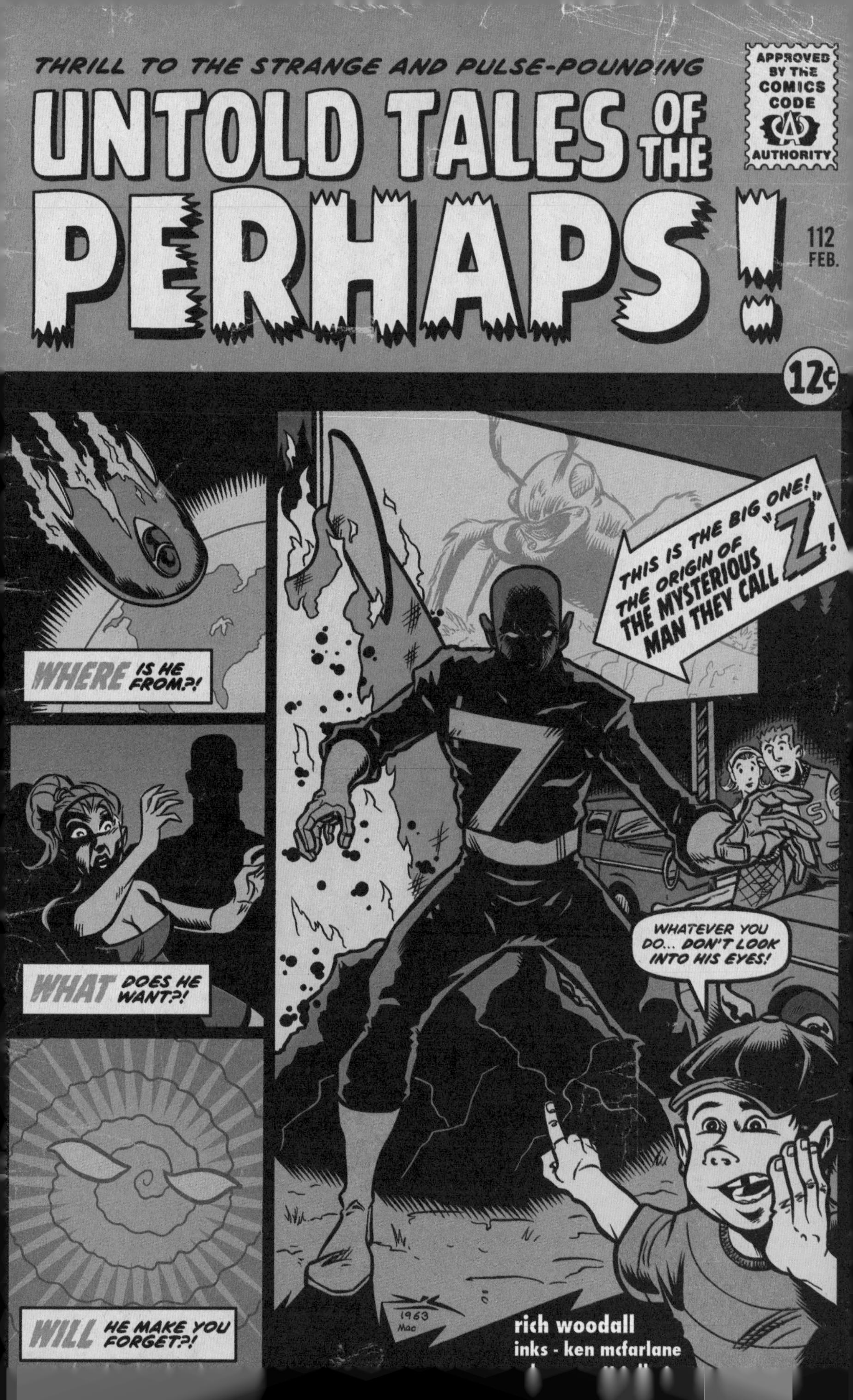
THRILL TO THE STRANGE AND PULSE-POUNDING
UNTOLD TALES OF THE PERHAPS!
APPROVED BY THE COMICS CODE AUTHORITY
112 FEB.
12¢
WHERE IS HE FROM?!
WHAT DOES HE WANT?!
WILL HE MAKE YOU FORGET?!
THIS IS THE BIG ONE! THE ORIGIN OF THE MYSTERIOUS MAN THEY CALL "Z"!
WHATEVER YOU DO... DON'T LOOK INTO HIS EYES!
1963 Mac
rich woodall
inks - ken mcfarlane

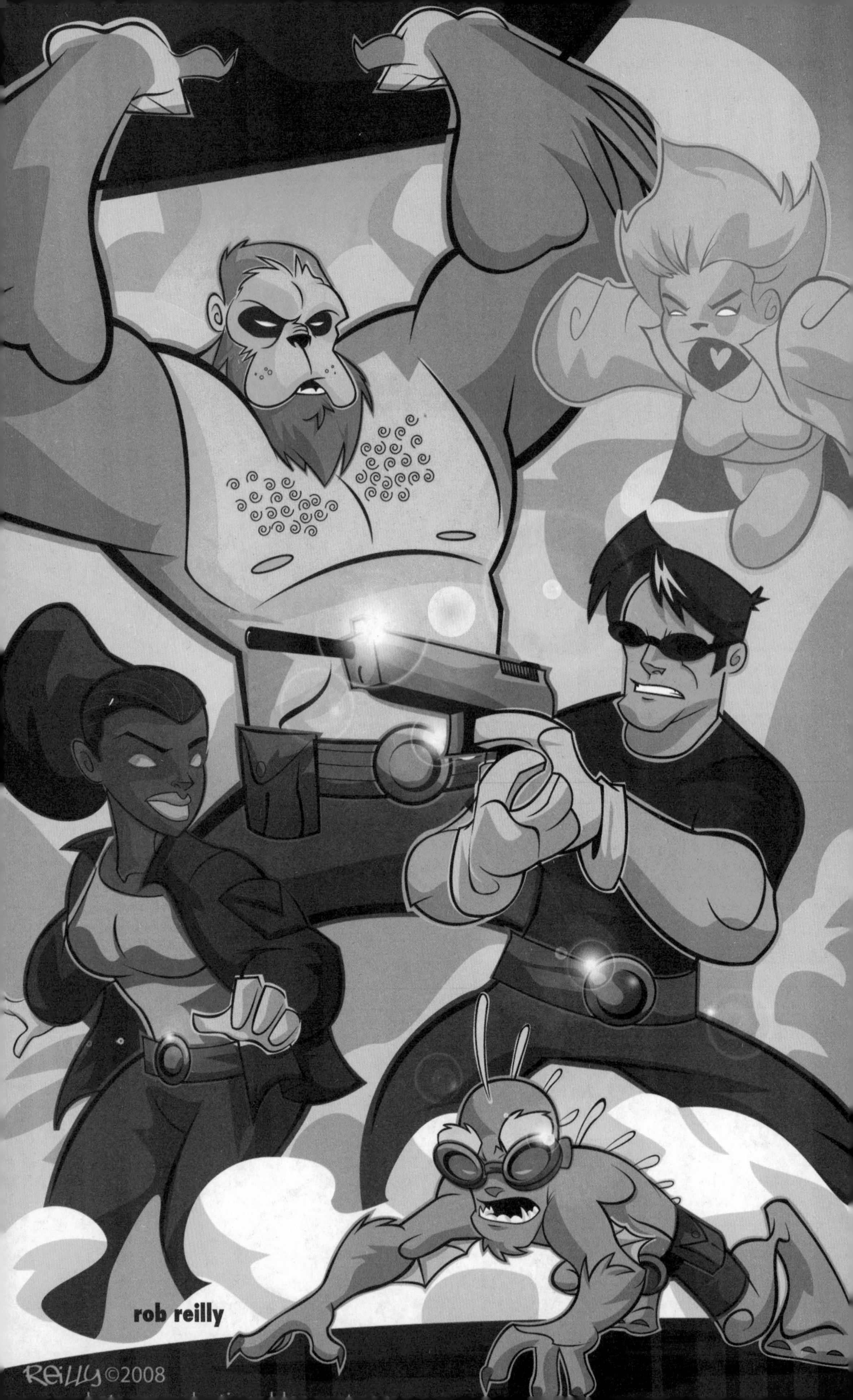
rob reilly
REILLY ©2008

deleted scenes
from perhapanauts 2

ARISA: THIS IS THE SYSTEM OF PNEUMATIC
TUBES THAT ACT AS HIGH-SPEED ELEVATORS
AROUND HERE.

ARISA: WE USED TO CALL THEM
"P-TUBES," UNTIL CHOO— ER, ONE OF OUR
CO-WORKERS THOUGHT THAT MEANT
SOMETHING ELSE.

"p-tubes"

"though i had come up with this gag years ago, it appeared that it was never going to see print as our relationship with dark horse continued to fade away. it was too funny a line not to use, so when i was asked to contribute one page to dc's special annniversary TEEN TITANS #50, i gave the joke to impulse. who knew that eric stephenson and joe keatinge would come and rescue the 'haps and we'd get a chance to tell that story? i left it out of the story 'cause i didn't want to be repetitious and 'cause there really wasn't any room, but we thought we'd include it here, where it originally belonged and 'cause it's just so damn choopie!" - todd

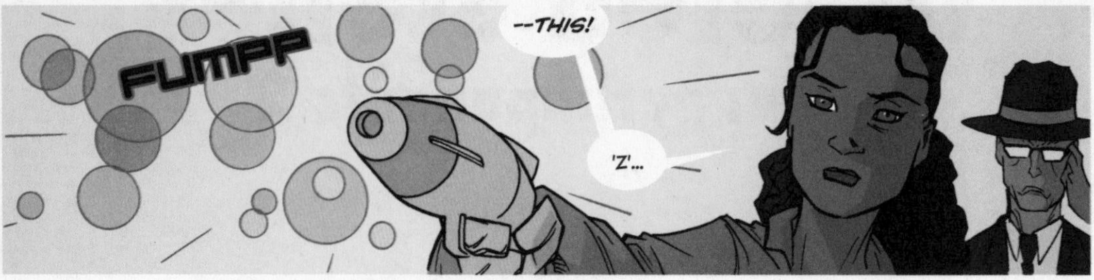
FUMPP
--THIS!
'Z'...

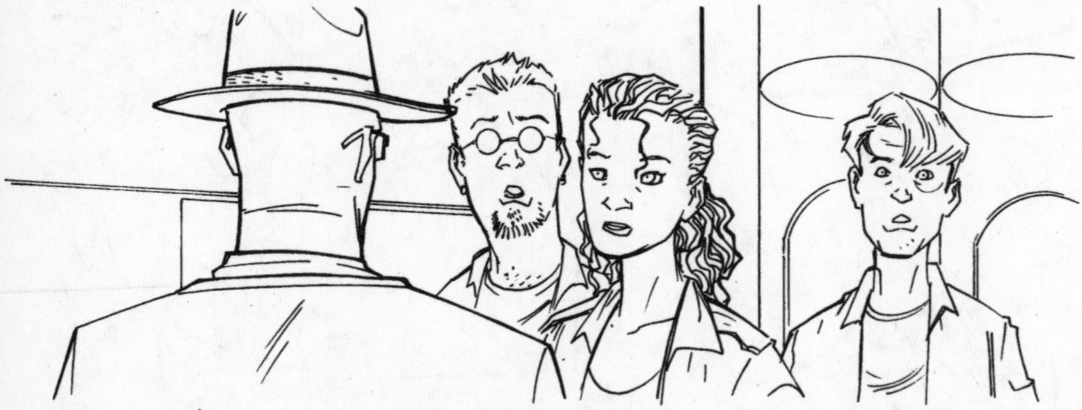

ARISA: OKAY, Z, NOW LISTEN. ALL I WANT YOU TO WIPE IS THE LOCATION OF BEDLAM AND THE STORAGE UNITS THAT GOT THEM IN HERE.

Z: VERY WELL, ARISA.

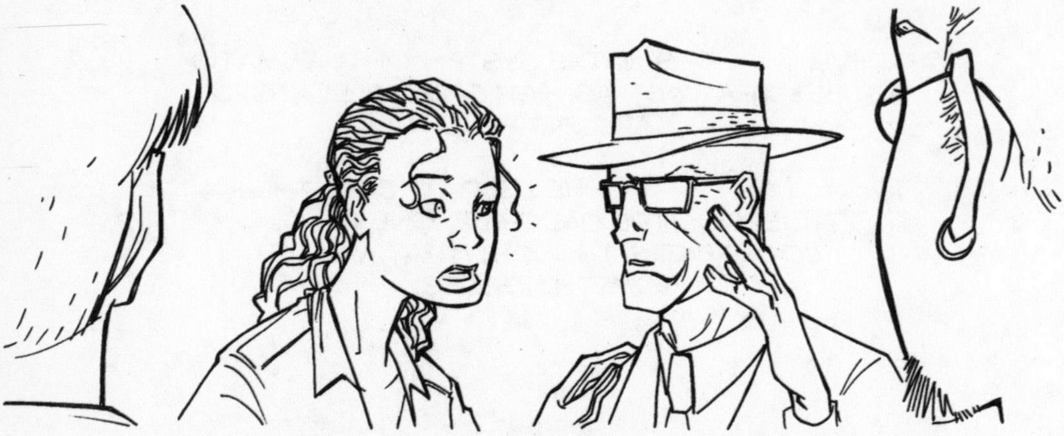

ARISA: OH, OH--AND THE GREMLINS! THEY SAW THE GREMLINS! THEY CAN'T REMEMBER THE GREMLINS.

Z: THE LOCATION AND THE GREMLINS. VERY WELL.

ARISA: OH, OH--WAIT! AND THAT I SHOT THEM WITH THIS GUN! THEY CAN'T THINK I SHOT THEM WITH THIS GUN!

ARISA: SO, THE LOCATION, THE GREMLINS, AND NO GUN! 'KAY?

Z: WILL THAT BE ALL?

ARISA: YUP. YES. THAT SHOULD DO IT.

ARISA: WAIT!

ARISA: NO, NO--THAT'S IT.

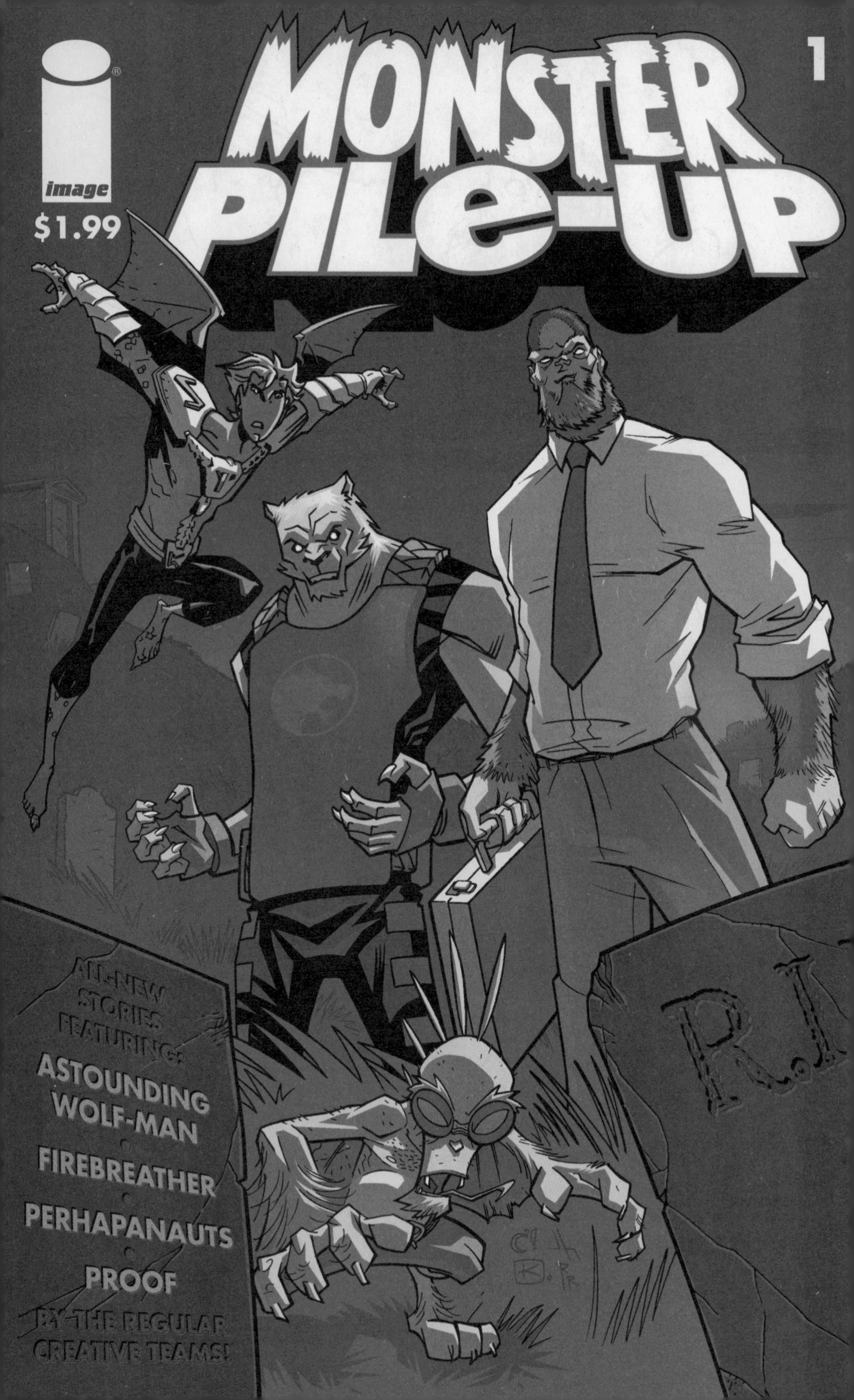

image
$1.99
MONSTER PILE-UP
1
ALL-NEW STORIES FEATURING:
ASTOUNDING WOLF-MAN
FIREBREATHER
PERHAPANAUTS
PROOF
BY THE REGULAR CREATIVE TEAMS!
R.I.

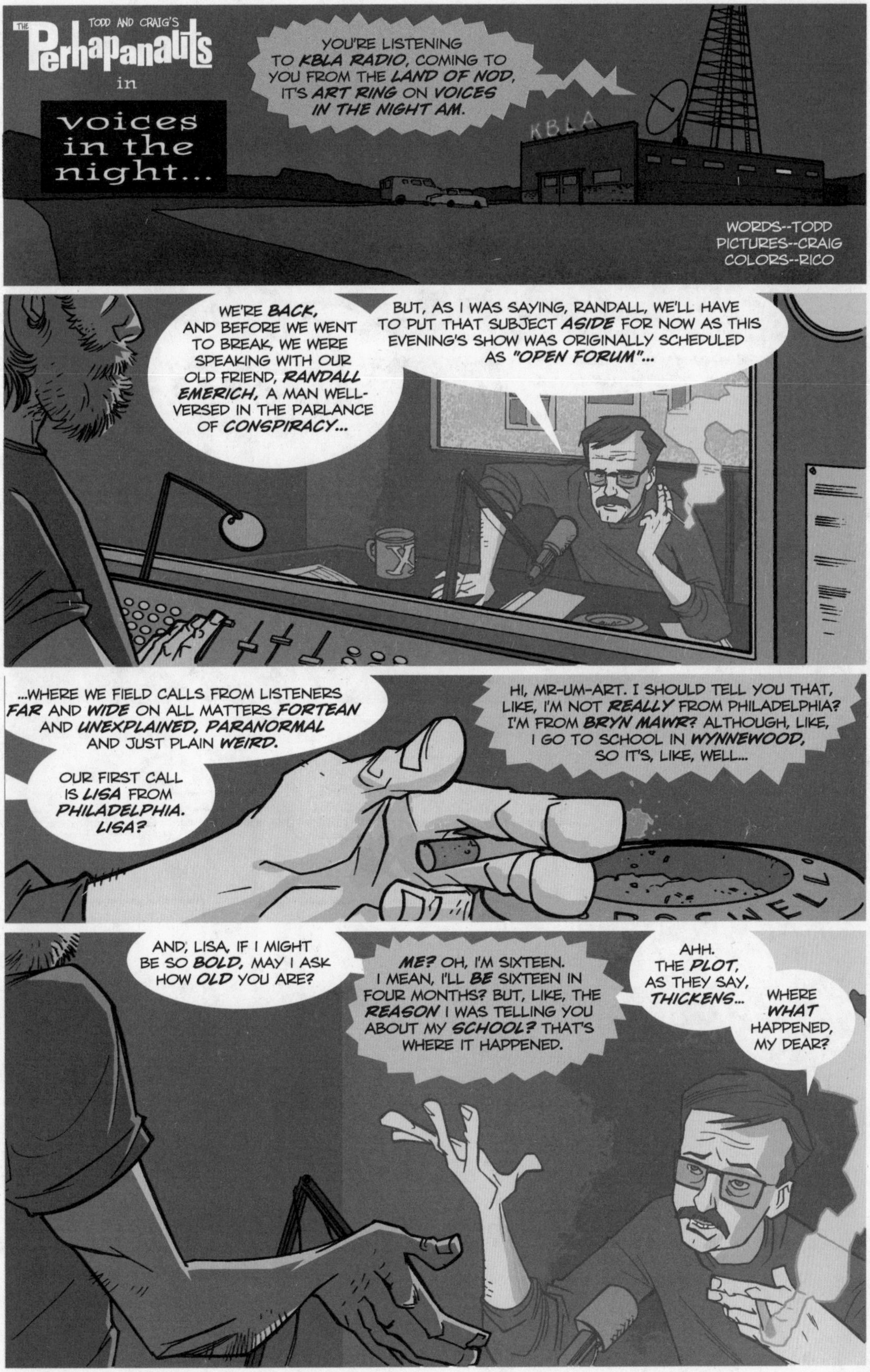
TODD AND CRAIG'S
THE Perhapanauts
in
voices in the night...
YOU'RE LISTENING TO KBLA RADIO, COMING TO YOU FROM THE LAND OF NOD, IT'S ART RING ON VOICES IN THE NIGHT AM.
KBLA
WORDS--TODD
PICTURES--CRAIG
COLORS--RICO
WE'RE BACK, AND BEFORE WE WENT TO BREAK, WE WERE SPEAKING WITH OUR OLD FRIEND, RANDALL EMERICH, A MAN WELL-VERSED IN THE PARLANCE OF CONSPIRACY...
BUT, AS I WAS SAYING, RANDALL, WE'LL HAVE TO PUT THAT SUBJECT ASIDE FOR NOW AS THIS EVENING'S SHOW WAS ORIGINALLY SCHEDULED AS "OPEN FORUM"...
...WHERE WE FIELD CALLS FROM LISTENERS FAR AND WIDE ON ALL MATTERS FORTEAN AND UNEXPLAINED, PARANORMAL AND JUST PLAIN WEIRD.
OUR FIRST CALL IS LISA FROM PHILADELPHIA. LISA?
HI, MR-UM-ART. I SHOULD TELL YOU THAT, LIKE, I'M NOT REALLY FROM PHILADELPHIA? I'M FROM BRYN MAWR? ALTHOUGH, LIKE, I GO TO SCHOOL IN WYNNEWOOD, SO IT'S, LIKE, WELL...
ROSWELL
AND, LISA, IF I MIGHT BE SO BOLD, MAY I ASK HOW OLD YOU ARE?
ME? OH, I'M SIXTEEN. I MEAN, I'LL BE SIXTEEN IN FOUR MONTHS? BUT, LIKE, THE REASON I WAS TELLING YOU ABOUT MY SCHOOL? THAT'S WHERE IT HAPPENED.
AHH. THE PLOT, AS THEY SAY, THICKENS...
WHERE WHAT HAPPENED, MY DEAR?

"'KAY, SO, LIKE, THIS HAPPENED, LIKE, TWO MONTHS AGO, RIGHT? MY FRIEND, *MAGS*, AND I WERE AT THIS *DANCE* THAT WAS S'POSED TO BE, LIKE, A *PROM*? BUT THEY DON'T *CALL* IT THAT ANYMORE 'CAUSE THEY THINK *THAT* CAUSES, LIKE, TOO MUCH *PRESSURE*? SO THEY CALL IT THE "END OF YEAR" COTILLION.

"'TEVER...

"MAGS AND ME *COULDA* HAD DATES, BUT WE REALLY DIDN'T WANNA HAFTA PUT UP WITH A COUPLE OF *BOYS* THAT NIGHT; WE JUST WANTED TO HAVE FUN *TOGETHER*.

"PLUS, THAT *SKANK* AMBER D'INTRONO? ASKED JEFF MORGAN BEFORE *MAGS* COULD, AND SHE DIDN'T REALLY WANNA GO WITH ANYBODY *ELSE*...

AND THAT'S WHEN I SAW IT...

"IT WAS LIKE--AT FIRST I THOUGHT MY EYES WERE PLAYING *TRICKS* ON ME? 'CAUSE, LIKE, THE LIGHTS WERE *LOW* AND THEY HAD ONE OF THOSE *DISCO-BALL* THINGY'S GOING...?

"BUT WHEN I GOT A REAL *LOOK*...? IT WAS *FREAKY*, 'CAUSE IT WAS A *GHOST!!* A REAL LIVE... WELL, NOT *LIVE* BUT, LIKE, *DEFINITELY* A GHOST!

"THERE WAS A *GIRL* STANDING *RIGHT THERE* BY THE LOCKER ROOM *DOORS* AND I COULD SEE *RIGHT THROUGH HER!* AND WHEN *SHE* SAW THAT *I* SAW HER-

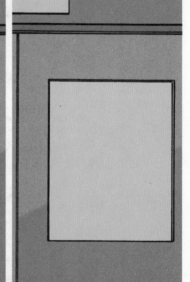

--SHE JUST *DISAPPEARED!*

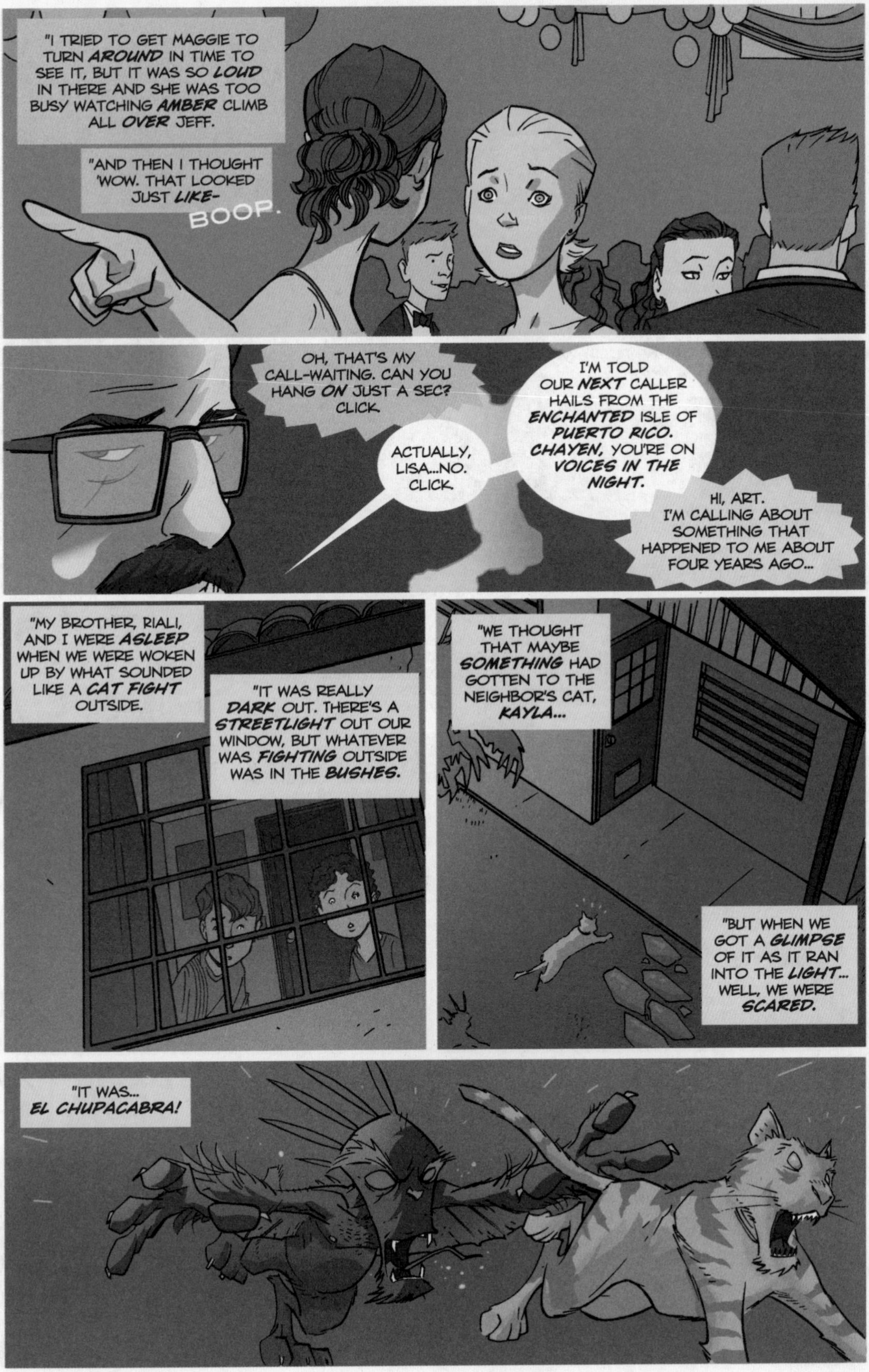
"I TRIED TO GET MAGGIE TO TURN AROUND IN TIME TO SEE IT, BUT IT WAS SO LOUD IN THERE AND SHE WAS TOO BUSY WATCHING AMBER CLIMB ALL OVER JEFF.
"AND THEN I THOUGHT 'WOW. THAT LOOKED JUST LIKE-
BOOP.
OH, THAT'S MY CALL-WAITING. CAN YOU HANG ON JUST A SEC? CLICK.
ACTUALLY, LISA...NO. CLICK.
I'M TOLD OUR NEXT CALLER HAILS FROM THE ENCHANTED ISLE OF PUERTO RICO. CHAYEN, YOU'RE ON VOICES IN THE NIGHT.
HI, ART. I'M CALLING ABOUT SOMETHING THAT HAPPENED TO ME ABOUT FOUR YEARS AGO...
"MY BROTHER, RIALI, AND I WERE ASLEEP WHEN WE WERE WOKEN UP BY WHAT SOUNDED LIKE A CAT FIGHT OUTSIDE.
"IT WAS REALLY DARK OUT. THERE'S A STREETLIGHT OUT OUR WINDOW, BUT WHATEVER WAS FIGHTING OUTSIDE WAS IN THE BUSHES.
"WE THOUGHT THAT MAYBE SOMETHING HAD GOTTEN TO THE NEIGHBOR'S CAT, KAYLA...
"BUT WHEN WE GOT A GLIMPSE OF IT AS IT RAN INTO THE LIGHT... WELL, WE WERE SCARED.
"IT WAS... EL CHUPACABRA!

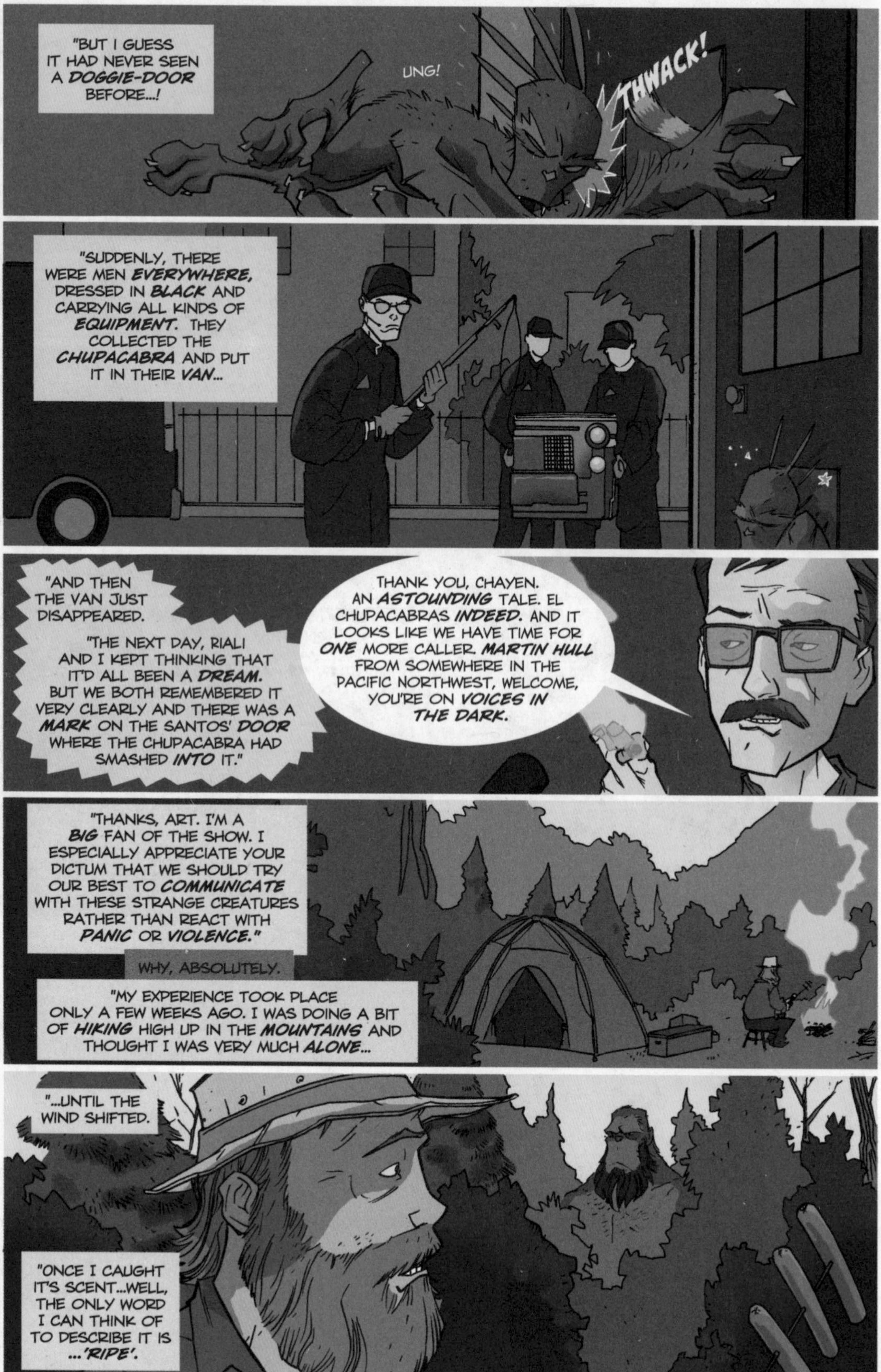
"BUT I GUESS IT HAD NEVER SEEN A DOGGIE-DOOR BEFORE...!
UNG!
THWACK!
"SUDDENLY, THERE WERE MEN EVERYWHERE, DRESSED IN BLACK AND CARRYING ALL KINDS OF EQUIPMENT. THEY COLLECTED THE CHUPACABRA AND PUT IT IN THEIR VAN...
"AND THEN THE VAN JUST DISAPPEARED.
"THE NEXT DAY, RIALI AND I KEPT THINKING THAT IT'D ALL BEEN A DREAM. BUT WE BOTH REMEMBERED IT VERY CLEARLY AND THERE WAS A MARK ON THE SANTOS' DOOR WHERE THE CHUPACABRA HAD SMASHED INTO IT."
THANK YOU, CHAYEN. AN ASTOUNDING TALE. EL CHUPACABRAS INDEED. AND IT LOOKS LIKE WE HAVE TIME FOR ONE MORE CALLER. MARTIN HULL FROM SOMEWHERE IN THE PACIFIC NORTHWEST, WELCOME, YOU'RE ON VOICES IN THE DARK.
"THANKS, ART. I'M A BIG FAN OF THE SHOW. I ESPECIALLY APPRECIATE YOUR DICTUM THAT WE SHOULD TRY OUR BEST TO COMMUNICATE WITH THESE STRANGE CREATURES RATHER THAN REACT WITH PANIC OR VIOLENCE."
WHY, ABSOLUTELY.
"MY EXPERIENCE TOOK PLACE ONLY A FEW WEEKS AGO. I WAS DOING A BIT OF HIKING HIGH UP IN THE MOUNTAINS AND THOUGHT I WAS VERY MUCH ALONE...
"...UNTIL THE WIND SHIFTED.
"ONCE I CAUGHT IT'S SCENT...WELL, THE ONLY WORD I CAN THINK OF TO DESCRIBE IT IS ...'RIPE'.

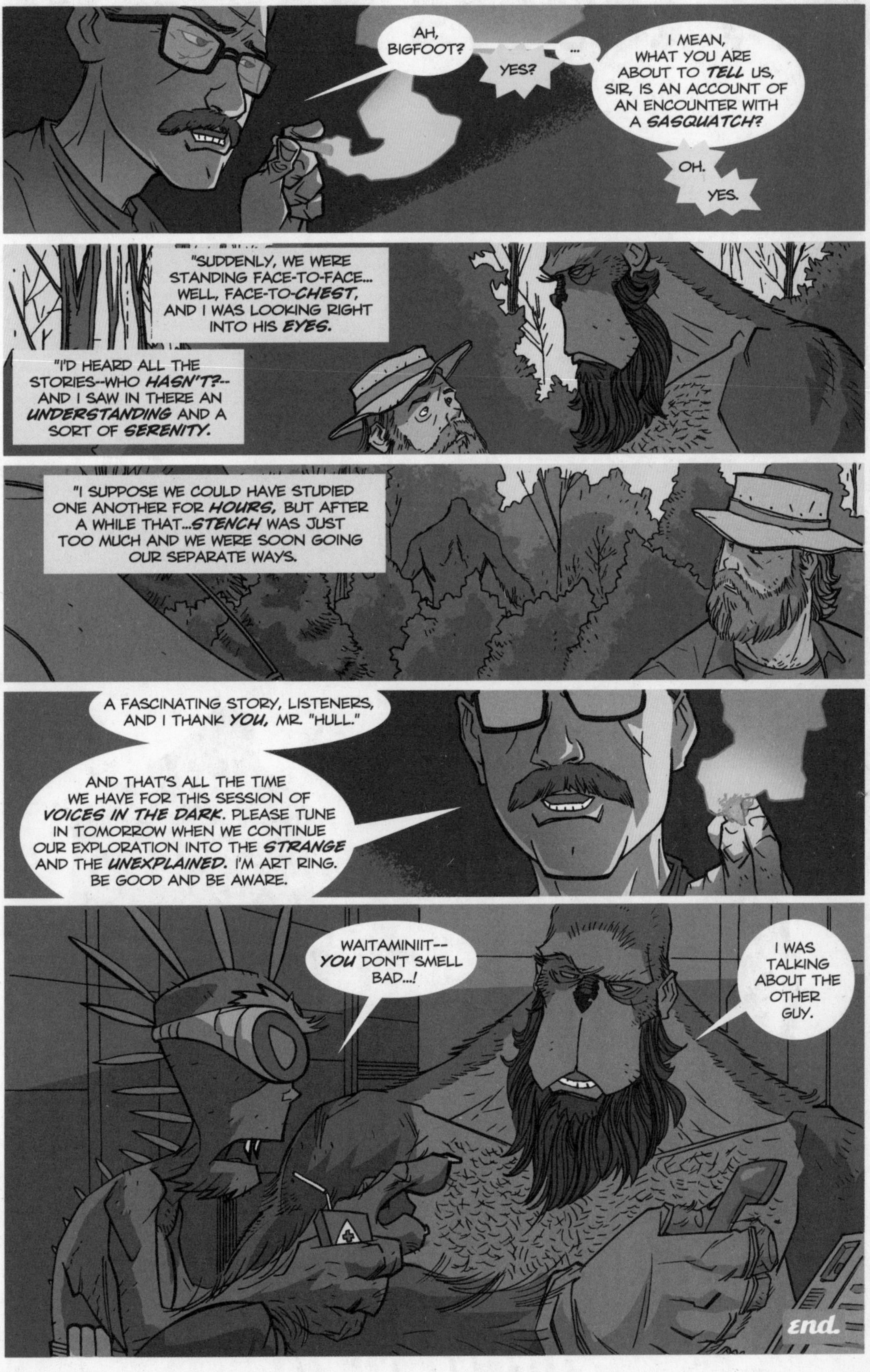
AH, BIGFOOT?
YES?
...
I MEAN, WHAT YOU ARE ABOUT TO TELL US, SIR, IS AN ACCOUNT OF AN ENCOUNTER WITH A SASQUATCH?
OH.
YES.
"SUDDENLY, WE WERE STANDING FACE-TO-FACE... WELL, FACE-TO-CHEST, AND I WAS LOOKING RIGHT INTO HIS EYES.
"I'D HEARD ALL THE STORIES--WHO HASN'T?--AND I SAW IN THERE AN UNDERSTANDING AND A SORT OF SERENITY.
"I SUPPOSE WE COULD HAVE STUDIED ONE ANOTHER FOR HOURS, BUT AFTER A WHILE THAT...STENCH WAS JUST TOO MUCH AND WE WERE SOON GOING OUR SEPARATE WAYS.
A FASCINATING STORY, LISTENERS, AND I THANK YOU, MR. "HULL."
AND THAT'S ALL THE TIME WE HAVE FOR THIS SESSION OF VOICES IN THE DARK. PLEASE TUNE IN TOMORROW WHEN WE CONTINUE OUR EXPLORATION INTO THE STRANGE AND THE UNEXPLAINED. I'M ART RING. BE GOOD AND BE AWARE.
WAITAMINIIT-- YOU DON'T SMELL BAD...!
I WAS TALKING ABOUT THE OTHER GUY.
end.

lost covers portfolio

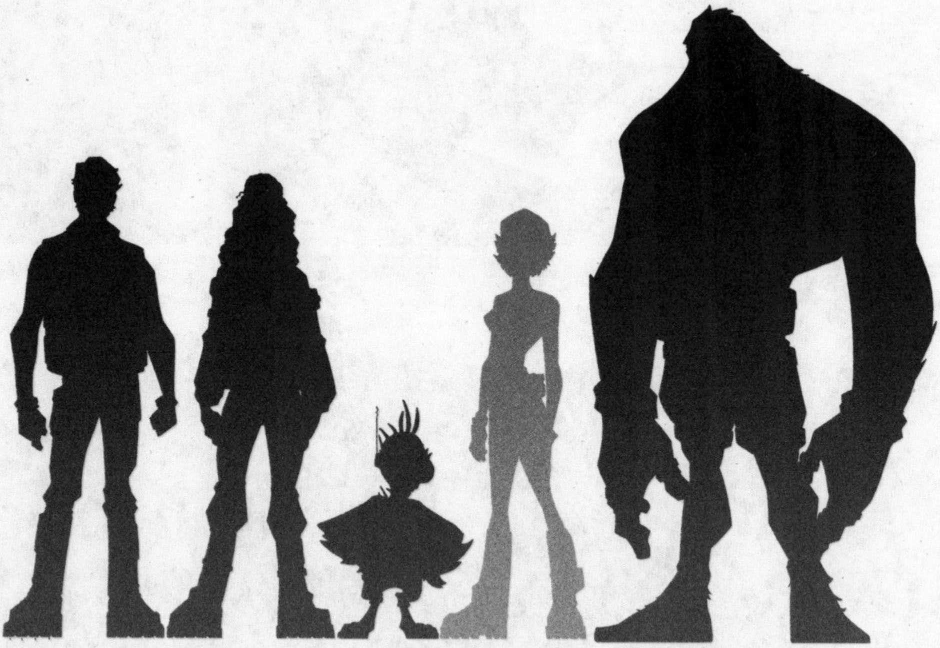

THE LOST COVERS
PORTFOLIO

As a kid, I was obsessed with two things; girls and comic books.

A shy, though imaginative kid, I didn't get too many girls. So I had a lot of comic books. (Yes, some may argue that the one may have discouraged the other, but I don't really think that's true...)

I loved comics. I would buy them and then devour them, get lost in them, live them. I thwipped webs in Manhattan, bounded over rooftops in Gotham City, power-ringed villains on the outer reaches of the galaxy! I would absorb those four-color stories into my mind and my memory, envelop myself in them. And when it was done, before I would file it away in my ever-growing library, I would read the letters page, reviewing the praise and problems my fellow Readers had for the previous issue (or in most cases, the issue from two or three months back). It would give me a chance to relive the story all over again and to share in the mostly silent community of comics Readers back then.

When the time came to publish the Perhapanauts, I decided to include a letters page that would, hopefully, bring back those bygone days, where a few well-placed letters could paraphrase and encapsulate an entire thrilling issue. Letters so enthralling that they would make the Reader want to run out and find that lost issue!
And so I wrote some. Using only the germ of an idea or relating stories I knew we'd never get a chance to tell, I wrote letters about issues that never existed.

And then we got letters.

We got letters and e-mails from many people, some bemused and some angry, who were confused by the whole experiment and went looking on ebay and/or throughout the internet to find these missing issues of the Perhapanauts.

Sorry. We never meant to create any anxiety over this. We just wanted to add the the 'Haps history and elude to some stories that, in another universe, we would love to tell.

So when Craig and I were spitballing the idea of doing a cool Perhapanauts Portfolio to showcase his awesome artwork, we thought it would be even cooler if the Portfolio had a theme of some sort. And Craig suggested doing a handful of the covers to the "lost" issues of the Perhapanauts.

And that's what this is all about.
The letters are in there, so you can read what there is.
Craig did an awesome job.
Enjoy!
todd

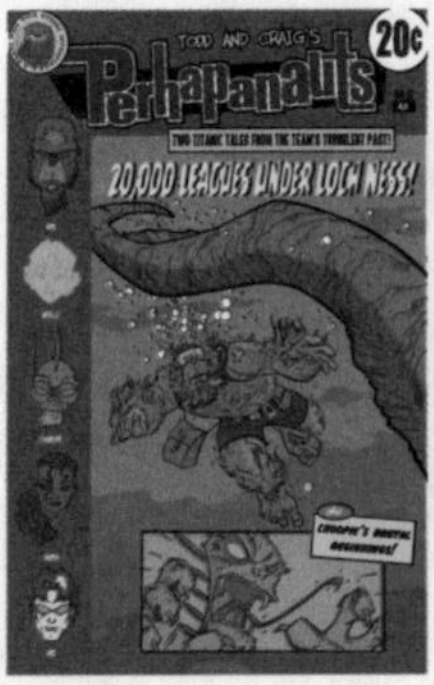
TODD AND CRAIG'S
20¢
Perhapanauts
20,000 LEAGUES UNDER LOCH NESS!

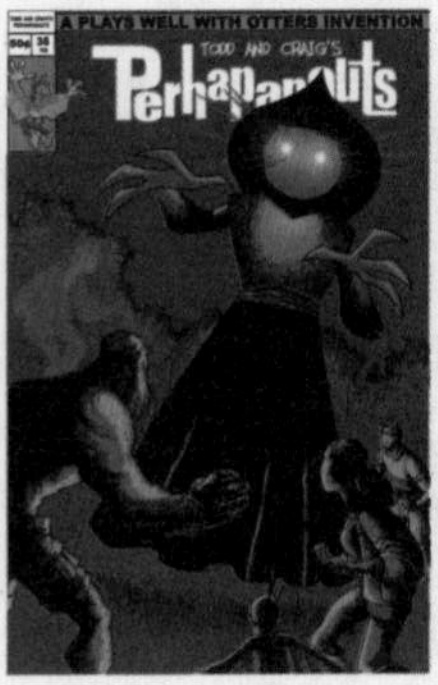
A PLAYS WELL WITH OTTERS INVENTION
TODD AND CRAIG'S
Perhapanauts

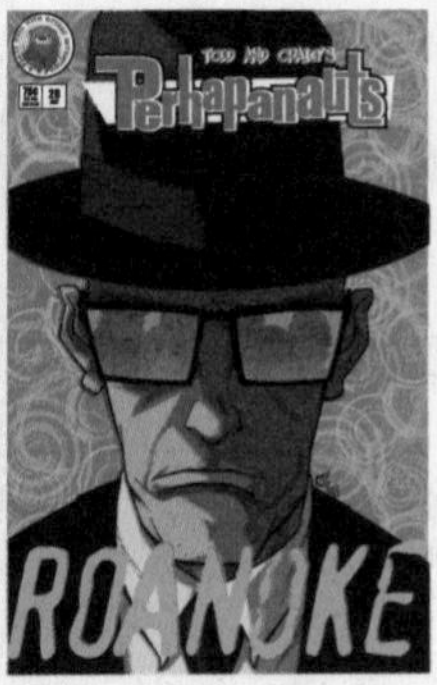
TODD AND CRAIG'S
Perhapanauts
ROANOKE

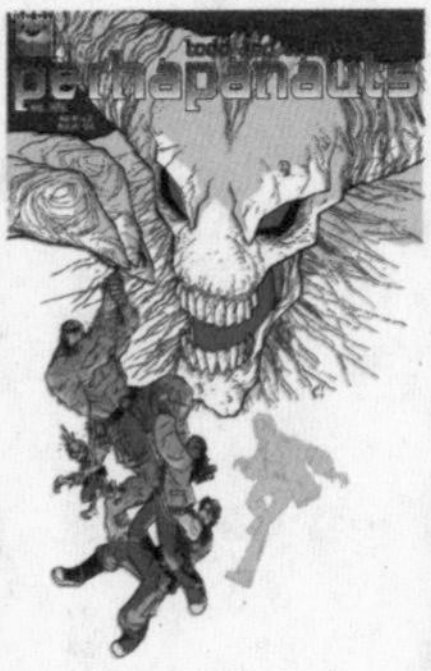

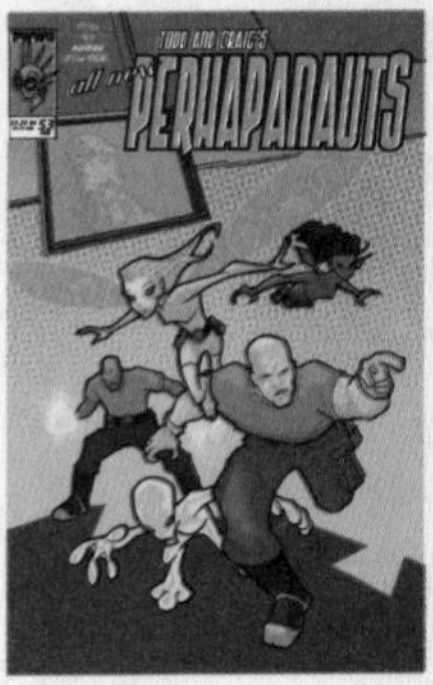
TODD AND CRAIG'S
PERHAPANAUTS

A PLAY WELL WITH OTTERS INVENTION

20

TODD AND CRAIG'S

Perhapanauts

NO 17
AUG

TWO TITANIC TALES FROM THE TEAM'S TURBULENT PAST!

20,000 LEAGUES UNDER LOCH NESS!

BIG

MOLLY

CHOOPIE

ARISA

MG

plus
CHOOPIE'S BRUTAL
BEGINNINGS!

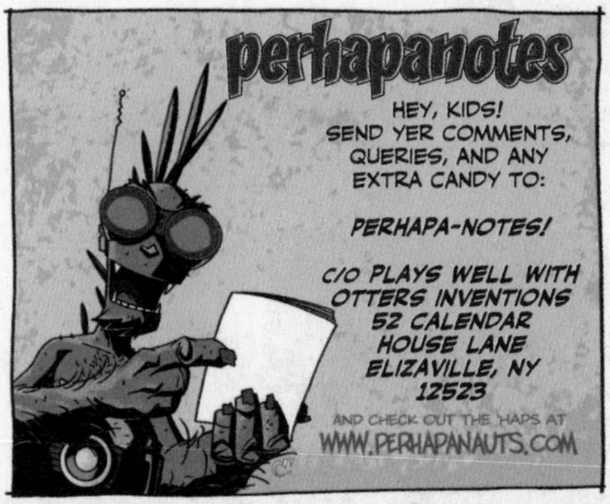
perhapanotes
HEY, KIDS!
SEND YER COMMENTS, QUERIES, AND ANY EXTRA CANDY TO:
PERHAPA-NOTES!
C/O PLAYS WELL WITH OTTERS INVENTIONS
52 CALENDAR HOUSE LANE
ELIZAVILLE, NY 12523
AND CHECK OUT THE HAPS AT
WWW.PERHAPANAUTS.COM

Dear Perhapanauts,

I am a huge Perhapanauts fan. Molly is my favorite and, like, all my friends say that I'm, y'know, just like her. We read the Perhapanauts together every month at lunch and I get to read Molly and MG's lines, Cameron gets to read Arisa's and Choopie's and Devon gets to read Big and everybody else. That's why I'm writing to you now about issue #17! There was no Molly! And no MG! (Well, just that little part in the very end.) I really liked the little solone stories of Big, Arisa, and Choopie, but I hardly got to read at all! No fair! I told Cameron it was no fair and she said that was tough. I said that I should get to read for Arisa or Choopie, but she said that they would probably be solone stories of Molly and MG in the next issue and that I'd just have to wait. We started yelling really loud and Cameron tried to hit me with the shoebox with the diorama that she made of George Washington crossing the Delaware but using the Perhapanauts action figures for Washingtom and his men because she can't draw and she's lazy but she missed and hit Devon who started to cry because the big Big action figure wearing his Washington three-cornered hat hit her right next to her eye but I don't think that it really hurt her. I think she was crying because Mrs. Yankitis said that it could've hit her right in the eye and she was crying because she was thinking about what it would be like being blind. Devon wouldn't talk to either of us for four days. Anyway, will there be any solone stories of Molly and MG? You should because if you don't that wouldn't be fair.

Marissa Butler
Chevy Chase MD

Your wish is our command, Marissa. You'll see more 'solone' adventures of the 'haps (including Molly and MG) as back-up features in future issues and in the upcoming Perhapanauts Annual. I hope you and Cameron and Devon will still be friends by then.--todd

Dear Craig and Todd,

While I had very much enjoyed the 3-part Lemuria adventure "A Close Shaver", in issues 14-16, the three solo stories in Perhapanauts 17, were a refreshing diversion. It was great to see all three in earlier pre-hapanauts tales. And while Choopie's story was funny, and Arisa's was aptly prophetic, it was the story of Big's coming-of-age, as it were, that touched me the most. Caught in that time between adolescence and adulthood--a period I'm sure we can all relate to--we see Big as he is confused and compromised, confronted by choice and finally makes a courageous decision to be his own man. A truly inspiring, triumphant story!
Thanks for another great issue!

Elliot Tomlinson
Sarasota FL

Dear Perhapanotes-

I loved the story of the young Big (in Perhapanauts #17), but where did you get your reference for Loch Ness? It's spot on! I live in Edinburgh and visit the lake once or twice a year (hoping to catch a glimpse), but when I turned the page I felt that I was right back there! It's perfect! Craig, have you ever been? And the underwater scenes were just brilliant! Of course, I've never been down to the bottom of the loch, but I felt I was there along with ol' Big chasin' after Ness. Kudos to your Rico Renzi; the colors were breathtaking! How did you possibly get that effect in those last three panels on page 11?
Thanks for another solid issue.

Rory Addison
Edinburgh, Scotland

Thanks, Rory. We think Rico is awesome too! It seems every time he sends us a newly colored page he gets Craig and I to 'ooh' and 'ahhh' over what he's done. And those underwater scenes were no exception! And Craig says he has never been to Scotland yet. --todd

Dear Todd,

Whyíd you do this? After building up such great momentum with the Lemuria/Hollow Earth stories in Perhapanauts 14-16, I was craving a new adventure, some more real time action. Instead you give us these three flashback stories (if you call Choopie's five pages a story) that just destroy the pace of a comic I rely on for fast-paced action and adventure. Don't get me wrong; I liked the stories, especially watching little Arisa as she (and her brothers) begin to discover that there's something different about her, not wanting to play cards or hide-and-seek with her anymore. Watching her realize that not everybody can do the things that she can, that she's different and, eventually deciding that she should hide her abilities. I liked that.
But, c'mon, man--keep the action coming! Don't pull me off the roller coaster just to go on the merry-go-round.

Sincerely--
Chris Maloney
Booth Bay Harbor ME

Sorry, Chris. I thought that after the "A Close Shaver" arc the 'haps deserved a little r&r. I'll try not to do it again.--todd

Dear Todd and Craig,

Choopie ís my favorite! I loved seeing how he got caught. It was hilarious! But why did he have to do that to those kittens?

Your #1 Fan,
Emma Botsford
Trunton TN

Dear Emma--I think we all tend to forget that Choopie is/was a wild animal--and a blood-sucking one at that!--and only doing what came to him instinctually to survive. It wasn't until he was put through Dr. Alazarís Evolvo-Ray that he began to be able to resist those urges, a battle he continues to fight everyday.

Thanks for the letters, everybody!
See ya here next month for more Perhapa-fun!
--todd

75¢
U.K. 50p
CAN $1.00

28
JULY

TODD AND CRAIG'S

Perhapanauts

ROANOKE

Well, to say that we got a ton of loquacious letters lauding our terrific time-tangled tale, "Manufractured History" (perhapanauts #28), would be, well...a bit of an exaggeration actually. Y'know, 'cause a ton would be a really lot. But we did get a bunch and apparently you were all tres impressed with the surprises, twists, and turns the story took, and especially the unique way in which Choopie chose to reward himself for following orders...but why am I telling you ?! Let's let the letters speak for themselves!

Dear Perhapa-dudes!
Perhapanauts 28 was the bomb, yo!
The aliens were the off the hook! Choopie was off the hook! It was all off the hook!
Justin Swent
Berkley, Ca

Dear Perhapa-people,
First of all, let me say that The Perhapanauts is the most awesome comic ever! It's my absolute favorite and I try to save it for last when I get my new comics. I try...but usually I can't wait! And issue #28 was the AWESOME-IST!! Right from the first page, where we saw the dark, ominous figure (could this have been Karl?...) hovering over the doomed community of colonial Roanoke, we knew that we were in for a tale rife with The Perhapanauts' trademark creepiness! But best part was definitely the end! I was so sure that Big and the rest were actually gonna let those poor confused colonists be taken away by the dominating aliens.
What a great twist! And then to find out what really happened to them! That's why I love this book! It's full of surprises, never predictable, and it always makes me think!
Thanks for the best book going!
Keep the adventure coming!
Josh Walberg
Kitchener, Ontario

Dear Todd and Craig,
I think you guys made a mistake. While it's true that all 116 members of the Roanoke colony disappeared into thin air sometime in the fall of 1591, only 17 of them were women. 9 were children. It looks as though you have them all paired off into couples. What up with that? Todd, you usually do your homework.
Otherwise, this was a truly enjoyable issue. I was moved by Molly's sorrow at being so rudely dismissed by the alien leader and I laughed out loud at how proud Choopie to have carried out his task so professionally! And Big, Arisa, and MG's solution in finding a home for the temporally displaced colonists...wonderful!
Thanks for another great issue!
Keep 'em coming!
Your Perhapa-fan!
Kaylea Jennings
Las Vegas, NV

Dear Perhapanotes,
Best use of an Ipod Mini EVER.
Rob Gentner
Adara, Alabama

Dear Craig and Todd,
There are a number of reasons why I didn't like Perhapanauts 28, but the biggest one is that I couldn't believe that Big and Arisa would even consider handing the Roanoke colonists over to the aliens to save the rest of the planet. This was completely out of character for them and, in the end, even though they proved me right, I was still too frustrated to enjoy their lame triumph.
I have read–and enjoyed–The Perhapanauts ever since issue 7, but you guys are slipping.
Hoping for better things,
Martin Eilenberg
Whippany, New Jersey

Dear Perhapanotes~~
Greetings and congratulations on producing what is arguably one of the most finely crafted comics on the market today. While Mr. Dezago's scripts continue to provoke wonder, laughs, and curious contemplation, it is Mr. Rousseau's truly beautiful artwork that I wish to expound upon here. His wonderfully animated characters and smooth, fluidic storytelling make the perhapanauts as much fun to watch as they are to read. Craig (if I may be so bold) has certainly been overlooked in this current industry and deserves much more recognition for his stunning work.
As an example, might I point out the sequence in issue 28 where the landing party discovers the eerie disappearance of the entire population of the small collective that was Roanoke, Virginia. In his masterful hands, Mr. Rousseau was able to make me feel, not only a sense of isolated aloneness, but an almost palpable dread that still gives me chills as I write about it now. Turning the page to find the familiar tableau of the perhapanauts 'family room' was more of a relief than I can easily put into words.
Of course that restful interlude lasted only so long. With the sudden appearance of the Klee M'Klee–an alien design so bizarrely unique I have never seen anything like it in comics–the Artist evoked in me the same sense of terror and helplessness as the team stood before their ominous gaze.
And finally, it was Craig's gradual and graceful pacing in both the conclusion and the revelatory epilogue that makes him a true master of sequential storytelling and this issue a pure treasure.
Sincerely,
Michael Brandeis
Hardington, Iowa

And that's it, Gang! More of your Merry Missives next issue! In the meantime, keep 'em comin' to:
Perhapa-Notes!
C/o Plays Well With Otters Inventions
52 Calendar House Rd
Elizaville NY 12523

And check out the 'haps at www.perhapanauts.com

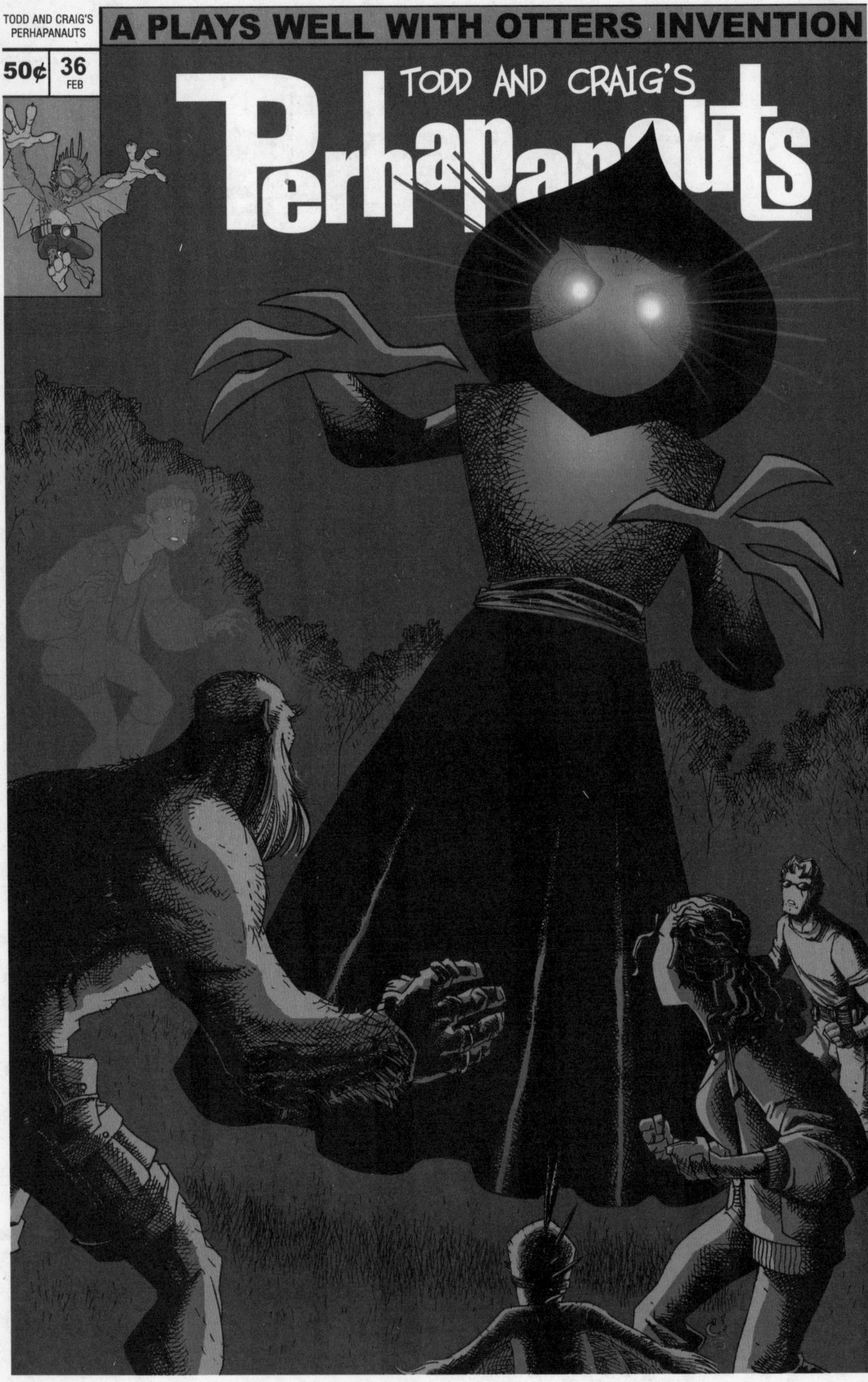

TODD AND CRAIG'S PERHAPANAUTS
A PLAYS WELL WITH OTTERS INVENTION
50¢
36
FEB
TODD AND CRAIG'S
Perhapanauts

perhapanotes

hi, perhapa-fans!
send your comments,
questions, and, y'know,
suggestions to:

perhapanotes@perhapanauts.com

tell'm molly sent ya.

AND CHECK OUT THE MAPS AT
WWW.PERHAPANAUTS.COM

Dear Todd and Craig,
I have to admit, I was never a big fan of the conspiracy episodes of The X-Files; I was more of a monster of the week fan, and the same holds true with the perhapanauts (Although maybe monster of the month would be a better moniker). Oh, don't get me wrong, I enjoy every issue, but nothing thrills me more than to pick up an issue that features the more horrifying creatures from rural legend and cryptozoology. The scarier the better! The Loveland Frogman, the Ingot(s), the Kelly Goblins, the Jersey Devil, all have given the 'haps a run for their money and all have given me nightmares because of the truth behind them. (Damn you, Todd, and your creepy research!) I love to see them, and am terrified by them at the same time. Does that make sense?
And I thought that I was definitely going to have another appalling vision to add to my gruesome files with perhapanauts #36. But just the way you guys were telling the story, I started to think that maybe this was going to be one of those stories where we never got to see the terror in the night, the horrific creature in the shadows, that the team (and it's poor victims) were the only ones who would view this particular beast. As a matter of fact, I convinced myself of that very fact as we got up to page 20, then 21...And I practically threw the book across the room when I turned to the final page and that...THING! was leering out at me!! I don't know how you guys did it; Craig, you are truly a Master! Rico, nothing has ever looked more real (not even the underwater scenes in perhapanauts #17), as if it were actually coming off the page at me!
So thanks, I guess, for another nightmare to add to my repertoire. This issue was truly amazing and everything I LOVE the perhapanauts for!
Your #1 fan,
Doug Fischella
Arlington, OH

Glad we could help, Doug. Hope we didn't give you TOO many nightmares.

Dear Perhapanotes,
Re: Perhapanauts #36.
I'm just glad that I live nowhere near West Virginia!
Fan Numero Uno,
Paul Spina
Westbury, NY

Dear Perhapanotes,
As Big points out in this issue of the perhapanauts, the original sighting/encounter with the Flatwoods Monster occurred back in 1952. Big goes on to mention the woman associated with the sighting, but your story doesn't include the virtually unbearable odor that the creature emitted or the fact that several of the nine people witnessing this contact soon after came down with severe cases of eye burn and conjunctivitis. More than likely you omitted these facts for the sake of what was ultimately a gripping and well-paced story.
What I didn't like about the issue, and perhaps I'm just an obsessive who cannot tolerate change, but I didn't care for the dialogue amongst the team. Dysfunctional is one thing, but after the recent loss of not one, but two of the original team, I found the exchange between characters to be hard enough without so much internal conflict. I only hope that this new perhapanauts team can find their common ground quickly.
Other than that, a four star issue!
Your Number One Fan,
Dennis Healy,
Carpenter, Kansas

Hopefully by now, Dennis, you've become a bit more accustomed to how this new team fits together--or doesn't. Not that the old team operated in constant harmony, but you have to admit, this new, more volatile combination certainly keeps things interesting.

Dear Perhapa-pals,
Thank you, thank you, thank you for perhapanauts #36! This issue was my absolute favorite and I can't thank you enough! The story of the gang investigating the Flatwoods Monster was great! I was thrilled to see you tackle this unexplained event in the perhapanauts, though, for more personal reasons. Being the nephew of one of the original witnesses, I can only tell you how much you captured the stories of the monster that my uncle would tell us around the campfire when the families went camping. (Mom wouldn't let him tell us until we were about 12 or 13; still too young, if you ask me. I still have nightmares!) He was just a kid when it happened but he can still remember exactly how it looked and smelled and hovered before them and especially the way it's eyes moved--that's the part he always sticks on. You can see it still spooks him! And it terrified all of us kids!
Thanks so much for bringing that story to life. You guys made it look just the way I always imagined it!
Your biggest fan,
James Coon,
Wheeling, WV

Wow! James, I would SO love to talk to your uncle. There is no record of the names of the other people who saw the creature besides Mrs. Kay's two sons, neither of which I could track down. That is so cool! Please let me know if he'd be game.

Dear Craig,
Just like with the first time we saw the Aswang,
that last page is gonna haunt me...
Great job!
Your #1 fan,
Laura Golloti
San Bernadino, CA

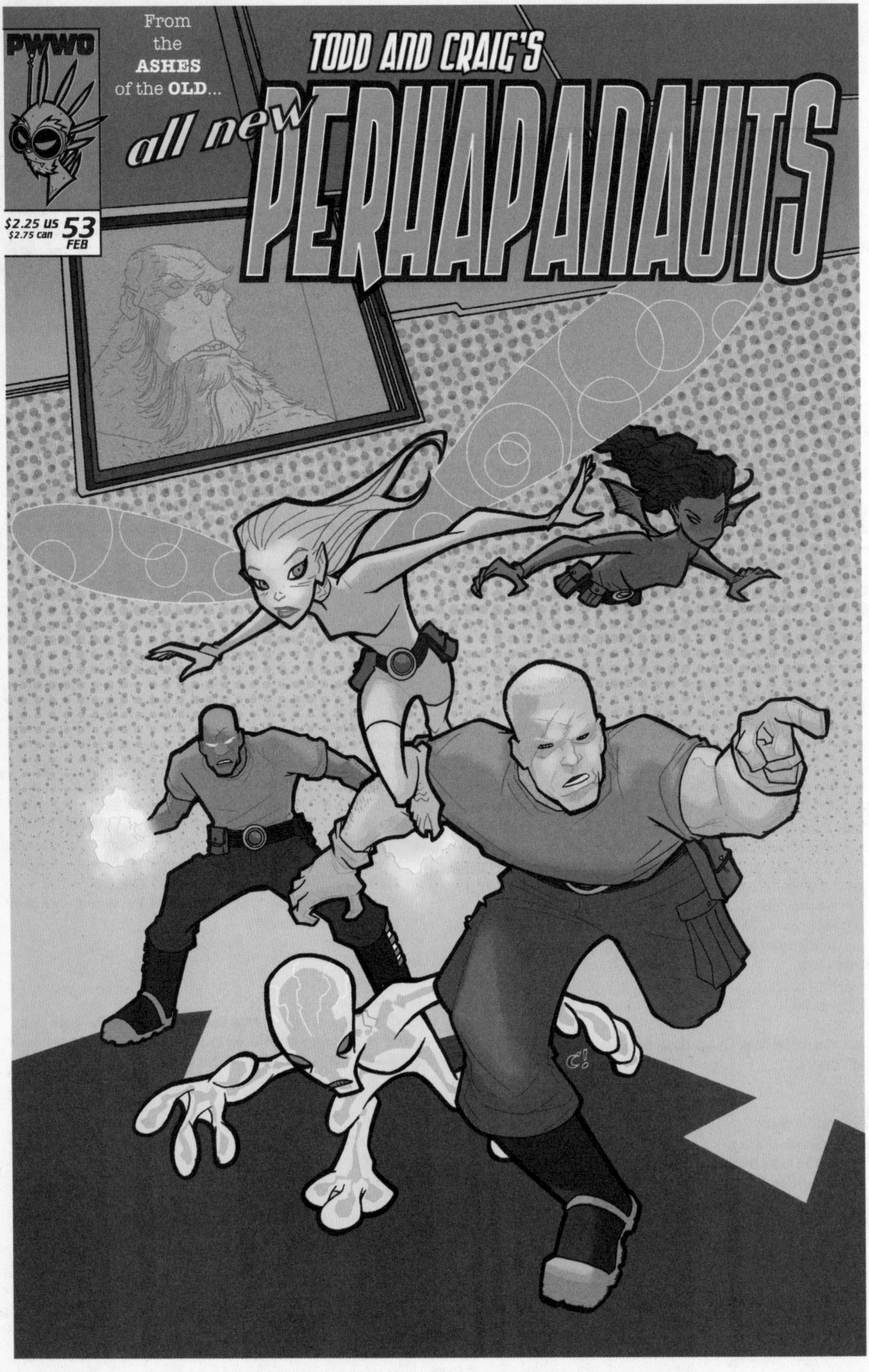
From the ASHES of the OLD...
PWWO
TODD AND CRAIG'S
all new
PERHAPANAUTS
$2.25 US
$2.75 can
53
FEB

PERHAPANOTES

C/O PLAYS WELL WITH OTTERS INVENTIONS 52 CALENDAR HOUSE ROAD ELIZAVILLE NY 12523

Dear Perhapanotes,
I have to admit that when I saw the cover to the latest issue, perhapanauts #53 featuring the ALL-NEW perhapanauts, my heart sank. I've been a loyal reader since before issue 1 (I still have my Classified:Dossier and my not gigantic color special #1 boarded and bagged and stored away where no one will ever get to them), and I always hate it when, in my favorite comics, the teams change or are broken up. And since all of this had been building up over the past four issues with Blue Team first being framed and then hunted down by Steris and his Sleepers (I was so sure that Arisa and Choopie were dead!), it was easy for me to believe that this truly was the end of the perhapanauts! After all, you killed MG and Molly for good, right? (Right…?) And after all those years of Hammerskold saying that he should run the Blue Team, now he was finally going to get his chance. I always liked Red Team…as Red Team, but there is NO TEAM that could ever replace the 'haps!! That's why the cover scared me so much! I mean, you've done some pretty crazy things over the years and I wouldn't be surprised if you didn't actually go ahead and kill them all! I held my breath through the whole story, waiting to make sure that this wasn't really happening, that it wasn't true. But you really did it, didn't you?
Still holding my breath,
Mary Wenstell
Des Moines, IA

Dear Craig and Todd,
I couldn't believe my eyes when I saw the cover for Perhapanauts #53! Was that the Aswang?! I knew that she would show up again sometime since her brief cameo way back in Second Chances #2, in panel 4 on page 7 (you guys thought nobody picked that up, didn't you?) I knew that, as much of a bitch as she is, that she'd be back and somehow become a part of BEDLAM! Thanks for proving me right!
Uetso Yakimada
Tokyo

Dear Perhapa-people, When I saw the cover, I almost didn't buy Perhapanauts #53, "Parmenides Lament"; I have no desire to see a bunch of second stringers try to live up to the legacy of the original Perhapanauts. I just don't care. And I was ready to give up this title permanently if that was what you were doing. Even if Big was supposedly overseeing this new team, it still would never be the real Perhapanauts. But I flipped through the comic anyway and almost put it back, when I caught the scene on page four where we saw that the "new" Perhapanauts were being ordered to hunt down and capture the old team.

I flipped a couple pages more and saw the beginning of the confrontation between Choopie and the Aswang and knew I just had to buy this book! And I wasn't disappointed! Not only did you deliver one of the blow-by-blow, nastiest, most brutal fight I've ever seen in a comic book, but, in the course of that battle, you made me switch sides, not because I felt sorry for the "new" team, but because they looked like they never stood a chance. And then when, with what seemed her dying breath, the Merrow was able to do the little bit of magic her kind can do, I was sold. I don't care that the old team are gone. I don't care if it won't be like the "old" Perhapanauts--Long Live the NEW Perhapanauts!
Dover Rules!
Jeff Dawson
Twin Lakes, WY

Dear Guys~
I can't believe you killed them all!
I hate you!
Michael Credendino
New York NY

Dear Perhapanotes,
Why is it that every time I think I know what's going on in this book, a story like "Parmenides Lament" comes along and makes me feel like I don't know nothin'?!
I was sure that you were going to find a way to redeem the 'Haps after Steris and his Minions took everything away from them. As I read, I kept trying to think of a way out of it all myself. But they did such a good job of painting the team as villains, as corrupted individuals. Why, they were even able to make Big mistrust his long time teammates! But the pacing and the timing of this issue was just so tight, I don't know how you did it. When they were finally able to get Thornton to overload all the surveillance equipment and free Arisa's mind to telepathically strafe them, I was certain that they were all dead. But when Merrrow was able to produce the glamour, I really didn't know what was going on. And Red Team's return to BEDLAM with the bodies convinced me that there was indeed going to be a big change in this book. And there WAS! When the 'Haps were finally back inside BEDLAM and Merrow's illusion came down, it was BOTH TEAMS that were standing there telling the Chief that history had been altered. And the visit to the Perhaps was enough to reveal that it was Saci Perer who had orchestrated the whole thing!
Very clever, Guys!
I never saw it coming!
Your fan for life!
Dave Goehring
San Bernadino CA

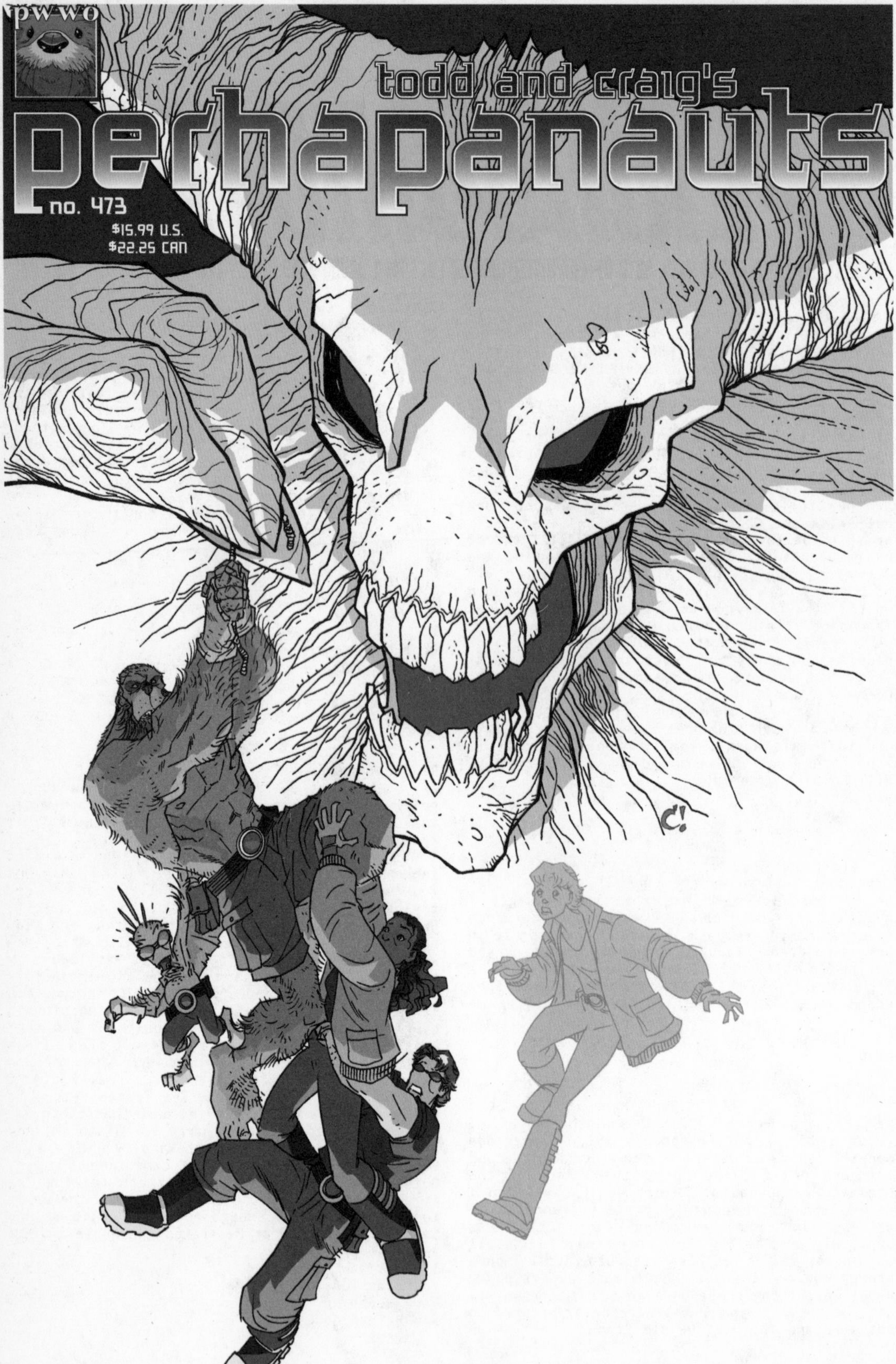
pw wo
todd and craig's
perhapanauts
no. 473
$15.99 U.S.
$22.25 CAN
C!

perhapanotes

c/o plays well with otters inventions 6158 Mulholland Hwy, Hollywood, CA 90068

Dear Perhapanotes,
Re: Perhapanauts #473.
Amazing! Just Amazing!
Amazing that, for this, the 35th Anniversary of the first appearance of the Perhapanauts, you could actually get both Mr. Dezago and Mr. Rousseau to come down from their lofty New Hollywood offices to once again work on the title that brought them each such great success! Amazing that, not only did you manage to reunite the original creative team, but that they were able to reunite the original Perhapanauts team, in an exciting, humorous, and at times, touching story worthy of the occasion! I have to say that I was one of the many that was sure that these two, after being away from comics so long, would have lost their sequential chops and that this landmark issue was going to be a huge disappointment (as we have seen so many times in the past...). But I needn't go any farther than page 3 (that moment with Molly and Choopie was beyond hilarious!) to see that we were not only back with the team that was born to do this book, but that they hadn't lost a bit of the charm that always made this book magic!
Donna Ricelinger
Instantentertainment.com

Greetings Perhapa-pals~
I had been waiting for the big anniversary issue featuring Todd and Craig's return ever since I saw it announced months ago on Instant Entertainment! Eager with anticipation, I ended up lining up at my comic post with all the other kids (I'm 44) two days before it hit the stands! And, of course, it was everything I'd dreamed of...and more!
With all the media coverage this event received, how, How, HOW did they keep the news of Rico's return a secret?! When I opened the book and saw Mr. Renzi's unmistakable colors adorning Craig's characters, I almost died! I would have told you it was impossible, that he was too busy, what with his many Gallery Shows and overseeing all of IndigoInk?!? It was such a shock to see his incredible hues that I had to go back and read the first five pages over again! Thank you all for a great story! But thank you especially for the great coloring surprise!
Rico Rules!
Mamby Toshu
Kenya

Dear Perhapanauts,
I loved Perhapanauts 473...up until the very end, when I realized that Craig and Todd weren't going to be back next issue. Don't let them go back to New Holly, don't they realize that this is where they belong?!
Micah Baily
Englewood NJ

Dear Perhapanotes,
It was wonderful to see that, after their well-publicized falling out several years ago, Mssrs Dezago and Rousseau would be able to put their differences aside to help us all celebrate the fantastic gift that they themselves gave us all those years ago...the Perhapanauts. Being a long-time Perhapanauts fan, I, like many, had been saddened by the news of their feud, and mourned the loss of one of comics' best creative teams to pass this way in a long time. Yet I was also tentative when the announcement came that they were to return to commemorate the anniversary with a special double-sized issue, afraid that this might cause even greater tension and result in a bitter and sorely-lacking story. I had nothing to worry about. This story was truly that; a celebration! It was easy to see that each of them put their all into every line and every word , creating what was, for me, a masterpiece! Hopefully, this project has given them pause and made them remember the wonderful friendship that was so apparent in the early days of this publication.
Thank you for a truly outstanding,
And hopefully, inspiring, book.
Renaldo DesPris
Florence Italy

Dear Perhapanotes,
I don't think they did this.
They're too busy, they don't like each other anymore, and I think somebody else wrote it.
I mean, seriously, how hard would it be to get somebody else to write and draw it for them?
Don't get me wrong, I thought the story was great and the artwork was awesome.
But I don't think they did it.
They were never this good.
Bryan Bryant
Mill Basin NY

more fund, one sheets and allen's ads

"this section contains some of the various and sundry other perhapanauts related stuff that didn't fit in the other categories. the first is a two-page story we did for sky dog press' **even more fund**, a book to benefit the comic book legal defense fund back in 2004.

"in 2006, craig and i thought it would be fun to start a series of perhapanauts prints to have available as exclusives at the various shows and conventions we do.

"the last page - as well as the ad for perhapanauts no.2 back in the cover gallery - features the genius of image production manager, allen hui. we were thrilled by his creativity and talent and, allen, man - we can't thank you enough!" - todd

postcard design

THE
TODD AND CRAIG'S
Perhapanauts

image
www.imagecomics.com
PLAYS WELL WITH OTTERS INVENTION
mail to
TO FIND A COMIC SHOP IN YOUR AREA
CALL: 1-888-266-4226
THE
TODD AND CRAIG'S
Perhapanauts
Remember when comics were FUN? When they were filled with CHARACTERS you liked and wanted to be? Heroes that went on ADVENTURES that were THRILLING and WILD, full of DANGER ad MYSTERY?
Remember when comics were fun?
The PERHAPANAUTS is about a team of agents sent out to deal with monsters and ghosts and things that go bump in the night! That this team is made up of monsters and ghosts and things that go bump in the night makes it all even more fun!
A Bigfoot, a chupacabra, a mothman, a ghost...!
Join The PERHAPANAUTS--Big, Molly, Choopie, Arisa, Karl, and MG-- each month in their very own adventures!
Now from IMAGE Comics!
www.perhapanauts.com
THE PERHAPANAUTS COPYRIGHT © 2008 TODD DEZAGO & CRAIG ROUSSEAU

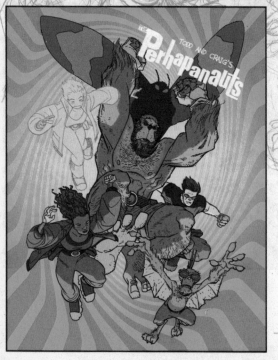

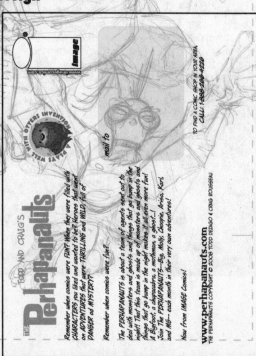

choopie swag

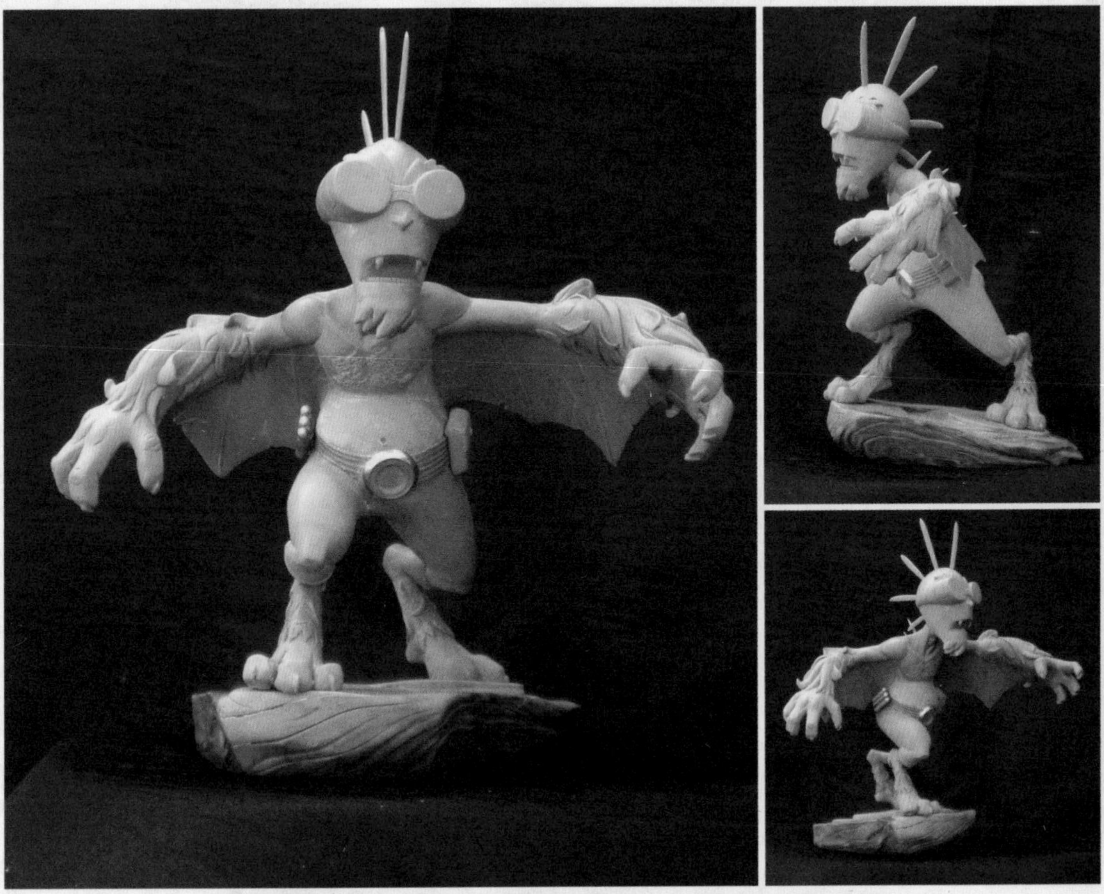

craig commissioned this sculpture of choopie from master sculptor, andrew wiernicki in 2006

Todd and Craig's Perhapanauts

Design for Choopie plush (prototype)

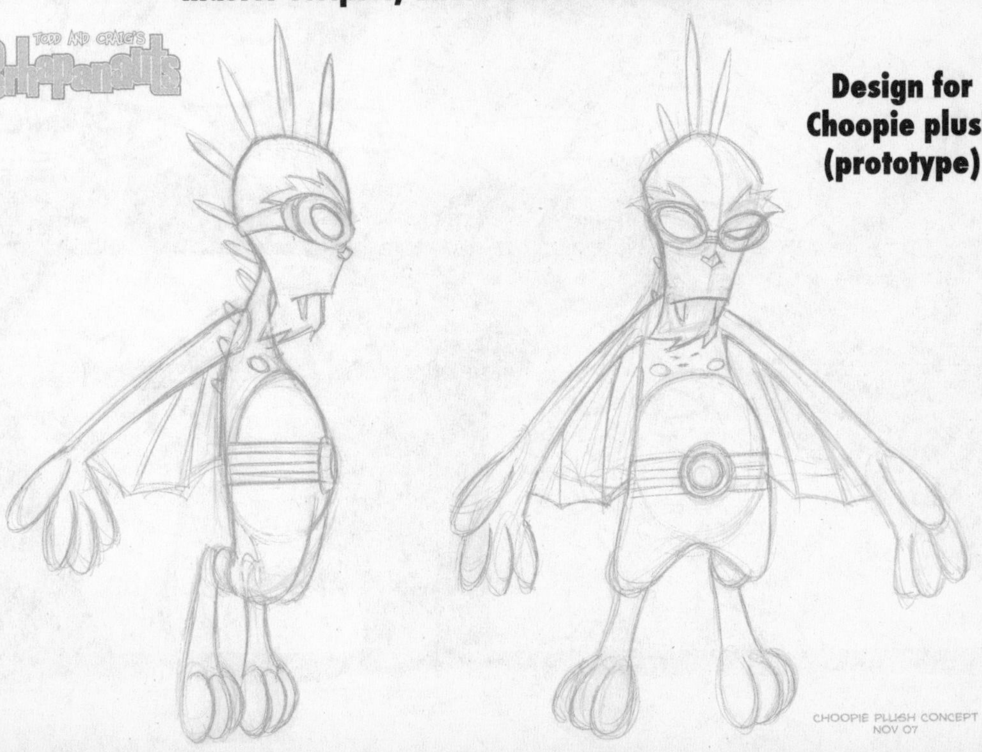
CHOOPIE PLUSH CONCEPT
NOV 07

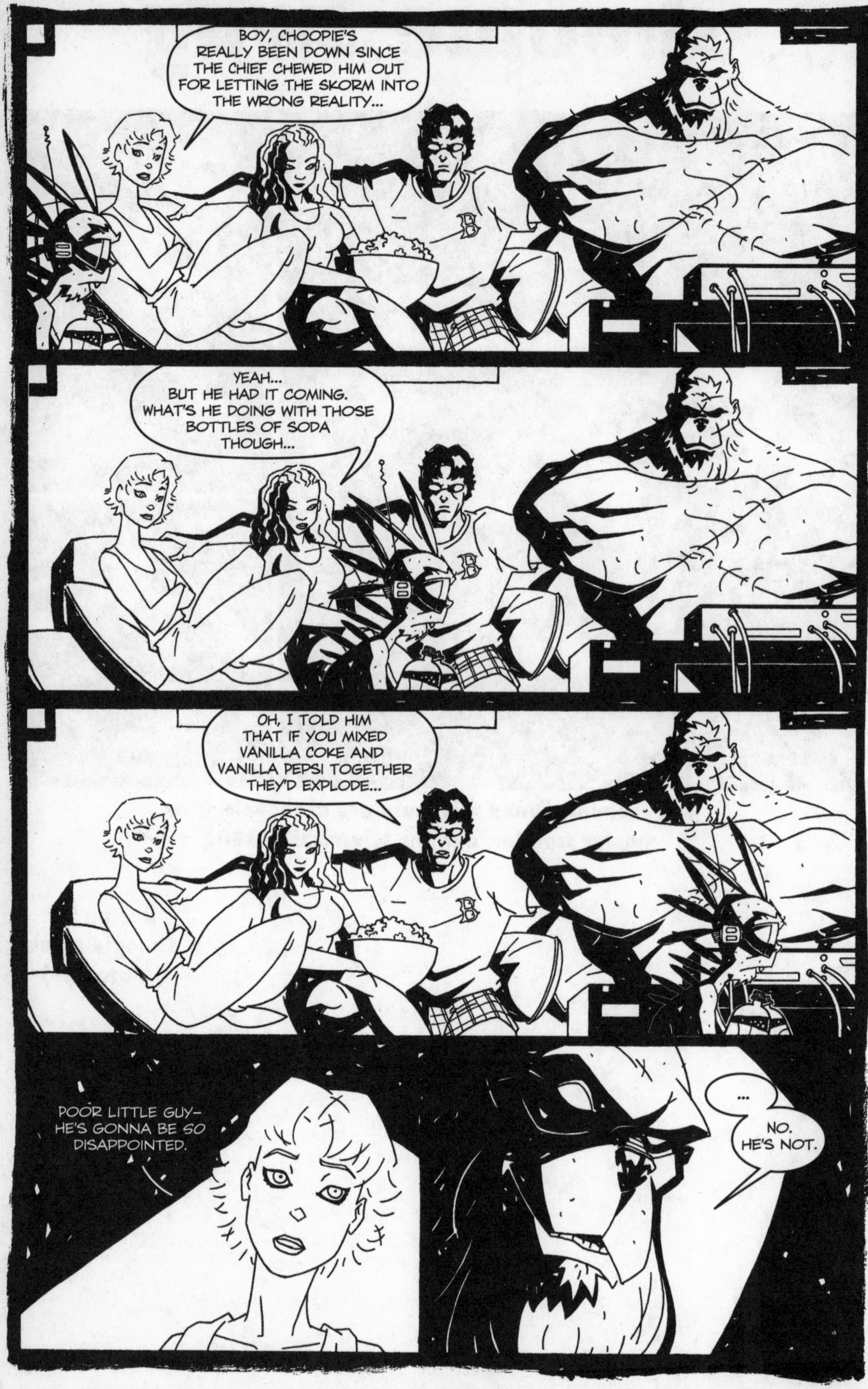
BOY, CHOOPIE'S REALLY BEEN DOWN SINCE THE CHIEF CHEWED HIM OUT FOR LETTING THE SKORM INTO THE WRONG REALITY...
YEAH... BUT HE HAD IT COMING. WHAT'S HE DOING WITH THOSE BOTTLES OF SODA THOUGH...
OH, I TOLD HIM THAT IF YOU MIXED VANILLA COKE AND VANILLA PEPSI TOGETHER THEY'D EXPLODE...
POOR LITTLE GUY– HE'S GONNA BE SO DISAPPOINTED.
...
NO. HE'S NOT.

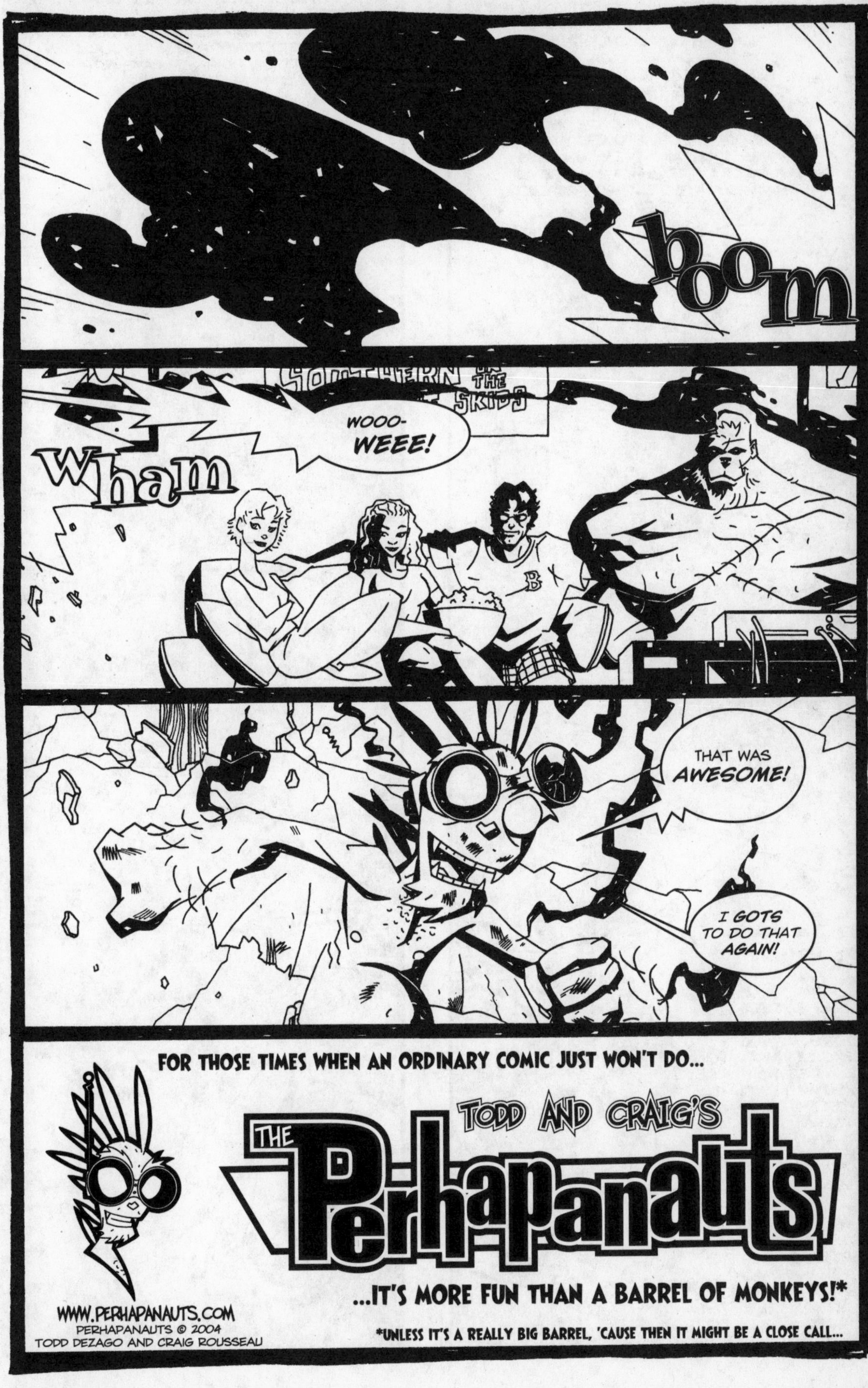
boom
Wham
WOOO-WEEE!
THAT WAS AWESOME!
I GOTS TO DO THAT AGAIN!
FOR THOSE TIMES WHEN AN ORDINARY COMIC JUST WON'T DO...
TODD AND CRAIG'S
THE Perhapanauts
...IT'S MORE FUN THAN A BARREL OF MONKEYS!*
WWW.PERHAPANAUTS.COM
PERHAPANAUTS © 2004
TODD DEZAGO AND CRAIG ROUSSEAU
*UNLESS IT'S A REALLY BIG BARREL, 'CAUSE THEN IT MIGHT BE A CLOSE CALL...

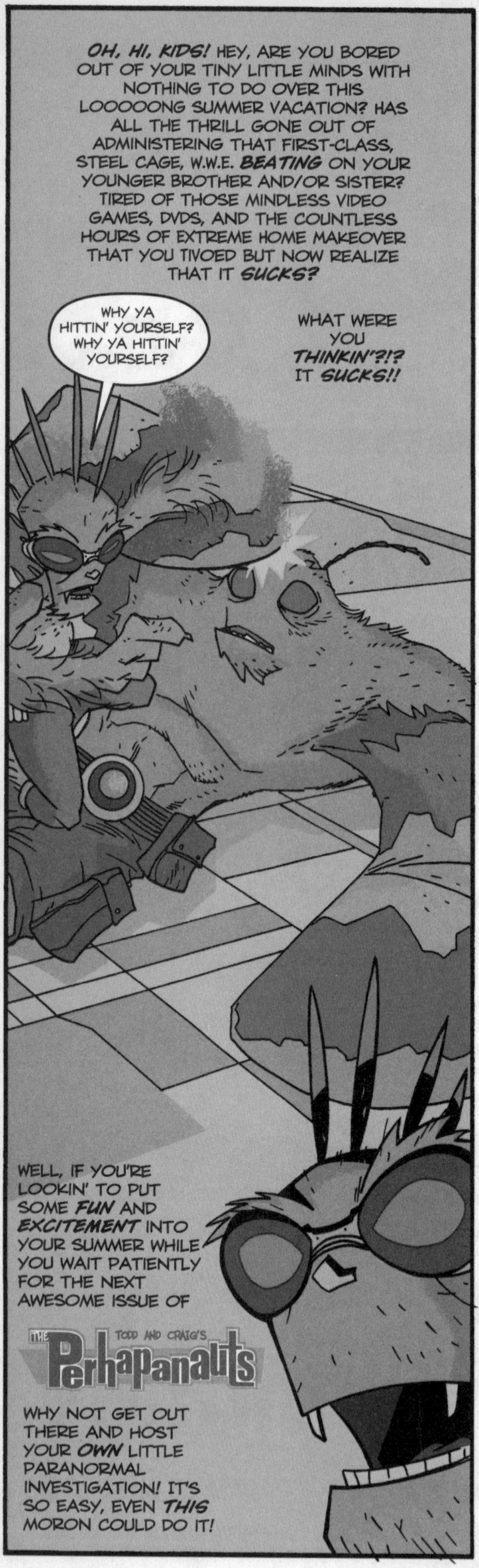
OH, HI, KIDS! HEY, ARE YOU BORED OUT OF YOUR TINY LITTLE MINDS WITH NOTHING TO DO OVER THIS LOOOOONG SUMMER VACATION? HAS ALL THE THRILL GONE OUT OF ADMINISTERING THAT FIRST-CLASS, STEEL CAGE, W.W.E. BEATING ON YOUR YOUNGER BROTHER AND/OR SISTER? TIRED OF THOSE MINDLESS VIDEO GAMES, DVDS, AND THE COUNTLESS HOURS OF EXTREME HOME MAKEOVER THAT YOU TIVOED BUT NOW REALIZE THAT IT SUCKS?
WHY YA HITTIN' YOURSELF? WHY YA HITTIN' YOURSELF?
WHAT WERE YOU THINKIN'?!? IT SUCKS!!
WELL, IF YOU'RE LOOKIN' TO PUT SOME FUN AND EXCITEMENT INTO YOUR SUMMER WHILE YOU WAIT PATIENTLY FOR THE NEXT AWESOME ISSUE OF
TODD AND CRAIG'S THE Perhapanauts
WHY NOT GET OUT THERE AND HOST YOUR OWN LITTLE PARANORMAL INVESTIGATION! IT'S SO EASY, EVEN THIS MORON COULD DO IT!
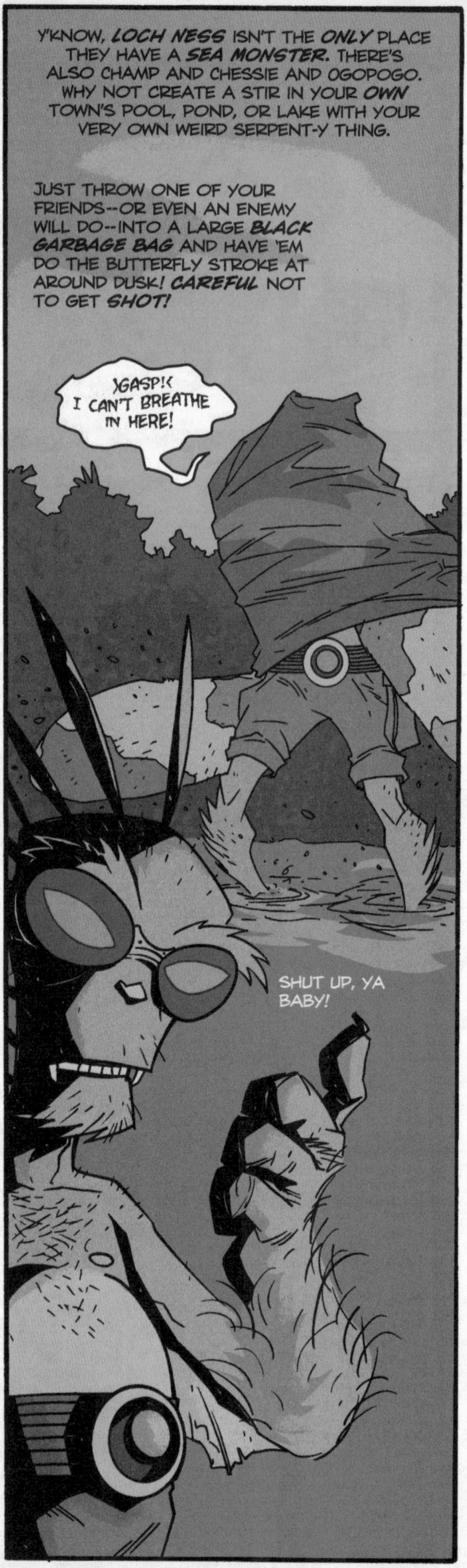
Y'KNOW, LOCH NESS ISN'T THE ONLY PLACE THEY HAVE A SEA MONSTER. THERE'S ALSO CHAMP AND CHESSIE AND OGOPOGO. WHY NOT CREATE A STIR IN YOUR OWN TOWN'S POOL, POND, OR LAKE WITH YOUR VERY OWN WEIRD SERPENT-Y THING.
JUST THROW ONE OF YOUR FRIENDS--OR EVEN AN ENEMY WILL DO--INTO A LARGE BLACK GARBAGE BAG AND HAVE 'EM DO THE BUTTERFLY STROKE AT AROUND DUSK! CAREFUL NOT TO GET SHOT!
GASP! I CAN'T BREATHE IN HERE!
SHUT UP, YA BABY!

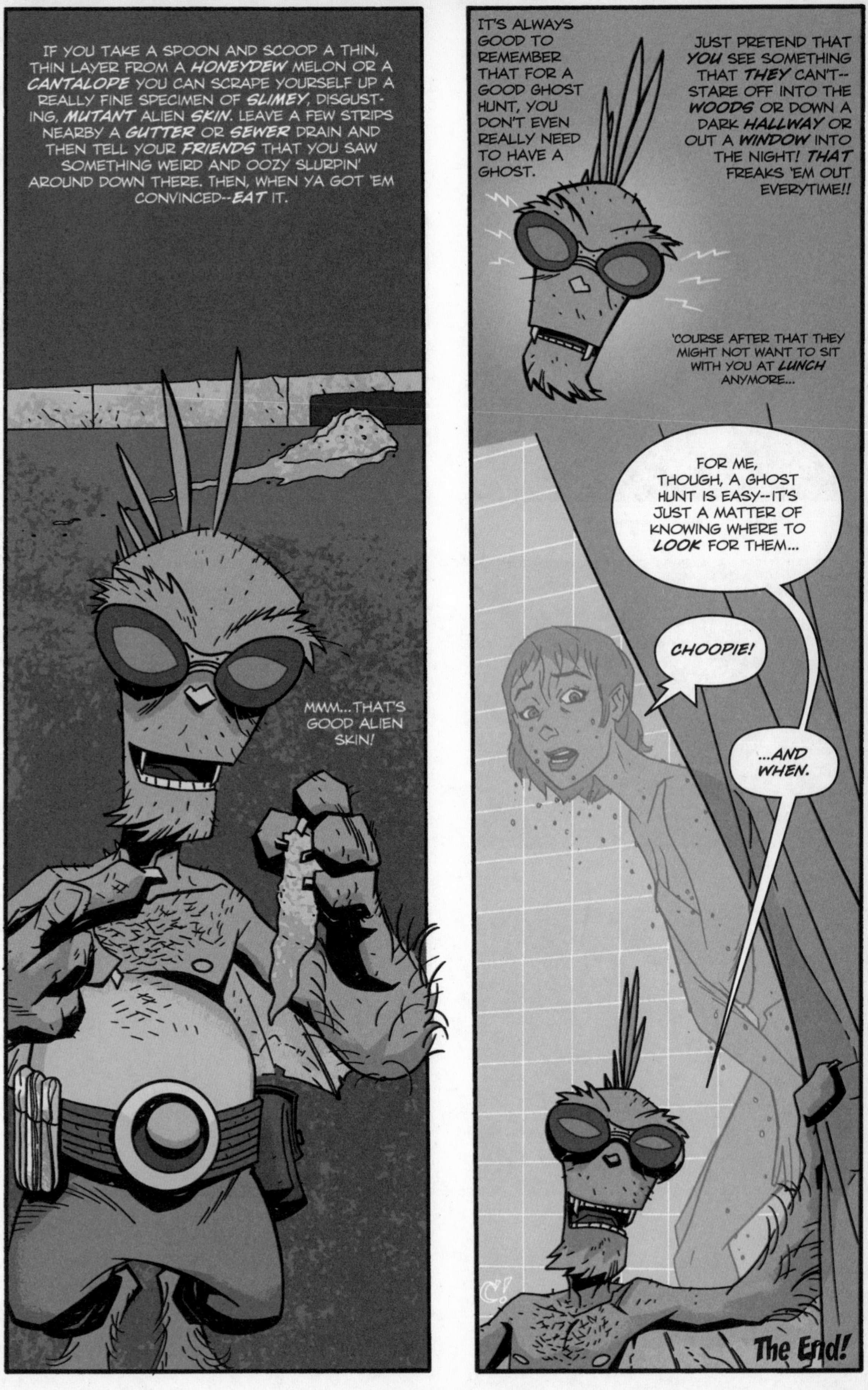
IF YOU TAKE A SPOON AND SCOOP A THIN, THIN LAYER FROM A HONEYDEW MELON OR A CANTALOPE YOU CAN SCRAPE YOURSELF UP A REALLY FINE SPECIMEN OF SLIMEY, DISGUSTING, MUTANT ALIEN SKIN. LEAVE A FEW STRIPS NEARBY A GUTTER OR SEWER DRAIN AND THEN TELL YOUR FRIENDS THAT YOU SAW SOMETHING WEIRD AND OOZY SLURPIN' AROUND DOWN THERE. THEN, WHEN YA GOT 'EM CONVINCED--EAT IT.
MMM...THAT'S GOOD ALIEN SKIN!
IT'S ALWAYS GOOD TO REMEMBER THAT FOR A GOOD GHOST HUNT, YOU DON'T EVEN REALLY NEED TO HAVE A GHOST.
JUST PRETEND THAT YOU SEE SOMETHING THAT THEY CAN'T--STARE OFF INTO THE WOODS OR DOWN A DARK HALLWAY OR OUT A WINDOW INTO THE NIGHT! THAT FREAKS 'EM OUT EVERYTIME!!
'COURSE AFTER THAT THEY MIGHT NOT WANT TO SIT WITH YOU AT LUNCH ANYMORE...
FOR ME, THOUGH, A GHOST HUNT IS EASY--IT'S JUST A MATTER OF KNOWING WHERE TO LOOK FOR THEM...
CHOOPIE!
...AND WHEN.
The End!

A PERHAPANAUTS ONE-PAGE--FIRST IN A SERIES!

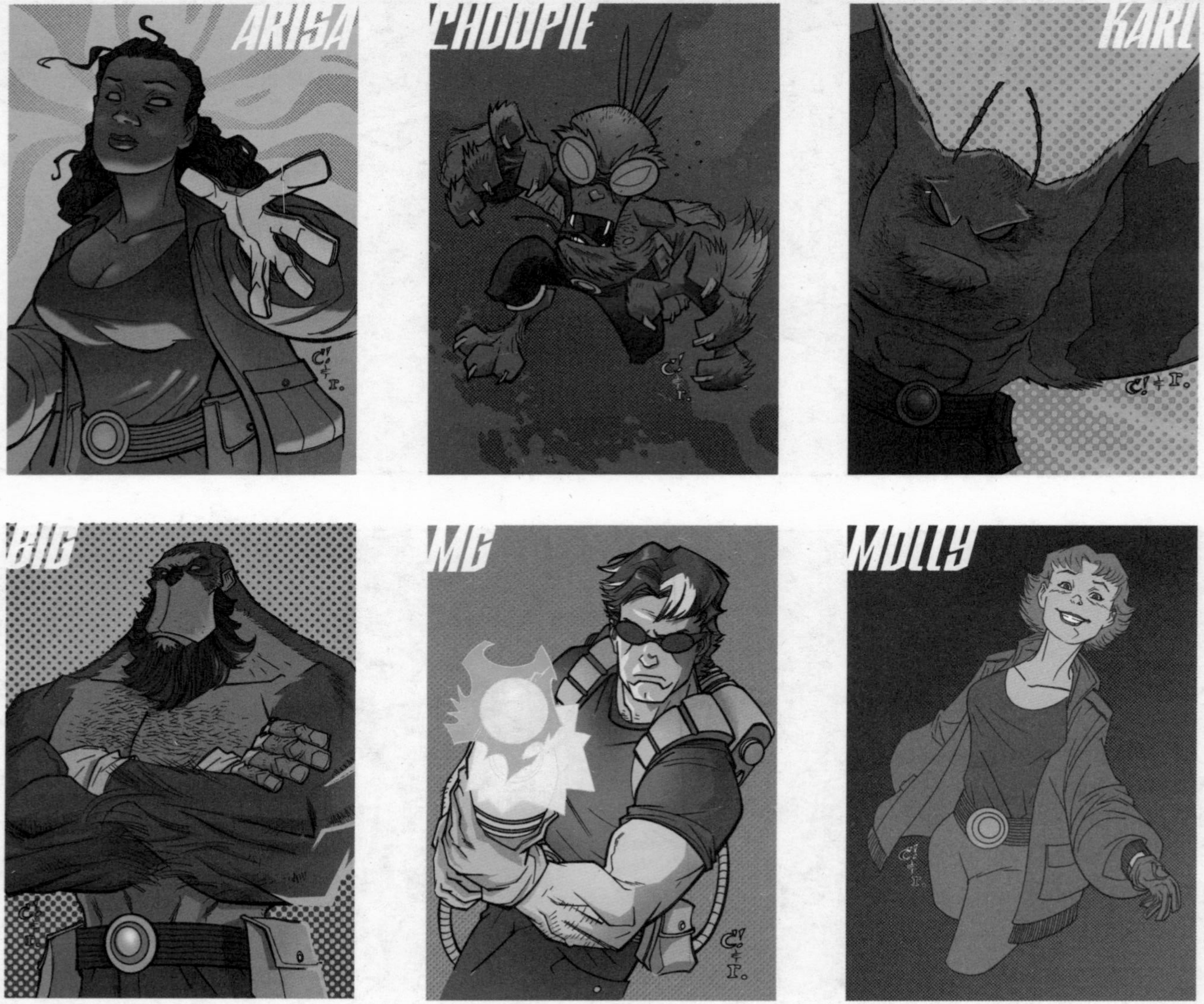
ARISA
CHOOPIE
KARL
BIG
MG
MOLLY

A PERHAPANAUTS ONE-PAGE--SECOND IN A SERIES!

A PLAYS WELL WITH OTTERS INVENTION

BEDLAM FILES

ARISA HINES
Leader, Blue Team

HIGH LEVEL TELEPATH. STRONG, RESOURCEFUL. SHE PLACES HER TEAMMATES ABOVE ALL ELSE. EVEN HERSELF.

A TEAM OF AGENTS OF THE SECRET ORGANIZATION KNOWN AS BEDLAM, THEY INVESTIGATE STRANGE AND UNEXPLAINED EVENTS, CONFRONT AND CONTAIN BIZARRE CREATURES NOT OF THIS EARTH, MAKING THE WORLD SAFE FROM THINGS THAT GO BUMP IN THE NIGHT...!

1 TODD AND CRAIG'S THE Perhapanauts

THE PERHAPANAUTS © 2008 TODD DEZAGO AND CRAIG ROUSSEAU

BEDLAM FILES

BIG
Bigfoot, a sasquatch

CAPTURED YEARS AGO BY BEDLAM, SUBJECTED TO EXPERIMENTAL EVOLVING DEVICE SOON BEGAN DEMONSTRATING INTELLECT TO MATCH HIS ALREADY DAUNTING STRENGTH.

A BUDDHIST AND PACIFIST, BIG SEEKS KNOWLEDGE AND ENLIGHTENMENT.

A TEAM OF AGENTS OF THE SECRET ORGANIZATION KNOWN AS BEDLAM, THEY INVESTIGATE STRANGE AND UNEXPLAINED EVENTS, CONFRONT AND CONTAIN BIZARRE CREATURES NOT OF THIS EARTH, MAKING THE WORLD SAFE FROM THINGS THAT GO BUMP IN THE NIGHT...!

4 TODD AND CRAIG'S THE Perhapanauts

THE PERHAPANAUTS © 2008 TODD DEZAGO AND CRAIG ROUSSEAU

BEDLAM FILES

CHOOPIE
El Chupacabras

BLOOD-SUCKING FREAK CREATURE OF LATIN AMERICAN MYTH AND LEGEND. (MIND OF AN 8-YEAR OLD)

A TEAM OF AGENTS OF THE SECRET ORGANIZATION KNOWN AS BEDLAM, THEY INVESTIGATE STRANGE AND UNEXPLAINED EVENTS, CONFRONT AND CONTAIN BIZARRE CREATURES NOT OF THIS EARTH, MAKING THE WORLD SAFE FROM THINGS THAT GO BUMP IN THE NIGHT...!

6 TODD AND CRAIG'S THE Perhapanauts

THE PERHAPANAUTS © 2008 TODD DEZAGO AND CRAIG ROUSSEAU

BEDLAM FILES

MG
Real Name Unknown

AN ENIGMA TO HIS TEAMMATES AND THE REST OF BEDLAM. BRILLIANT MIND, WITH THE ABILITY TO "SLIDE" BETWEEN OUR DIMENSION AND OTHERS NEARBY.

A TEAM OF AGENTS OF THE SECRET ORGANIZATION KNOWN AS BEDLAM, THEY INVESTIGATE STRANGE AND UNEXPLAINED EVENTS, CONFRONT AND CONTAIN BIZARRE CREATURES NOT OF THIS EARTH, MAKING THE WORLD SAFE FROM THINGS THAT GO BUMP IN THE NIGHT...!

2 TODD AND CRAIG'S THE Perhapanauts

THE PERHAPANAUTS © 2008 TODD DEZAGO AND CRAIG ROUSSEAU

BEDLAM FILES

KARL
Mothman

AN OUTCAST FROM HIS CLAN, THE HARBINGERS OF DOOM CALLED THE MOTHMEN, KARL IS EAGER TO PROVE HIMSELF AS AN AGENT OF BEDLAM. CAN PROJECT WAVES OF INTENSE AND PARALYZING FEAR.

A TEAM OF AGENTS OF THE SECRET ORGANIZATION KNOWN AS BEDLAM, THEY INVESTIGATE STRANGE AND UNEXPLAINED EVENTS, CONFRONT AND CONTAIN BIZARRE CREATURES NOT OF THIS EARTH, MAKING THE WORLD SAFE FROM THINGS THAT GO BUMP IN THE NIGHT...!

5 TODD AND CRAIG'S THE Perhapanauts

THE PERHAPANAUTS © 2008 TODD DEZAGO AND CRAIG ROUSSEAU

BEDLAM FILES

MOLLY MacALLISTER
Ghost

ABLE TO PHASE THROUGH SOLID OBJECTS, BECOME INVISIBLE AND INHABIT THE BODIES OF UNCONSCIOUS OR SEMI-CONSCIOUS PEOPLE. (NOT HAPPY ABOUT BEING DEAD.)

A TEAM OF AGENTS OF THE SECRET ORGANIZATION KNOWN AS BEDLAM, THEY INVESTIGATE STRANGE AND UNEXPLAINED EVENTS, CONFRONT AND CONTAIN BIZARRE CREATURES NOT OF THIS EARTH, MAKING THE WORLD SAFE FROM THINGS THAT GO BUMP IN THE NIGHT...!

3 TODD AND CRAIG'S THE Perhapanauts

THE PERHAPANAUTS © 2008 TODD DEZAGO AND CRAIG ROUSSEAU

"...WAY TO LIBERATE THEIR SIX TEAMMATES FROM THE MAGICAL VINES THAT BOUND THEM.

CHOOPIE HURLED HIMSELF THROUGH THE DENSE UNDERGROWTH, THE TROPICAL FOLIAGE DOING ITS BEST TO SLOW HIS MAD RACE! HE DARE NOT PAUSE TO LISTEN BUT WAS CERTAIN THAT HE COULD HEAR THE CRACK OF BRANCH AND CRUNCH OF LEAVES AND THE SHARP GUTTURAL GRUNTS THAT SIGNALED THE TINY TERROR'S CLOSE PURSUIT! HE THREW HIMSELF FORWARD, HOPING FOR A SLIGHT CLEARING WHERE HE COULD TURN AND FACE THE LITTLE MASKED FREAK! WITH OR WITHOUT HIS GUN, HE WAS GONNA MESS THIS THING UP!

FROM HER VANTAGE POINT ABOVE THE TREES, MOLLY DARTED AFTER THE TWO. SHE COULD SEE THEM ONLY AS A TRAIL OF RUFFLING BUSHES THROUGH THE EXOTIC FLORA. SHE MISSED ARISA. WITHOUT HER BEST FRIEND'S TELEPATHY TO LINK THE TEAM, SHE, MOLLY, HAD NO WAY TO COMMUNICATE WITH THE FLEEING CHUPACABRA, NO WAY OF TELLING HIM HER PLAN--IF IT WAS A PLAN. SHE WAS QUITE CERTAIN IT WAS THE MASK THAT WAS POSSESSING THE TINY ABORIGINE. WHAT SHE DIDN'T KNOW WAS IF THE MASK COULD POSSESS HER...

SUDDENLY, THEY WERE THERE, JUST BELOW HER--CHOOPIE IN A QUICK SERIES OF GLIMPSES, BREAKING INTO AN AREA WHERE THE VEGETATION WAS SPARSER, THE ANGERED TIKI MASK BOBBING MERE FEET BEHIND. AND AS THE SMALL, INCENSED FIGURE SPRUNG TO ATTACK HER PARTNER, MOLLY MADE A LEAP OF HER OWN... INTO THE EVIL TIKI, INTO THE UNKNOWN..."

--FROM THE PERHAPANAUTS, ISLE OF THE UNKNOWN

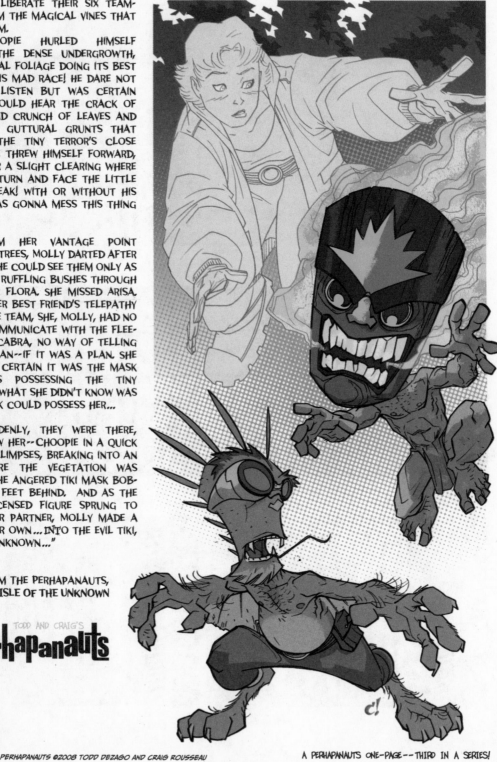

TODD AND CRAIG'S THE PERHAPANAUTS

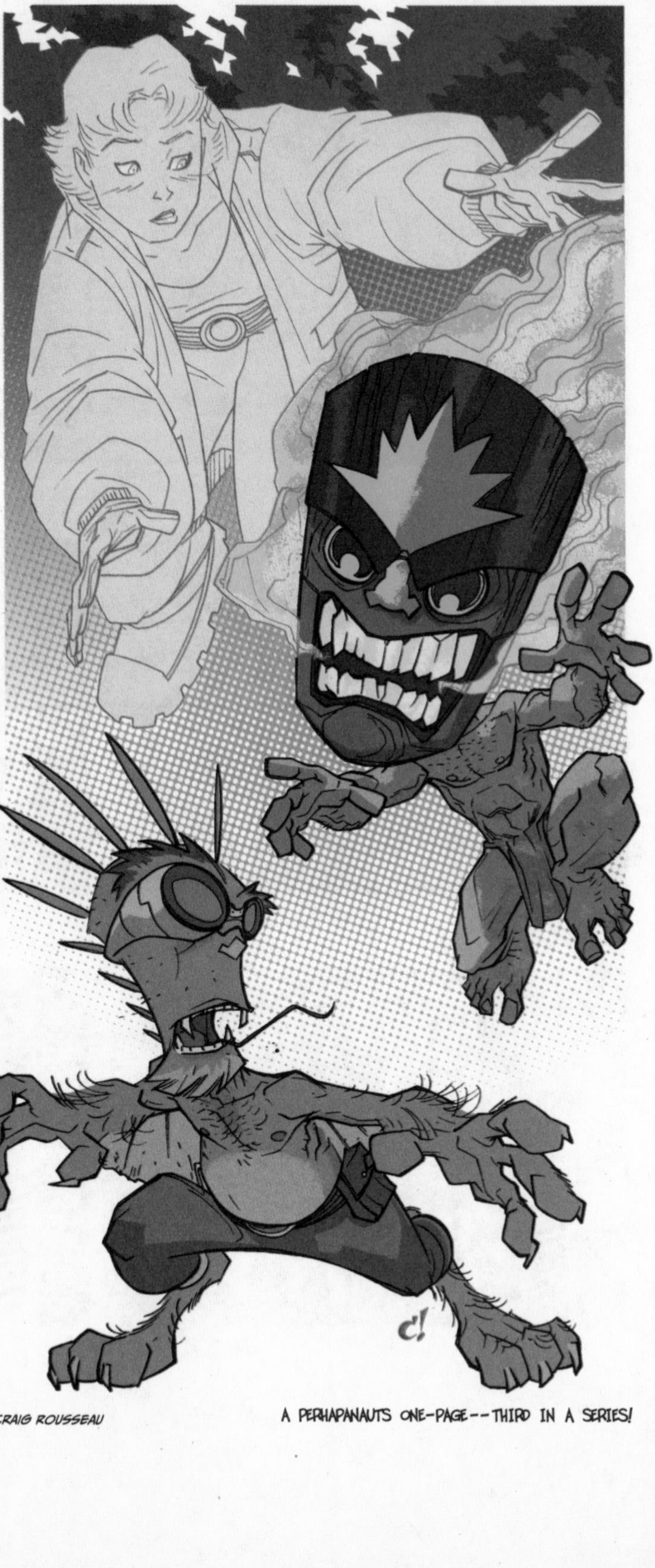

A PERHAPANAUTS ONE-PAGE--THIRD IN A SERIES!

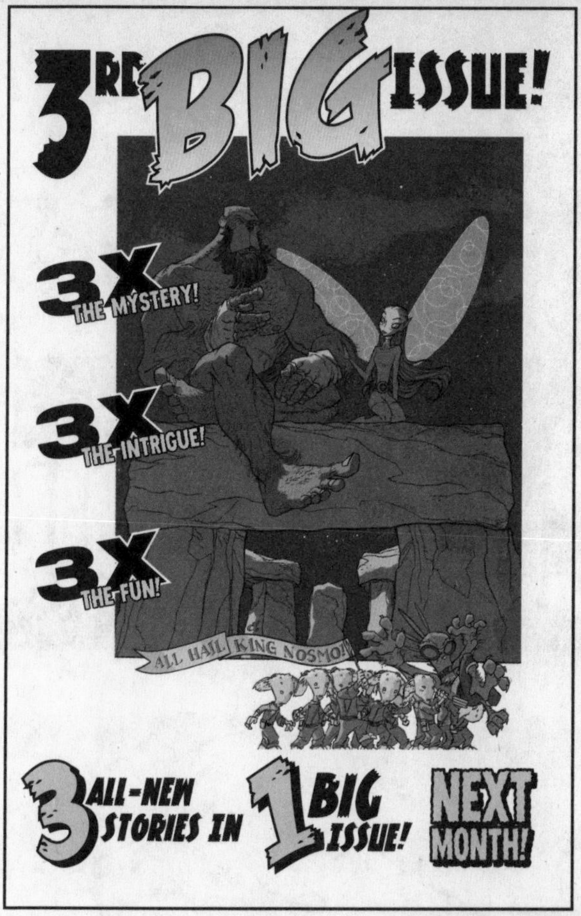
3RD BIG ISSUE!
3X THE MYSTERY!
3X THE INTRIGUE!
3X THE FUN!
ALL HAIL KING NOSMO!
3 ALL-NEW STORIES IN 1 BIG ISSUE!
NEXT MONTH!

NEXT ISSUE AD FOR
THE PERHAPANAUTS #3

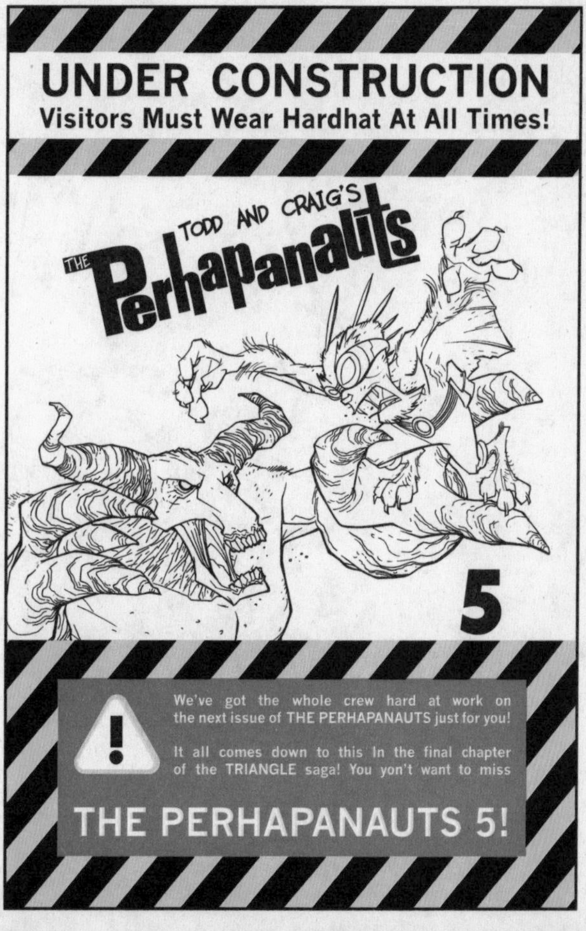
UNDER CONSTRUCTION
Visitors Must Wear Hardhat At All Times!
TODD AND CRAIG'S
THE Perhapanauts
5
We've got the whole crew hard at work on the next issue of THE PERHAPANAUTS just for you!
It all comes down to this In the final chapter of the TRIANGLE saga! You yon't want to miss
THE PERHAPANAUTS 5!

NEXT ISSUE AD FOR
THE PERHAPANAUTS #5

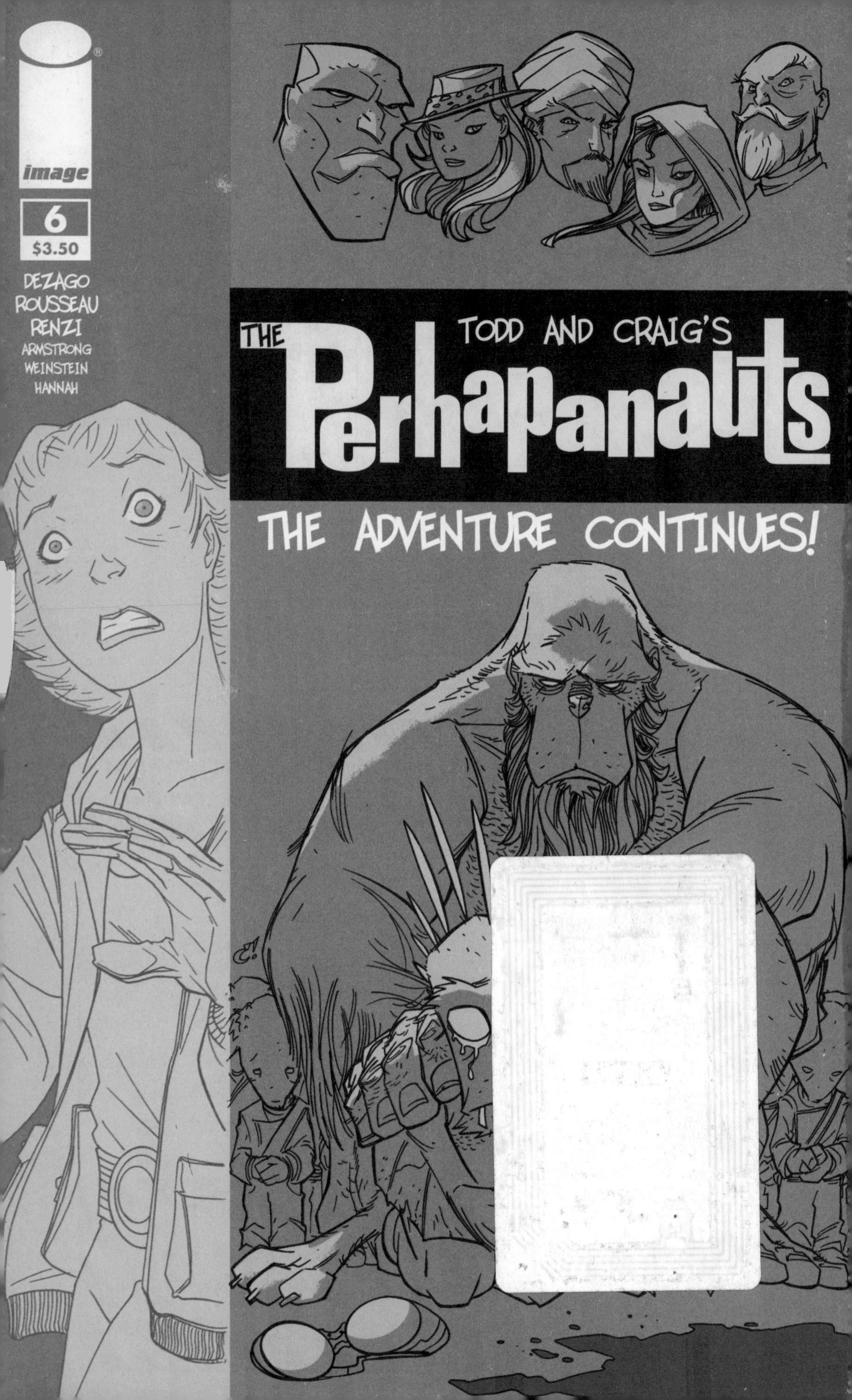
image
6
$3.50
DEZAGO
ROUSSEAU
RENZI
ARMSTRONG
WEINSTEIN
HANNAH
TODD AND CRAIG'S
THE Perhapanauts
THE ADVENTURE CONTINUES!